Learning to Teach England and the United States

The Evolution of Policy and Practice

Maria Teresa Tatto, Katharine Burn,
Ian Menter, Trevor Mutton and
Ian Thompson

Routledge
Taylor & Francis Group

LONDON AND NEW YORK

First published 2018 by Routledge

2 Park Square, Milton Park, Abingdon, Oxfordshire OX14 4RN
52 Vanderbilt Avenue, New York, NY 10017

Routledge is an imprint of the Taylor & Francis Group, an informa business

First issued in paperback 2019

British Library Cataloguing in Publication Data
A catalogue record for this book is available from the British Library

Library of Congress Cataloguing in Publication Data
A catalog record for this book has been requested

ISBN: 978-1-138-93374-3 (hbk)
ISBN: 978-0-367-36864-7 (pbk)

Typeset in Galliard
by Wearset Ltd, Boldon Tyne and Wear

Learning to Teach in England and the United States

Learning to Teach in England and the United States studies the evolution of initial teacher education by considering some of the current approaches in England and the United States. Presenting empirical evidence from these two distinct political and historical contexts, the chapters of this thought-provoking volume illustrate the tensions involved in preparing teachers who are working in ever-changing environments. Grounded in the lived experiences of those directly affected by these shifting policy environments, the book questions if reforms that have introduced accountability regimes and new kinds of partnership with the promise of improving teaching and learning, have contributed to more powerful learning experiences in schools for those entering the profession.

The authors consider the relationships between global, national and local policy, and question their potential impact on the future of teacher education and teaching more generally. The research adopts an innovative methodology and sociocultural theoretical framework designed to show greater insights into the ways in which beginning teachers' learning experiences are shaped by relationships at all of these levels. A key emerging issue is that of the alignment – or not – between the values and dispositions of the individuals and the institutions that are involved.

This book will appeal to academics, researchers and postgraduate students in the fields of teacher education, comparative education, higher education, and education policy and politics.

Maria Teresa Tatto is a Professor in the Division of Educational Leadership and Innovation at Arizona State University, and the Southwest Borderlands Professor of Comparative Education at the Mary Lou Fulton Teachers College.

Katharine Burn is an Associate Professor of Education at the University of Oxford and Director of the Oxford Education Deanery.

Ian Menter is an Emeritus Professor of Teacher Education at the University of Oxford and a Fellow of the Academy of Social Sciences.

Trevor Mutton is an Associate Professor at the University of Oxford where he is the Director of Professional Programmes.

Ian Thompson is an Associate Professor of Education at the University of Oxford where he is the lead English curriculum tutor on the PGCE course.

Routledge Research in Teacher Education

The Routledge Research in Teacher Education series presents the latest research on teacher education and also provides a forum to discuss the latest practices and challenges in the field.

Books in the series include:

Learning to Teach in England and the United States
The Evolution of Policy and Practice
Maria Teresa Tatto, Katharine Burn, Ian Menter, Trevor Mutton and Ian Thompson

Teacher Education in England
A Critical Interrogation of School-based Training
Tony Brown

Preparing Classroom Teachers to Succeed with Second Language Learners
Lessons from a Faculty Learning Community
Edited by Thomas H. Levine, Elizabeth R. Howard and David M. Moss

Interculturalization and Teacher Education
Theory to Practice
Cheryl A. Hunter, Donna K. Pearson and A. Renee Gutiérrez

Community Fieldwork in Teacher Education
Theory and Practice
Heidi L. Hallman and Melanie N. Burdick

Portrait of a Moral Agent Teacher
Teaching Morally and Teaching Morality
Gillian R. Rosenberg

Observing Teacher Identities Through Video Analysis
Practice and Implications
Amy Vetter and Melissa Schieble

Navigating Gender and Sexuality in the Classroom
Narrative Insights from Students and Educators
Heather Killelea McEntarfer

Teacher Education in Taiwan
State Control Vs Marketization
Edited by Sheng-Keng Yang and Jia-Li Huang

We dedicate this book to Harry Judge

Contents

Contributors

Katharine Burn is an Associate Professor of Education at the University of Oxford and Director of the Oxford Education Deanery, an extended partnership between the university and local schools, committed to supporting teachers' initial and continued professional learning through research engagement and collaboration. She taught history for 10 years in state secondary schools and retains a strong commitment to history education, both through her Postgraduate Certificate in Education (PGCE) teaching and supervision of higher degree students and as chair of the Historical Association Secondary Committee and co-editor of the professional journal *Teaching History*.

Ian Menter is an Emeritus Professor of Teacher Education at the University of Oxford and a Fellow of the Academy of Social Sciences. Before retirement in 2015, he was the Director of Professional Programmes at the Department of Education at the University. He is a former President of the British Educational Research Association (2013–2015) and holds visiting professorships at a number of United Kingdom universities. He is a founding member of the United Kingdom-wide research group, The Teacher Education Group and has published in a wide range of journals, mainly on aspects of teacher education.

Trevor Mutton is an Associate Professor at the University of Oxford where he is the Director of Professional Programmes. He has a background teaching Modern Foreign Languages in secondary schools and currently contributes to the modern languages PGCE and masters programmes at the university. He has been involved in a number of research projects focusing on the professional development of beginning teachers and the role of school–university partnerships in teacher education, as well as having a research interest in the development of teacher education policy.

Maria Teresa Tatto is a Professor in the Division of Educational Leadership and Innovation at Arizona State University, and the Southwest Borderlands Professor of Comparative Education at the Mary Lou Fulton Teachers College. She is the principal investigator for the Teacher Education and Development Study in Mathematics, and for the First Five Years of Mathematics Teaching

Study, both designed to explore the connections between pre-service preparation and what is learned on the job during the first years of teaching. She is a former President of the Comparative and International Education Society, and studies the effects of educational policy on school systems.

Ian Thompson is an Associate Professor of Education at the University of Oxford where he is the lead English curriculum tutor on the PGCE course. He is also the co-convenor of the Oxford Centre for Sociocultural and Activity Theory Research. Ian taught English in state secondary schools for 16 years. He has been involved in research projects from sociocultural and activity theory perspectives on: collaborative learning; the effects of poverty on learning; school exclusions; and literacy across the curriculum.

Foreword

This book is about initial teacher education in the United States and England today. It reports one of the few genuine research studies conducted on the subject on both sides of the Atlantic at the same time.[1] But although it is about contemporary practice, it is important to recognise that the stories that are told here have a long history. Much of that history, including my own involvement in this topic, goes back to the 1980s.

In 1983, the English government published a White Paper on *Teaching Quality* which included the following announcement.

> Initial teacher training of all qualified teachers should include studies closely linked with practical experience in school and involve the active participation of experienced practising school teachers. Satisfactory local arrangements to this end would have to be established. *The Department of Education and Science has recently commissioned a research project to monitor and evaluate four examples of such arrangements, so as to assist the development of good practice* [emphasis added].
>
> (Department of Education and Science, 1983)

As a newly appointed lecturer in the Department of Education at the University of Cambridge, I, together with the then head of department, the philosopher Paul Hirst, led the research, which evaluated these early experiments in what at the time was called 'school-based' initial teacher education (Furlong, Hirst, Pocklington & Miles, 1988). The significance of the project was that it was the first move by an English government to encourage a greater role for schools in initial teacher education.

At more or less the same time, in 1986, the Holmes Group in the United States (a highly influential consortium of elite universities involved in teacher education) set out a similar aspiration for strengthening the links between their universities and schools. The Group had five principal goals for the overall improvement of education in America, one of which was:

> To connect our own institutions [university faculties of education] to schools. If university faculties are to become more expert educators of

teachers, they must make better use of expert teachers in the education of other teachers, and in research on teaching. In addition, schools must become places where both teachers and university faculty can systematically inquire into practice and improve it.

(Holmes Group, 1986)

As these examples show, at more or less the same time, similar policy conversations were therefore taking place on both sides of the Atlantic. But despite these similarities this brief history also reveals important differences between the two countries as well. The development of schools' contribution in England was something that was centrally supported and then centrally driven by the English government. After 1984, long before the Cambridge evaluation was complete, an increased role for schools became mandatory (Department of Education and Science, 1984). The English government was able to use its responsibility for setting standards of entry into the teaching profession and its control and funding of higher education to insist on its own preferred model of teacher education. A decade later, the establishment of a national inspectorate, Ofsted (Office for Standards in Education, Children's Services and Skills), that covered university departments of education as well as schools, gave the government even more control over the sector. By contrast, the 1980s debate in America on the future of teacher education was led not by a government department, but by the Holmes Group, a self avowedly elite group of Deans of Education. That was because the policy context in the United States was and is fundamentally different from that of England. Not only is each of the individual states responsible for their own educational systems, including standards for entry into the teaching profession, the higher education system, still the dominant provider of programmes, is much more diversified, both in terms of its funding and its management. And of course, there is no national inspectorate. Despite the development of some national organisations such as the Council for the Accreditation of Educator Preparation, or the National Board for Professional Teaching Standards, teacher education policy and practice therefore, remains far more diverse and decentralised in the United States than it does in England.

But that is the policy context; what of the world of practice? The two teacher education programmes that are the main focus of research for this book are in many ways iconic not only because they were amongst the earliest examples of genuinely collaborative teacher education, but also because of the depth of thinking and research behind them. From England, the focus is very much on the Oxford Internship Scheme, a model of collaborative provision that itself was established in the late 1980s under the leadership of Donald McIntyre and his various colleagues (Benton, 1990; Hagger & McIntyre, 2006). From the United States, the example used is Michigan State University's internship scheme, again a scheme with a long history developed under the leadership of Lee Shulman and Judith Lanier, herself a leading figure in the Holmes Group (1986, 1990, 1995). The aim of the empirical research presented in this book is to document what the experience of teacher education is actually like for novitiate teachers today on these two iconic programmes; programmes that to some extent have common intellectual histories, though they differ from each other in their day-to-day practice.

A great deal has happened in this field on both sides of the Atlantic since the 1980s. England has seen centrally driven reform after centrally driven reform with the common theme of an ever-greater role for schools. Under the current Schools Direct model of teacher education (Department for Education, 2010), schools themselves can now be the 'lead provider' of programmes, attracting government funding, admitting students and deciding for themselves how much, if any, university support they wish to 'purchase'. The result has been a kind of centrally mandated diversification with the number of different providers of initial teacher education now running into the thousands (Whiting et al., 2016). The United States has also seen a greater diversification with large numbers of states now offering a whole raft of 'alternative' employment-based routes, the most popular of which has been the Teach for America programme (the model for the English Teach First, which is also reported on in this volume). Yet despite this diversification, the two programmes that form the basis of the research reported here – the Oxford and Michigan State internship schemes – have maintained their position as leading examples of very high-quality collaborative provision. I suspect that that has something to do with the fact that, in contrast to so many of the more recently invented forms of provision, the development of these programmes is based on rigorous research and scholarship – both when they were established and today.

Exploring the changing face of teacher education in the United States and England through the lens of these two key programmes is then an important opportunity for all of us with an interest in this topic to learn from each other. But as the authors rightly point out, cross-national comparisons are challenging; context is all. That is why the common analytical framework set out early in the book is so important. Using that framework, contributors from both countries are able to ask parallel questions not only about the day-to-day experiences of student teachers but also about the national, state and institutional contexts in which these programmes operate. The result is a fascinating account of that difficult and challenging process of becoming a new teacher in two very different educational contexts.

In 1983, when I took on the task of evaluating England's first national scheme for a collaborative model of initial teacher education, I was not to know how long it would take for the lessons we learned to be understood and appreciated across the system as a whole. Nor did I appreciate how leading teacher educators in the United States were going through a similar learning process at more or less the same time. Now, with this book, for the first time, we have the opportunity to explore both the English and the American experience of collaborative teacher education in a coordinated and scholarly way. It does I think add significantly to our understanding of the complex yet vitally important process of learning to be a teacher in today's schools.

John Furlong
Oxford
June 2017

Note

1 Harry Judge's groundbreaking work in 1994 (Judge et al., 1994) is one of the few other examples of which I am aware.

References

Benton, M. (Eds.). (1990). *The Oxford internship scheme: Integration and partnership in initial teacher education*. London: Calouste Gulbenkien.

Department for Education. (2010). *The importance of teaching: The Schools White Paper 2010*. Command 7980. London: Department for Education.

Department of Education and Science. (1983). *Teaching quality* (White Paper). Command 8836. London: HMSO.

Department of Education and Science. (1984). *Initial teacher training: Approval of courses (Circular 3/84)*. London: Department of Education and Science.

Furlong, J., Hirst, P., Pocklington, K. & Miles, S. (1988). *Initial teacher training and the role of the school*. Buckingham: Open University Press.

Hagger, H. & McIntyre, D. (2006). *Learning teaching from teachers*. Buckingham: Open University.

Holmes Group. (1986). *Tomorrow's teachers: A report of the Holmes Group*. East Lansing, MI: Holmes Group. Retrieved from https://eric.ed.gov/?id=ED270454.

Holmes Group. (1990). *Tomorrow's schools: Principles for the design of Professional Development Schools*. East Lansing, MI: Holmes Group. Retrieved from https://eric.ed.gov/?id=ED328533.

Holmes Group. (1995). *Tomorrow's schools of education: A report of the Holmes Group*. East Lansing, MI: Holmes Group. Retrieved from https://eric.ed.gov/?id=ED399220.

Judge, H., Lemosse, M., Paine, L. & Sedlak, M. (1994). *The university and the teachers: France, the United States, England*. Wallingford: Triangle Books.

Whiting, C., Black, P., Hordern. J., Parfitt, A., Reynolds, K., Sorensen, N. & Whitty, G. (2016). *Towards a new topography of ITT. A profile of Initial Teacher Training in England 2015–16*, Occasional Paper No 1. Bath: Bath Spa Institute for Education.

Preface

In an era when disruption of established practices seems to be the order of the day, and simplistic views about teaching and teacher education abound, this book seeks to undertake an in-depth examination of the challenges entailed in learning to teach. The study we present demonstrates the complexity of this endeavour and shows how policies that bypass teacher education, albeit with the aim to accelerate the placement of teachers in every classroom, may have serious unintended consequences.

Simplistic ideas about teaching such as the primacy of subject content over pedagogy and the notion that one can learn to teach almost exclusively in schools have nourished the notion that many can teach without much in the way of specialised knowledge of how people learn. Whilst these policies have not taken hold in every country, the globalised nature of reform movements make these simplistic ways of thinking about how one learns to teach dangerously attractive. These sweeping reforms merit careful examination.

Indeed, these reforms fly in the face of research evidence showing that quality teachers are the most important school level variable affecting student learning outcomes and that teacher education is key to improving the knowledge, skills and dispositions of future teachers. Learning to teach in an era of increasingly specialised curriculum and a growingly diverse student population is, indeed, a complex but needed undertaking that goes beyond knowing school subjects or engaging in classroom teaching regardless of relevant knowledge and experience.

Substantial responses to the recent global call (by UNESCO [United Nations Educational, Scientific and Cultural Organization]), to ensure inclusive and equitable quality education and promote lifelong learning opportunities for all, are unsustainable without qualified teachers. There is, however, widespread variation about the level and depth of the knowledge that high-quality teachers of diverse populations require. Arguments as to whether teachers are 'born' or 'made' lie at the centre of the controversial nature of teacher education yet most individuals need specialised education to be effective teachers. Answers to the question of how, where and by whom teachers are educated reveal fundamental societal views about the purposes of education, the knowledge that is valued and what it means to be an effective teacher. Understanding past and current changes in teacher education provides a window into the nature of the state, the theories as to how societies mould their citizens, whose culture and knowledge is valued, and the role of globalisation, education and the economy in this dynamic.

As the school curriculum becomes more complex it is important to understand how the diversification of teacher education can support the knowledge required of teachers. This book presents evidence from two distinct historical, political, cultural and social contexts and asks whether, how and under what conditions the professional education of teachers can occur in higher education institutions or in schools, or in both via partnerships, or other arrangements. Of interest, is the examination of whether reforms that have introduced market models, standards, and external systems of quality assurance into teacher education have contributed to more powerful teaching and learning in schools, and in schools of education.

This book arises from a transatlantic collaboration between Maria Teresa Tatto and a group of four teacher educators at the Department of Education at the University of Oxford. When the project commenced Maria Teresa Tatto was working at Michigan State University, although by the end of the project she had moved to Arizona State University.

Intrigued by the rapid transformation that teacher education in England had undergone in the 1980s and the emergence of similar forces in the United States over the next 30 years, Maria Teresa Tatto developed a research proposal to investigate the evolution of teacher education policy in these two countries. The central idea was to study the impact of accountability and market-based policies on these systems, and specifically as these affect how teachers learn to teach in their last stage of their preparation: during the internship. Michigan State University supported the proposal as part of Maria Teresa Tatto's sabbatical research, as did the University of Oxford's Department of Education. An invitation from the then Director of the Department on behalf of the Oxford University team ensued and Maria Teresa Tatto took up a Visiting Research Fellowship in Oxford in September 2013. She spent the following academic year and part of the next academic year based in Oxford where the team discussed the proposal and further refined the research project reported in this volume.

Since Maria Teresa Tatto's year in Oxford, she has continued to make visits on a regular basis and these visits, together with numerous Skype calls and emails, have enabled us to continue to collaborate in completing this project. It has been a complex process, writing together and especially developing our theoretical ideas together, but it has been an enormous pleasure and not only are we all still talking to each other, we are continuing to collaborate!

Our strategy was to study our two programmes as renowned examples of university and school partnerships with a long history of sustained success in each country. The study needed to include observations in classrooms and analyses from outsiders looking in, as well as interviews with programme designers and policy makers.

All of us were well aware of the depth of insights that might be gained from working together on a comparative study as a way to analyse how similar reforms act in different contexts and how these comparisons may help to highlight what is universal and what is culture specific.

As teacher educators, we were very interested in the possibilities of seeking to 'make sense' of what was going on in the processes of becoming a teacher in the new climate of accountability, competition and standards in both countries. How and what do beginning teachers learn and when and where do they learn it? How do pressures introduced by new reforms affect their opportunities to learn in schools? In both England and the United States, there had been considerable debate about the best approaches to pre-service teacher education and these debates were creating considerable uncertainty about policy and practice on both sides of the Atlantic. These debates not only continue but have become more intense and widespread as countries engage in reforms to improve their education systems in a constantly changing global dynamic.

We hope that the data we collected and the framework we developed to analyse the complex dynamics in learning to teach will be helpful for others and that our work will contribute to deeper understandings of the issues involved in promoting the development of knowledgeable and committed teachers for all children and youth.

Maria Teresa Tatto, Katharine Burn, Ian Menter,
Trevor Mutton and Ian Thompson
July 2017

Acknowledgements

There are several friends and colleagues whom we wish to thank for their support and encouragement. We are thankful to Dr Harry Judge, the former Director of the then Department of Educational Studies at the University of Oxford and an important source of inspiration for this project. Not only did he make an indelible impression during his first conversations with Maria Teresa Tatto back in 1988 in Michigan but his work and insights foresaw with uncanny accuracy current policy trends in teacher education not only in England and in the United States but in other parts of the world.

We also want to thank another former Director of the Department of Education at the University of Oxford, Professor John Furlong, not only for writing the Foreword to this book, but for his continuing inspiration and support throughout this research. We thank Professor Ernesto Macaro for supporting the study, which occurred during his tenure as Director of the Department of Education. We are also very grateful to Tessa Blair, an Assistant Head Teacher and part-time doctoral student at Oxford who advised on the project and facilitated some of the data collection.

Although we cannot mention them by name, we are thankful to all the interns and mentor teachers in England and in the United States who agreed to be observed and interviewed, and the vice-principals and head teachers who graciously granted us permission to carry out fieldwork in their schools and classrooms.

We are thankful to Professors David Labaree (Stanford University) and Geoff Whitty (Bath Spa University, United Kingdom and Newcastle University, Australia) for acting as discussants at a symposium sponsored by the World Education Research Association at the '2016 Annual Meeting' of the American Educational Research Association at which we reported on this project. They both offered us very helpful critical feedback. We are thankful to Peter Youngs, University of Virginia, for his helpful feedback on the United States' section of the book.

Maria Teresa Tatto would like to acknowledge colleagues who shared their time and expertise to inform the study. In England, she is grateful to Sir Tim Brighouse, John Furlong, Bob Moon, Kate Reynolds, David Phillips, Richard Pring, Anne Watson and Geoff Whitty for sharing their insights on England's education systems and policies. In the United States, she is grateful to the Michigan State University teacher education programme and the secondary team of faculty and students. She acknowledges the support of Michigan State University during her sabbatical year and the support of Arizona State University for providing time and space to finish this book.

The research reported in this book was supported in part by the United States National Science Foundation under award number DRL-0910001. Any opinions, findings and conclusions or recommendations expressed in this material are those of the authors and do not necessarily reflect the views of the National Science Foundation.

Abbreviations

AACTE	American Association of Colleges for Teacher Education
AERA	American Educational Research Association
CAEP	Council for the Accreditation of Educator Preparation
CCCU	Canterbury Christ Church University
CCSS	Common Core State Standards
CPD	Continuing professional development
EAL	English as an Additional Language
edTPA	Teacher Performance Assessment
ESSA	Every Student Succeeds Act
GCSE	General Certificate of Secondary Education
GERM	Global Education Reform Movement
GPA	Grade point average
HEFCE	Higher Education Funding Council for England
HEI	Higher education institution
HQT	Highly qualified teacher
IHE	Institutions of higher education
InTASC	Interstate Teacher Assessment and Support Consortium
IOE	Institute of Education – part of the University of London
MFL	Modern Foreign Languages
MSU	Michigan State University
NCATE	National Council for Accreditation of Teacher Education
NCLB	No Child Left Behind
NCSS	National Council for Social Studies
NCTM	National Council of Teacher of Mathematics
NCTQ	National Council on Teacher Quality
OECD	Organisation for Economic Cooperation and Development
OfC	Opportunities for change
OfD	Opportunities for development
Ofsted	Office for Standards in Education, Children's Services and Skills
OIS	Oxford Internship Scheme
PDS	Professional Development Schools
PGCE	Postgraduate Certificate in Education
PISA	Programme for International Student Assessment

QTS	Qualified Teacher Status
SCITT	School-Centred Initial Teacher Training
SEND	Special educational needs and disability
SOAPPSTone	Subject, Occasion, Audience, Purpose, Point of view, Speaker, Tone
STEM	Science, Technology, Engineering and Mathematics
TDA	Training and Development Agency
TEAC	Teacher Education Accreditation Council
TEACH	Teacher Education Assistance for College and Higher Education
TEDS-M	Teacher Education and Development Study in Mathematics
TIMSS	Trends in International Mathematics and Science Study
UNESCO	United Nations Educational, Scientific and Cultural Organization
WWI	World War I

Part I
Learning to teach
Theory, methods and contexts

1   Introduction and background

Learning to teach has long been recognised as a developmental process that is highly complex and demanding. This learning involves adopting and developing several identities in order to negotiate the tacit or explicit rules and demands of different institutions and social practices. In addition to their own experiences as students themselves, student teachers may learn: from their peers; from the expertise of other teachers operating in particular settings; from their own pedagogical interactions with young people and their reflections on practice; from critical incidents involving mistakes made by themselves and those teachers they observe; or from testing and critiquing theories in practice. They learn in the social and cultural settings of schools and universities as well as at the desks where they complete academic assignments. They also learn at particular historical junctures within particular teacher education programmes and partnership schools that are reacting to policy changes as well as political constraints and demands. The development of these student teachers is both intensely personal, and highly social, requiring almost constant interaction with other adults and children.

A series of research studies has explored these and other aspects of learning to teach and whilst there seems to be agreement that the process is developmental, complex and deeply personal, there is lack of consensus in other areas. Some scholars document development as occurring in discrete stages (Berliner, 1994; Feiman-Nemser, 2001), whilst others argue for a non-linear and more complex model (Huberman, 1992; Maynard & Furlong, 1993, 1995; McIntyre & Hagger, 1993; Rusznyak, 2008; Shulman, 1986, 1987). Studies exploring the situational nature of learning to teach have argued that teacher education programmes' impact on student teachers is exiguous (Berliner, 1994; Feiman-Nemser, 1983), only to revise their position in later work (Berliner, 2001; Feiman-Nemser, 2001), and more recently rigorous studies have found that teacher education programmes have an important influence on knowledge outcomes depending on the programmes' selectivity and the opportunities to learn (Darling-Hammond, 2006; Tatto et al., 2012). Other studies have shown the nuanced ways in which schools may support or undermine learning and how individual student teachers in the same schools may undergo dramatically different experiences (Burn, Hagger, Mutton & Everton, 2003). Scholars have

the delicate balance and degree of collaboration that must exist
different institutions in which teachers learn to teach, revealing a
of arrangements and results (Furlong, Barton, Miles, Whiting &
); McIntyre, 2006; Holmes Group, 1986; Cochran-Smith & Lytle,
ll as different reactions to policy demands (Cochran-Smith, 2001).
ies have extensively documented the deeply personal and affective
aspects of learning to teach (Hammerness et al., 2005; Hobson et al., 2008;
Lortie, 1975; Calderhead & Robson, 1991). New understandings of how individuals learn, and of how institutions accommodate increasingly complex internal and external demands influenced by global forces, make this an important moment to examine learning to teach within a socio-historical and comparative framework.

This book presents evidence from the two distinct historical, political and social contexts of England and the United States to shed light on the ways in which the professional education of teachers is being reshaped by rapid, contemporary changes in teacher education policy. We consider how the contributions of the two main sites of learning for student teachers – the school and the university – play their respective parts in the various new dispositions that have been arrived at (see Dewey, 1904/1965). We argue that student teachers face at least two social situations of development (Vygotsky, 1987) as they begin to teach: one from their position as learners within the academic environment of a university; and another as novice teachers within the specific professional contexts of their placement schools. Their engagement with these social situations may be influenced by factors such as their previous experience of education and their existing and possibly naïve understanding of social and cultural norms in addition to their cultural capital from family and community. These social situations intersect in complex and dialectical interplay between theory and practice. The sociocultural research framework developed in this book enables us to explore student teachers' acquisition of the knowledge and the psychological tools required for effective pedagogy and their engagement with the cultural assumptions that govern what are deemed to be appropriate ways of being a teacher in a particular school and in society as a whole. We focus on the education of future secondary level teachers as a window to examine these questions as such teachers are expected to attain deep knowledge of the particular disciplines and to be able to teach them to a diverse population of pupils.

The book also examines how policy affecting teacher education is constructed and examines the evidence that is currently used to support such policies. We explore, for example, through documentary analysis and our empirical data whether or not the surge of market models, standards and external systems of quality assurance in the two countries has contributed to more powerful teaching and learning in schools and in university-based teacher education programmes. We begin by addressing the issue of initial teacher education more broadly as a policy problem before considering specific policies and practices in the two nations in more depth in future chapters.

Initial teacher education as a policy problem

The education of teachers has generally been seen as a key policy tool to improve the quality of education (McKinsey & Company, 2007; Tatto, 2007/2009). There is much research evidence internationally that shows that good teachers make a difference to the schooling of children (e.g. Hattie, 2003). Less agreement, however, exists about the level and depth of the knowledge that high-quality teachers require; arguments as to whether teachers are 'born' or 'made' lie at the centre of the controversial nature of teacher education (Lortie, 1975). Much debate also exists about what form of initial teacher education is required, with initial teacher education in England, in particular, subject to radical and ongoing reform.

The question of how, where and by whom teachers are educated reveals fundamental societal views about the purposes of education, the knowledge that is valued and the teacher's role in this dynamic. Understanding past and current changes in teacher education provides a window into the nature of the state and into its theories and assumptions as to how societies and its citizens are to be transformed, whose culture and knowledge is to be transmitted and the role of education and the economy in this process (Cochran-Smith & Demers, 2008; Judge, Lemosse, Paine & Sedlak, 1994; Menter, 2016).

As the school curriculum becomes more complex it is important to understand how the diversification of teacher education can support the development of the knowledge required of teachers (McKinsey & Company, 2007; Menter, 2009; Tatto et al., 2012). Burn, Hagger and Mutton (2015) argue the need to acknowledge the complexity of this learning, focusing not merely on the different kinds of knowledge that teachers need to be an effective professional but also on the process of learning to teach, which requires the sustenance of a dual identity as both learner and teacher.

In England and the United States, teacher education programmes, schools and teachers have been under intense scrutiny over the last 10 years in light of political concerns that pupils are underperforming when measured against world standards. However, the evidence provided by recent international comparisons such as the Programme for International Student Assessment (PISA) indicates that pupils in England are achieving above average in science and just above average in mathematics and reading and that the level has been maintained over the last 10 years. Seventy-one countries participated in PISA 2015, including all members of the Organisation for Economic Cooperation and Development (OECD).

> The average science, mathematics and reading scores of pupils in England have not changed since 2006. Our 15-year-olds continue to perform significantly above the OECD average in science whilst they remain at the OECD average for mathematics. For the first time in 2015, pupils in England perform significantly, but only just, above the OECD average in reading.
>
> (Jerrim & Shure, 2016, p. 4)

In some exercises, such as the Trends in International Mathematics and Science Study (TIMSS), England has shown steady improvement in the mathematics achievement of their primary level pupils (Year 5, aged 9–10) since 1995, the point at which TIMSS began tracking countries longitudinally, whilst secondary level pupils (Year 9, aged 13–14) showed significant improvement between 2003 and 2007, stayed about the same in 2011, and again improved in 2015.[1] The study shows that those pupils with higher average achievement had teachers who reported 'lower levels of teacher challenge (with *challenge* defined as having too many teaching hours or difficulty keeping up with curriculum changes)'. Yet the same study also found that 'teachers in England report relatively challenging teaching conditions ... [and that] job satisfaction among Year 5 and 9 teachers in England is low compared to teachers in most countries' (Greany, Barnes, Mostafa, Pensiero & Swensson, 2016, p. 13). Indeed, there is considerable evidence suggesting that many teachers in England have become very disenchanted with their work, with almost a third leaving teaching within 5 years of qualifying.[2] According to a YouGov survey carried out in 2015 for the National Union of Teachers, around 60 per cent of teachers were considering leaving the profession in the next 2 years.[3] Yet neither the positive nor the negative outcomes such as these have been examined in relationship to England's sweeping reforms in teacher education.

England's higher education monopoly of teacher education was broken in the early 1980s under the Thatcher government; allowing the market to operate in the provision of teacher education and facilitating an important role for schools in the education of future teachers (see Judge et al., 1994). Later, under the Labour administrations of Tony Blair and Gordon Brown, the nature of the teaching profession and of professional knowledge was re-defined and reforms were introduced, which resulted in a further move away from higher education and towards schools which were seen as responsible for defining best practices within a national framework (Furlong, 2008). Currently, the system of teacher education in England is highly diversified. According to Furlong (2008), by 2008 there were 36 different routes by which to enter the teaching profession, including Teach First and the Graduate Teacher Programme, and more recently, School Direct (both salaried and fee-paying options) and Troops to Teachers, all contributing to the creation of new models of teacher education. According to English scholars the 'technical rationalist vision of teacher professionalism' that has tended to predominate within the new models stands in sharp contrast with other approaches that see teachers' professional knowledge as capable of supporting inquiry and innovation in schools. A study carried out across England between 2015 and 2016 came to the conclusion that not only is the system now incredibly complex, it is extremely difficult to obtain the full range of data required to make sense of what is actually being provided (Whiting et al., 2016).

Similarly, in the United States, teacher education has become far more diversified in the past 20 years than ever before. There has always been a variety of approaches to teacher education across widely varying institutions, but the programmes now include an even broader range of institutions and a wider range of theories of teacher learning. As occurred earlier in England, concerns with the quality of teaching and student learning resulted in an increase of regulatory policy in teacher education. The latest attempts at policy intervention were the proposed federal regulations to evaluate the quality of teacher education using as the ultimate criteria for success the results of student achievement tests (USDOE, 2014). Whilst these regulations were rescinded on March 2017 under a new administration, the individual states are still required under Title II of the Higher Education Act (USDOE, 2016) to report outcomes and other evidence of programme quality. As in England, the TIMSS results in mathematics show steady improvement over the years, with the highest improvement yet between 2011 and 2015 for both primary and secondary pupils. Yet the general discourse of crisis in education and particularly as concerns teachers, which began in earnest as a result of the *A Nation at Risk* report in 1983, continues to ignite policy change, often without the support of evidence (USDOE, 1983).

In contrast with England, market-driven alternative routes to certification in the United States have had a more arrested development since they first emerged in the early 1980s, and whilst some models have found fertile ground in other national contexts, most notably Teach for America, the majority of teachers in the United States (close to 90 per cent) are prepared in traditional pre-service programmes in higher education institutions (HEIs) (USDOE, 2015). Nevertheless, ongoing concerns with teacher quality have fuelled criticism of traditional teacher education programmes and continue to stimulate the growth of alternative approaches.

Remarkably, given the similarities with policy trends in England, there has been little exchange between these two countries regarding their approaches to teacher education, their rationale for those approaches, or the kinds of teachers that are now entering practice as a result of these policy and programme changes.

One of the purposes of this book is to study the evolution of university-based teacher education, and emergent alternative approaches in England and the United States with an emphasis on the last 10 years and their consequences for the future of the profession in these two countries. England is chosen as a focus, as opposed to the United Kingdom as a whole, because each of the four nations in the United Kingdom has separate, devolved education systems and demographically it is overwhelmingly the largest of the nations. More specifically, the study reported in this book, asks how and under what conditions the current approaches to teacher preparation in England and in the United States contribute to the initial education of teachers in an era when the school curriculum is becoming more complex and the student population more diverse, within an increasingly contested terrain dominated by neoliberal policy and accountability and market-oriented regimes.

The book draws on data from a 2-year study undertaken by Michigan State University (MSU) and the University of Oxford. The data on learning to teach come from observations, interviews and questionnaires conducted with beginning secondary level teachers in English and United States schools, and from teacher preparation programme documentation on the different routes to learn to teach in both countries, as well as from interviews with faculty and school personnel working with student teachers following these routes into teaching. The study also analyses policy documents and draws upon interviews with programme designers.

The study in both countries was driven by the following questions:

- How has emergent policy affected the structure, content and practice of teacher education?
- What are the specific skills, attributes and cognitive demands made of the beginning teachers and of the teacher educators at different organisational levels and in different settings?
- How have the conceptions of teaching and teacher education changed for schools and for universities?
- How may changes in teacher education policy affect professional knowledge and day-to-day practice in schools?

The book is presented in three parts. The first part provides an account of the study as a whole, establishes its theoretical framework and provides a detailed, contextualised account of the specific institutions within which the research was conducted in each country. The second part presents findings from the empirical work, examining the experiences of a range of beginning teachers, each learning to teach within a highly specific school-university partnership. The third part offers a comparative review and analysis of the significance of the findings.

Part I sets out the background to the study in greater depth. In particular, in the rest of this chapter (Chapter 1) we look at recent literature on policy and practice in teacher education, especially as it affects England and the United States, but also considering how these two countries compare with other parts of the world. We then identify some of the challenges in undertaking comparative study in educational research in order to sensitise the reader to the complexity of the analysis that we seek to undertake. The chapter concludes with a brief description of the sites chosen for the empirical work. Chapter 2 presents the sociocultural theoretical framework and explains how it informed the design of the study, including the methods for data collection and analysis. Chapter 3 offers an account of the contemporary policy context for the two sites of study, in England and the United States respectively. Chapters 4 and 5 present in greater detail how the HEIs and schools within this study have each developed their teacher education practices, in response to – but not entirely driven by – the policy mandates outlined in Chapter 3 as they have engaged in the challenging process of preparing future secondary teachers.

Part II, opens with an account in Chapter 6 of the innovative analytical typology that has emerged from the study, setting out five categories that encapsulate some of the different kinds of alignment experienced by the beginning teachers within their particular social situations of development, shaped not only by the departmental and institutional assumptions and practices of specific school and university contexts but also by each individual's prior experiences and agendas. The next five chapters (Chapters 7 to 11) each present a single example, representing one case of each of these categories, supported by evidence drawn from other cases (there were 18 cases in all). The section concludes with Chapter 12, in which the five cases are reviewed and the insights revealed by this typology are summarised.

Part III, in Chapter 13 offers a comparative analysis of the findings, assessing the extent of the similarity and the kinds of differences between the English and the United States contexts. The chapter also seeks to identify wider implications for teacher education policy and practice, wherever it takes place. The concluding chapter, Chapter 14, reviews the strengths and weaknesses of the study and suggests areas and methods for future research on teacher education.

Policy development in initial teacher education

Global trends

Across the world the general increase in political attention that is given to education has led to a corresponding effect on initial teacher education. As we have seen governments becoming more concerned about educational attainment and as the general consensus has been that 'teaching matters', so there have been attempts to improve outcomes and standards through focusing on the quality of teaching and teachers. The 'Global Education Reform Movement (GERM)', as Sahlberg (2011) called it, has echoed through the reforms of initial teacher education around the world over the last 10 years.

The five factors that Sahlberg identified as key characteristics of the GERM were: an increased emphasis on 'standards' in teaching and learning; a strong focus on literacy and numeracy; an increasingly centrally prescribed curriculum for teacher education; increased accountability measures with a focus on the measurement of teachers' performance; and the introduction of market forces into the provision of teacher education (Sahlberg, 2011, p. 103).

In the four main jurisdictions of the United Kingdom (as well as in the Republic of Ireland) a rapid series of teacher education reviews – often more than one in just a few years – has indicated governments' anxieties to be seen as 'improving' teaching and teacher education (see Teacher Education Group, 2016, for a full account). But there have also been major reviews in Australia, Norway and Austria. In the United States, since the Holmes Group Report of 1986, there has been a relentless series of federal and state-backed investigations and reports (Holmes Group, 1986).

One recent collection of accounts of eight national systems demonstrated how these patterns of reform and investigation had developed and revealed a number of common themes as well as some less common aspects. Darling-Hammond and Lieberman (2012) suggest that amongst the common developments have been efforts to increase the quality of teaching by:

- Recruiting, selecting, preparing and retaining high-quality individuals via, for instance, the introduction of salary incentives, establishing supportive induction models, supporting professional development, promoting career ladders and promoting profession-wide capacity building.
- Increasing the relevance and rigour of teacher education by including, modifying or creating routes into teaching that offer connections between theory and practice through integration with clinical practice in the case of programmes in HEIs, or by creating school-based routes (Darling-Hammond & Lieberman, 2012, pp. 137–138).

However, they also point out that in some settings we may also see patterns of:

- *diversification* in entry into the profession; and
- movement by governments away from a clear stipulation of *what it means to qualify as a teacher* (Darling-Hammond & Lieberman, 2012, pp. 137–138).

They suggest that England and the United States are amongst those settings where these two developments are clearly visible. We examine each of these four trends below.

Recruiting, selecting, preparing and retaining high-quality individuals

There has been much discussion about the importance of recruiting and select-ing both high quality and sufficient numbers of teachers to meet the demand in ways that match the changing demography of the school population. In the United States, the entry standards into initial teacher education have not been very rigorous. Setting the bar relatively low has, over the years, guaranteed a steady supply of teachers, especially for the primary grades. More recently, however, the number of young people choosing to become teachers has dropped due to more employment opportunities for women and minorities, increased pressure on teachers brought about by accountability demands, and an increasingly poor public opinion of the profession. This is happening at a time when the population of young children attending school has increased due to the influx of immigrant populations in many of the southern states. Whilst most teachers are still prepared in programmes housed in universities, alternative routes into teaching including such approaches as Teach for America, Troops to Teachers and the Urban Teacher Residency programmes, amongst others, have been steadily increasing in response to the demand for qualified teachers, par-ticularly in urban and underserved areas. These approaches will be described in detail in Chapter 3.

In other countries, including England, it has also proved very difficult at times to meet the demand, and steps have had to be taken by successive govern-ments to ensure that there are sufficient teachers at any given time. Again, these steps have included the introduction of different routes into teaching, designed to recruit suitable people who might not otherwise consider entering the profession. But they have also included a range of financial incentives often targeted at especially challenging aspects of recruitment, such as the bursaries provided for those training to teach particular shortage subjects. The English variants of these approaches, including the introduction of 'employment-based routes', are also discussed in more detail in Chapter 3.

However, in addition to the basic demand to fill teaching posts within the system, the growing attention to the quality of teaching has also led to attempts to ensure that the best-qualified recruits are attracted into the profession. The notion of 'best-qualified' has usually been taken to refer to applicants' academic qualifications. The Teach First programme in the United Kingdom, following the model set by Teach for America years before, was designed to attract graduates from the best universities with the best degree classifications in order to meet this aspiration. It was claimed that many of these people would not otherwise have joined teaching and also that their high calibre would make them well suited to working in the most challenging schools (Hutchings, Maylor, Mendick, Menter & Smart, 2006). In spite of this focus on candidates' previous qualifications, there is remarkably little evidence from anywhere in the world to support the view that those teachers with the strongest academic qualifications become the best teachers.

Testing the proposition obviously begs the question about how teaching quality might be defined. Most commonly it is asserted that teaching quality can be measured by student outcomes. In other words, the best teachers are those whose pupils achieve the highest test or exam results. However, even on this somewhat narrow definition, there is little evidence that such outcomes are achieved by pupils of the teachers with the best academic qualifications. In England, for example, the only evidence that the Department for Education could cite in the 2011 *Training Our Next Generation of Outstanding Teachers. An Improvement Strategy for Discussion* (DfE, 2011) to back up the view that studies show that teachers with good subject knowledge are more effective, was a book written by an educational consultant Fenton Whelan (2009). In the United States, a recent review of the research literature revealed mixed results (Tatto et al., 2016).

It has also been suggested that what actually matters most in recruiting teachers and ensuring that the most suitable people enter the profession is actually the standing of the profession within society. In other words, the status of teaching as an occupation seems to be very significant in ensuring that there is active competition to become a teacher, making it possible to select on grounds of quality or potential rather than accepting all those who apply. That is certainly part of the case argued in Finland by Sahlberg (2011) who notes that there are up to 10 applicants for each place in teacher education programmes and that this ratio compares favourably with medical education for doctors. Similarly, in both parts of Ireland, there is intense competition for places which enables providers of teacher education to be more selective when they are organising admissions to their programmes. The status of the teaching profession is very different in the

United States and in England, as will become apparent in contextual discussions in Chapter 3.

The other factor that affects the supply and demand of teachers is that of retention. In the past, it has often been assumed that a teacher will stay in the profession for the whole of her or his working life, perhaps with a career break for childrearing purposes. However, in the late 20th and early 21st centuries, as we have seen changes in employment patterns across the whole economy, so we have seen increasing numbers of people leaving the teaching profession after only a few years. Indeed, in some settings a significant number of the people qualifying as teachers do not even take up a regular post in a state school. Increasing numbers of teachers trained in England, for example, opt to go abroad to work, or choose to work in the private school sector, whilst others decide teaching is not for them after all – perhaps because they are unable to get a teaching post in their preferred geographical area (Foster, 2016).

But a factor which seems to be increasing the number of teachers leaving the profession in both countries is actually the changing nature of the work. Teacher educators and scholars in the United States and teacher unions in England, have been expressing concern about the number of teachers who are quitting because they find the job too stressful or that it is very different from what they expected. Increased levels of bureaucratic demand and paperwork have led to some teachers expressing severe disenchantment with the work. They may say they came into the profession to work with children and to develop positive pedagogical relationships with them, only to find that what the work actually entails is much time on administration, even when they are in the classroom. They may find the increased demands for accountability that come accompanied by heightened levels of surveillance by managers and inspectors to be over burdensome (Greany et al., 2016; Tatto et al., 2016).

Relevance and rigour of teacher education and the changing role of higher education

During the 20th century, universities and colleges of higher education steadily came to play a very major role in the provision of initial teacher education. In the United States, the United Kingdom and many other European and Anglophone countries, as teaching became increasingly professionalised, so much of the education of teachers came to be the responsibility of these HEIs. Prior to these developments, the training of teachers was essentially taken on by schools themselves through various forms of 'apprenticeship', with novice teachers learning from experienced practitioners. However, as educational sciences developed and it was recognised that learning is a complex and intellectual process, so beginning teachers were understood to require some understanding of, for example, psychology. At no time was the importance of practical experience or 'experiential learning' actually denied, but it was increasingly thought necessary for this to be balanced with the systematic study of education as well, of course, as the study of the subject knowledge to be taught.

Other established professions such as law, medicine and engineering preceded teaching in establishing their strong training base within higher education and it was symbolic of the maturation of teaching as a profession that teacher education moved into the academy during the 20th century (see Furlong, 2013). However, it became clear that this base was not a secure one, especially in the United States and in England. During the 1980s and in subsequent decades, a number of strident attacks were launched against the university contribution to teacher education, which began to influence government policy on teacher education. We discuss the specific details of these attacks and the thrust of government policy in the United States and England in more detail in Chapter 3, but suffice it to say that the struggle between 'school-based/school-led' and 'university-led/partnership-based' approaches to initial teacher education in these countries became a contest of enormous significance in teaching and teacher education in these countries, at a time when several other countries, including Scotland, Australia and Austria (for example) were consolidating or enhancing the university contribution within their systems of teacher education.

Standards in teacher education

A common trend in teacher education in many countries during the last part of the 20th century and then into the 21st century, has been the introduction of the concept of teaching standards. Whilst the term 'competences' was originally used in many contexts, the adoption of the word 'standards' to describe the list of skills and attributes that teachers should have and be able to demonstrate has become widespread. Indeed, as mentioned above, 'standardisation' is identified by Sahlberg as one of the main characteristics of the GERM (Sahlberg, 2011). More specifically the adoption of standards may be seen as an aspect of the concern to increase accountability within teacher education. Provision of national teacher education systems represents a major demand on the public purse and it is therefore, rational to expect that providers of teacher education should be held accountable for the investment that the state makes. In order to assess 'value for money' as well as to ensure that the quality of teaching is appropriately high for modern schooling, it was argued that there should be a baseline against which to judge the performance of beginning teachers (Ryan & Bourke, 2013).

Indeed, in some systems the idea of standards has been developed into a series of statements designed to cover different stages of a teacher's career or a different range of responsibilities. In England, it has been the responsibility of the government through its appropriate agency – currently the National College for Teaching and Leadership – to develop and apply the standards, albeit with some form of consultation with the profession.

In the United States, the development of standards to regulate teacher education and the profession has a long history of failed attempts. Recently, due to increasing federal pressure, proposals to regulate teacher education took hold and the Interstate Teacher Assessment and Support Consortium (InTASC) standards are now being used in programme accreditation efforts[4] by a number of states (CCSSO, 2013). These standards were constructed as 'progressions' and are seen as also regulating teacher performance in the early years. Whilst the strongest regulatory discourse has emerged at the federal level, the responsibility to develop or select standards for qualification falls to the individual states, and programmes still maintain a reasonable degree of autonomy (as will be discussed in Chapter 3).

Comparison of teaching standards in different countries reveals both similarities and differences. One similarity is the overall structure of standards statements, which almost all include declarations about what a teacher should know and about what a teacher should be able to do. Where there is less commonality is both in the detail of what is included under each of these headings and in whether or not attention is given to a third area, that of teacher dispositions and/or values. There has been anxiety in some settings about stipulating the values that should be held by teachers as these are either seen to be a matter of personal belief or perhaps to interfere politically with some things that should be apolitical. Statements that do not steer away from these issues suggest, for example, that teachers should demonstrate a commitment to democracy, equality and fairness. Interestingly, in England where there is a notable reluctance to stipulate these matters, there is nevertheless, a statement that teachers should not undermine 'fundamental British values' in their work. In other words, there are no positive statements about the values that the teacher should themselves hold; the value statement is instead couched in the essentially negative terms of how they should not behave. Furthermore, of course there is much discussion to be had on what is actually meant by 'fundamental British values!'

The use of standards statements, including a statement about values, has led to a situation where the assessment of student teachers is largely based on judgements made by school-based mentors and/or university-based tutors about whether or not the appropriate standards have been met by each individual student teacher. If they have been met, then that person is judged to be 'ready' to enter the profession and to be awarded at least provisional qualification as a teacher.

In the United States, the discourse on values again varies by state and often by programme. Whilst there is great variability across programmes, values respecting human diversity tend to dominate. Nevertheless, the notion of values, whilst it consumes a great deal of effort, is less important than in England as far as certification is concerned. The award of Qualified Teacher Status is typically provided by a HEI based on the combined evaluation of the candidate's performance throughout the programme including performance during the school internship. Programmes typically use as criteria: the candidate's knowledge of the learner and learning process (which include learner development and learning differences as well as an understanding of learning environments); the knowledge of the subject (which includes knowledge of the content and its application); the quality of their instructional practice (which includes assessment, planning for instruction and knowledge of instructional strategies); and their level of professional responsibility (which includes professio[...] and ethical practice, and leadership and collaboration) (CCSSO, 2013[...]

Diversification

When teacher supply issues become politically sensitive, it is not uncommon fo[r] policy makers to look for solutions that seek to attract people from different backgrounds into the profession. At various times – particularly around major wars – governments have resorted to 'emergency training' of teachers, which has typically involved a radical shortening of the period of time required before entering the profession. Attempts to boost supply have also focused on widening the pool – or creating alternative pools – from within which applicants might be found: encouraging people into the profession at later stages in life, for example, by recruiting women who have raised families and are looking for a new career. The recognition of this market pressure on the supply pool of teachers has sometimes led to the creation of part-time entry routes or indeed to distance learning routes. Distance learning has also been an approach favoured in remote areas ranging from sub-Saharan Africa to the Scottish Highlands, where student teachers may find it impractical to attend a teacher education centre in person. But there have also been other initiatives involving the recognition of overseas qualifications or even employing unqualified teachers, sometimes because of a particular skill, such as musical ability or sporting prowess. It is examples such as these that Darling-Hammond and Lieberman (2012) are alluding to when they write:

> In these countries candidates can choose from an array of different pre-service preparation models or undertake a pathway that provides 'on-the-job training', generally through a graduate program. Some teachers can receive a permit to teach before receiving any training. Standards that have evolved on paper are not universally enforced. It is unclear what these governments think a *qualified* teacher looks like.
>
> (p. 153)

What it means to be a qualified teacher

In considering the standards that have been developed in any particular setting, one may detect how teaching itself is understood in that setting. Whilst there may be much common ground, for example, about teachers possessing the requisite subject knowledge to teach the official curriculum, and agreement about the need for teachers to be able to communicate effectively and organise classrooms and manage pupils' behaviour appropriately, there may be far less agreement about some other matters. The extent to which teachers should be seen as agents of change, for example, actually challenging injustice or inequality or the extent to which teachers should be carrying out original enquiry into their own classrooms and making use of the latest educational research are y be considerable variation in the ways in which teaching

…ure review of teacher education (Menter, Hulme, Elliot & …m of us suggested that there may be a range of models or …ing, which may influence not only the ways in which teaching …ned but also the ways in which teacher education systems are …other words, the curriculum, assessment and pedagogy of initial …ion essentially reflect the particular model of teaching that is …in the setting. We suggested that it may be possible to distinguish …radigms. We called these:

- the effective teacher;
- the reflective teacher;
- the enquiring teacher; and
- the transformative teacher.

In general terms, these paradigms may be seen as being placed along a spectrum, ranging from a relatively restricted view of teaching professionalism to a much more extended view, to use Hoyle's terms from the 1970s (Hoyle, 1974). But they may also be seen as 'cumulative', in that the later models build upon the earlier ones. In a nutshell, a transformative teacher is one who is also enquiring and reflective, and effective.

Similarly, in an earlier work, Stuart and Tatto (2000) in their examination of initial teacher education approaches in five international settings (England and Wales, Malawi, Mexico, South Africa and the United States) in the context of wide-ranging educational reforms, discuss the delicate balance between the political and the epistemological debate in teacher education and the consequences in the conceptions and formation of future teachers as transmitters or mediators of the school curriculum. In the first conception, teaching is regarded as a mechanical or routine procedure, where learning is seen as a series of procedures or steps to accomplish and teachers tend to end up primarily reacting to external mandates and guidelines. Consequently, the teacher education curriculum under this conception is:

> [O]ccupied with strategies to help teachers deal with classroom routines as a series of steps or tasks to accomplish, and to comply appropriately with external demands on them. Under this view teaching requires little specialized knowledge, and the teacher education curriculum primarily reflects the curriculum that teachers will deliver in the school.
>
> (Stuart & Tatto, 2000, p. 499)

In contrast, when teaching is conceived as a complex undertaking where the teacher is seen as a highly qualified professional able to help pupils to develop problem-solving capabilities, the teacher education curriculum 'aims to develop norms about what good teaching is, and to provide teacher learners with the knowledge, skills and dispositions needed to reach and sustain such norms' (Stuart & Tatto, 2000, p. 500).

These distinctions seem important in trying to make sense of the contexts in which beginning teachers are learning and will inform our attempt to make sense of the learning experiences of beginning teachers in some particular settings in England and the United States.

Teaching and learning in teacher education: what the research tells us

Having given some thought to the ways in which teacher education is shaped by policy developments; we turn now to consider some aspects of the learning (and teaching) that are undertaken when people are entering the teaching profession. As we noted above, teaching standards are now the most common formal expression of what it is that teachers should know and be able to do. However, the nature of the relevant professional knowledge has been discussed and at times contested and our analysis needs to acknowledge the differences at the heart of that debate. But we also wish to consider the nature of 'expertise' – what is it that teachers come to be able to do on the basis of their professional knowledge? Understandings of expertise are closely linked with concepts of teachers' professional identities. What are the processes which help or hinder successful professional learning? We need to consider the nature of work-based learning and the relationships between theory and practice in becoming a teacher.

Professional knowledge

The most widely accepted accounts of professional knowledge are those developed from the work of Shulman in the 1980s (Shulman, 1986, 1987). He suggested that as well as subject or content knowledge, teachers need to learn professional knowledge, which Shulman initially called curricular knowledge. But his initial original contribution was to identify a third form of professional knowledge, which he called pedagogical content knowledge, which may be seen as knowing a subject in a way that facilitates teaching (and learning) that subject (Shulman, 1987). In later work, Shulman (1987) further elaborated these three categories into seven, as follows (see Philpott, 2014 for a full account):

1   content knowledge;
2   general pedagogical knowledge;
3   curriculum knowledge;
4   pedagogical content knowledge;
5   knowledge of learners and their characteristics;
6   knowledge of educational contexts; and
7   knowledge of educational ends, purposes and values.

We can see how this list creates a skeletal curriculum for a teacher education programme, but in itself it says nothing about how or where these seven aspects are best learned. What it does, however, demonstrate is that learning to teach is not necessarily as straightforward as some of the earlier models, especially simple apprenticeship models, may have implied.

The relationship between experience and cognition in professional learning is a complex one but there have been serious efforts to understand it. McIntyre (1993) and later Hagger and McIntyre (2006) have, for example, developed the concept of practical theorising in an attempt to capture the synergetic relationship between these aspects of learning. This involves questioning educational theories, presented in the form of suggestions for practice, trying them out in specific school settings, and testing them against diverse criteria. Practical theorising was developed as an alternative to reflective practice models (e.g. Schön, 1983) because of the lack of experience of most student teachers. This model is very influential in the University of Oxford Internship scheme, to be discussed further in Chapter 4.

Sustained work carried out by some members of our research team has given close attention to the nature of beginning teachers' learning. Indeed, on the understanding that teachers develop their capabilities through a process of inter-action between intellectual activity and experience in real contexts of teaching and learning, Burn et al. (2015) prefer to talk about the developing expertise of beginning teachers. Working from close study and analysis of student teachers' claims as to what and how they were learning from experience during their teacher education programmes they identified five characteristics that may affect any individual's orientation towards their professional learning. These they call:

- aspiration – the extent of the student teacher's aspirations for their own and their pupils' learning;
- intentionality – the extent to which the student teacher deliberately plans for their own learning;
- frame of reference – the value that the student teacher ascribes to looking beyond their experience in order to make sense of it;
- response to feedback – the student teacher's disposition towards receiving feedback and the value that they attribute to it; and
- attitude to context – the student teacher's attitude to the positions in which they find themselves and the approaches that they take to the school context (Burn et al., 2015).

In their work, Burn et al. (2015) demonstrate and draw attention to the ways in which an individual's orientations may change during the learning process, and subsequent doctoral work by Tessa Blair (Blair, 2017) is exploring the extent to which a typology such as this may be used as an aid to improve the learning not only of the student teacher her/himself, but also of the experienced teacher (mentor) who may be working with them.

In the United States, teacher education has been framed by a constructivist view of teaching and learning with the MSU programme exemplifying this approach by ensuring that student teachers develop a deep understanding of both subject and pedagogical knowledge, and can use their own experiences to develop their own theory and practice over time. Under this model, teaching is seen as a complex undertaking based on constructing, acting and reflecting on one's actions, whilst helping students to develop problem-solving abilities. Teachers are considered as 'actors' who take initiatives to improve their own practice and are capable of challenging the status quo in schools, and to proactively work towards stated societal as well as instructional goals; notions of democracy, community, equity and inclusion characterise the aims of teacher preparation (Stuart & Tatto, 2000). The curriculum is aimed at developing norms about good teaching, and providing student teachers with the knowledge, skills and dispositions needed to reach and sustain such norms.

Partnerships designed to create a collaborative approach between HEIs, schools and classrooms to prepare teachers capable of dealing effectively with the problems of practice and to manage themselves as responsible professionals also characterises the MSU programme.

In the United States, complex models for teacher preparation have evolved, for instance the MSU programme combines consecutive and concurrent elements, and at the same time attempts to ensure coherence through a kind of 'progressive focusing' by first studying over 4 years a subject-oriented degree, and from the third year onwards combining this with professional courses aimed at helping student teachers to 'think and know like a teacher'. This sequence leads into the postgraduate internship year where they learn to 'act like a teacher', whilst continuing to study professional issues. According to Stuart and Tatto (2000), this arrangement clearly indicates the intention to bring private tacit and public propositional knowledge together in a reflective manner in a programme that as a whole is both knowledge and practice-oriented.

These more complex models of professional learning in teacher education indicate why it is erroneous to polarise or oversimplify the processes of becoming a teacher. Whilst it is foolish to advocate a simple apprenticeship model of learning to teach, it would be equally erroneous to suggest that all the theoretical learning in a teacher education programme should emanate entirely from a university. There are elements of becoming a teacher that are very firmly based on the craft aspects of the work and this is why the interactions between beginning and more experienced teachers are so crucial. But to suggest that 'modelling' is the only contribution to be made by school-based staff is as short-sighted as suggesting that university staff should not be discussing and analysing practice with student teachers.

Although there is some uneasiness with terminology that adopts language drawn from the field of medicine, the development of what have come to be known as 'research-informed clinical practice' models in teacher education (AACTE, 2010; Burn & Mutton, 2014; Grossman, Hammerness & McDonald, 2009) has been built upon understandings of professional learning as needing both context-specific and abstract or decontextualised elements. Crucially such models imply close cooperation and collaboration between school-based and university-based staff. The promotion of partnership in teacher education is another element of these developments, although, as has been shown in some earlier studies in England (Furlong et al., 2000), partnerships have sometimes been quite limited or formalistic in their conception.

Coherence in teacher education

Previous studies of educational reform and its influence on different approaches to teacher education in the United States and elsewhere have revealed that programmes that have been judged to be successful are those defined as highly coherent (Tatto, 1996, 1998, 1999a, 1999b). Coherence in this sense however, is not defined as compliance with external standards and regulations, but rather as a process that emerges internally within the programme faculty in the process of curriculum formation and through extensive conversations concerning programme aims and strategies. Faculty members in successful programmes were found to hold consistent beliefs about what constitutes a successful teacher, and about how each of the experiences within the programme, including the school practicum, were key to supporting young people learn to teach. Coherent programmes had developed the necessary tools to help future teachers develop their knowledge and skills in a manner consistent with a programme's aims. The key characteristic of these successful programmes was their approach to teaching as inquiry, which required from future teachers: a strong knowledge of the subject and an ability to engage in sense-making; understanding themselves and their pupils as learners; understanding that knowledge (the curriculum) is socially constructed and enacted in sociocultural situations; and learning to teach in a community of learners, amongst others. The findings from these studies and others (e.g. Grossman, Hammerness, McDonald & Ronfeldt, 2008) inform in part the theoretical framework developed for this study and the analysis of the data which seeks to identify instances of alignment across the different contexts in learning to teach as conducive to creating and enabling teacher learners to recognise the opportunities open to them in order to develop and change.

Challenges in the comparative study of teacher education

In Chapter 2, we discuss the sociocultural theoretical framework and the methodology that was adopted for the investigation reported in this book. Here, however, we wish to discuss some aspects of the comparative nature of this study, set, as it is, in specific local contexts within two different national settings.

Importing and adapting policy in embedded contexts

One of the major effects of what Sahlberg (2011) has called the GERM, has been a marked increase in policy makers' attention to education policies elsewhere. We have seen an increasing amount of policy importation and adaptation, sometimes described as 'policy borrowing', where reports of educational improvements in one setting attract the interest of researchers or policy makers from elsewhere and there then follows the adoption of a similar policy, albeit with some adaptation, in the visitor's homeland. Examples of this in England would include some aspects of the national numeracy strategy, which appeared to have been adapted from numeracy teaching practices in South Korea and more recently the promotion by the government in England of 'mastery maths' following approaches used in Singapore and Shanghai. Similarly, the Swedish 'free schools' provided part of the inspiration for the Conservative party's introduction of a similar kind of new school in England from 2010 onwards. And even before that, the United States' charter schools influenced the creation of self-governing academies in England, under the Labour administration (see Adonis, 2012).

There are, however, many problems, both potential and real, in importing policies that appear to be successful in one context and implanting them in another. These problems include the possibility that the policy itself may not continue to be successful in its original context. Such was the case with the Swedish free schools which were subsequently found to have created greater social division in communities and not to have led to sustained improvements in educational attainment.[5] But even where the original has proved successful, the simple transference of a policy from one context to another on the assumption that it will have the same effect in the new context is based on the naïve view that context is not important. We have seen time and again over the course of history how strongly educational systems and the policies and practices within them are shaped by the particular social and cultural contexts in which they operate.

Alexiadou and Jones (2001) have drawn attention to the interaction between what they call 'travelling policy' and the 'embedded contexts' in which the policies 'arrive'. An interesting case in point might be the way in which the Teach First programme was developed in England, initially in London, on the basis of the experience of Teach for America in the United States. Teach First, although adopting some of the key principles of the American scheme, nevertheless, developed in a distinctively English way to such an extent that there is sometimes a denial that they are in any meaningful sense the same programme. Nevertheless, it is worth noting that employment-based, fast track schemes of this kind have now been launched in many different countries. There is indeed an international network (see Ball, 2012) of such schemes. Clearly the policy has travelled far and wide but in each case it has been developed in a way that is responsive to the local context and may be judged as more or less successful.

Rizvi and Lingard (2010), in their analysis of how education policy has become increasingly globalised talk about 'vernacular globalisation' or even 'glocalisation', terms that recognise the significance of the interaction between the global forces and the history and culture of educational provision in the particular setting.

The need to be sensitive to context

These complex interactions create something of a challenge for scholars in comparative education. The historical origins of this field of study lay in somewhat imperialistic descriptions of how education systems 'elsewhere' are organised. Indeed, one of the early classic comparative education texts in Britain was called *Other Schools and Ours* (King, 1967). The main purpose of comparative education was to identify similarities and differences in the policies and practices in different national contexts. As comparative studies in education have developed, there has been growing awareness of the complexity of making such comparisons. It has been suggested that we should not be assuming that we are comparing 'like-with-like'; that we can only begin to understand education within any society by analysing it in terms of its own contexts, especially the historical, social and cultural. So comparativists such as Crossley and Watson (2003) and many others have stressed the significance of 'context sensitivity' in such studies. One of the most sustained examples based on such an approach was Alexander's major comparative work on primary education in five national settings. The title of his work *Culture and Pedagogy* (Alexander, 2000) reflects from the start his conviction that it is only possible to make sense of policies and practices in primary schools by looking at their histories and their relationship to aspects of the wider culture within the particular society. This does not prevent us from making comparisons, but rather it will tend to ensure that we do not make simplistic judgements about practices, their origins or motivations.

These considerations have influenced the present study significantly. Even within the apparently limited context of the United Kingdom, considerations of the different contexts in England, Northern Ireland, Scotland and Wales are seen as very important and indeed help to shed great light on what can be revealed through 'home international' study (Hulme, 2016). Similarly, the ambitious study reported by Tatto et al. (2012) of teacher education in 17 countries whilst using a comparative methodology was carefully crafted to take into account history, culture and context. In the present study, we certainly seek to avoid over-simple comparisons between the two settings and, indeed, we spend some time discussing the distinctive nature of the two policy contexts in Chapter 3.

Sites of research in the Learning to Teach in England and the United States study

This study looks at teacher education practices in two national contexts, England and the United States. The research in the English context has been carried out in two settings, one within London, where we consider the experiences of some Teach First participants and those who are working with them. The other focuses on the experiences of student teachers on two slightly different routes in Oxfordshire, one long-established and one much newer, but both associated with the University of Oxford. The Teach First participants were training in a London school that had been quick to embrace that particular route into teaching whilst the Oxford Internship Scheme had developed from an explicit commitment to partnership models that predated national requirements. The two Oxfordshire schools' commitment to the School Direct route was driven in large part by concerns to secure an adequate supply of teachers in a region facing an increasing shortage of teachers.

In the United States, the relevant macro policy context is not only the national one but also that of the state. The sites we investigated for this study were schools associated with MSU, well known for educating teachers using a research evidence-based curriculum and for its year-long internship, and with a history of fruitful partnerships with local schools.

It is important to be clear that in both England and the United States, our empirical work was carried out in the school setting – as explained in Chapter 2 – in the context of partnership programmes of *different* kinds. Moreover, the specific relationship of each school to its university partner(s) meant that in every specific case the nature, depth and history of those partnerships varied considerably.

Summary and conclusion

Our aim in this chapter has been to set the scene for the study that is reported. We have identified a number of the key questions in teacher education that emerge from a broad overview of the literature. Although the study itself is tightly focused on a limited number of particular settings and individuals, we designed it in such way that it would shed light on each of these questions. The selection of the student teachers was based on the notion of 'the best case scenario' within each of the programmes studied and the data collection and analysis was geared towards the production of detailed 'snapshots' of practice including the planning, teaching and reflection of each student teacher. Thus, whilst we refer to England and the United States, the purpose of this study was the deep analysis of initial teaching practice across different subjects and contexts as seen through the practices of individuals going through the process of learning to teach. The study is not meant to be representative of each country or of the general teaching practices within them. Its purpose is to build theory and strategies to understand the complexity of learning to teach in the fast-paced contexts of changing policy and curriculum standards, in an environment of increased accountability. Through doing parallel work in two national settings and in a number of specific sites it was our intention to achieve new insights into the nature of professional learning for student teachers, including the relative influence of different sites of learning and the interaction between the student teachers and the school contexts in which they find themselves.

In the next chapter, we set out some of the wider theoretical and methodological starting-points for the study and then move into a description of how the particular case sites were approached and investigated. Then, in Chapter 3, before reporting on our findings about the experience of learning to teach, we offer a more detailed account of the distinctive policy and institutional contexts on each side of the Atlantic, in order to help us locate the student teachers within them, and make sense of each distinctive social situation of development.

From the outset, therefore, we are suggesting that the processes of learning to become a teacher are not simple; they are complex and multifaceted. This of course, is one reason why the study of teacher education is so deeply fascinating and why it provides such effective illumination of wider educational processes and theories.

Notes

1 See http://timss2015.org/timss-2015/mathematics/student-achievement/trends-in-mathematics-achievement/ (TIMSS & PIRLS International Study Center, 2016).
2 www.theguardian.com/education/2016/oct/24/almost-third-of-teachers-quit-within-five-years-of-qualifying-figures (Weale, 2016).
3 www.teachers.org.uk/news-events/press-releases-england/nutyougov-teacher-survey-government-education-policy (NUT, 2015).
4 In the United States accreditation of teacher preparation falls under the Council for the Accreditation of Educator Preparation http://caepnet.org/ (CAEP, 2015).
5 See: www.newstatesman.com/politics/education/2016/06/why-sweden-s-free-schools-are-failing (Wigmore, 2016).

References

Adonis, A. (2012). *Education, education, education: Reforming England's schools.* London: Biteback.
Alexander, R. (2000). *Culture and pedagogy.* Oxford: Blackwell.
Alexiadou, N. & Jones, K. (2001). *Travelling policy/local spaces.* Paper presented to the Congress Marx International 111: Le capital et l'humanité, Université de Paris-X Nanterre-Sorbonne, 26–29 Septembre.
American Association of Colleges for Teacher Education (AACTE). (2010). *The clinical preparation of teachers: A policy brief.* Washington, DC: AACTE. Retrieved from http://oacte.org/pdf/ClinicalPrepPaper_03-11-2010.pdf.
Ball, S. (2012). *Global Education Inc.* London: Routledge.
Berliner, D. (1994). The wonder of exemplary performances. In J. N. Mangieri & C. C. Block (Eds.), *Creating powerful thinking in teachers and students* (pp. 161–186). Fort Worth: Harcourt Brace.
Berliner, D. (2001). Learning about and learning from expert teachers. *International Journal of Educational Research, 35,* 463–482.
Blair, T. (2017). Paper presented at Teacher Education Advancement Network conference, May 2017, University of Aston, Birmingham, UK.
Burn, K., Hagger, H. & Mutton, T. (2015). *Beginning teachers' learning.* Northwich: Critical Publishing.
Burn, K., Hagger, H., Mutton T. & Everton, T. (2003). The complex development of student-teachers' thinking. *Teachers and Teaching: Theory and Practice, 9*(4), 309–321.
Burn, K. & Mutton, T. (2014). *Review of 'research-informed clinical practice' in initial teacher education.* London: BERA, available at bera.ac.uk.
Calderhead, J. & Robson, M. (1991). Images of teaching students' early conceptions of classroom practice. *Teaching and Teacher Education, 7*(1), 1–8.

Cochran-Smith, M. (2001). Constructing outcomes in teacher education: Policy, practice and pitfalls. *Education Policy Analysis Archives, 9*(11), 1–57.

Cochran-Smith, M. & Demers, K. (2008). How do we know what we know? Research and teacher education. In M. Cochran-Smith, S. Feiman-Nemser, D. McIntyre & K. Demers (Eds.), *Handbook on research in teacher education* (pp. 1009–1016). New York: Routledge.

Cochran-Smith, M. & Lytle, S. (1999). Relationships of knowledge and practice: Teacher learning in communities. *Review of Research in Education, 24,* 249–306.

Council for the Accreditation of Educator Preparation (CAEP). (2015). *Homepage.* Retrieved from http://caepnet.org/.

Council of Chief State School Officers (CCSSO). (2013). *Interstate Teacher Assessment and Support Consortium InTASC model core teaching standards and learning progressions for teachers 1.0: A resource for ongoing teacher development.* Washington, DC: Author.

Crossley, M. & Watson, K. (2003). *Comparative and international research in education.* London: Routledge Falmer.

Darling-Hammond, L. (2006). *Powerful teacher education: Lessons from exemplary programs.* San Francisco: Jossey-Bass.

Darling-Hammond, L. & Lieberman, A. (2012). Teacher education around the world: What can we learn from international practice? In L. Darling-Hammond & A. Lieberman (Eds.), *Teacher education around the world* (pp. 151–169). London: Routledge.

Department for Education (DfE). (2011). *Training our next generation of outstanding teachers: An improvement strategy for discussion.* London: DfE. Retrieved on 25 April 2017, from www.gov.uk/government/publications/training-our-next-generation-of-outstanding-teachers-an-improvement-strategy-for-discussion.

Dewey, J. (1965). The relation of theory to practice in education. In M. Borrowman (Ed.), *Teacher education in America: A documentary history* (pp. 140–171). New York: Teachers College Press. (Original published in 1904).

Feiman-Nemser, S. (1983). Learning to teach. In L. S. Shulman & G. Sykes (Eds.), *Handbook of research on teaching and policy.* New York: Longman.

Feiman-Nemser, S. (2001). From preparation to practice: Designing a continuum to strengthen and sustain teaching. *Teachers College Record, 103*(6), 1013–1055.

Foster, D. (2016). *Teachers: Supply retention and workload* (Briefing Paper 2777). London: House of Commons Library.

Furlong, J. (2008). Making teaching a 21st century profession: Tony Blair's big prize. *Oxford Review of Education, 34*(6), 727–739.

Furlong, J. (2013). *Education: An anatomy of the discipline.* London: Routledge.

Furlong, J., Barton, L., Miles, S., Whiting, C. & Whitty, G. (2000). *Teacher education in transition.* Buckingham: Open University.

Greany, T., Barners, I., Mostafa, T., Pensiero, N. & Swensson, C. (2016). *Trends in Maths and Science Study (TIMSS): National report for England.* London: Department for Education.

Grossman, P., Hammerness, K. M. & McDonald, M. (2009). Redefining teaching, re-imagining teacher education. *Teachers and Teaching, 15*(2), 273–289.

Grossman, P., Hammerness, K. M., McDonald, M. & Ronfeldt, M. (2008). Constructing coherence: Structural predictors of perceptions of coherence in NYC teacher education programs. *Journal of Teacher Education, 59*(4), 273–287.

Hagger, H. & McIntyre, D. (2006). *Learning teaching from teachers.* Buckingham: Open University.

Hammerness, K. M., Darling-Hammond, L., Bransford, J., Berliner, D., Cochran-Smith, M., McDonald, M. & Zeichner, K. (2005). How teachers learn and develop. In L. Darling-Hammond & J. Bransford (Eds.), *Preparing teachers for a changing world: What teachers should learn and be able to do* (pp. 358–389). San Francisco: Jossey-Bass.

Hattie, J. (2003). *Teachers make a difference: What is the research evidence?* Paper presented at the Australian Council for Educational Research conference: Melbourne.

Hobson, A., Malderez, A., Tracey, L., Giannakaki, M., Pell, G. & Tomlinson, P. (2008). Student teachers' experiences of initial teacher preparation in England: Core themes and variation. *Research Papers in Education, 23*(4), 407–433.

Holmes Group. (1986). *Tomorrow's teachers: A report of the Holmes Group*. East Lansing, MI: Holmes Group. Retrieved from https://eric.ed.gov/?id=ED270454.

Hoyle, E. (1974). Professionality, professionalism and control in teaching. *London Education Review, 3*(2), 13–19.

Huberman, M. (1992). Teacher development and instructional mastery. In A. Hargreaves & M. G. Fullan (Eds.), *Understanding teacher development* (pp. 122–142). New York: Teachers College Press.

Hulme, M. (2016). Analysing teacher education policy: Comparative and historical approaches. In Teacher Education Group (Ed.), *Teacher education in times of change* (pp. 37–54). Bristol: Policy Press.

Hutchings, M., Maylor, U., Mendick, H., Menter, I. & Smart, S. (2006). *An evaluation of innovative approaches to teacher training on the Teach First programme: Final report to the Training and Development Agency for schools*. Accessed on 16 February 2017, from http://archive.londonmet.ac.uk/metranet.londonmet.ac.uk/londonmet/fms/MRSite/Research/ipse/FINAL%20Report%20Teach%20First%20July06.pdf.

Jerrim, J. & Shure, N. (2016). *Achievement of 15-year-olds in England: PISA 2015 national report*. London: Department for Education.

Judge, H., Lemosse, M., Paine, L. & Sedlak, M. (1994). *The university and the teachers: France, the United States, England*. Didcot: Symposium Books.

King, E. (1967). *Other schools and ours* (3rd ed.). London: Holt, Rinehart and Winston.

Lortie, D. (1975). *Schoolteacher: A sociological study*. Chicago: University of Chicago Press.

Maynard, T. & Furlong, J. (1993). Learning to teach' and models of mentoring. In D. McIntyre, H. Hagger & M. Wilkin (Eds.), *Mentoring: Perspectives on school-based teacher education* (pp. 69–85). London: Kogan Page.

Maynard, T. & Furlong, J. (1995). *The growth of professional knowledge: Mentoring student teachers*. London: Routledge.

McIntyre, D. (1993). Theory, theorizing and reflection in initial teacher education. In J. Calderhead & P. Gates (Eds.), *Conceptualizing reflection in teacher development* (pp. 97–114). London: Falmer Press.

McIntyre, D. (2006). Opportunities for a more balanced approach to ITE: Can we learn again from research and other experience? *Scottish Educational Research, 37*, 5–19.

McIntyre, D. & Hagger, H. (1993). Teacher expertise and models of mentoring. In D. McIntyre, H. Hagger & M. Wilkin (Eds.), *Mentoring: Perspectives on school-based teacher education* (pp. 86–102). London: Kogan Page.

McKinsey & Company. (2007). *How the world's best-performing schools come out on top*. Retrieved 5 February 2017, from http://mckinseyonsociety.com/how-the-worlds-best-performing-schools-come-out-on-top/.

Menter, I. (2009). Teachers for the future: What have we got and what do we need? In S. Gewirtz, P. Mahony, I. Hextall & A. Cribb (Eds.), *Changing teacher professionalism: International trends, challenges and ways forward* (pp. 217–228). London: Routledge.

Menter, I. (2016). Introduction. In Teacher Education Group (Ed.), *Teacher education in times of change* (pp. 3–18). Bristol: Policy Press.

Menter, I., Hulme, M., Elliot, D. & Lewin, J. (2011). *Literature review on teacher education in the twenty-first century*. Edinburgh: The Scottish Government.

National Union of Teachers (NUT). (2015). *NUT/YouGov teacher survey on government education policy*. Retrieved from www.teachers.org.uk/news-events/press-releases-england/nutyougov-teacher-survey-government-education-policy.

Philpott, C. (2014). *Theories of professional learning*. Northwich: Critical Publishing.

Rizvi, F. & Lingard, B. (2010). *Globalizing education policy*. London: Routledge.

Rusznyak, L. (2008). *Learning to teach: Developmental teaching patterns of student teachers*. (Unpublished doctoral dissertation). Wits School of Education, University of Witwatersrand: Johannesburg.

Ryan, M. & Bourke, T. (2013). The teacher as reflexive professional: Making visible the excluded discourse in teacher standards. *Discourse: Studies in the cultural politics in education, 34*(3), 411–423.

Sahlberg, P. (2011). *Finnish lessons*. New York: Teachers' College.

Schön, D. (1983). *The reflective practitioner: How professionals think in action*. New York: Basic Books.

Shulman, L. S. (1986). Those who understand: Knowledge growth in teaching. *Educational Researcher, 15*(2), 4–14.

Shulman, L. S. (1987). Knowledge and teaching: Foundations of the new reform. *Harvard Educational Review, 57*(1), 1–22.

Stuart, J. & Tatto, M. T. (2000). Designs for initial teacher preparation programs: An international view. *International Journal of Educational Research, 33*, 493–514.

Tatto, M. T., Schwille, J., Senk, S. L., Ingvarson, L., Rowley, G., Peck, R., Bankov, K., Rodriguez, M. & Reckase, M. (2012). *Policy, practice, and readiness to teach primary and secondary mathematics in 17 countries. Findings from the IEA Teacher Education and Development Study in Mathematics (TEDS-M)*. Amsterdam: International Association for the Evaluation of Student Achievement (IEA).

Tatto, M. T. (1996). Examining values and beliefs about teaching diverse students: Understanding the challenges for teacher education. *Educational Evaluation and Policy Analysis, 18*, 155–180.

Tatto, M. T. (1998). The influence of teacher education on teachers' beliefs about purposes of education, roles and practice. *Journal of Teacher Education, 49*, 66–77.

Tatto, M. T. (1999a). Improving teacher education in rural Mexico: The challenges and tensions of constructivist reform. *Teaching and Teacher Education, 15*, 15–35.

Tatto, M. T. (1999b). The socializing influence of normative cohesive teacher education on teachers' beliefs about instructional choice. *Teachers and Teaching, 5*(1), 111–134.

Tatto, M. T. (Ed.) (2009). *Reforming teaching globally*. Charlotte, NC, USA: Information Age Publishers. (Reprinted from *Reforming teaching globally*, M. T. Tatto, 2007 Oxford, UK: Symposium Books).

Tatto, M. T., Savage, C., Liao, W., Marshall, S., Goldblatt, P. & Contreras, M. L. (2016). The emergence of high-stakes accountability policies in teacher preparation: An examination of the U.S. Department of Education's proposed regulations. *Education Policy Analysis Archives, 24*(25). doi: http://dx.doi.org/10.14507/epaa.24.2322.

Teacher Education Group. (2016). *Teacher education in times of change*. Bristol: Policy Press.

TIMSS & PIRLS International Study Center. (2016). *TIMSS 2015 international results in mathematics: Trends in mathematics achievement*. Retrieved from http://timss2015.

org/timss-2015/mathematics/student-achievement/trends-in-mathematics-achievement/.

U.S. Department of Education (USDOE). (1983). *A nation at risk: The imperative for educational reform. A report to the Nation and the Secretary of Education.* Washington, DC: National Commission on Excellence in Education. Retrieved from http://files.eric.ed.gov/fulltext/ED226006.pdf.

U.S. Department of Education (USDOE). (2014). Teacher education issues. Proposed Rule. Federal Register, *79*, 232, [consulted December 3, 2014].

U.S. Department of Education (USDOE). (2015). *Highly qualified teachers enrolled in programs providing alternative routes to teacher certification or licensure.* Washington, DC: United States Department of Education, Office of Planning, Evaluation and Policy Development, Policy and Program Studies Service. Retrieved from www2.ed.gov/rschstat/eval/teaching/hqt-teacher-certification/report.pdf.

U.S. Department of Education (USDOE). (2016). *Preparing and credentialing the nation's teachers: The secretary's 10th report on teacher quality.* Washington, DC: Office of Postsecondary Education, USDOE. Retrieved from www2.ed.gov/about/reports/annual/teachprep/index.html.

Vygotsky, L. S. (1987). Thinking and speech. In L. S. Vygotsky (Ed.), *Collected works: Volume 1.* New York: Plenum Press.

Weale, S. (2016, October 24). Almost a third of teachers quit state sector within five years of qualifying. *Guardian.* Retrieved from www.theguardian.com/education/2016/oct/24/almost-third-of-teachers-quit-within-five-years-of-qualifying-figures.

Whelan, F. (2009). *Lessons learned: How good policies produce better schools.* London: Fenton Whelan.

Whiting, C., Black, P., Hordern, J., Parfitt, A., Reynolds, K., Sorensen, N. & Whitty, G. (2016). *Towards a new topography of ITT: A profile of Initial Teacher Training in England 2015–16.* An Occasional Paper from the IFE No. 1. Retrieved on 25 April 2017, from http://researchspace.bathspa.ac.uk/8254/1/8254.pdf.

Wigmore, T. (2016, June 18). Why Sweden's free schools are failing. *New Statesman.* Retrieved from www.newstatesman.com/politics/education/2016/06/why-sweden-s-free-schools-are-failing.

2 A sociocultural framework and methods for the analysis of teacher education policy and practice in England and the United States

Introduction

This chapter presents the sociocultural framework used by the study *Learning to Teach in England and the United States* in order to conduct a comparative analysis of initial teacher education in these two very different contexts. We contend that the politics and concerns of national and regional government education departments that have helped shape the policy landscapes of teacher education in each country are played out in very different ways in the particular and situated contexts of student teachers' development. However, questions of initial teacher education remain both highly politicised and contested in both the United States (e.g. Cochran-Smith, 2008; Tatto et al., 2016; Zeichner, Payne & Brayko, 2015) and the United Kingdom (e.g. Burn & Mutton, 2015; Whitty, 2016). Our focus in this research was simultaneously on: the macro element of the policies and practices of teacher education; the meso element of historically and culturally defined practices within institutions; and the micro element of individual behaviour and action. Rather than viewing the macro, meso and micro as separate levels, a sociocultural approach views these elements as being in constant dialectical interplay. Our primary objective in developing this framework from a sociocultural theoretical perspective was to explore the social, cultural and historical factors, which mediate the experience and understandings of student teachers as they negotiate both the national contexts of teacher training and the particular experiences of their school and university contexts.

The analysis of student teachers' social situations of development presented in this chapter explores the complex relationship between individual learning and the social situations in which that learning occurs. As Edwards (2010) argues, examining 'learning in practice' requires 'a focus on the changing relationship between learner and social situation of development' (p. 65). This in turn demands the development of a language of analysis to describe the ways learners respond to the demands of the social situation in which their learning takes place. In order to develop this complex language of analysis, we have developed a sociocultural framework that draws both on the work of the sociologist Bernstein (1990) on knowledge structures, and on Hedegaard's (2004,

2012) work on the contending motives of individual learners and societal demands from the perspective of cultural-historical activity theory.

Why sociocultural theory?

One of the dilemmas for researchers of initial teacher education is how to frame research designs that look at the interactions between: the complexity of the social organisation of schools and universities as institutions and the consequent pedagogical design of curriculum; the social relations within that institution (at both staff and pupil level); and the development of individual learning competences within these social settings. This form of research involves a combined focus on the dialectic between systemic cultural-historical practices and contradictions, social interactions and individual development (Daniels, 2008; Edwards & Daniels, 2004). This requires a dual focus on both the psychology of student teacher development in initial teacher education as well as a sociological focus on the nature and structure of educational developments in society. The development of student teachers is particularly complex as their experience is refracted through the multiple lenses that they encounter within schools and academia.

We have adopted a sociocultural framework for our analysis since we are interested in exploring the social, cultural and historical factors that have shaped the patterns of initial teacher education in each country and, which mediate the experience and understandings of student teachers as they negotiate both the national contexts of teacher training and the particular experiences of their school contexts. Sociocultural theory and cultural-historical activity theory developed from the research and theoretical focus of the Russian psychologist Lev Vygotsky from the 1920s and 1930s. These closely related theoretical approaches view the mechanisms of individual psychological development (behaviour and consciousness) as being rooted in the society and culture that a person lives in (Edwards & Daniels, 2004). Cultural-historical activity theory was developed by Cole (1996) from the activity theory work of Vygotsky's former colleague work of Leontiev (1978). Leontiev's research moved away from attention on the mind in society to a focus on the object of social activity. Leontiev formulated a distinction between goal-oriented actions that are conscious, tool-mediated operations, which he called 'the methods for accomplishing actions' (Leontiev, 1978, p. 65), and collective activity as a unit that involves both actions and operations.

The concept of object motive is a key element in cultural-historical activity theory research not least because of the possibility of conflicting or contradictory object motives within an activity. Researchers in the sociocultural tradition (e.g. Penuel & Wertsch, 1995; Holland, Lachicotte, Skinner & Cain, 1998) point to the fundamental role of mediation for the study of identity formation. Sociocultural theory stresses the importance of social interaction and cultural contexts in the development of individual consciousness and learning. This theoretical framework views the mechanisms of individual psychological development (behaviour and consciousness) as being rooted in the society and culture in which a person lives. An analysis of a social situation of development is crucial to an understanding of human development as it is both through inter-action with other people, and through our response to our material conditions, that we learn to make sense of the world. As Edwards (2010) puts it, 'relation-ships change as learners take in what is culturally valued, consequently interpret their social worlds differently and therefore, act in and on them in newly informed ways, which in turn impact on the social situations' (p. 64). In this sense, learners are active participants in their own learning by being both changed by social situations and renegotiating them.

Social situations of development in initial teacher education

Secondary level student teachers are both subject specialists with strong aca-demic credentials and subject learners within the sociocultural settings of schools and classrooms. Developing the pedagogy necessary to teach a discipli-nary subject to a variety of young people, alongside the ability to use formative and summative assessment to help those pupils to progress, are complex devel-opmental processes for student teachers. The focus on the complexity of devel-opment in this study develops a view of teaching and learning as a process through which student teachers take on what is valued in a culture and hope-fully, in turn, develop the agency that allows them to begin to contribute to that culture.

Vygotsky's (1987, 1998) concept of the social situation of development is characterised by changes in personality and consciousness of the social world at particular ages. Vygotsky, from the perspective of the child, argued that develop-ment can involve critical periods as the learner encounters contradictions between their own psychological development and the demands of the learning situation. However, Edwards (2009) and others have applied the concept of the social situ-ation to adults' learning in social settings. Thus, an analysis of student teachers' social situations of development explores the complex relationship between indi-vidual learning and the social situations in which that learning occurs. Vygotsky (1997) argued that in critical periods the learner encounters contradictions between their own psychological development and the demands of the learning situation. These changes occur when the developmental needs of a person are not met or are frustrated by the current available social means of their satisfac-tion. When there is a clash between the personal and the social, a person through interaction with others, can begin to envisage things in a new way. These moments are both personal to the particular need and history of the individual but also socially experienced and mediated by interaction with others. Each social situation of development differs according to a person's particular situation and the responses of those around them. Moreover, the key to development lies in the ability of individuals to perceive the limitations of the situation they are in and to imagine a different role for themselves (Holland et al., 1998). Neverthe-less, as Edwards (2017) has argued, 'in contrived and time-limited learning situations, such as schools and teacher education programmes, mediation from a more expert other is also needed' (p. 9).

Student teachers face at least two social situations of development: their position as learners, within the academic environment of a university; and within the specific professional contexts of their placement schools. Their experience is also mediated by both university and school educators acting as tutors and mentors. At times, these social situations intersect in a complex and dialectical interplay between theory and practice (McIntyre, 1993). At other times, the immediacy of the school or university setting may dominate the student teachers' time and thoughts. Their engagement with these social situations may be influenced by factors such as: their previous experience of education; their existing and possibly naïve understanding of social and cultural norms (e.g. Lortie, 2002; Tatto, 1999; Thompson, McNicholl & Menter, 2016); and their cultural capital acquired from family and community.

Yet just as language and thought have potential developmental functions, so context has a formative role. It matters where and how we learn as well as who we learn from and with. Claxton (2007) has described the importance of 'potentiating environments' that 'stretch learners' (p. 125). This suggests the need to create learning environments for initial teacher education that allow risk and experimentation, mediated by interaction with university tutors and school mentors. One of the key constructs from sociocultural and activity theory is the insight that our development as human beings is mediated through our interactions with others and through the use of mediational tools, especially psychological tools or signs (Daniels, 2014; Vygotsky, 1987). Student teachers are not only acquiring the psychological tools for effective pedagogy but also engaging with the cultural assumptions that govern what are deemed to be appropriate ways of being a teacher in a particular school and in society as a whole. Wertsch (2007) makes the distinction between explicit and implicit mediation within a social situation of development. Guile (2010) contends that the post-Vygotskian distinction between mediation by activity and semiotic mediation introduces 'the role of objects, practices and discourses more explicitly into our understanding of mediation' (p. 7). For initial teacher education, the explicit mediation of university settings and mentor meetings is balanced and sometimes countered by the implicit mediation of personal experience and the cultural norms and expectations of the school staff or subject room setting. The student teachers' ideas are formed and developed through this dialectical interplay between the explicit mediation of teacher education and the implicit mediation of learning to teach in the classroom.

Thus, a curriculum task set by a university tutor or school mentor may be the deliberate introduction of a stimulus designed to mediate the experience for the student teacher of teaching a particular concept in a subject within a classroom setting. An example of this explicit mediation in the early stages of teaching practice is where the student teacher might be asked to plan a lesson, which is actually taught by the mentor. In this form of practical theorising, the experience of planning for learning is mediated both through observing the success of the lesson and through the subsequent discussion of the learning observed. More implicit mediation might come from the experience of the student teacher planning and delivering a lesson that goes wrong. Task design in the classroom involves the ways teachers translate the curriculum into the tasks and activities that can engage both the cognitive and affective processes involved in learners' development (Thompson, 2015). However, the teaching of these tasks is mediated by the social interaction involved in classroom activities. Doyle (1977) has described the ways in which classroom tasks are negotiated between the pupils and the teacher, both anxious to avoid a breakdown in the social order. The mediation of the student teacher's learning here is implicit and sometimes difficult to grasp. All too often, attempts to reflect on this process result in discussions around behaviour management strategies rather than the pedagogic appropriateness of the task for the pupils' learning.

Leontiev's (1978) distinction between object motives involved in goal-oriented actions and the unit of collective activity is helpful here. The concept of object motive is a key element in cultural-historical activity research not least because of the possibility of conflicting or contradictory object motives within an activity. The object motive for teachers and the reason they design classroom activities are their pupils' learning trajectories. The object motive for the pupils involved in these activities may well be very different.

Researching the object motives of activities involves a dual focus on the cultural and historical practices that shape activity. Rogoff (2003) has argued that in much traditional educational research on developmental psychology, cultural factors are treated as separate entities and hence, research often ignores the influence of culture on the individual. On the other hand, a sociocultural approach explores the social, historical, institutional and cultural factors in which the individual is embedded. Rogoff talks of observing sociocultural activity on three interrelated 'planes': participatory appropriation (personal); guided participation (interpersonal); and apprenticeship (community process). However, Sawyer (2002) has critiqued Rogoff's analysis as being an example of treating society and the individual as separable units of analysis despite her claims of inseparability. Sawyer contends that within sociocultural theory there has long been a debate between the advocates of inseparability between the individual and society (e.g. Rogoff, 2003; Lave & Wenger, 1991) or partial separability (e.g. Wertsch, 1993; Cole, 1996; Valsiner, 1998). This debate matters for sociocultural research, and for the research in this book, as we explore the development of individuals and institutions within specific social and cultural contexts and at a particular historical time. As Mercer (2013) argues, whilst there is much research to suggest that collaborative learning, in certain conditions, benefits individual learning, there is not enough research focused with a social conception of the way people learn in specific contexts. The argument that is advanced in the research presented in this book recognises the impossibility of separating the cognitive and affective development of student teachers from societal and historical pressures and demands. At the same time, individual transitions will differ and be affected by specific contexts and experiences. Our

analysis, therefore, needs to focus both on the micro level of individual transitions and development, the meso level of practice and cultures of particular schools and local environments, and the macro, societal level of historical and current educational policy.

Multiple identities of student teachers

Dreier (1999) has argued that we must conceptualise individual subjects as 'always situated in local contexts of social practice and involved from there in primarily practical relations with social structures of practice' (p. 6). However, Dreier also points out that individuals are engaged in multiple social contexts and 'play different parts in a social practice, often from different positions and with different scopes of possibilities, concerns, and obligations' (ibid.). Identity formation is therefore, both relational in terms of being formed in social practices and situated in particular places and cultures. The identity formation of student teachers reflects the social and cultural demands and multiple motives involved in becoming a professional. These demands are multiple and may, at times, be contradictory. Holland and Lachicotte define identity as 'a self-understanding to which one is emotionally attached and that informs one's behaviour and interpretations' (Holland & Lachicotte, 2007, p. 104). Holland et al. (1998) developed the concept of positionality in order to point out that an individual's participation in activities in practice takes place from a particular stance or perspective. Identities that develop in activities in action emerge as a 'heuristic means to guide, authorize, legitimate, and encourage their own and others' behaviour' (Holland et al., 1998, p. 18). This heuristic development of identity requires two distinctive forms of agency: improvisation (the openings whereby change comes about) and appropriation (the adoption and re-shaping of professional knowledge).

Holland and Lachicotte (2007) argue that the identities that individuals develop are 'social and cultural products' (p. 134). These identities are both mediated through social and professional experience and through interactions with others (Edwards, 2010). Identity is premised as one's objectified self-image in relation to 'the ways of inhabiting roles, positions, and cultural imaginaries that matter to them' (Holland & Lachicotte, 2007, p. 103). Norton-Meier and Drake, drawing on Holland et al. (1998), argue that one of the challenges for initial teacher education programmes is 'to understand how to help university students integrate their histories of personal figured worlds of schooling and past relational identities' (Norton-Meier & Drake, 2010, p. 204). Holland and Lachicotte's concept of the figured world refers to the way that individuals position themselves in relation to the 'socially and culturally constructed realms of interpretation and performance' (Holland & Lachicotte, 2007, p. 115).

Sociocultural transitions

Student teachers are in a process of complex transition from learner to practitioner as they attempt to translate their own domain expertise to the subject pedagogy required to teach young people. This negotiation is dynamic in that whilst the learner develops within particular social contexts, and this learning is mediated by the social relations they encounter, they are also part of that context and bring their own experiences and understandings to their learning. An understanding of learning to teach needs to go beyond the concept of the transferable acquisition of pedagogical knowledge in different settings towards a more complex understanding of the transitions involved. These transitions, between school and university and between school placements present both pedagogical challenges and opportunities.

Crafter and Maunder (2012) have highlighted three sociocultural frameworks for addressing transitions: consequential transitions that have an impact on both the individual and their social context (Beach, 1999); symbolic transitions and identity rupture (Zittoun, 2006); and transitions within a community of practice (e.g. Lave & Wenger, 1991; Wenger, 1998). Beach's (1999) sociocultural typology of four categories for understanding consequential transitions is particularly helpful in understanding the transitional layers encountered by student teachers within teacher education programmes. The categories comprise of: lateral transitions (movement from historically-related settings such as school to university); collateral transitions (relatively simultaneous involvement in related activities); encompassing transitions (where an individual adapts to a new or changing social activity); and mediational transitions (simulated involvement in an educational activity not yet experienced in teaching practice). The student teacher experiences all these contexts as they move from academic success in a university to learning pedagogy in schools at a time of rapid and profound change in both schooling and initial teacher education. Zittoun's (2006) portrayal of symbolic transitions and identity rupture engendered through changes in cultural contexts, relationships or interactions points to potential moments of crisis for student teachers. From this perspective, transitions for student teachers can only be understood by taking into account the social and cultural situatedness of individual thought and action. Lave and Wenger's (1991) concept of communities of practice also reminds us that many student teachers need to negotiate the practices in both the university and school settings. However, Dreier (1999, 2009) argues for the need for research to focus on the learning of individuals over time and across the different social practices that they encounter in order to examine what he terms their 'learning trajectories'. For student teachers these learning trajectories are complex (Burn, Hagger, Mutton & Everton, 2003) and may not be linear (Furlong & Maynard, 1995). This twin lens, on the individual and on the social practices in which they learn, calls for a non-dualist and dialectical account of learning to teach that combines a focus on both the cognitive and emotional experience within development (van Huizen, van Oers & Wubbels, 2005).

Analysing activity settings

Some recent sociocultural research in teacher education has drawn on discourse and the role of semiotic mediation (e.g. Blanton, Berenson & Norwood, 2001) as well as from the perspective of cultures of practice (e.g. Goos, 2005; Moll & Arnot-Hopffer, 2005). Blanton et al. (2001) used Vygotsky's concept of language as a developmental mediating tool to investigate the discourse of prospective mathematics teachers and their university supervisors. Moll and Arnot-Hopffer (2005) drew on the concept of confianza (mutual trust) in their theoretical research perspective in order to explore the social and cultural contexts of schooling. Other research (e.g. Ellis, 2008; Liu & Fisher, 2010) has looked at the process of change within the activity settings of initial teacher education.

Activity theory takes historically changing and evolving collective activity systems as the prime units of analysis (e.g. Engeström, 2010). Through analysing the internal contradictions based on the different object motives within an activity system, and by making these contradictions apparent through an intervention, activity theorists explore systemic developmental transformations. Engeström (1987, 1999, 2007) has developed Leontiev's (1981) description of activity systems by extending Vygotsky's concept of action constituting a subject, an object and mediational tools to account for the social relations that affect the mediational process. In particular, he highlights the importance of rules and division of labour within activity. Engeström's theory of expansive learning views joint activity, as opposed to individual actions, as the central unit of activity. Internal contradictions of this activity are 'the motive force of change and development' (Engeström, 1999, p. 9). Mediated activity changes not only the subject but also the social context of the activity system. The 'reflective appropriation of advanced models and tools' as 'ways out of internal contradictions' result in the development of new activity systems (Cole & Engeström, 1993, p. 40). Internal contradictions of this activity are identified as the motive force of change and development.

However, Hedegaard's (2004, 2012) version of cultural-historical activity theory argues for a research focus on the individual's social situation of development within an activity setting. Her research focuses more on what happens in practices rather than systemic analyses. Hedegaard (2012) has developed a framework based on planes of analysis (Table 2.1) from the context of activity theory with its focus on the study of the complexity of human social behaviour within activity settings and in specific contexts. Hedegaard's three interrelated

Table 2.1 Hedegaard's planes of analysis

Entity	Process	Dynamic
Society	Tradition	Societal needs/conditions
Institution	Practice	Value motive/objectives
Activity setting	Situation	Motivation/demand
Person	Activity	Motive/intentions
Human's biology	Neurophysiological process	Primary needs

Source: Hedegaard, 2012, p. 19.

planes of entity, process and the dynamic are designed to explore the dialectic between the object motives of the individuals and the societal and cultural demands of the setting and the relationships within that context.

Hedegaard's framework was developed to analyse the dynamic relations in child learning and development, but similar analyses have been applied by Edwards (e.g. 2010) in accounts of professional learning using an earlier iteration of Hedegaard's planes of analysis. However, whilst Hedegaard's framework helpfully focuses the research on the social situations of development and the contending motives of individual learners and societal demands, Daniels (2008) argues that this kind of analysis alone lacks a language of description to explain both institutional practices and the particular forms of pedagogic discourses that operate within educational institutions. As Abreu and Elbers (2005) have also argued, 'in order to understand social mediation it is necessary to take into account ways in which the practices of a community, such as school and the family, are structured by their institutional context' (p. 149). Daniels (2008) suggests that in order to develop a language of description we can turn to the work of the sociologist Bernstein (1990) on knowledge structures and societal practice.

Bernstein (1990) argued that institutional pedagogic discourse is produced through three hierarchically related fields of: the production of specialised knowledge (universities and research institutes); the re-contextualisation of specialised knowledge (departments of education, teacher education and education journals); and reproduction – the teaching of knowledge (schools, colleges and universities). Bernstein believed that in the case of schools: 'Pedagogic discourse is a principle for appropriating other discourses and bringing them into a special relationship with each other for the purposes of their selective transmission and acquisition' (Bernstein, 1990, pp. 183–184). Bernstein (2000) also established more broadly that pedagogic discourse is made up of regulative discourse, the dominant values of a society that regulate how knowledge is transmitted, and instructional discourse or the way that knowledge is transmitted.

Bernstein (2000) distinguished between 'horizontal discourse', which is mundane or everyday knowledge that is context-specific, and esoteric discourse consisting of the 'unthinkable' or 'yet to be thought' (p. 30). Here, knowledge becomes potentially transformational and can 'become (not always) a site for alternative possibilities, for alternative realisations between the material and immaterial' and can 'change the relations between the material and immaterial' (Bernstein, 2000, p. 31). Beck and Young (2005) point out that Bernstein was interested in language in the process of identity formation and the conditions in which they are formed.

In order to capture this complex language of analysis we have developed the following sociocultural framework (Table 2.2) that draws on both the sociology of Bernstein and the cultural-historical approach of Hedegaard. The aim of this framework is to maintain a multiple focus on the social situations of development faced by student teachers.

Table 2.2 Social situations of development in initial teacher education

Cultural and historical demands	Motives/ engagement	Pedagogic practice	Pedagogic discourse
Societal	Student/teacher performance	Teacher standards	Knowledge production: theory, research
Institutional/ activity setting	Values Context History	Contextual rules and practices Structures and support	Re-contextualisation of knowledge
Individual transitions	Beliefs Context History	Planning Classroom teaching Reflection	Re-contextualisation of knowledge

Sources: Bernstein, 1990, pp. 183–184; Hedegaard, 2012, p. 19.

The use of this sociocultural framework in our study of *Learning to Teach in England and the United States* allows us to analyse contradictions and alignments in student teachers' teaching practices and reflections on subject pedagogy and learning. It prompts us to pay attention to the macro, meso and micro elements of learning to teach through a combined focus on: the cultural and historical demands on the student teacher; motives and engagement; pedagogic practice; and pedagogic discourse. At the macro level, the cultural and historical demands are societal and focus on the performance of teachers and pupils, the standards that regulate teachers and the production of knowledge. At the meso level, these demands are re-interpreted and re-contextualised at institutional levels and within the activity settings of schools and university. At the micro level we focus on the individual transitions involved in the re-contextualisation of knowledge in learning to teach.

A sociocultural understanding of initial teacher education

To sum up, this discussion of our sociocultural theoretical framework, we posit that student teachers face at least two social situations of development as they begin to teach: their position as learners, within the academic environment of a university; and within the specific professional contexts of their placement schools. Their engagement with these social situations may be influenced by factors such as their previous experience of education, their existing and possibly naïve understanding of social and cultural norms, plus their cultural capital from family and community. These social situations intersect in complex and dialectical interplay between theory and practice. The sociocultural framework developed in this book enables us to explore the extent to which student teachers are acquiring the psychological tools required for effective pedagogy and their engagement with the cultural assumptions that govern what are deemed to be appropriate ways of being a teacher in a particular school and in society as a whole. This approach also demands a sociocultural understanding of initial teacher education where learning for the student teacher is situated in multiple sites and cultures of practice.

Research design

Informed by this sociocultural framework, the research design that we adopted focused on individual student teachers, using a case study approach to examine their experiences in the contexts of the specific schools within which they were then teaching, either as part of an 'internship programme' within the more traditional initial teacher education programmes in each country, or as 'participants' in an alternative and largely employment-based route. In England, most of the student teachers taking part in the study were engaged in partnership programmes associated with the University of Oxford. In the United States, they were all enrolled in the initial teacher education programme at Michigan State University (MSU). Both institutions are recognised within their respective countries for the quality of their provision and for their commitment to collaboration with their school partners. Whilst alternative routes into teaching were becoming increasingly prevalent in *both* contexts, an emphatic shift towards 'school-led' forms of provision in England, to which the coalition government was deeply committed at the time when the data was being collected, prompted us to include in the sample prospective teachers who were undergoing their training in two of the most popular alternative routes: the School Direct non-salaried training route and the Teach First Leadership Development Programme. We therefore, included a number of student teachers within the Oxford Internship Scheme who had applied to train through the School Direct route and a separate cohort of Teach First participants who were placed in one London school, working in association with two different higher education institutions (HEIs) and with the Teach First organisation. The choice of Teach First allowed us to focus on participants learning to teach in a school with a 10-year history of involvement in that particular alternative route and a similarly deep commitment to it.

We chose the individual prospective teachers as our units of analysis because of our focus on student teacher development or transitions as they negotiate the specific social situations of development within their placement schools, each embedded in particular forms of institutional partnership. In England, the case studies were drawn from two schools working in partnership with the University of Oxford and one school in London associated with Teach First. In the United States, the case study interns were selected from four different schools associated with the MSU initial teacher education programme. Detailed accounts of the different programmes and of the participating institutions – both HEIs and schools – are presented in Chapters 4 and 5 respectively.

Selection procedures

All the fieldwork was conducted during the academic years 2013–2015, focusing on the interns in the two HEIs, and on Teach First participants as they began to negotiate their social situations of development in school. Within each programme we focused on a single cohort of prospective secondary teachers in their school placements across five different subject disciplines. In England and in the United States, we followed ethical procedures designed to protect human subjects.[1] Once we had identified particular programmes as the specific contexts for our study, we then needed to make a similarly purposive selection of schools, identifying those that would represent 'best case scenarios' for learning to teach and to seek consent both from the schools and from the individual participants within them. Chapter 5 explains in detail the nature of each school's commitment to the particular teacher education programme in which they were engaged and thus, illustrates the basis of our selection.

Within each school the invitation to participate was extended to principals or head teachers, professional mentors (senior leaders in charge of initial teacher education), all eligible student teachers, and their mentors/class teachers. Although some declined, the majority of the targeted individuals agreed to participate. In England, all 4 of the eligible Teach First participants agreed to take part whilst 6 out of 20 in the Oxford programmes declined or discontinued participation. In the United States, 8 out of 13 potential participants agreed to take part in the study. Reasons for declining were attributed by the student teachers to the sense of pressure or stress that they were already experiencing in school.

Whilst we collected extensive data from a range of student teachers in each programme and across the different schools, we have selected a smaller sample from amongst them to discuss in this book. The criteria for inclusion here were: the degree to which the data collected for each case study was complete; the need to encompass examples from across the range of five different subjects; and the need to ensure an adequate representation of the degree of variability of experiences we uncovered as a result of our analyses. The collection of cases therefore, should be seen as snapshots of the interns' or participants' practice embedded in best case scenarios (Patton, 2014), and whilst they illustrate the challenges that programmes, schools and student teachers encounter in an ever-changing and challenging policy environment, these cases cannot be seen as representative of student teachers in these programmes, schools or countries.

Participant characteristics

Because of the recent policy changes affecting how HEIs and schools negotiate their roles, we decided to examine the implementation of these routes in schools that can be seen as some of the best case scenarios of organisational learning under the current fast-paced reform in England and in the United States. All the schools selected were regarded as being effective providers of initial teacher education provision. The three schools in the United States were officially classified as located in rural districts in Michigan, and all were public schools, meaning they were state-funded via tax revenues and subject to state oversight in relation to attendance, compliance with state-approved curriculum, testing and standards and teacher certification. The three schools had a long history of collaboration with the teacher education programme at MSU.

All of the three of the schools served predominantly white populations. Two of these, a high school and a middle school, which we are calling Midfield High School, and Midfield Middle School were located in rural areas a fair distance away from the MSU campus in East Lansing. These two schools had a large proportion of their pupils eligible for free or reduced lunch, which is used as a rough indicator of economic disadvantage and for pupils that may be at risk of school failure. In contrast, the other school which we are calling Nearfield High School, was a relatively small school, and was located closer to the MSU campus. Whilst also in a rural area, it had different demographics. The school served a predominantly white population with about a third of the pupils considered as eligible for free or reduced school lunch. All of the schools reported that they were aligned to the Common Core Standards and other professional standards in subject areas. All of these three schools followed an inquiry-based approach to teaching and learning.

The school in London, which we have named Eastside Academy, had a relatively long history of training teachers through the Teach First route in collaboration with two universities. It was a medium-sized, inner city school with a diverse and ethnically mixed cohort. The other English schools offered places to student teachers who had applied directly to Oxford, as well as to prospective teachers who made their application directly to the school through the salaried and non-salaried School Direct routes. Riverside Academy was a large city school that served some of the wealthier and poorer areas of the city. Groveside Academy was in a medium-sized rural town with a mixed socio-economic intake. At the time of the research, these three schools represented three instances amongst many of programme implementation and change. Eastside Academy had accepted participants within the Teach First programme since 2004 and was fully committed to recruiting and preparing new teachers through this route, whilst Riverside and Groveside Academies (which both played a leading role in a county-wide Teaching Schools Alliance) had a long history of working with the University of Oxford Department of Education, but had also recently embraced the opportunity to participate in the School Direct initiative.

Since all the schemes use specific terms to refer to their prospective teachers, we have used 'student teacher' as a common term for ease of reference where we are referring to any prospective teacher engaged in one of the teacher preparation programmes based in HEIs, and more specific terms, such as 'intern' (used both by Oxford and MSU) or 'participant' (used by Teach First) where we are referring to those within a particular programme. To avoid confusion we have used the word 'pupil' rather than 'student' for schoolchildren. All names of schools and individuals are pseudonyms. However, the universities involved have been named because of the need to identify specific institutional policies and historical practices. Every effort has been made to avoid identifying specific schools and individuals.

Most of the student teachers in the English context had undergraduate degrees from a variety of universities in England and abroad and were in their mid- to late twenties. Many of them came with previous experience of teaching overseas or working as teaching assistants in English schools. In contrast, the student teachers in the United States all had their undergraduate degrees from MSU, were in their early twenties, and had no previous employment as teachers. Tables 2.3, 2.4, and 2.5 (see pp. 43–46) show the distribution of the student teachers across routes and school settings, as well as their subjects, preparation and teaching experience previous to enrolling in the English and United States programmes, and their gender.

Data sources

The data relating to the student teachers in England were collected between the end of January and mid-April 2014 and related to schools in which the interns had been placed for 2 or 3 days a week since September and full-time from January. The interns in the United States were also teaching full-time from January onwards and data was collected between the end of January and mid-April 2015. Policy data comes from document analysis. Programme documents were analysed in order to develop a profile of the initial teacher education programme. Documents describing the schools, some retrieved from their websites, were analysed to describe the contexts in which the prospective teachers were learning to teach, along with additional information from the school-based mentors, programme personnel within the university and from the student teachers themselves. A survey was sent to all enrolled student teachers in each institution who agreed to participate, and a sample was selected for videotaped or audiotaped observation, and pre- and post-observation interviews. In selecting a focus for the observation, the student teachers were asked to suggest particular lessons within the data collection period(s) that they would be willing to share with the observer. The field work schedule accommodated all of the student teachers and participants' requests. Data collection also included lesson plans and other materials that could provide information about the resources used by the participants to plan (and evaluate) their lesson. In addition, and to the extent that it was possible, the researcher observed any post-lesson debriefing conversations that took place between the mentor (or the regular class teacher) and the student teachers. Separate interviews were conducted with the student teachers, their school-based subject mentors (or occasionally with the regular teacher of that particular class) and with the professional mentor.

Data analysis

The research team met regularly throughout the course of the study (from December 2013 to December 2016) to develop the research design and the methods of analysis, although all the observations, student teacher and mentor interviews were conducted by just one researcher. Once the data had been collected, the team worked through a series of stages for coding and analysis in line with the framework explained above. The first step was to complete an analytical

Table 2.3 London participants in the first year of the Teach First Leadership Development Programme (which leads at the end of the year to a PGCE and Qualified Teacher Status) by subject, school context, previous experience of teaching and gender

Name	Subject	Route	School context	Degrees/qualifications	Previous experience in teaching	Gender
Naomi	Maths	Teach First	Eastside Academy, London – urban	BSc Mathematics and Music Part-time Postgraduate Certificate in Education (PGCE) (not completed)	Yes	Female
Aneesha	English	Teach First	Eastside Academy, London – urban	BA English	No	Female
Sheila	Science	Teach First	Eastside Academy, London – urban	BSc Biochemistry and Biology	No	Female
Nereen	History	Teach First	Eastside Academy, London – urban	BA History	No	Female

Table 2.4 Oxford interns following the traditional PGCE route or the PGCE route via School Direct by subject, school context, previous experience teaching and gender

Name	Subject	Route	School context	Degrees/qualifications	Previous experience in teaching	Gender
Doug	History	PGCE	Riverside Academy, Oxfordshire – suburban	BA History and MA History	Yes: 1 year as a Teaching Assistant in a United Kingdom secondary school	Male
Leslie	MFL (French and German)	PGCE	Riverside Academy, Oxfordshire – suburban	MA in Modern Languages and MSt in European Literature	Yes: 1 year as a Foreign Languages Assistant at a secondary school in Germany	Female
Sandrine	MFL	School Direct (non-salaried)	Riverside Academy, Oxfordshire – suburban	Bachelor's degrees in Journalism and in Sciences of Education (from French universities)	Yes: 2 years as a Foreign Languages Assistant at Riverside Academy. Experience as an Activity Leader and as a Campus Manager in a language summer school	Female
Megan	English	School Direct (non-salaried)	Riverside Academy, Oxfordshire – suburban	BA English and Modern Languages MSc and PhD in Education	Yes: voluntary mentoring (reading support) in primary schools and 6 months' work as a Teaching Assistant in a United Kingdom secondary school	Female
Jane	Science	PGCE	Groveside Academy, Oxfordshire – rural	BSc in Biochemistry	No	Female
Joseph	History	PGCE	Groveside Academy, Oxfordshire – rural	BA Middle East Studies (Medieval and Modern History and Arabic)	Yes: 2 years teaching humanities and music in an international school in Africa	Male

Name	Subject	Qualification	School	Degree	Experience	Gender
Michael	Maths	PGCE	Groveside Academy, Oxfordshire – rural	BSc in Maths and MSc in Economics	Yes: 3 years part-time English conversation classes; 6 years maths and science teaching and tuition in Far East	Male
Jacqueline	MFL (French)	PGCE	Groveside Academy, Oxfordshire – rural	Bachelor's degree and master's degree in French (obtained at French university)	Yes: 3 years part-time as a French and English tutor in a French language college and 1 year as a Foreign Languages Assistant in a United Kingdom secondary school	Female

Table 2.5 MSU interns, engaged in the pre-service internship year (i.e. a fifth-year programme, following 2 years of academic study and 2 years of university-based initial teacher education) by subject, school context, previous experience teaching and gender

Name	Subject	Route	School context	Degrees/qualifications	Previous experience in teaching	Gender
William	Science (Biology)	Traditional pre-service route + 1-year internship	Highfield High School, Michigan – rural	BSc – major in Biological Sciences	No	Male
Irene	History	Traditional pre-service route + 1-year internship	Midfield Middle School, Michigan – rural	BA – major in Social Studies, with minor in English as a Second Language	No	Female
Alyson	Maths	Traditional pre-service route + 1-year internship	Midfield Middle School, Michigan – rural	BA – major in Mathematics	No	Female
Jason	English	Traditional pre-service route + 1-year internship	Hightown High School, Michigan – rural	BA – major in English	No	Male
Sophia	English	Traditional pre-service route + 1-year internship	Nearfield High School, Michigan – rural	BA – major in English	No	Female

grid for each participant that followed the structure of Table 2.2. This allowed us to map out the key features of the macro and meso levels in each context and so begin to make visible their interplay with the micro level of individual transitions, creating the highly specific social situations of development that each individual faced. The policy and documentary analysis at the macro and meso levels that informed the construction of these grids will be presented in detail in Chapters 3, 4 and 5 of this book. Once we had used this data to map out, at the societal and institutional levels, the cultural and historical demands and motives for engagement, along with the pedagogic practices and discourse within which all individual transitions took place, we could move on to the data relating to each individual's experience. This allowed us to trace these same features at the personal level, so creating a full picture of each individual's particular social situation of development. In every case, we used our observation of the teaching and our interview data to create a summary account of the ways in which the student teacher re-contextualised (subject) knowledge for their pupils, through the processes of planning, teaching and evaluation and of the ways in which those processes were explicitly or implicitly related to the specific context in which they were placed; to the student teachers' stated beliefs about learning and teaching; and to any previous experiences as learner or teacher that they cited in seeking to account for their decisions and actions.

The mapping process – locating individual transitions in the context of what we had learned about the institutional values, context and history of the relevant HEI and of the placement school (in general and in subject-specific terms) – helped us to identify the extent of the alignment between the macro, meso and micro levels (both horizontally and vertically) and to discern any possible tensions or contradictions that might arise. In referring to the 'institutional/activity setting' in Table 2.2 it should be noted that this encompassed a further degree of complexity at the meso level since both HEI and schools, although working in partnership, obviously each functioned as individual institutions and were (for most of the time) experienced as such by the student teachers. This meant that there was either close alignment in terms of the motives and practices of both institutions within a collective teacher education partnership, or that there were potentially differing motives and practices between the partners, giving rise to specific tensions and challenges (horizontally, within the meso level). Examples of potential differences included: differing conceptions of pupil learning (either generally or within a subject-specific context); differing approaches to planning lessons; and differing approaches to what constituted effective assessment practice. Tensions also arose from insufficient integration between the university and school-based elements of the programme; from the misunderstanding of specific roles and responsibilities on both sides; or from the misinterpretation of commonly agreed principles and approaches (Douglas, 2014). Such tensions resulted in an inevitable degree of vertical misalignment since individual student teachers experienced either inconsistency or, in some cases, clear conflict between the motives and practices of each of the respective institutional partners.

Vertical misalignment was not restricted, however, to cases where the student teachers experienced misalignment between the object motives of the university and school actors at the meso level. For some, the impetus for change came from strong personal motives at the individual level, such as an ambition to improve and to change the social situation. For others, contradictions *within* the learner (at an intra-personal level) related to transitions of identity within the social situation and led to contradictions at the horizontal level. For example: somebody who saw themselves as a high achiever but who struggled with the process of learning to teach; somebody who saw themselves as non-confrontational yet had to be assertive with individuals in the classroom context; somebody who had a strong work ethic who found that hard work alone was not enough to get through the challenges; and somebody who had strong pre-conceptions about what constituted effective teaching yet was failing to engage the learners. It is important to emphasise again the individual nature of learners and their transitions within particular social situations of development.

Following Hedegaard and Vygotsky's dialectical conception of potential development, we see these contradictions and tensions as 'opportunities for development (OfD)' and 'opportunities for change (OfC)' that emerge from enacting practice. OfD is the term that we use to identify the potential for individuals' development within a social situation that is specifically created by the experience of tension or contradiction brought about by a lack of alignment between the ideal and the reality. This lack of alignment *may* reflect contradictions between ideas and practices espoused by the individual and those promoted by one or more of the institutions within which they are seeking to learn; or between those of the two institutions; or they may arise from internal contradictions such as ambition to improve despite the constraints of the social situation. OfC refer to individuals' recognition of the limitations of the situation they are in and their ability to imagine a different role for themselves as teachers. The argument here is not that all learning comes from contradictions and tensions, but that where these seem to arise then they have the potential to offer OfD and OfC. In some cases, this represented the mediational means through which the learner might renegotiate or re-contextualise a particular problem, critical point in development or even a crisis in development. The possibility of change here depends not only on individuals' recognition of the existing limitations of their current situation but also on the tools available to them; both those that derive from their own previous experience and those that are made available to them through the institutions in which they are seeking to learn as teachers: their HEI, and their placement school.

The process of developing a coding system required repeated viewing of the video data from classroom lessons taught by the student teachers. These were considered alongside the interview and questionnaire data, which served to contextualise and explain student teachers' decision-making and evaluation processes. In addition, we examined accounts of the student teachers' learning and experience of the programme given by the different teacher educators working with them. The coding system that emerged (see p. 49) allowed us to identify and examine the intensity or availability of particular features within each individual's social situation of development. These included the individual's experience of transition, often, but not exclusively, a product of a lack of alignment at the meso level between the institutional practices and demands of both school and HEI, or, at the micro level between those of the two institutions and of the individual student teacher. Other important features of the social situation of development derived from the extent to which the student teachers were equipped by their different contexts and by their own personal histories with appropriate mediational tools and from their own dispositions to develop and change. One other distinctive feature was the prominence assumed by the nature of the subject they were teaching or by particular conceptions of subject pedagogy within the student teacher's experience of crisis or amongst the mediational tools employed by the student teachers and those working with them.

Coding system

The coding system for each individual's experience as reflected in the single observed lesson and all the data associated with it included four key features:

1 OfD – the situations that emerge when enacting practice from inherent contradictions within or between different planes.
2 OfC:
   2.1 provided by mediational tools offered by the *HEI*: tools such as the theoretical frameworks presented within the HEI programme; particular short- or medium-term planning pro formas; or the specific advice of a university-based curriculum tutor;
   2.2 provided by mediational tools offered by the *school*: tools such as established school policies or routine practices; particular short- or medium-term planning pro formas; or the specific advice or feedback of a school-based mentor; and
   2.3 provided by *individual* mediational tools, such as the individual's prior experience, knowledge of the subject, sense of agency or particular processes of reflection.
3 The individual's disposition to recognise the scope for development and change:
   3.1 individual disposition to recognise OfD; and
   3.2 individual disposition to recognise OfC.
4 The relative prominence of the subject (or subject pedagogy) in consideration of the need for development or change:
   4.1 the relative prominence of the subject in OfD; and
   4.2 the relative prominence of the subject in OfC.

This coding system helped us uncover the extent of alignment (and thus, of the scope for tensions or contradictions) between the individual, HEI and school and more specifically, the extent of alignment and scope for contradictions between the individual student teacher's motives for engagement, and pedagogic discourse and practices. We then developed the final category descriptions outlined below and used in Chapters 7 to 11 to report our findings. These types of situations of development are represented here as distinct categories, although there are considerable variations within the individual social situations of development within each type.

Typology of analytical categories

Vertical and horizontal alignment with few apparent contradictions/ tensions

These cases represent instances of horizontal and vertical alignment between the individual, their placement school and the HEI partner within the teacher education programme with few apparent contradictions/tensions. In different ways, these individuals have developed through their social situations as student teachers to become knowledgeable and reflective educators able to draw on a range of mediational tools in their continued development.

Vertical alignment across institutions but a high level of contradictions/tensions at the individual level, which were addressed through effective mentoring

In these cases, critical points or crises of social situations of development at the individual level were apparent (either because the individual was clearly struggling in the classroom or expressed serious concerns about their practice in the observed lesson, or because the individual was challenging school's norms that in his or her view impeded pupils from engaging with the subject more deeply). In these cases, the developmental and change processes were mediated through the use of effective tools such as strong school and/or university mentoring.

Unacknowledged contradictions across institutions (school and HEI), which resulted in low levels of support for the individual

In these cases, the assumptions and practices of the school and HEI partner were nominally aligned and the student teachers were perceived to be making good or steady progress. However, OfD and OfC contradictions and tensions that were apparent to the research team on issues such as pupil learning or subject pedagogy were neither acknowledged nor addressed by the actors involved. As a result, fewer mediational tools were apparent.

Vertical alignment between the individual and school culture and practices (but not with the HEI)

The dominance of school culture and practices in these cases meant that although some limited OfD and OfC tensions/contradictions were apparent, the potential for development was limited as the student teacher's practice (which replicated general whole school and/or departmental practices) was not seen as something that needed to be challenged.

Vertical alignment between the individual and HEI (but not with the school)

The dominance of the programme's aims and conceptions of the subject and pedagogy held by the individual in these cases clashed with those of the school and meant that there were important OfD and OfC tensions/contradictions apparent to the individual and to the classroom teacher or mentor, yet the potential for development represented an individual struggle even if such a struggle was not visible to the HEI educators, with the consequence that the student teachers' practice was not seen as something that needed negotiation in order to arrive at a productive resolution.

The next chapters in Part I describe in detail the policy, and institutional contexts in England and in the United States. Part II describes our findings in detail in relation to the typologies outlined above. Part III will draw on our analysis across all three levels, in discussing the overall findings and implications of our study.

Note

1 MSU approval of a project involving human subjects, IRB: i048121. Oxford Department of Education CUREC Application Approval 25 April 2014.

References

Abreu, G. & Elbers, E. (2005). The social mediation of learning in multi-ethnic schools: Introduction. *European Journal of Psychology of Education, 20*(1), 3–11.

Beach, K. D. (1999). Consequential transitions: A sociocultural expedition beyond transfer in education. *Review of Research in Education, 24*, 101–139.

Beck, J. & Young, M. F. D. (2005). The assault on the professions and the restructuring of academic and professional identities: A Bernsteinian analysis. *British Journal of Sociology of Education, 26*(2), 183–197.

Bernstein, B. (1990). *Class, codes and control: Volume IV – The structuring of pedagogic discourse.* London: Routledge.

Bernstein, B. (2000). *Pedagogy, symbolic control and identity: Theory, research and critique* (2nd ed.). Lanham, MD: Rowman & Littlefield Publishers.

Blanton, M., Berenson, S. & Norwood, K. (2001). Using classroom discourse to understand a prospective mathematics teacher's developing practice. *Teaching and Teacher Education, 17,* 227–242.

Burn, K. Hagger, H., Mutton, T. & Everton, T. (2003). The complex development of student teachers' thinking. *Teachers and Teaching: Theory and Practice, 9*(4), 309–331.

Burn, K. & Mutton, T. (2015). A review of 'research-informed clinical practice' in Initial Teacher Education. *Oxford Review of Education, 41*(2), 217–233.

Claxton, G. (2007). Expanding young people's capacity to learn. *British Journal of Educational Studies, 55*(2), 115–134.

Cochran-Smith, M. (2008). The new teacher education in the United States: Directions forward. *Teachers and Teaching: Theory and Practice, 14*(4), 271–282.

Cole, M. (1996). *Cultural psychology.* Cambridge Mass: The Belknap Press of Harvard University Press.

Cole, M. & Engeström, Y. (1993). A cultural-historical approach to distributed cognition. In G. Salomon (Ed.), *Distributed cognitions: Psychological and educational* considerations (pp. 1–46). New York: Cambridge University Press.

Crafter, S. & Maunder, R. (2012). Understanding transitions using a sociocultural framework. *Educational and Child Psychology, 29*(1), 10–18.

Daniels, H. (2008). *Vygotsky and research.* London and New York: Routledge.

Daniels, H. (2014). Vygotsky and dialogic pedagogy. *Cultural-Historical Psychology, 10*(3), 19–29.

Douglas, A. S. (2014). *Student teachers in school practice: An analysis of learning opportunities.* London: Palgrave Macmillan.

Doyle, W. (1977). Learning the classroom environment: An ecological analysis. *Journal of Teacher Education, 28*(6), 51–55.

Dreier, O. (1999). Personal trajectories of participation across contexts of social practice. *Outlines. Critical Practice Studies, 1*(1), 5–32.

Dreier, O. (2009). Persons in structures of social practice. *Theory and Psychology, 19*(2), 193–212.

Edwards, A. (2009). From the systemic to the relational: Relational agency and activity theory. In A. Sannino, H. Daniels & K. Gutiérrez (Eds.), *Learning and expanding with activity theory* (pp. 197–211). Cambridge, UK: Cambridge University Press.

Edwards, A, (2010). How can Vygotsky and his legacy help us to understand and develop teacher education? In V. Ellis, A. Edwards & P. Smagorinsky (Eds.), *Cultural-historical perspectives on teacher education and development* (pp. 63–77). London: Routledge.

Edwards, A. (2017). The dialectic of person and practice: How cultural-historical accounts of agency can inform teacher education. In J. Clandinin & J. Husu (Eds.), *International handbook on research on teacher education.* Thousand Oaks, CA: Sage.

Edwards, A. & Daniels, H. (2004). Using sociocultural and activity theory in educational research. *Educational Review, 56*(2), 107–111.

Ellis, V. (2008). Exploring the contradictions in learning to teach: The potential of developmental work research. *Changing English: Studies in Culture and Education, 15*(1), 53–63.

Engeström, Y. (1987). *Learning by expanding: An activity-theoretical approach.* Helsinki: Orienta-Konsultit.

Engeström, Y. (1999). Activity theory and individual and social transformation. In Y. Engeström, R. Miettinen & R. L. Punamäki-Gitai (Eds.), *Perspectives on activity theory* (pp. 19–38). New York: Cambridge University Press.

Engeström, Y. (2007). Putting Vygotsky to work: The change laboratory as an application of double stimulation. In H. Daniels, M. Cole & J. Wertsch (Eds.), *The Cambridge companion to Vygotsky* (pp. 363–382). New York: Cambridge University Press.

Engeström, Y. (2010). Activity theory as a framework for analyzing and redesigning work. *Ergonomics, 43*(7), 960–974.

Furlong, J. & Maynard, T. (1995). *Mentoring student teachers: The growth of professional knowledge.* London: Routledge.

Goos, M. (2005). A sociocultural analysis of the development of pre-service and beginning teachers' pedagogical identities as users of technology. *Journal of Mathematics Teacher Education, 8*(1), 35–59.

Guile, D. (2010). *The learning challenge of the knowledge economy.* Rotterdam, The Netherlands: Sense.

Hedegaard, M. (2004). A cultural-historical approach to learning in classrooms. *Outlines. Critical Practice Studies, 6*(1), 21–34.

Hedegaard, M. (2012). The dynamic aspects in children's learning and development. In M. Hedegaard, A. Edwards & M. Fleer (Eds.), *Motives in children's development* (pp. 9–17). New York: Cambridge University Press.

Holland, D. & Lachicotte, W. (2007). Vygotsky, Mead and the new sociocultural studies of identity. In H. Daniels, M. Cole & J. Wertsch (Eds.), *The Cambridge companion to Vygotsky* (pp. 101–135). New York: Cambridge University Press.

Holland, D., Lachicotte, W., Skinner, D. & Cain, C. (1998). *Identity and agency in cultural worlds.* Cambridge MA: Harvard University Press.

Lave, J. & Wenger, E. (1991). *Situated learning: Legitimate peripheral participation.* New York: Cambridge University Press.

Leontiev, A. N. (1978). *Activity, consciousness, and personality.* Englewood, Cliffs, NJ: Prentice-Hall.

Leontiev, A. N. (1981). *Problems of the development of mind.* Moscow: Progress.

Liu, Y. & Fisher, L. (2010). What have we learnt after we had fun? An activity theory perspective on cultures of learning in pedagogical reforms. In V. Ellis, A Edwards & P. Smagorinsky (Eds.), *Cultural-historical perspectives on teacher education and development: Learning teaching* (pp. 180–195). London and New York: Routledge.

Lortie, D. C. (2002). *Schoolteacher* (2nd ed.). Chicago: University of Chicago Press.

McIntyre, D. (1993). Theory, theorizing and reflection in initial teacher education. In J. Calderhead & P. Gates (Eds.), *Conceptualizing reflection in teacher development* (pp. 97–114). London: Falmer Press.

Mercer, N. (2013). The social brain, language, and goal-directed collective thinking: A social conception of cognition and its implications for understanding how we think, teach, and learn. *Educational Psychologist, 48*(3), 148–168.

Moll, L. C. & Arnot-Hopffer, E. (2005). Socio-cultural competence in teacher education. *Journal of Teacher Education, 56*(3), 242–247.

Norton- Meier, L. A. & Drake, C. (2010). When third space is more than the library. In V. Ellis, A. Edwards & P. Smagorinsky (Eds.), *Cultural-historical perspectives on teacher education and development* (pp. 196–211). London and New York: Routledge.

Patton, M. Q. (2014). *Qualitative research and evaluation methods.* Los Angeles, CA: Sage.

Penuel, W. R. & Wertsch, V. J. (1995). Vygotsky and identity formation: A sociocultural approach. *Educational Psychologist, 30*(2), 83–92.

Rogoff, B. (2003). *The cultural nature of human development.* New York: Oxford University Press.

Sawyer, R. K. (2002). Unresolved tensions in sociocultural theory: Analogies with contemporary sociological debates. *Culture & Psychology, 8*(3), 283–305.

Tatto, M. T. (1999). The socializing influence of normative cohesive teacher education on teachers' beliefs about instructional choice. *Teachers and Teaching, 5*(1), 111–134.

Tatto, M. T., Savage, C., Liao, W., Marshall, S., Goldblatt, P. & Contreras, M. L. (2016). The emergence of high-stakes accountability policies in teacher preparation: An examination of the U.S. Department of Education's proposed regulations. *Education Policy Analysis Archives, 24*(25). doi: http://dx.doi.org/10.14507/epaa.24.2322.

Thompson, I. C. (2015). Introduction: Tasks, concepts, and subject knowledge. In I. E. Thompson (Ed.), *Designing tasks in secondary education: Enhancing subject understanding and student engagement* (pp. 3–12). London: Routledge.

Thompson, I., McNicholl, J. & Menter, I. (2016). Student teachers' perceptions of poverty and educational achievement. *Oxford Review of Education, 42*(2), 214–229. doi: 10.1080/03054985.2016.1164130.

Valsiner, J. (1998). *Culture and the development of children's action: A theory of human development.* New York: John Wiley & Sons.

van Huizen, P., van Oers, B. & Wubbels, T. (2005). A Vygotskian perspective on teacher education. *Journal of Curriculum Studies, 37*(3), 267–290.

Vygotsky, L. S. (1987). Thinking and speech. In L. S. Vygotsky (Ed.), *Collected works: Volume 1.* New York: Plenum Press.

Vygotsky. L. S. (1997). The history of the development of higher mental functions. In L. S. Vygotsky (Ed.), *Collected works: Volume 4.* New York: Plenum Press.

Vygotsky, L. S. (1998). Child psychology. In L. S. Vygotsky (Ed.), *Collected works: Volume 5.* New York: Plenum Press.

Wenger, E. (1998). *Communities of Practice: Learning, meaning and identity.* New York: Cambridge University Press.

Wertsch, J. V. (1993). Commentary. *Human Development, 36,* 168–171.

Wertsch, J. V. (2007). Mediation. In H. Daniels, M. Cole & J. Wertsch (Eds.), *The Cambridge companion to Vygotsky* (pp. 178–192). Cambridge: Cambridge University Press.

Whitty, G. (2016). *Research and policy in education.* London: Sage.

Zeichner, K., Payne, K. A. & Brayko, K. (2015). Democratizing teacher education. *Journal of Teacher Education, 66*(2), 122–135.

Zittoun, T. (2006). *Transitions: Development through symbolic resources.* Greenwich: Information Age Publishing.

3   The policy landscapes for teacher education in England and the United States

Introduction

England and the United States have been sites of considerable upheaval in teacher education policy for several decades. Our purpose in this chapter is to set out the major developments that have occurred in each country with a view to developing a contextual backdrop for the study. The chapter uses a chronology of key events with special emphasis on the last 10 years (although necessarily also looking further back), based on an analysis of significant policy documents. We thus, offer a depiction, mainly at the macro level, of the context in which our institutional and individual investigations were conducted, before examining what is actually occurring in teacher education programmes in specific sites in England and in the United States respectively. That meso level of analysis is reported in Chapters 4 and 5, whilst the micro level analysis is reported in various chapters of Part II.

There are two major sections to this chapter, one depicting each of the national contexts, before a summary and conclusion.

England

It has been suggested that teacher education policy in England has become so distinctive and different from elsewhere in the United Kingdom that the country should be regarded as something of an outlier (Teacher Education Group, 2016). The extent to which policy in England differs from that of the United States is obviously a central focus of this study, and it is important to note in making this comparison that a very different policy trajectory has emerged in England from those pursued respectively, in Scotland, Wales or Northern Ireland or indeed the Republic of Ireland. In this section, we offer a short chronology outlining policy development in England, drawing in part on earlier work by Childs and Menter (2013).

In the second half of the 20th century, teaching was moving to becoming an all-graduate profession. Entry into teaching was typically through one of two main routes. The first route was free-standing degree programmes, leading to the award of the Bachelor of Education, mainly for entry into primary teaching and lasting up to 4 years. The second route was the 1-year programme for candidates already possessing a first degree. This programme led to the award of a Postgraduate Certificate in Education (PGCE). Although the origins of the second route were very much associated with secondary school teaching, increasingly during the latter part of the 20th century this option also became more widely available for intending primary teachers. Both types of programme were provided by higher education institutions (HEIs), including colleges of education, polytechnics and universities. Towards the end of the century there was a gradual 'harmonisation' of the higher education sector so that by the early 21st century, nearly all HEIs were designated as universities. However, as we discuss below, this was also a time when a number of other routes into teaching were being introduced.

Writing as long ago as 1984, Alexander reviewed a great deal of 'organisational change' in teacher education over the previous 20 years but noted that this had been within 'a context of cultural and epistemological continuity' (Alexander, 1984, p. xviii). But there has subsequently been some serious disruption to that continuity, both cultural and epistemological. Indeed, in 1983, the then Conservative government issued a White Paper entitled *Teaching Quality,* which signalled a growing interest by politicians in matters of teaching (DES, 1983). This led in 1984 to the first direct intervention into teacher education provision by the government in the form of a circular on the initial training of teachers, Circular 3/84 (DES, 1984). This stipulated a number of matters about the lengths of various initial teacher education programmes, the time to be spent by student teachers respectively in school and higher education and the Circular also established a national body that would be responsible for the accreditation of teacher education programmes, the National Council for Accreditation of Teacher Education (NCATE) (McIntyre, 1991).

This proved to be just the first in a continuing series of circulars which steadily brought in greater central regulation, a process that continued under New Labour when they came to power in 1997. However, there were several other very significant developments before that point. Perhaps most notable amongst them was the pair of circulars published in 1992–1993: Circular 9/92 for secondary teacher education provision and Circular 14/93 for primary (DfE, 1992, 1993). These circulars contained new regulations about the amount of time that was to be spent by beginning teachers in school and also required for the first time that teacher education providers should enter into formal partnership agreements with the schools with which they were working. The Secretary of State for Education at the time, Kenneth Clarke, had initially announced that the school/university time balance for trainees should be 75:25 on 1-year programmes, the previous typical balance having been 33:67. The 75:25 ratio was actually adjusted to 67:33 when the circulars were actually published, representing a more or less mirror image of what had existed before. It was thus, clear that this requirement would lead to a significant reduction in most programmes for the time available for HEI-based study.

The creation of HEI – school partnerships

Although some providers had already developed partnership agreements before this time, the agreements that were introduced in response to these circulars ensured that in all situations school-based staff had an important role in the processes of teacher education and, in view of that responsibility, required that a part of the resources allocated to the HEI to provide the training programme should be transferred to the school concerned.

In 1992, the government also created a new inspection agency for schools, the Office for Standards in Education, Children's Services and Skills (Ofsted). Ofsted was subsequently to take over from the fully independent Her Majesty's Inspectorate in the inspection of teacher education provision. However, this inspection regime only really got under way following the creation in 1994 of a new funding agency for teacher education, initially called the Teacher Training Agency. Until that time teacher education provision had essentially been funded by the Higher Education Funding Council for England (HEFCE), alongside all other higher education provision in the country. This route for funding had, however, been complemented by another in 1988 when the government decided that it wished to introduce teacher training programmes led by schools. Initially these were 'employment-based routes' known as the Articled Teacher Scheme and the Licensed Teacher Scheme, but they were soon followed by School-Centred Initial Teacher Training (SCITT). None of these school-led schemes could be funded by HEFCE, whose remit was limited to higher education provision, and so the government decided that rather than having two funding streams for teacher education, they would create one new body, the Teacher Training Agency, which would fund all teacher education. This effectively replaced the traditional governance of teacher education with a new arrangement, removing it from mainstream higher education. In due course, the full significance of this became clear. At the time, although a number of universities and their senior managers expressed some concerns, especially about the apparent encroachment into the long-established principle of academic autonomy for universities, their voices were not strong enough to prevent it happening (see Furlong, 2013).

When New Labour took office in 1997 their education policies were published in the Green Paper *Teachers: Meeting the Challenge of Change* (New Labour, 1998). This introduced performance management into teaching and also compulsory 'skills tests' into teacher education (in literacy, numeracy and information and communications technologies). The Paper also led to a wider development in the schools' workforce, with a major expansion of teaching assistant positions in schools. When it became clear that the Teaching Training Agency would take on some responsibility for the development of this new element it changed its name to become the Training and Development Agency (TDA) for schools. The emphasis on performance management throughout teaching led to the development in teacher education of teaching competences, soon to be called standards, as mentioned in Chapter 1. So it was that the new government used Circular 9/97 to set out a list of observable behaviours that

beginning teachers would have to demonstrate in order to achieve their qualification (DfEE, 1997). Following this, the government also introduced a heavily
prescribed 'curriculum for Initial Teacher Training' in specific subject areas
including science, English, mathematics as well as for Information and Communication Technologies provision, which cut across all subject areas.

In 2002, Teach First was launched as a radical new approach aiming to
attract the 'brightest' graduates from the best universities into teaching, particularly those who might not otherwise have joined the profession. This was an
employment-based route in which the beginning teachers would be based in a
school in challenging circumstances, assume full responsibility for teaching
during their first year, with some involvement of a university, and then stay in
that school for a further year. Whilst it was hoped that some participants would
stay in teaching beyond these 2 years, the commitment that participants made
was to the 2-year Leadership Development Programme, after which they would
arguably be better equipped to take up other careers, perhaps with one of the
private sector organisations that sponsored the scheme. This route into teaching
took inspiration from and was modelled in part on Teach for America, although
it operated independently (Ellis et al., 2016).

The inspection regime had also been developing through this period so that
resourcing of teacher education providers was directly linked to the grades they
achieved in Ofsted inspections. At the most extreme, providers judged by
Ofsted to be poor would completely lose their allocation of training places. This
led to an increasingly compliant culture within teacher education, some people
at the time called it 'a climate of fear' (Gilroy, 2014), such was the pressure on
delivering what government required. At the time when New Labour was focusing very heavily on raising standards in literacy and numeracy through the introduction of the 'skills tests' mentioned above, it was perhaps not surprising that
literacy teaching in particular became the subject of very tight prescription
within initial teacher education at the primary level.

Where the interventions in the 1980s had been fuelled by a series of pamphlets
produced by a range of right-wing think tanks, such as the Adam Smith Institute,
the Hillgate Group and the Centre for Policy Studies (see Whitty & Menter,
1989), the 'discourse of derision' (Ball, 1990) that had been applied to teachers
themselves increasingly became targeted at teacher educators and what the politicians insisted on calling 'the teacher training colleges'. Furlong (2013) has written
a very important account of the steady marginalisation of the input of universities
and higher education over the course of the second half of the 20th century.

Teacher education in a 'school-led' system

So it was that when the coalition government, that is a joint administration of the
Conservative and Liberal Democratic parties, took power in 2010 and Michael
Gove was appointed as Secretary of State for Education, his first White Paper, *The
Importance of Teaching* (DfE, 2010), signalled a further marginalisation of higher
education within teacher education. This announced the expansion of a new form

of 'school-led' teacher education that was to be called School Direct. The TDA had by this time become The Teaching Agency and was soon merged with the National College for School Leadership into the National College for Teaching and Leadership, a branch of the ministry of the Department for Education and no longer at arm's length from government. This coalition government also confirmed its intention to expand Teach First.

The creation of essential standards

It was also Gove who oversaw a 'simplification' of the teaching standards for initial teacher training. On the basis that he saw the standards then operating as over-elaborate and imbued with unwarranted complexity, Gove established a working group that was charged with reducing the standards to what was essential in teaching. So it was that during 2011, the 32 standards inherited from the previous administration were reduced to 8 (DfE, 2011). Although each of these eight had about four sub-clauses, making them actually look remarkably similar to their predecessors, this simplification significantly reshaped the ways in which professional knowledge was presented and also downplayed issues of diversity amongst school pupils. The new *Teachers' Standards* (DfE, 2011) were intended not to be only for initial entry into the profession but were to replace the rather disparate sets of standards that applied to differing stages of the career. Thus, whilst the new *Teachers' Standards* were to set the requirements for entrance into the profession (DfE, 2011), the same standards would also serve as the criteria for disciplinary action against teachers in cases where competency procedures were being undertaken. The introduction to these standards makes clear that they are to be used *relative* to the particular stage of development that a teacher is at.

Part 1 of the standards concern 'Teaching' and include eight main headings, as follows (which applied during the time of the fieldwork for this study):

A teacher must:

1   Set high expectations which inspire, motivate and challenge pupils
2   Promote good progress and outcomes by pupils
3   Demonstrate good subject and curriculum knowledge
4   Plan and teach well-structured lessons
5   Adapt teaching to respond to the strengths and needs of all pupils
6   Make accurate and productive use of assessment
7   Manage behaviour effectively to ensure a good and safe learning environment
8   Fulfil wider professional responsibilities.

(DfE, 2011)

Part 2 of the standards concerns 'Personal and Professional Conduct' and states:

A teacher is expected to demonstrate consistently high standards of personal and professional conduct. The following statements define the behaviour and attitudes which set the required standard for conduct throughout a teacher's career.

- Teachers uphold public trust in the profession and maintain high standards of ethics and behaviour, within and outside school, by:

  - treating pupils with dignity, building relationships rooted in mutual respect, and at all times observing proper boundaries appropriate to a teacher's professional position
  - having regard for the need to safeguard pupils' well-being, in accordance with statutory provisions
  - showing tolerance of and respect for the rights of others
  - not undermining fundamental British values, including democracy, the rule of law, individual liberty and mutual respect, and tolerance of those with different faiths and beliefs
  - ensuring that personal beliefs are not expressed in ways which exploit pupils' vulnerability or might lead them to break the law.

- Teachers must have proper and professional regard for the ethos, policies and practices of the school in which they teach, and maintain high standards in their own attendance and punctuality.
- Teachers must have an understanding of, and always act within, the statutory frameworks which set out their professional duties and responsibilities.

(DfE, 2011)

Over the whole period from 1984 to the present, we can see the impact of neo-liberal and neoconservative thinking on teacher education in a way that both illustrated the marginalisation of higher education but also showed the relative lack of power of any of the professionals involved in the processes of teaching and teacher education (Childs & Menter, 2013). This was a period during which ideology drove policy much more than evidence (Whitty, 2016, Chapter 2). Through the creation of 'diverse routes' into teaching, successive governments sought to bring a market element into initial teacher education, offering potential teaching recruits a consumer style choice about how they would seek to join the profession. With one eye on standards and the measures of effectiveness that so dominate the thinking of education ministers around the world (Sahlberg, 2011), these governments also exerted very strict controls on the outcomes that student teachers would need to demonstrate. At many points in this story they did, as we have seen, control the content of programmes very tightly.

By the time the fieldwork for the study being reported in this book was carried out there was thus, a range of routes into teaching and one of the main purposes of the study was to investigate whether we could detect significant differences between them in relation to the motivations and experiences of the student teachers or indeed of others who were involved in providing the programme. Each programme was based on particular arrangements and responsibilities for school and HEI staff and the programmes were organised in different ways.

Early in 2015, the report *Carter Review of Initial Teacher Training* in England was published (Carter, 2015). We have presented a more detailed analysis of the content of this report elsewhere (Mutton, Burn & Menter, 2016), but, in summary, it was somewhat less technocratic in its orientation than many commentators had anticipated, recognising the complexity of teaching, even though it still set out the 'core elements' of initial teacher education in a managerial fashion. It was also less explicitly 'anti-higher education' than many had expected and indeed appears to take for granted the importance of partnerships between schools and higher education. The review had been established whilst Gove was still Secretary of State. It was he who appointed as its leader Sir Andrew Carter, the head teacher of a primary school and group of academies (self-managing schools) that was already operating as a SCITT. Sir Andrew in turn, appointed an advisory group that included only one mainstream university-based teacher educator. It may be that Gove's departure from the Department for Education during the period of the review and his replacement by Nicky Morgan was another factor that led to some moderation in the approach of the report. Our close analysis has shown there are many ambiguities and tensions in the report, but it certainly cannot be read as the final nail in the coffin for university involvement in teacher education in England, as some had feared or predicted.

However, the review did lead to the establishment of 'expert' groups tasked with implementing the findings and recommendations of the report. In early 2016, these working groups reported on their respective areas: a framework of core content for initial teacher training; developing behaviour management content for initial teacher training; and national standards for school-based initial teacher training mentors (DfE, 2016a). It is perhaps significant that one of the working groups was chaired by the government's 'behaviour guru', Tom Bennett, who has frequently asserted that more should be done to train beginning teachers in effective behaviour management in classrooms, a view subsequently reflected in the recommendations. Interestingly none of the recommendations of these reports have been made mandatory, although the expectation that teacher training providers will be accountable for the way in which the recommended core content is being delivered has since become a focus of Ofsted inspections. It should be noted, however, that the core content recommended by the expert group was, in fact, far less prescriptive than had been anticipated and was framed in such a way as to link it directly to the *Teachers' Standards* (DfE, 2011). Separately, but at the same time, the government published a new continuing professional development (CPD) standard (DfE, 2016b) produced by the Teachers' Professional Development Expert Group, whose findings reflected existing research into what is known about effective CPD.

The more direct challenges to universities involved in teacher education have emerged from other directions, most especially in the ways in which teacher training places have been allocated to providers over the past year and into the future. In 2015, the government agency that allocates these places, the National College for Teaching and Leadership, effectively prioritised school-led approaches, in particular SCITTs and School Direct, rather than the traditional core provision offered by university-led partnerships. This led to severe reductions in the number of funded places available for university partnerships to secure both in primary provision and in secondary subjects. Whilst this created an enormous sense of uncertainty across the whole sector, universities in particular are becoming extremely exercised by the volatility that this brings into their resource planning. For many institutions, it has become impossible to sustain any degree of confidence in future plans and budgeting for teacher education. At least three universities have pulled out of teacher education in recent years, largely as a consequence of this uncertainty – The Open University (which had been a leading provider of distance learning routes), the University of Bath (a provider judged to be outstanding by Ofsted) and Anglia Ruskin University (a very large provider of primary places in the east of England).

At the same time as these developments in teacher education provision, we have seen a continuing overhaul of the wider governance of schooling in England towards what ministers call 'a school-led system', with a government White Paper published in March 2016 that planned to enforce 'academisation' on all schools within the next 5 or 6 years (DfE, 2016c). Although this process was softened, following the demise of David Cameron's leadership and his replacement by Theresa May, who appointed Justine Greening as Secretary of State for Education in 2016, it remains likely that local authorities will have still less influence on or responsibility for the provision, management or governance of schools. At present, the great majority of primary schools are still under local authority control, although the majority of secondary schools are already 'free-standing' academies. The likely interaction of this process with teacher education and training is to create even more uncertainty in the system. It is already the case that academies do not have to employ teachers who have recognised teaching qualifications. The new laws are likely to mean that we will see a proliferation of unqualified teachers working across all sectors. Indeed, the White Paper also suggests that teachers could work towards accreditation whilst in post (DfE, 2016c). In other words, they could apply for recognition as qualified teachers at such point as they decide they are ready. This seems likely to lead to the side-lining of national agreements on pay and conditions for teachers, as academies are free to make their own decisions about levels of pay and working hours and other aspects of conditions of service.

Summary

In summary, over recent years we have seen the emergence of an atomised schooling system in England where the regulatory framework for teachers' qualifications and employment are both breaking down. There is no research evidence to support any of these developments. What the research and other evidence that is available have shown includes:

- very variable success in the outcomes achieved by academies (to the extent that the Chief Inspector of Schools has expressed some concern) (House of Commons Education Committee, 2015);
- increasing numbers of academies where there have been alleged breaches of financial guidelines;[1]
- great instability in teacher supply, with some parts of the country finding major difficulties in recruitment of teachers, especially in some 'shortage subjects' (Foster, 2016);
- growing concern about teacher retention – and not only in schemes such as Teach First, which had always been designed to attract teachers for a relatively short term (Foster, 2016); and
- difficulties in recruiting suitable people to take on school leadership.[2]

At the same time as this marketisation and quasi-privatisation is apparently leading to greater uncertainty and instability (some would say chaos) in schooling and in teacher education, there are some other tendencies which may have something of a countervailing effect. Amongst these we may cite the designation of Teaching Schools where good practice in professional development, as well as successful outcomes for pupils, have been identified and the schools with this designation are required to undertake initiatives on teacher development (including initial teacher education) and in research and development. Funding to support these developments, however, is at a very low level especially after the initial 3 years of operation. Second, a new independent Chartered College of Teaching was established in 2017 (albeit with an initial injection of government funding) to serve as a professional body for teachers that may eventually set the standards for teaching and oversee professional development. All three other UK jurisdictions, as well as the Republic of Ireland, now have well-established General Teaching Councils or equivalent bodies. If successful, the Chartered College would effectively fill the space created by Gove's abolition of the General Teaching Council for England in 2010–2011. This emergent body also supports the notion of evidence-informed teaching, a principle which the Department for Education itself has been promoting. Rhetoric around this continues to pervade the White Paper although the Department for Education's own practice in relation to the use of evidence does make this claim seem somewhat paradoxical (Menter, 2016).

One final note of importance in this disturbing story is the almost total absence of any effective opposition or alternative voice being influential in teacher education policy. Providers themselves have not been effective in resisting most of the developments – although perhaps the policies might have been even more extreme without the influence of some university vice-chancellors and organisations such as the Universities' Council for the Education of Teachers.

The teachers' unions have on the whole been opposed to the policy developments in teacher education (see for example, ATL, 2013) but rarely have these issues reached the top of their agenda for activity. The political opposition in Parliament has failed to fully engage with these developments, let alone to articulate clear alternatives. The most critical voice in Parliament has actually been that of the House of Commons Select Committee on Education, a cross-party committee which has several times expressed serious concern about the trajectory of developments (as noted by Childs & Menter, 2013 and by Whitty, 2016). The other voice that has sounded some alarm bells has been the National Audit Office, which in their 2016 report on these matters suggested that some elements of the current policy carry a high-risk of failure (Comptroller and Auditor General, 2016).

United States

In this section, we look at educational reform in the United States, particularly in relation to schools and schooling, and discuss the effects of such reforms on teacher education policy and practice.

Systemic education reform

A brief history of policy changes and its effects on teacher education illustrates the quick pace of change for the profession in recent years. As Labaree (2008) has pointed out, after a brief attempt at adopting a critical stance in education, since the 1930s schools of education adopted a 'functional role supporting the existing system of schooling' (p. 286) with teacher education programmes defining their raison d'être as that of preparing teachers to teach the school curriculum. Since then, the future of teacher education has been closely linked to policy changes in K-12 education. The 1983 report *A Nation at Risk* marked an important time for education reform in America as it revealed that many pupils' academic performance was beneath desirable levels (USDOE, 1983). These concerns led to measures aimed at increased monitoring of the school curriculum and teaching including the *Goals 2000: Educate America Act* (Public Law 103–227), signed into law in early 1994 by President Clinton, which set the basic principles for standards-based education reform, with an emphasis on outcomes-based education (U.S. Congress, 1994).

Whilst the Goals 2000 are seen by many as the precursor to the standards movement (U.S. Congress, 1994), it was not until 2001 with the *No Child Left Behind Act of 2001* (NCLB) that the education landscape in the United States changed dramatically (U.S. Congress, 2002). This Act of Congress which re-authorised the *Elementary and Secondary Education Act of 1965* (U.S. Congress, 1965) introduced a workable system-wide framework for standards-based education reform including measurable goals to improve individual outcomes in education. In order to receive federal funding, the Act required states to develop and administer pupil assessments to measure yearly progress towards stated goals

(U.S. Congress, 1965). The Act used a five-fold strategy: annual state-wide standardised testing; schools' demonstration of annual academic progress (adequate yearly progress); system/school report cards; teacher qualifications; and funding changes (U.S. Congress, 1965). Importantly for teacher education, this Act also re-defined the meaning of 'highly qualified teacher' by requiring teachers to have a bachelor's degree and full state certification, and to demonstrate content knowledge in the subjects they teach (U.S. Congress, 1965). The Act gave states the freedom to define certification according to their needs including the creation of alternate routes, an action that explicitly de-emphasised the importance of pedagogy preparation, or of clinical practice (U.S. Congress, 1965). Whilst the initial reaction to these changes was not very strong, by 2007–2008, 38 states, and as a consequence teacher education programmes, began requiring teachers a passing grade on tests of basic literacy and numeracy skills with 41 states mandating a passing grade on tests of content knowledge according to teachers' specialisation.

In 2009, as part of the *American Recovery and Reinvestment Act of 2009* (U.S. Congress, 2009), the U.S. Department of Education created 'Race to the Top', a US$4.35 billion contest in which states competed to implement policy mandates such as the establishment of performance-based standards for teachers and principals; articulation of a reform agenda in compliance with nationwide standards including turning around low achieving schools (which in some cases meant promotion of charter schools and privatisation of education); and introduction of data systems to support instruction and most importantly to keep track of academic progress.

Important curricular and assessment changes for K-16 education came in the form of the development and implementation of the Common Core State Standards (CCSS) for several core subjects with an emphasis on Science, Technology, Engineering and Mathematics (STEM) subjects. The development of the CCSS was launched in 2009 by state leaders, including governors and state commissioners of education from 48 states, two territories and the District of Columbia, through their membership in the National Governors Association Centre for Best Practices and the Council of Chief State School Officers.

Touted as a 'success story of meaningful, state-led change to help all students succeed' the CCSS outlined what pupils are expected to know and understand by the time they graduate from high school (also known as the college- and career-readiness standards), and the K-12 standards, which address expectations for elementary school through high school.[3] More specifically the CCSS developed two sets of standards – the general English language arts and literacy standards, and the more specific Mathematics standards. The English language arts and literacy standards' main focus is on reading, writing, language, speaking and listening skills for each grade level. These standards also incorporate literacy expectations beyond the English language to touch upon other subjects such as social studies and specifically history, and science including technical subjects. The Mathematics standards are more detailed including specifics about the mathematical concepts and skills pupils should learn at each grade level (e.g.

mastering skills such as problem-solving, reasoning, and modelling in algebra and geometry).

The development of the CCSS did not occur in a vacuum. The effort was in part informed by (and complemented) standards that had been developed over the years by education organisations bringing together groups of education scholars and practitioners with the general goal of improving access to quality teaching and learning in the subject areas. These organisations and standards included the National Council of Teachers of Mathematics, the Next Generation of Science Standards, the National Council of Teachers of English and the National Curriculum Standards for Social Studies. The key difference however, is that the CCSS are standards that the states have now the power to enforce by, for instance, requiring schools to align their curriculum according to these standards. According to Achieve (2010), a bipartisan, non-profit organisation which has worked with states to develop and align standards with graduation requirements, assessments and accountability systems, the CCSS for mathematics are similarly rigorous, and comparable in coherence and focus (e.g. conceptual understanding, procedural skills and problem-solving) with the National Curriculum Standards for Social Studies standards, yet the former are of necessity more specific.

The standards came accompanied by the introduction (by the states) of a more formal system of school and teacher evaluations. This was followed by calls from multiple fronts for close scrutiny of traditional teacher education programmes' curriculum and outcomes, as poor results in teacher evaluations were seen as a result of the 'mediocre' preparation teachers received in their programmes (Levine, 2006). These calls were quickly followed by a review of teacher education programmes by a conservative group called the National Council on Teacher Quality (NCTQ) claiming an interest on 'raising the bar on teacher preparation'. The group, which was founded in 2000, is currently sustained by foundations and private donors, yet initially received funding by the U.S. Department of Education during the Bush administration to help create an online programme (currently known as the American Board for Certification of Teacher Excellence) that would quickly create teachers for every classroom. The NCTQ, which had in its advisory board and technical panel Sir Michael Barber and some other well-known educators and economists including the founder of Teach for America, published a report in 2013 that was highly critical of teacher education programmes (NCTQ, 2013). Upon careful scrutiny, it was found that the report had followed a flawed methodology which discredited these results at many levels. Whilst a number of educators and institutions (including MSU) were critical of such a methodology and of the review that was produced (Darling-Hammond, 2013), these developments began to create a negative climate for teacher education (Keller, 2013).

Accreditation requirements and federal and state scrutiny of teacher education programmes began to change rapidly and a number of programmes that were not able to comply with the requirements closed. For instance, in 2012 Michigan officials suspended six teacher education programmes at Lake Superior

State University, citing falling licensing-test scores and other problems. Several states also reported closing programmes.[4] At the same time, some institutions of higher education (IHE) voluntarily got out of the business of preparing teachers (for instance, Finlandia University, a private university in Hancock, Michigan closed its teacher education programme in 2013).

On 10 December 2015, President Obama signed into law the *Every Student Succeeds Act (ESSA)* (U.S. Congress, 2015), which updated (and renamed) the *Elementary and Secondary Education Act of 1965* (U.S. Congress, 1965) the primary federal education law in the United States mentioned above. This law effectively devolved power to the states, districts and schools to make decisions about their content standards, assessments and teacher-evaluation requirements, and it was seen as a way to 'fix' the NCLB emphasis on testing and accountability, which had been under federal control. The law also excluded important policy incentives that had been introduced at the federal level to catalyse change such as the Race to the Top education reform effort, and the School Improvement Grant Programme. These changes did not remove annual assessments in reading and mathematics across selected grades K-12. Whilst states were still expected to set their own academic goals for schools, they were also expected to evaluate teachers and schools, and starting in the 2017–2018 school year to submit improvement plans at the federal level for approval (this was especially relevant for schools that were seen as failing). With this devolution of responsibility to maintain accountability to the states, the U.S. Department of Education lost its ability to influence states' adoption of standards, a decision that was seen as weakening the initial drive of the CCSS. With the change in administration in 2017, the direction of change is uncertain.

The increased regulation of schools and teachers during the Bush and Obama administrations also had an effect on teacher education. Increased scrutiny of teacher education systems in individual states revealed great variability with some states providing general guidelines, whilst others mandating specific requirements concerning liberal arts courses, subject matter courses and pedagogy courses. The states – and as a consequence teacher preparation programmes – also varied with regard to requirements for practicum experience (for instance, until recently, of the 50 states 39 required between 5 and 18 weeks of practice teaching). The recognition that the preparation of teachers across the country was highly uneven fuelled the notion that teacher education may be an important factor contributing to poor teaching and low pupil achievement in areas such as mathematics and science.

Increased accountability demands gave rise to a more complex system of accreditation for teacher preparation programmes and the creation of a new set of standards. In early 2015, the U.S. Department of Education, under the leadership of the then secretary Arne Duncan, announced a federal regulatory plan for teacher education programmes and other approaches to preparing teachers. Whilst this proposal was seen as a possible positive move to improve the quality of teacher education programmes and other routes into teaching by some, others reacted critically to this proposal, including the American Association of Colleges for Teacher Education (AACTE), which represents more than 800 post-secondary institutions. They collected more than 4,500 comments; almost all were in opposition to the regulations. The major concern had to do with the cost burden of implementation. The federal regulations proposal called for a programme of periodic accreditation aligned with the recently established (in 2013) Council for the Accreditation of Educator Preparation (CAEP), and an ongoing requirement that providers collect yearly data to allow them to demonstrate the level of success of graduates as indicated by knowledge and satisfaction at graduation, 3-year employment outcomes and pupil outcomes. Teacher education programmes and alternative routes would be accountable to the state, which, according to this plan, would produce ratings and allocate incentives (e.g. the Teacher Education Assistance for College and Higher Education or TEACH grants) to those providers that demonstrated success according to the aforementioned indicators. In October 2016, the U.S. Department of Education (2016a) officially released its revised regulations for teacher education programmes, which after much resistance have been subsequently rescinded in March of 2017. Whilst the rejection of these regulations means a relaxation of the role of the federal government on teacher education, it also means that the regulatory role mostly belongs to the individual states.

In sum, the introduction of the accountability movement and of the teacher education regulations came at a time of increasing criticism of higher education, more generally, and of teacher education programmes in particular, and signalled an important turn on the social perception of the teaching profession. The emergence and notoriety of the NCTQ as a private, self-appointed teacher education evaluation body, albeit non-recognised by the teacher education profession, was indicative of a worrisome trend and represented a direct challenge to the profession.

Publications by Levine (2006) documenting efficiency problems with teacher education programmes, and the constant evaluation reports coming from the NCTQ (albeit with questionable methods) have emerged with only moderate responses from the field. Some teacher education programmes seemed to have accepted and some have enthusiastically embraced the need to integrate programme evaluation routines into their day-to-day activities in preparation for and anticipation of the next accreditation wave. The new accreditation agency, the CAEP, continues to work in the development, refinement and implementation of new standards for teacher education programmes, as will be described below. In short, teacher education programme regulation seems to have become a permanent fixture in the pursuit of education quality.

The reformation and diversification of initial teacher education

In the 1980s, the Holmes Group first published the report *Tomorrow's Teachers*, a document that demanded more rigorous standards for the education of teachers, and urged universities to reconnect teacher education to schools and classrooms (Holmes Group, 1986). A follow-up report *Tomorrow's Schools* (Holmes Group, 1990) urged the creation of 'Professional Development Schools (PDSs)', focusing on professional preparation, school research and the improvement of teaching. A later report, *Tomorrow's Schools of Education* (Holmes Group, 1995), influenced a large number of teacher education programmes, resulting in 3-4 year teacher certification programmes with the final year being an internship in a school, including PDSs, and opened the possibility for yet more innovative reforms.

These reports also influenced the reform of teacher education. The reformed programmes focused on the development of an inquiry-based curriculum with a stronger emphasis on school subjects, a longer period of school practice, and a tightening of selection criteria to enter teacher education programmes. However, given the highly decentralised system of education in the United States these changes were not universal. At the same time, there has been increased diversification mostly through the introduction of alternative routes, some attached to universities in the form of induction programmes, and some operating independently.

Alternate routes to licensure have grown significantly. These routes, which have been adopted widely throughout the nation (with the exception of a few states), have been defined by states as avenues to meet the need for teachers in specific, high-need subject matter areas or high-need locations. According to the most recent data from the U.S. Department of Education (2016b), in 2011–2012, a total of 62,961 individuals were enrolled on alternative routes and 551,166 in traditional routes across the country, with approximately 30,000 individuals entering teaching through alternative routes every year. The highest concentration of recruitment of alternative route teachers has been in growing states such as Texas, followed by North Carolina, New York and Florida. In contrast, approximately 170,000 individuals continue to enter the profession from traditional routes (USDOE, 2015, p. 30). Whilst traditional programmes have been subject to regulations via accreditation since the 1950s, it was not until 2015 that the U.S. Department of Education issued a proposal for regulations that would apply to all routes to certification including alternative routes.

In sum, the emergence of market approaches to teacher education alongside increased regulation has resulted in the closing or in a reduction in enrolments in traditional teacher education programmes across the country. The most affected programmes are those in small HEIs as compliance with regulations exerts a heavy demand of internal resources to document programme process and outcomes over time. In spite of continued criticism, traditional teacher education programmes continue to prepare more than 85 per cent of future teachers in the nation. Yet a downward trend, which began in 2010 and reached a decline of nearly 20 per cent in 2012–2013, has affected enrolment in teacher education programmes country-wide. A recent report by the U.S. Department of Education (2016b) based on data collected in 2013–2014 shows that enrolments have continued to decline, but not as sharply as before. Alternative routes have been equally affected, including the prominent Teach for America. Overall, the landscape of teacher education in the United States has been altered dramatically over the last 10 years with the field increasingly signalling a turn towards more practice-oriented teacher education (Zeichner, 2012).

The development of a new model for teacher education

As mentioned above, the mid-1980s marked a period of vigorous reform in teacher education in the United States. Calls emerged for the need to have well-educated teachers to redesign the schools of the future, and indicated a reliance on the 'science of teaching' as a way to guide these efforts (see Labaree, 1992, p. 124). These calls for reform were in reaction to the top-down mandates that had dominated what was seen as an ineffective system; the solution sought 'less bureaucracy, more professional autonomy and more leadership for teachers' (as cited in Labaree, 1992, p. 130). These reform proposals for teacher education were backed by prominent education scholars such as Shulman and others who argued for the introduction of a market strategy to teacher certification (Shulman & Sykes, 1986). Further, education scholars such as Lanier and Little (1986) argued for the professionalisation of the teacher educators, who, they suggested, should fully participate in constructing the scholarship of teaching by 'contributing better knowledge and understanding of teaching and schooling' (Labaree, 1992, p. 135) – an important goal considering the traditionally weak position of teacher educators within the university and within colleges of education. This movement resulted in the creation of a more central role for teacher education within colleges of education and the universities, the expansion of teacher education research via federally funded centres in universities (the most prominent in MSU), the publication of the third edition of the *Handbook of Research on Teaching* (Wittrock, 1985), and importantly the creation of the now powerful Division K *Teaching and Teacher Education* in the American Educational Research Association (AERA) the most important association of education researchers in the United States (AERA, 2017).

Whilst the field was energised by these reforms, the decentralised nature of the United States system meant that the changes were uneven. Some programmes that implemented changes, as proposed by the reformers, demonstrated important gains whilst others made no changes (Tatto, 1996, 1998, 1999). In spite of a steady decade of progress in research and innovation in teacher education (from the 1980s to the mid-1990s when the Goals 2000 emerged [U.S. Congress, 1994]), traditional teacher education programmes came again under close scrutiny and were asked to demonstrate whether they were achieving desired outcomes. The emergence in force of international testing programmes such as the Trends in International Mathematics and Science Study highlighted the middling performance of the United States' pupils vis-à-vis their peers in other nations reviving the concerns about teacher effectiveness that had been raised after the publication of *A Nation at Risk* (USDOE, 1983). However, this time the attribution of failure encompassed not only teachers but also the programmes that prepared them.

These shifts in definition of the 'policy' problem in teacher education in a space of over 50 years has been characterised by Cochran-Smith and Fries (2005) as one of training (1960s to early 1980s), one of learning (1980s to 2000s), and one of outcomes (2000–on). The last shift, signals an attempt at controlling the processes and outcomes of teacher education under the argument that there is a need to improve teacher quality and ultimately pupil learning.

The introduction of standards and regulations in teacher education

Despite being historically a highly decentralised country at all levels, in the 1990s the United States began a gradual shift towards centralisation of the teacher licensure requirements as a result of the federal NCLB legislation (U.S. Congress, 2002). More recently, during the Obama administration, the push at the federal level for the development of a core curriculum accompanied by the creation of subject standards and calls for increased accountability via accreditation criteria began to create synergies towards more homogeneity in the provision of teacher education, albeit still controlled and regulated at the state level. These changes towards more standardisation whilst slow coming were welcomed by critics of teacher education who had noted that whilst all states require teacher education programmes to get state approval for what they offer, approval standards varied across states (Levine, 2006; Youngs & Grogan, 2013). This was a cause for concern given that as a result of local control and privatisation, more than 1,300 public and private colleges and universities as well as school districts, state agencies, and private organisations offer teacher education for future primary and secondary teachers (Youngs & Grogan, 2013).

Indeed, there is great variation in levels of certification offered by universities, colleges and alternative routes in the 50 American states. For instance, there are six main types of programmes offered in HEIs – one for each of the three phases: primary, lower secondary and secondary, each offered in both a concurrent and a consecutive version (Youngs & Grogan, 2013). Because grade spans overlap, teachers in grades generally identified with primary school can be prepared in a lower secondary programme-type, and teachers in grades usually identified with lower secondary can be prepared in either a lower secondary or a lower-plus-upper-secondary programme-type. The differences in content preparation for teachers at any of these grade levels may, therefore, vary considerably with primarily upper secondary teachers prepared as subject specialists. Alternative routes have introduced an added level of variability and because they have not been subjected to accreditation it has been difficult to know how effective they actually are. In addition, there is variability in who enters teacher education: aside from the mandatory completion of upper secondary school, many teacher preparation institutions and states have set additional requirements that applicants must meet (e.g. minimum grade point average, previous course requirements, scores on university entrance examinations [SAT/ACT], and, in some cases, state licensure test scores) but these are not uniform across or even within the states. This degree of variability was used to justify the elusive search for standards in teacher education.

The re-definition of a qualified teacher to a highly qualified teacher

One of the first steps towards homogenisation came as a result of the federal NCLB (U.S. Congress, 2002), which introduced high-stakes accountability measures in the form of tests and standards across the education system. At the same time, this legislation re-defined the notion of Qualified Teacher Status to that of a highly qualified teacher (HQT). Whilst typically to receive full state certification graduates were required to have a bachelor's degree, proficiency in the subject matter they will teach, preparation on pedagogical content knowledge and pedagogy and acceptable performance at the practicum stage, amongst others, the re-definition of HQT in actuality narrowed the knowledge and skills expectations for graduates. To be considered a HQT, the requirements were reduced to that of having a bachelor's degree, full state certification or licensure (which could be obtained via traditional or alternatives routes into teaching) and proficiency in the subject matter they will teach. Thus, teachers could now hold the HQT status with only a portion of the requirements expected in traditional teacher education programmes. The new definition of a HQT was quickly adopted and operationalised. According to a U.S. Department of Education report, in the year 2012–2013 states reported that 97 per cent of core academic classes in public schools were taught by teachers designated as HQT with about 15 per cent of those, graduating from alternative routes (USDOE, 2015) signalling an important shift in the demand for alternative routes into teaching.

Until then, and in comparison to other teacher education systems in the world, entry into teacher education in the United States had not been rigorous. But as a result of the changes introduced by the NCLB legislation in 2001 (U.S. Congress, 2002), programmes began to develop more restrictive criteria to comply with the requirements set for HQT. These changes saw a quick reduction in enrolment in teacher education programmes and in master programmes as well, reinforcing the notion that there was indeed a problem with the quality of teacher education and opened the door to a proposal to regulate teacher education at the federal level.

The failed attempt at federal regulation of teacher education programmes

Initiatives to regulate teacher education in the United States at the federal level have had mixed results. The last attempt at federally regulating the evaluation of teacher education lasted less than 3 years from 2014 when they were announced to 2017 when they were rescinded by the United States Congress, yet the evolution of this movement and its repercussion for the future of the accountability movement in teacher education needs analysis. Late in 2014, the federal government issued a proposal to regulate teacher education given the great variation in the offer across the country described above. The regulatory action was in accordance with Section 205 of the *Higher Education Opportunity Act* (U.S. Congress, 2008), which requires states and IHE annually to report on various characteristics of their teacher preparation programmes, including an assessment of programme performance. The justification for the regulation and programme reporting at the federal level was stated by the U.S. Department of Education as follows:

> These reporting requirements exist in part to ensure that members of the public, prospective teachers and employers (districts and schools), and the states, IHEs, and programs themselves have accurate information on the quality of these teacher preparation programs. These requirements also provide an impetus to States and IHEs to make improvements where they are needed. Thousands of novice teachers enter the profession every year and their students deserve to have well-prepared teachers.
>
> (Federal Register, 2017)

In October 2016, the U.S. Department of Education officially released its revised regulations for teacher preparation programmes. These regulations called for an annual rating of such programmes according to four indicators (reproduced here from the AACTE resource library[5]):

1   Student learning outcomes calculated for all novice teachers. States must use student growth, teacher-evaluation measures, another State determined measure that is relevant to calculating student learning outcomes, including academic performance, and that meaningfully differentiates amongst teachers, or a combination of the three.
2   Employment outcomes.
   a   Placement rates. The State must calculate annually a teacher's placement rate, a placement rate in high-needs schools, a retention rate, and a retention rate in high-need schools. The State is permitted to assess traditional, alternative route, and distance education teacher prep programs differently, 'provided that differences in assessments and reasons for those differences are transparent and that assessments result in equivalent levels of accountability and reporting irrespective of the type of program [or] where the program is physically located'. A state is not *required* to calculate placement rates for alternative routes to certification programmes.
   b   Retention rates. Retention rate is reported for each of the three cohorts of novice teachers immediately preceding the current Title II report year. This will start in the 2018 reporting year with only one cohort and it builds each year until accounting is for three cohorts.
3   Report on characteristics and performance of teacher preparation programmes, including measures of satisfaction with the teacher preparation

programme from the student teachers, and from the principal where the teacher is employed using survey data collection methods.

4   Evidence of programme approval or specialised accreditation (there is no requirement of rigorous entry qualifications but there is a requirement to prove rigorous exit qualifications).

The U.S. Department of Education established a link 'between the State's classification of a teacher preparation program's performance under the Title II reporting system and that program's identification as "high-quality" for TEACH Grant eligibility purposes' (USDOE, 2016a).

Whilst the regulations did not come to fruition the requirement to report teacher education programme's performance under Title II still holds (U.S. Congress, 2008). It is also important to note that in spite of a number of issues raised when announced in November 2014 and much feedback from the public, there were few changes in the regulations; however some of these changes were significant. For instance, the authorisation into law of the *Every Student Succeeds Act* (U.S. Congress, 2015) did away with federal requirements for teacher evaluations, devolving this power to the states. In addition, the regulations included the evaluation of online teacher education programmes, which prepare a large number of teachers (nationally and internationally across the country) and include for-profit, not-for-profit and public institutions. The expectation was for the design and implementation of a data system that would have been ready in 2017 when the regulations were expected to enter a 'pilot year' coordinating with Title II reporting requirements in 2018. In 2021–2022, states were expected to assign TEACH[6] grants to programmes deemed successful.[7]

Whilst the federal control of the regulations was rescinded in 2017, states are still expected to demonstrate that teacher education programmes are of high quality as per Title II as mentioned earlier. Because teacher education programme accountability is closely tied to accreditation, the next section of this chapter describes the overall mechanism to accredit teacher preparation and to control the quality of graduates.

Accreditation and the emergence of new outcome standards for teacher preparation providers

Traditional teacher education programmes housed in universities had been accredited by two bodies, the long-standing NCATE created in the mid-1950s and later by the Teacher Education Accreditation Council (TEAC), which emerged in the mid-1990s as a more organic programme-driven evaluation and as a reaction to the NCATE. Although these two organisations still mediate accreditation processes, a new organisation, CAEP, was created in 2013 to merge the two whilst still maintaining NCATE and TEAC accreditation processes under a legacy arrangement to honour the processes begun by institutions before the creation of the CAEP. It is expected that eventually CAEP will function as the only accrediting institution. CAEP's accreditation process is guided by five standards that were created after extensive consultation. Here, we include a brief description of each as stated by CAEP (2015):

> Standard 1: Content and Pedagogical Knowledge: The provider ensures that candidates develop a deep understanding of the critical concepts and principles of their discipline and, by completion, are able to use discipline-specific practices flexibly to advance the learning of all students toward attainment of college- and career-readiness standards.
>
> Standard 2: Clinical Partnerships and Practice: The provider ensures that effective partnerships and high-quality clinical practice are central to preparation so that candidates develop the knowledge, skills, and professional dispositions necessary to demonstrate positive impact on all P-12 students' learning and development.
>
> Standard 3: Candidate Quality, Recruitment, and Selectivity: The provider demonstrates that the quality of candidates is a continuing and purposeful part of its responsibility from recruitment, at admission, through the progression of courses and clinical experiences, and to decisions that completers are prepared to teach effectively and are recommended for certification. The provider demonstrates that development of candidate quality is the goal of educator preparation in all phases of the program. This process is ultimately determined by a program's meeting of Standard 4.
>
> Standard 4: Program Impact: The provider demonstrates the impact of its completers on P-12 student learning and development, classroom instruction, and schools, and the satisfaction of its completers with the relevance and effectiveness of their preparation.
>
> Standard 5: Provider Quality Assurance and Continuous Improvement: The provider maintains a quality assurance system comprised of valid data from multiple measures, including evidence of candidates' and completers' positive impact on P-12 student learning and development. The provider supports continuous improvement that is sustained and evidence-based, and that evaluates the effectiveness of its completers. The provider uses the results of inquiry and data collection to establish priorities, enhance program elements and capacity, and test innovations to improve completers' impact on P-12 student learning and development.
>
> (CAEP, 2015)

These standards were developed in coordination with the U.S. Department of Education to support the proposed regulations and the AACTE amongst others, although the latter was highly critical of Standards 4 and 5. What is remarkable in these standards is not only the change in the language used (for instance, the change from 'teacher education' to 'teacher preparation' in an attempt to encompass not only traditional routes to preparation but also alternative pathways into teaching, and from 'programmes' to 'providers' a term also used in England), but also the steep requirements to receive accreditation. Whilst ensuring that student teachers graduate with adequate knowledge of the discipline(s) and of pedagogy has been the raison d'être of teacher education programmes in the United States, the standards also seek to regulate how this is to be accomplished (e.g. by increasing programme selectivity, and engaging in productive partnerships to procure high-quality clinical practice, amongst others).

The most demanding developments, however, are the criteria in Standard 4, which require programmes to demonstrate impact using as an indicator the learning and development attained by the P-12 pupils' of graduates, and in Standard 5, which require the maintenance of a highly complex longitudinal database that can be used to demonstrate evidence of sustained impact and quality. Critics of these standards (and of the federal regulations that proposed compliance with these standards) have argued that whilst it is reasonable to demonstrate impact based on graduates' knowledge and skills, using measures of pupils' performance to demonstrate programmes' success lacks validity, especially for traditional routes and favours school-based routes. As far as a maintenance of a quality assurance system is concerned, critics argue that the standards (and the regulations) failed to consider that the majority of the programmes (or providers) would need to first develop such a system in addition to maintaining it, resulting in significant costs that would need to be incurred by the programmes themselves (Tatto et al., 2016), a situation that whilst desirable may be difficult to attain in a short time period and without significant funding.

Developmental standards for teachers

The CAEP process relies on the 2011 *Interstate New Teachers Assessment and Support InTASC Model Core Teaching Standards and Learning Progressions for Teachers 1.0: A Resource for State Dialogue* (CCSSO, 2011). These standards provide curriculum guidelines for teacher education programmes, and for evaluation of programme graduates once in the field. The standards have now been adopted by most states across the nation, and use a developmental model of teacher learning. The standards document describes the actual standards and details assessment criteria including 'performances', 'essential knowledge', and 'critical dispositions', which are summarised into 'progression indicators' as described in Table 3.1 (see pp. 77–79).[8]

What is remarkable about these standards is that whilst they were released in the late 1990s they are only gaining traction now. The standards are important in their comprehensiveness, in the notion that learning to teach is developmental, and in their intent to serve as a guide in the knowledge and skills required of graduates as well as their development once in the classroom. The standards thus, serve as a counterbalance to the input and output models used to evaluate teachers promoted by value-added models and by the NCLB

Table 3.1 Summary of InTASC teaching standards and learning progressions for teachers

Learner development and learning differences

Standard #1: The teacher understands how learners grow and develop, recognising that patterns of learning and development vary individually within and across the cognitive, linguistic, social, emotional and physical areas and designs and implements developmentally appropriate and challenging learning experiences

Progression indicators:

1 The teacher uses understanding of how learners grow and develop (in cognitive, linguistic, social, emotional and physical areas) to design and implement developmentally appropriate and challenging learning experiences

Standard #2: The teacher uses understanding of individual differences and diverse cultures and communities to ensure inclusive learning environments that enable each learner to meet high standards

2 The teacher uses understanding of learners' commonalities and individual differences within and across diverse communities to design inclusive learning experiences that enable each learner to meet high standards

Learning environments

Standard #3: The teacher works with others to create environments that support individual and collaborative learning, and that encourage positive social interaction, active engagement in learning and self-motivation

Progression indicators:

1 The teacher collaborates with others to build a positive learning climate marked by respect, rigour and responsibility

2 The teacher manages the learning environment to engage learners actively

Content knowledge

Standard #4: The teacher understands the central concepts, tools of inquiry and structures of the discipline(s) he or she teaches and creates learning experiences that make these aspects of the discipline accessible and meaningful for learners to assure mastery of the content

Progression indicators:

1 The teacher understands the central concepts, tools of inquiry and structures of the discipline(s) he or she teaches

2 The teacher creates learning experiences that make the discipline accessible and meaningful for learners to assure mastery of the content

Application of content

Standard #5: The teacher understands how to connect concepts and use differing perspectives to engage learners in critical thinking, creativity and collaborative problem-solving related to authentic local and global issues

Progression indicators:

1 The teacher connects concepts, perspectives from varied disciplines and interdisciplinary themes to real world problems and issues

2 The teacher engages learners in critical thinking, creativity, collaboration and communication to address authentic local and global issues

continued

Table 3.1 Continued

Assessment

Standard #6: The teacher understands and uses multiple methods of assessment to engage learners in their own growth, to monitor learner progress and to guide the teacher's and learner's decision-making

Progression indicators:

1 The teacher uses designs or adapts multiple methods of assessment to document, monitor and support learner progress appropriate for learning goals and objectives

2 The teacher uses assessment to engage learners in their own growth

3 The teacher implements assessments in an ethical manner and minimises bias to enable learners to display the full extent of their learning

Planning for instruction

Standard #7: The teacher plans instruction that supports every student in meeting rigorous learning goals by drawing upon knowledge of content areas, curriculum, cross-disciplinary skills and pedagogy, as well as knowledge of learners and the community context

Progression indicators:

1 The teacher selects, creates and sequences learning experiences and performance tasks that support learners in reaching rigorous curriculum goals based on content standards and cross-disciplinary skills

2 The teacher plans instruction based on information from formative and summative assessments as well as other sources and systematically adjusts plans to meet each student's learning needs

3 The teacher plans instruction by collaborating with colleagues, specialists, community resources, families and learners to meet individual learning needs

Instructional strategies

Standard #8: The teacher understands and uses a variety of instructional strategies to encourage learners to develop deep understanding of content areas and their connections, and to build skills to apply knowledge in meaningful ways

Progression indicators:

1 The teacher understands and uses a variety of instructional strategies and makes learning accessible to all learners

2 The teacher encourages learners to develop deep understanding of content areas, makes connections across content and applies content knowledge in meaningful ways

Professional learning and ethical practice
Standard #9: The teacher engages in ongoing professional learning and uses evidence to continually evaluate his/her practice, particularly the effects of his/her choices and actions on others (learners, families, other professionals and the community) and adapts practice to meet the needs of each learner

Progression indicators:
1 The teacher engages in continuous professional learning to more effectively meet the needs of each learner
2 The teacher uses evidence to continually evaluate the effects of his/her decisions on others and adapts professional practices to better meet learners' needs
3 The teacher practices the profession in an ethical manner

Leadership and collaboration
Standard #10: The teacher seeks appropriate leadership roles and opportunities to take responsibility for student learning, to collaborate with learners, families, colleagues, other school professionals and community members to ensure learner growth, and to advance the profession

Progression indicators:
1 The teacher collaborates with learners, families, colleagues, other school professionals and community members to ensure learner growth
2 The teacher seeks appropriate leadership roles and opportunities to take responsibility for student learning and to advance the profession

Source: CCSSO, 2013, pp. 16–47.

re-definition of a HQT. Indeed, these standards attempt to bring back the notion of teachers as learners that was so central to the development of the profession in the 1980s and 1990s. But whilst the standards have been carefully drafted, and enjoy support from teacher educators, there is much disagreement about the development of measures to assess the degree to which graduates are reaching these standards.

Assessing student-teachers' knowledge and performance

Because programme accreditation requires measurable outcomes, a number of assessments of teacher knowledge have emerged. One of these, the edTPA (Teacher Performance Assessment developed and owned by Stanford University), will be described here because it is the most comprehensive, has been in use since the end of 2013, some states however, and may yet develop their own measures. The edTPA has received wide support from educators and psychometricians, teacher education programmes, the AACTE and the U.S. Department of Education as a vital component in the evaluation of teacher education outcomes (edTPA, 2014). The assessment is also well aligned with the CAEP and the InTASC standards and its creators and promoters cite decades of educational research and the 'foundational work' of the National Board for Professional Teaching Standards as building blocks for the assessment.

The edTPA assesses whether teacher candidates have the knowledge and classroom skills necessary to ensure pupils are learning, it is administered by the testing corporation Pearson, and costs student teachers US$300 dollars. According to their website:[9]

> [E]dTPA is a performance-based, subject-specific assessment and support system used by more than 600 teacher preparation programs in some 40 states to emphasize, measure and support the skills and knowledge that all teachers need from Day 1 in the classroom. Developed by educators for educators, edTPA is the first such standards-based assessment to become nationally available in the United States. It builds on decades of work on assessments of teacher performance and research regarding teaching skills that improve student learning.
>
> (AACTE, 2017b)

But whilst a number of states are in various stages of exploration, adoption and implementation, critics to this assessment cite validity and reliability problems, and its inability to discriminate between high and low performers (e.g. in an exploratory study in the state of New York the pass rate was 83 per cent) (Singer, 2014). Others have expressed concerns about the test's narrow scope, the undue burden it imposes on candidates and on the programme staff who find themselves preparing student teachers to complete a highly prescribed test (Dover & Schultz, 2016; Cronenberg et al., 2016).

In sum, in spite of criticism from several fronts, the profession and the U.S. Department of Education under the past administration managed to build a cohesive system to regulate teacher preparation programmes and the teaching profession more generally. Whether any of these efforts will survive is yet to be seen.

Summary

Teacher education since first becoming part of the higher education system after a period of reform had enjoyed a history of relative stability in the United States. However, in the early 1980s, experience-based routes into teaching began to emerge. Currently a greater variety of programmes and approaches are being tried. But there has not been as radical a shift as in England. Since the early 2000s, the stability of teacher education in the universities in the United States has begun to erode as a result of the introduction of market models in the provision of teacher education, increased standards for accreditation, which have been applied unevenly to traditional and alternative programmes and strong criticism of the teaching profession, which has failed to produce amongst teacher educators a coherent and defensible response.

After a period of growth and productive reforms, the re-definition of what it means to be a qualified teacher in the early 2000s combined with high-stakes teacher evaluations of novice teachers served to challenge the traditional curriculum offering of teacher education programmes. Successful evaluations of novice teachers once in schools has taken priority over preparing future teachers to plan, teach, assess and reflect. Because teacher performance evaluations are tied to pupils' tests results (under the increasingly popular value-added approaches) teaching practice is in many cases dominated by teaching to the test. Increased standardisation has also affected pedagogy in teacher education in response to accreditation demands. Scholars argue that the current shift in teacher education is 'from focus on bodies of knowledge (e.g. cultural foundations, learning theory) to a focus on depictions of practice' (Kennedy, 2016, p. 6) or set of core practices, and that this shift has resulted on educators paying less attention to the purposes that are served by those behaviours arguing for a focus towards universal requirements of teaching including enacting the curriculum, enlisting pupil participation, exposing pupil thinking, containing pupil behaviours and accommodating personal needs.

But accreditation waves seem to regulate the ebb and flow of teacher education programme activity distracting teacher educators from the complex work of teacher preparation. Standards are changing relatively quickly after years of more stable approaches as regulated by the NCATE and TEAC. The newly constituted accreditation agency for teacher education CAEP in 2013 re-introduced the *InTASC Model Core Teaching Standards and Learning Progressions for Teachers 1.0: A Resource for Ongoing Teacher Development* (CCSSO, 2013). Because the standards are expected to regulate teacher education, support accreditation and extend beyond the first years of teaching, a number of teacher education programmes have acted quickly to align their course offerings with these standards. The *Every Student Succeeds Act* authorisation (U.S. Congress, 2015) and the official release of the federally mandated regulations of teacher preparation at the end of 2016 served to bring the profession together, albeit with the goal of rejecting the regulation initiative in early 2017. At the time of writing, there seems to be a high degree of uncertainty in the field. Even if the federal regulations were rescinded, the emergence of unabated criticism, standards and a regulatory discourse has served to create a new modus operandi for teacher education programmes characterised by further dependence on state administrators and policy makers, and increased pressure to respond to constant accountability demands, all of which has reduced time for reflection and growth, and may mean a weakened position of teacher education programmes in HEIs.

Conclusion

It is against these two backdrops that the study's efforts to understand what is happening within the processes of learning to teach within the two national contexts should be considered. The two accounts illustrate the enormous complexity of making sense of learning to teach in contexts which are continuing to change on a very rapid basis. Each country is very complex in itself, with variations in practice reflecting the opportunities and challenges created by this constantly shifting policy context.

Amongst the similarities that we may observe in what is happening in policy in England and the United States, we may note first of all the continuing condition of turbulence. In both countries, teacher education continues to be a major focus for politicians and policy makers. We can also see increasing elements of intervention in the governance and control of teacher education. This is evidenced through the creation and implementation of standards for teaching and specifically for entry into the profession. In both settings however, this central intervention is accompanied by increasing diversity and 'marketisation' of the processes by which it is possible to become a teacher. Although the challenges to universities' engagement in teacher education are manifest in rather different forms, there is no doubt that in both countries these institutions are experiencing major threats.

The main differences we have identified of course include the fact, in relation to teacher education, that England is a unitary state, with one government department that is responsible for issuing the various mandates and regulations concerning teacher education. In the United States, by contrast, many elements of teacher education policy (including the determination of standards) are decided at the level of the state rather than the federal government. This may be one reason that the changes in England appear overall to have been more radical than in the United States, in that a single entity following a clear political agenda has the authority to act. There are also significant differences between the two contexts in the higher education elements of teacher education provision, reflecting the different national histories of teacher education, which will be discussed in more detail in later chapters.

Looking at these two macro contexts, it can certainly be said that we are living through the consequences of the impact of neoliberal approaches to social policy, including education. However, our study aims to help ascertain the real impact on the processes of learning to teach in these turbulent environments. What is it that student teachers are learning? How are they learning it? Who are they learning it from? What are the impacts of schools, universities and other agencies/institutions on these learners? It is questions such as these that the study seeks to address in the belief that these things matter – teaching and teachers matter, teacher education and teacher educators matter. Social policies, including policies in teacher education, have very real impacts on human lives. Following the methodological outline presented in Chapter 2, we look next, at Chapters 4 and 5, respectively at the HEI and school contexts in more detail, moving into the meso level. These are the two social situations of development which our beginning teachers experience in the process of becoming teachers.

Notes

1 www.theguardian.com/education/2015/oct/24/academy-chain-fees-griffin-accountability-trustees (Boffey & Mansell, 2015).
2 www.theguardian.com/education/2016/nov/11/english-schools-shortage-of-19000-heads-by-2022-report (Press Association, 2016).
3 www.corestandards.org/about-the-standards/development-process/ (Common Core Standards Initiative, 2017).
4 See the report in www.edweek.org/ew/articles/2014/12/16/states-slow-to-close-faltering-teacher-ed.htm (Education Week, 2017).
5 https://secure.aacte.org/apps/rl/resource.php?resid=648&ref=rl (AACTE, 2017a).
6 'The TEACH Grant Program provides grants of up to US$4,000 a year to pupils who are completing or plan to complete course work needed to begin a career in teaching' (Federal Student Aid, 2017a). 'A TEACH-Grant-eligible program is a program of study that is designed to prepare individuals to teach as a highly qualified teacher in a high-need field and that leads to a bachelor's or master's degree, or is a post-baccalaureate program' (Federal Student Aid, 2017b).
7 https://studentaid.ed.gov/sa/sites/default/files/teach-grant.pdf (Federal Student Aid, 2017c).
8 These are described in more detail in: www.ccsso.org/Documents/2013/2013_INTASC_Learning_Progressions_for_Teachers.pdf (CCSSO, 2013).
9 edtpa.aacte.org (AACTE, 2017b).

References

Achieve. (2010). *Achieving the Common Core: Comparing the Common Core State Standards in Mathematics and NCTM's Curriculum Focal Points*. Washington, DC: Achieve. Retrieved from www.achieve.org/files/CCSSandFocalPoints.pdf.
Alexander, R. (1984). Innovation and continuity in the initial teacher education curriculum. In R. Alexander, M. Craft & J. Lynch (Eds.), *Change in teacher education. Context and provision since Robins* (pp. 103–160). London: Holt, Rinehart and Winston.

American Association of Colleges for Teacher Education (AACTE). (2017a). *Resource library.* Retrieved from https://secure.aacte.org/apps/rl/resource.php?resid=648&ref=rl.

American Association of Colleges for Teacher Education (AACTE). (2017b). edTPA. Retrieved from edtpa.aacte.org.

American Educational Research Association (AERA). (2017). Teaching & teacher education (K). Retrieved from www.aera.net/Division-K/Teaching-Teacher-Education-K.

Association of Teachers and Lecturers (ATL). (2013). *Select committee inquiry on school direct and college of teaching* (July 2013). Retrieved from: www.atl.org.uk/Images/atl-response-select-committee-school-direct.pdf.

Ball, S. (1990). *Politics and policy making in education.* London: Routledge.

Boffey, D. & Mansell, W. (2015, October 24). Academy chain's fees for 'consultants' put schools programme under scrutiny. *Guardian.* Retrieved from: www.theguardian.com/education/2015/oct/24/academy-chain-fees-griffin-accountability-trustees.

Carter, A. (2015). *Carter review of initial teacher training (ITT).* London: Department for Education.

Childs, A. & Menter, I. (2013). Teacher education in the 21st Century in England: A case study in neo-liberal policy. *Revista Espanola de Educacion Comparada (Spanish Journal of Comparative Education), 22,* 93–116.

Cochran-Smith, M. & Fries, K. (2005). Researching teacher education in changing times: Paradigms and politics. In M. Cochran-Smith & K. Zeichner (Eds.), *Studying teacher education: The report of the AERA panel on research and teacher education* (pp. 69–110). Mahwah, NJ: Lawrence Erlbaum Press.

Common Core Standards Initiative. (2017). *Development process.* Retrieved from www.corestandards.org/about-the-standards/development-process/.

Comptroller and Auditor General. (2016). *Training new teachers.* London: National Audit Office.

Council for the Accreditation of Educator Preparation (CAEP). (2015). *The CAEP Standards.* Retrieved from http://caepnet.org/standards/introduction.

Council of Chief State School Officers (CCSSO). (2011). *Interstate Teacher Assessment and Support Consortium (InTASC) model core teaching standards: A resource for state dialogue.* Washington, DC: Author.

Council of Chief State School Officers (CCSSO). (2013). *Interstate Teacher Assessment and Support Consortium InTASC model core teaching standards and learning progressions for teachers 1.0: A resource for ongoing teacher development.* Washington, DC: Author. Retrieved from www.ccsso.org/Documents/2013/2013_INTASC_Learning_Progressions_for_Teachers.pdf.

Cronenberg, S., Harrison, D., Korson, S., Jones, A., Murray-Everett, N.C., Parrish, M. & Johnston-Parsons, M. (2016). Trouble with the edTPA: Lessons learned from a narrative self-study. *Journal of Inquiry & Action in Education, 8*(1), 109–134.

Darling-Hammond, L. (2013). *Why the NCTQ teacher prep ratings are nonsense. Washington Post.* Retrieved on June 18, 2013 from www.washingtonpost.com/blogs/answer-sheet/wp/2013/06/18/why-the-nctq-teacher-prep-ratings-are-nonsense/.

Department for Education (DfE). (1992). *Initial teacher training (secondary phase), Circular 9/92.* London: DfE.

Department for Education (DfE). (1993). *The initial training of primary school teachers: New criteria for course approval, Circular 14/93.* London: DfE.

Department for Education (DfE). (2010). *The importance of teaching: The Schools White Paper 2010.* Command 7980. London: HMSO.

Department for Education (DfE). (2011). *Teachers' standards.* London: HMSO.

Department for Education (DfE). (2016a). *Initial teacher training: Government response to Carter review*. Retrieved from www.gov.uk/government/publications/initial-teacher-training-government-response-to-carter-review.

Department for Education (DfE). (2016b). *Standard for teachers' professional development*. Retrieved from www.gov.uk/government/publications/standard-for-teachers-professional-development.

Department for Education (DfE). (2016c). *Educational excellence everywhere* (White Paper). Command 9230. London: DfE.

Department for Education and Employment (DfEE). (1997). *Initial teacher training: Approval of courses (Circular 9/97)*. London: HMSO.

Department of Education and Science (DES). (1983). *Teaching quality* (White Paper). London: HMSO.

Department of Education and Science (DES). (1984). *Initial teaching training: Approval of courses (Circular 3/84)*. London: DES.

Dover, G. A. & Schultz, B. D. (2015). Troubling the edTPA: Illusions of objectivity and rigor. *The Educational Forum, 80*(1), 95–106.

edTPA. (2014). Educative assessment & meaningful support: 2014 edTPA administrative report. Retrieved from https://secure.aacte.org/apps/rl/res_get.php?fid=2183&ref=rl.

Education Week. (2017). *Teaching the teachers: States slow to close faltering teacher ed. programs*. Retrieved from www.edweek.org/ew/articles/2014/12/16/states-slow-to-close-faltering-teacher-ed.html.

Ellis, V., Maguire, M., Tom Are Trippestad, T., Liu, Y., Yang, X. & Zeichner, K. (2016). Teaching other people's children, elsewhere, for a while: The rhetoric of a travelling educational reform. *Journal of Education Policy, 31*(1), 60–80.

Federal Register. (2017). *Teacher preparation issues: A rule by the Education Department on 10/31/2016*. Retrieved from www.federalregister.gov/documents/2016/10/31/2016-24856/teacher-preparation-issues.

Federal Student Aid. (2017a). *What is a TEACH grant?* Retrieved from https://student aid.ed.gov/sa/types/grants-scholarships/teach.

Federal Student Aid. (2017b). *What is a TEACH-Grant-eligible program?* Retrieved from https://studentaid.ed.gov/sa/types/grants-scholarships/teach.

Federal Student Aid. (2017c). *TEACH Grant Program*. Retrieved from https://student aid.ed.gov/sa/sites/default/files/teach-grant.pdf.

Foster, D. (2016). *Teachers: Supply retention and workload*. (House of Commons Briefing 7222). London: House of Commons Library.

Furlong, J. (2013). *Education – An anatomy of the discipline: Rescuing the university project?* London: Routledge.

Gilroy, P. (2014). Policy intervention in teacher education: Sharing the English experience. *Journal of Education for Teaching, 40*(5), 622–632.

Holmes Group. (1986). *Tomorrow's teachers: A report of the Holmes Group*. East Lansing, MI: Holmes Group. Retrieved from https://eric.ed.gov/?id=ED270454.

Holmes Group. (1990). *Tomorrow's schools: Principles for the design of Professional Development Schools*. East Lansing, MI: Holmes Group. Retrieved from https://eric.ed.gov/?id=ED328533.

Holmes Group. (1995). *Tomorrow's schools of education: A report by the Holmes Group*. East Lansing, MI: Holmes Group. Retrieved from https://eric.ed.gov/?id=ED399220.

House of Commons Education Committee. (2015). *Academies and free schools*. Fourth Report of Session 2014–15 (HC258). London: The Stationery Office.

Keller, B. (2013, October 20). An industry of mediocrity. *New York Times*, p. A21.

Kennedy, M. (2016). Parsing the practice of teaching. *Journal of Teacher Education, 67*(1), 6–17.

Labaree, D. F. (1992). Power, knowledge, and the rationalization of teaching: A genealogy of the movement to professionalize teaching. *Harvard Educational Review, 62*(2), 123–155.

Labaree, D. F. (2008). An uneasy relationship: The history of teacher education in the university. In M. Cochran-Smith, S. Feiman-Nemser & D. J. McIntyre (Eds.), *Handbook of research on teacher education: Enduring issues in changing contexts* (3rd ed.) (pp. 290–306). Washington, DC: Association of Teacher Educators.

Lanier, J. E. & Little, J. W. (1986). Research on teacher education. In M. C. Wittrock (Ed.), *Handbook of research on teaching* (pp. 527–569). New York: Macmillan.

Levine, A. (2006). *Educating school teachers*. Washington, DC: The Education Schools Project.

McIntyre, G. (1991). *Accreditation of teacher education: The story of CATE 1984–1989.* London: Falmer Press.

Menter, I. (2016). The use, misuse and abuse of research in the Education White Paper. Available at: www.timeshighereducation.com/blog/use-misuse-and-abuse-research-education-white-paper.

Mutton, T., Burn, K. & Menter, I. (2016). Deconstructing the Carter Review: Competing conceptions of quality in England's 'school-led' system of initial teacher education. *Journal of Education Policy, 32*(1), 14–33.

National Council on Teacher Quality (NCTQ). (2013). *Teacher prep review 2013*. Washington, DC: National Council on Teacher Quality. [www.nctq.org/dmsView/Teacher_Prep_Review_2013_Report].

New Labour. (1998). *Teachers: Meeting the challenge of change* (Green Paper). London: HMSO.

Press Association. (2016, November 11). Teacher shortages: English schools 'may face shortage of 19,000 heads by 2022'. *Guardian*. Retrieved from www.theguardian.com/education/2016/nov/11/english-schools-shortage-of-19000-heads-by-2022-report.

Sahlberg, P. (2011). *Finnish lessons*. New York: Teachers' College Press.

Singer, A. (2014, July 14). The 'big lie' behind the high-stakes testing of student teachers. *The Huffington Post, The Blog*. Retrieved from www.huffingtonpost.com/alan-singer/the-big-lie-behind-the-hi_b_5323155.html.

Shulman, L. & Sykes, G. (1986). *A national board for teaching? In search of a bold standard*. Paper prepared for the Task Force on Teaching as a Profession. Carnegie Forum on Education and the Economy, pp. 24–26.

Tatto, M. T. (1996). Examining values and beliefs about teaching diverse students: Understanding the challenges for teacher education. *Educational Evaluation and Policy Analysis, 18*(2), 155–180.

Tatto, M. T. (1998). The influence of teacher education on teachers' beliefs about purposes of education, roles and practice. *Journal of Teacher Education, 49*(1), 66–77.

Tatto, M. T. (1999). The socializing influence of normative cohesive teacher education on teachers' beliefs about instructional choice. *Teachers and Teaching, 5*(1), 111–134.

Tatto, M. T., Savage, C., Liao, W., Marshall, S., Goldblatt, P. & Contreras, M. L. (2016). The emergence of high-stakes accountability policies in teacher preparation: An examination of the U.S. Department of Education's proposed regulations. *Education Policy Analysis Archives, 24*(21). http://dx.doi.org/10.14507/epaa.24.2322

The Teacher Education Group. (2016). *Teacher education in times of change*. Bristol: Policy Press.

U.S. Congress. (1965). *Elementary and Secondary Education Act of 1965*. Public Law 89–100. Washington, DC: Government Printing Office.

U.S. Congress. (1994). *Goals 2000: Educate America Act*. Public Law 103–227. Washington, DC: Government Printing Office.

U.S. Congress. (2002). *No Child Left Behind Act of 2001*. Public Law 107–110. Washington, DC: Government Printing Office.

U.S. Congress. (2008). *Higher Education Opportunity Act*. Public Law 110–315. Washington, DC: Government Printing Office. Retrieved from https://title2.ed.gov/public/TA/HEA_2008_Sections%20205_208.pdf.

U.S. Congress. (2009). *American Recovery and Reinvestment Act of 2009*. Public Law 111–115. Chicago: CCH.

U.S. Congress. (2015). *Every Student Succeeds Act*. S.177. Public Law 114–195. Washington, DC: Government Printing Office.

U.S. Department of Education (USDOE). (1983). *A nation at risk: The imperative for educational reform. A report to the Nation and the Secretary of Education*. Washington, DC: National Commission on Excellence in Education. Retrieved from http://files.eric.ed.gov/fulltext/ED226006.pdf.

U.S. Department of Education (USDOE). (2015). *Highly qualified teachers enrolled in programs providing alternative routes to teacher certification or licensure*. Washington, DC: Policy and Program Studies Service, Office of Planning, Evaluation and Policy Development, USDOE. Available at www2.ed.gov/about/offices/list/opepd/ppss/reports.html.

U.S. Department of Education (USDOE). (2016a). *Teacher preparation issues: Final regulations*. Washington, DC: Office of Postsecondary Education, Department of Education. Available at: www.federalregister.gov/documents/2016/10/31/2016-24856/teacher-preparation-issues.

U.S. Department of Education (USDOE). (2016b). *Pathways to teaching*. USDOE, Office of Postsecondary Education. Higher Education Act Title II Reporting System. Washington, DC: USDOE. Retrieved 5 February 2, 2017 from https://title2.ed.gov/Public/46608_Final_Title_II_Infographic_Booklet_Web.pdf.

Whitty, G. (2016). *Research and policy in education*. London: UCL IoE Press.

Whitty, G. & Menter, I. (1989). Lessons of Thatcherism: Education policy in England and Wales 1979–88. In A. Gamble & C. Wells (Eds.), *Thatcher's law* (pp. 42–64). Cardiff: GPC Books.

Wittrock, M. (Ed.). (1985). *Handbook of research on teaching* (3rd ed.). London: Macmillan.

Youngs, P. & Grogan, E. (2013). Preparing teachers of mathematics in the United States of America. In J. Schwille, L. Ingvarson & R. Holdgreve-Resendez (Eds.), *TEDS-M encyclopedia*. Amsterdam, the Netherlands: International Association for the Evaluation of Educational Achievement (IEA).

Zeichner, K. (2012). The turn once again toward practice-based teacher education. *Journal of Teacher Education*, *63*(5), 376–382.

4 Teacher education programmes as settings for learning to teach

Responses to policy and social pressures in England and in the United States

This chapter moves to the meso level, first to examine the response of teacher preparation programmes based in higher education institutions (HEIs) to the societal and policy pressures (discussed in Chapter 3) that have shaped the field in England and the United States. Following a very brief discussion of the different positions generally adopted by HEIs in response to external (state/federal) and internal (within university) pressures, we look more closely at individual institutions, focusing in each country on just one well-established HEI, widely recognised for: (a) the quality of its teacher education programmes and its graduates; (b) the stability of its partnerships with schools; and, (c) its research-based practices.

Thereafter, since one of the most important trends in both countries has been the development of alternative routes into teaching in which the third sector plays a prominent role, we focus on one significant and well-established example of this phenomenon from within the Teach for All movement, a network of social enterprises, coordinated by a board 'drawn from the worlds of finance, consulting and logistics as well as education' (Ellis et al., 2016). Since this kind of initiative depends on private and philanthropic funds, as well as those from public sources, and since it introduces institutions other than universities and schools into initial teacher education partnerships, there is a separate section devoted to the specific case study that we have chosen – Teach First in England. Within that section, we examine the nature both of the organisation itself and of the relationship that it established with particular universities. (Detailed attention is given to a particular school's engagement with Teach First in Chapter 5).

In both countries and in the different kinds of partnership our interest is only in programmes preparing future *secondary* teachers, since this allows us to hold constant the need for the specialist subject knowledge expected of teachers at this level. Given our assumption that institutions, experiencing their own internal pressures, produce different responses to external demands, we do not presume that any of these particular institutions represents what may be happening elsewhere; rather we treat their responses as 'best case scenarios' (Patton, 1990) that may illuminate the possible outcomes that may arise.

England and teacher education at the University of Oxford

Against the background of the destabilisation of teacher education in England (see Chapter 3) individual programmes have continued to develop in very specific ways, often in response to the policies of central government or related agencies, particularly, of course, where these have carried statutory force. Institutional obligations to respond have also been influenced both by government use of the inspection regime – with the identification of priority areas as the focus for scrutiny by the Office for Standards in Education, Children's Services and Skills (Ofsted) – and by the structural mechanisms used to create and promote particular routes into teaching, specifically the channelling of increasing numbers of potential applicants, after 2010, into what were defined as 'school-led' routes.

Developed from 1984 onwards, the innovative approach of the Oxford Internship Scheme (OIS) was in many ways the precursor to Circulars 9/92 and 14/93 (DfE, 1992, 1993). Based on a set of clearly articulated principles (see McIntyre, 1990), the model required student teachers (known as 'interns') to spend at least 120 days in school classrooms, an approach to the practicum which was intended to overcome two key problems identified from research. These were the 'disconnectedness of university-based studies from student teachers' work in schools' (McIntyre, 1997, p. 9) and the position of teacher education at the time as a 'marginal activity' in schools, which meant that the conditions for student teachers' learning were often poor (ibid.). Both issues were subsequently recognised in Circulars 9/92 and 14/93 (DfE, 1992, 1993), as were other key aspects of the programme: innovative approaches to school-based mentoring; the development of partnership approaches; and agreed indicators of expected intern performance.

The OIS can thus, be seen as initially anticipating national policy developments in many areas. More recently, however, it has drawn on its underlying principles and commitment to delivering a fully integrated, collaborative programme to inform its response to subsequent policy initiatives. Given the existing role of schools within the OIS, the emphasis of government policy on 'school-led' provision was seen less as a challenge to established ways of working and more as an opportunity to re-emphasise the collaborative nature of the partnership. What the Oxford programme emphatically rejected, however, – just as it had done originally on the basis of research evidence – was the promotion of an apprenticeship model of learning to teach. In the face of such a view (promoted by the Secretary of State for Education at the time), the OIS continued to emphasise its core beliefs, particularly the principle that interns should be explicitly encouraged to 'use ideas drawn from *diverse* sources ... including their own personal histories as well as university and school sources, to inform their thinking and their teaching' (McIntyre, 1990, p. 32).

Adapting to policy changes over time

The University of Oxford, like all other initial teacher education providers in England, has obviously had to adapt to the requirements of changing national policy. Key changes, such as the frequent revisions to the National Curriculum in England (in 1994, 2000, 2008 and 2013) and related changes to national assessment frameworks were followed by adaptations to the initial teacher education curriculum, planned through joint discussions between the schools and the university (many of them at the subject level) to determine exactly how knowledge about the school curriculum should be effectively integrated within the teacher education programme as a whole.

Overall, the OIS approach has focused not on simply adjusting the university-based programme to accommodate new additions to the curriculum or to 'fill the gaps' following policy changes, but rather on adopting a research-informed partnership perspective and working collaboratively with school colleagues to decide how and where new aspects of the programme would be delivered and, if appropriate, assessed.

The secondary programme at Oxford

As explained above, the OIS is underpinned by a set of specific principles (McIntyre, 1990), which form the basis of the 'Partnership Agreement' between the university and local schools and shape the structure of the course. The first term commencing in October, comprises a series of 'Joint Weeks', in which time is shared between the university and the school. From January onwards, the interns are in the same school on a full-time basis until the end of the second term (usually around late March), with the exception of a week spent back at the university in mid-February. The final term begins with a further week in the university, followed by approximately 8 weeks of a second school placement. At the end of the course, in late June, the interns return to the university for 2 final days.

The academic programme

The University of Oxford selects around 180 highly qualified graduates for its initial teacher education programme each year. The programme is designed not only to enable interns to gain the knowledge, skills and understanding required to teach their specific subject but also to provide a broader understanding of issues related to schools and schooling. This broader strand is addressed primarily (but not exclusively) in the Professional Development Programme, which complements the strong, central, subject-specific curriculum strand. The underlying rationale for this integrated range of learning experiences is that no single one of them in itself would be sufficient to provide interns with both a contextualised understanding and a wider conceptual awareness of the range of issues involved. The programme thus, capitalises fully on the opportunities offered by a university-school partnership; opportunities that are severely restricted for trainees on employment-based routes that provide little insight into practice beyond one specific school context.

Integration within the teacher education course

The *integration* of the various elements of the programme is most strongly reflected in the pattern of 'Joint Weeks' outlined above. This enables university-based subject tutors (or tutors) and school-based subject mentors (or mentors) to develop a detailed weekly programme that allows the interns to focus on specific issues in the teaching of their particular subject: examining them in depth at the university at the beginning of the week; exploring them individually in their school settings; and reflecting collectively on the implications of their analysis of these different learning experiences back at the university, within their subject group. This structure allows for an appropriate pace of development, sensitive both to the demands of the course and to the individual intern's progression within it.

During the following term, the interns are based in school full-time, allowing them to plan, teach and evaluate longer-term sequences of lessons that focus on effective progression and to build productive learning and teaching relationships that depend on more extensive knowledge of individual learners and routine school procedures. Formal assignments require them to integrate theoretical understandings (including those drawn from relevant reading) with their own exploration of pupils' perspectives and with the views and observed classroom practices of the experienced teachers with whom they are working, and to adopt an inquiry-focused approach to their own teaching in order to make sense of – and draw conclusions from – the diverse sources from which they are learning.

Preparation in the subject areas

As indicated above, a strong feature of the OIS is its emphasis on individual subject teaching, focusing on the development both of subject knowledge (where appropriate) and of subject-specific pedagogy. Following Shulman's (1986, 1987) acknowledgement of the importance of 'pedagogical content knowledge', and his elaboration of its key components, the curriculum strands in each subject include exploration of: the underpinning concepts of the subject; the different ways of introducing them to young learners; and ways of sequencing them to support effective progression. This is accompanied by detailed consideration of pupils' existing 'everyday' concepts and of the ways in which these might be built upon, as well as the likely misconceptions to which they may give rise. The relative autonomy of the different curriculum teams within the programme has meant that the OIS firmly resisted the shift towards a more generic approach – variously promoted by the cross-curricular emphases within the 2008 National Curriculum (later reversed in 2014) and by the shift to 'school-led' forms of training, involving many smaller programmes within which subject-specific groups were simply not viable and/or experienced subject mentors might not be available.

Given the importance of the subject dimension within Oxford interns' experience of learning to teach, we have outlined below the specific ways in which the curriculum programme in five main subjects (those relevant to the case studies in Part II) has responded to national debates and policy requirements.

English

The English curriculum strand is designed to reflect the core OIS values of: critical exploration of the relationship between theory and practice through the principle of practical theorising (McIntyre, 1993); issues of social justice relating to the teaching of English; and learning to teach in a culturally diverse society. In common with all OIS subjects, strenuous efforts are made to ensure that English mentors are actively engaged with university tutors in the design, delivery and assessment of the programme.

The English curriculum has been subjected to almost continual change since the introduction of the National Curriculum. It is also one of the subjects that generate the most controversy and argument in relation to both curriculum design and delivery. This tension can be reflected in school departments' often very different responses to successive curriculum changes, particularly in the lower secondary years where interns in different schools have to negotiate different interpretations and understandings of what has been prescribed. The structure of the OIS English programme in fact reflects the multi-layered nature of the subject as it is experienced within the school departments that host the interns.

English teaching at secondary school level involves pedagogical understanding of: a variety of literary forms and narrative structures; linguistics and the history of the English language in use; grammar and spelling conventions; as well as media, film and cultural studies. The range of subject knowledge thus, required of English teachers represents a challenge for the majority of interns who are literature graduates and often feel uncomfortable, especially at first, teaching linguistics and grammar. The fact that this is also true of the majority of qualified English teachers can be an additional complication for interns in their placements.

English has traditionally been both a high-status and a high-stakes subject. Results in public examinations at 16+ (the General Certificate in Secondary Education, or GCSE) in English and Maths have been used as key indicators of school success in national league tables and English has also been at the forefront of examination changes at both GCSE and Advanced level (18+). The pressures on English teachers of this high-stakes testing alongside constant curriculum change can lead to tensions and contradictions within the OIS English programme. When English departments feel under pressure themselves, there is a tendency for some mentors and other teachers working with interns to adopt an apprenticeship approach to their learning that contrasts with the OIS philosophy.

In addition, the programme also has to address both the contested and politicised nature of English as a subject. Issues such as standards of grammar usage, spelling accuracy, the ability to write an 'extended text' or the acquisition of reading skills are all highly politicised, with debates polarised around views of literacy as a skills-based activity and literacy as a tool for making meaning of the world. The OIS programme puts forward the view that literacy is best viewed as social and cultural practices rather than an exercise in technical skills or competencies. At the same time, English as a subject is also about the creation and understanding of language and literary processes and products such as written texts. English pedagogy is concerned with pupils' meaning making within social and cultural environments and with pupils' ways of knowing and acting on the world around them, although these conceptions can run counter to government edicts on aspects of literacy. The OIS English programme therefore, encourages interns to examine research claims and evidence critically.

History

History teaching in England has tended to provoke considerable political debate, crudely characterised in the media either as a conflict between visions of learning history as mastery of a body of knowledge and the development of critical thinking skills (particularly associated with the critical evaluation of sources) or as a struggle between different bodies of historical knowledge – the kind of 'canon' that should be taught. Views of 'our island story' compete with a much more diverse range of topics and more inclusive notions of who might be encompassed within the history of these islands. Although the OIS history programme is deliberately constructed around a model of learning history that embraces the essential need for substantive knowledge *and* understanding of the second-order concepts that shape the discipline – concepts such as 'continuity and change, cause and consequence, similarity, difference and significance' (DfE, 2013) – echoes of the tensions between them can, nonetheless, be seen in the different emphases given to particular approaches by the university-based tutors and school-based mentors.

Precisely because school history departments continue to enjoy considerable freedom to make their own choices about the substantive content that they teach, the taught curriculum of the programme is most obviously built around the second-order concepts of the discipline, which can be guaranteed to feature (albeit in more or less explicit ways) within any topic. Subject knowledge development sessions and individual developmental priorities vary depending on the needs of individual interns in particular school contexts. As a result, there can be tensions between the apparent emphasis of the university programme on interns' learning about potential misconceptions and patterns of development in pupils' thinking in relation to disciplinary concepts and each school's concern with their interns' familiarity with highly specific topics. The university tutors have sought to redress this balance by establishing opportunities for interns to learn from subject specialists within the university, from mentors and from each other's expertise.

There is one element of the history programme that the university tutors promote very deliberately, although they acknowledge that it is not universally employed in schools. This is the use of enquiry-based planning (Riley, 2000): sequences of lessons structured around a single overarching historical question. Whilst this approach has deep roots in the history education community and has been widely popularised in various series of textbooks, many history departments regard it as impractical, especially when pupils have only one history lesson a week or where their teachers feel obliged to cover a wide range of content at high speed. Nevertheless, enquiry-based teaching forms the basis of one of the interns' assignments and schools are therefore, obliged to accommodate interns' planning in this way for at least one short sequence of lessons, even if this approach does not reflect their normal practice.

A third source of potential tension relates to the university's concern to equip interns to think critically about different kinds of curriculum structure and approaches to assessment whilst mentors' priorities tend to be driven by the need to familiarise interns with particular exam specifications and mark-schemes. The university programme introduces interns to research-based models of progression in historical thinking and encourages them to consider using examples of historians' work to frame their thinking about what getting better at the subject involves. In contrast, the formulaic nature of many high-stakes exam questions may mean that interns are encouraged in school to teach particular response structures that turn historical method into a prescribed series of steps that can be systematically reproduced, sometimes with limited understanding of the process or its purpose.

Mathematics

Whilst mathematics undoubtedly involves learning and using definitions, properties and procedures, it also encompasses much more than this. It is a way of thinking about and viewing the world that involves reasoning, communicating and problem-solving. It can also be creative and enjoyable. No mathematics teacher would disagree with this dynamic conception of the subject, but how it is interpreted and treated within schools and classrooms varies enormously. For some, 'problem-solving' is a specific lesson that they teach at the end of the week; for others it is embedded within the majority of tasks and activities. For some, teaching involves offering definitions, giving examples, allowing pupils to practise and then applying what they have learned to more challenging problems. Others begin by working on problems that they know will lead to pupils recognising their need to learn new definitions or procedures, which are then introduced as part of the problem-solving process. The mathematics programme uses the overall principles of the OIS to deal with this diversity by expecting interns to draw on and synthesise evidence from a wide range of different sources including mathematics education research, observations of experienced teachers and discussions with others.

The mathematics programme emphasises pupils constructing their own understanding of mathematics and making sense of key ideas within mathematics. The tutors seek to bring together research on the difficulties and different conceptions pupils may have when working on particular topics, with examples of how teachers may approach these topics. The programme devotes considerable time to working with the mathematics itself, using a variety of representations, perspectives and tasks, and tutors expect the interns to synthesise the similarities and differences in what they have experienced to inform their own decisions when teaching. This can lead to tensions with some teachers or schools where there are particular methods or approaches that are endorsed as the 'best' way to teach a topic. Unlike subjects such as history or science, where interns may find themselves teaching particular topics that they have not studied in any depth, interns are usually very familiar with the mathematical content of the curriculum. The emphasis for subject knowledge development is therefore, on developing awareness of what could be considered when planning and teaching this mathematics.

Science

Although less well-publicised and fiercely debated in the media than controversies within English or history education, the science curriculum in England has also been characterised by tensions between views of subject learning as mastery as a body of knowledge and those that focus on the development of young people's understanding of the processes of enquiry that are recognised and validated by the discipline. These contrasting views are encapsulated in the argument advanced by Millar and Osborne (1998) in their report *Beyond 2000: Science Education for the Future* which calls for the teaching of 'scientific literacy', an approach that was influential in the 2008 revision of the National Curriculum. Unsurprisingly, these ideas were challenged in 2013 by the curriculum reforms of the incoming coalition government, which reiterated the importance of pupils acquiring a secure grasp of a defined body of substantive knowledge.

The OIS science programme has consistently encouraged interns to adopt a critical approach, examining and evaluating the objectives of different curricular models and thinking equally critically about the specific purposes that they are seeking to achieve within any given lesson. Whilst the science tutors endorse an essentially constructivist model of learning and teaching, they do not similarly ratify or promote any particular teaching strategies but rather invite interns to evaluate the different strategies suggested to them.

The tutors are well aware that the departments with which they work in partnership schools have adopted a range of different approaches to the teaching of 'scientific literacy', reflected in the particular GCSE specifications that they choose to follow. Whilst some made as few changes as possible, others worked in experimental ways to develop, trial and critique methods and resources focused on the teaching of scientific literacy. Others who sought to embrace it found that a lack of professional training left them highly dependent on pre-packaged purchased materials.

With the emphasis on 'core knowledge' reflected in the introduction of a new National Curriculum in 2013 and changes planned for GCSE and

Advanced level, the extent of variability between schools began to decline. Whilst the position of science as a compulsory core subject has tended to encourage approaches to teaching that reflect the nature of the assessment tasks used in public examinations, the science tutors are able to identify important differences between departments in terms of the freedoms that they perceive to adopt different strategies, particularly with younger pupils.

In explaining the nature of the joint curriculum programme the tutors emphasise that one of the most important influences on beginning teachers' practice and professional learning is the fact that science teachers are regularly required to teach subjects in which they have not specialised. This is a product both of the way in which science teaching tends to be organised up to the age of 16, and of the particular shortage of physics graduates within the profession. One of the strategies that schools use to try to ensure that non-specialist teaching is as effective as possible is the creation of shared schemes of work, in which detailed lesson plans and resources are designed and selected by specialists for others to use. Tutors are aware that whilst these schemes are an invaluable source of support and guidance for interns, the ways in which they are perceived and employed in schools also vary significantly. Departmental cultures thus, interact in important ways both with the explicit commitment of the OIS science team to encouraging interns to determine, in each context, the most appropriate route to their particular objective and with the interns' own reactions to different degrees of choice and prescription.

Modern Foreign Languages

The Modern Foreign Languages (MFL) programme reflects the overall principles of the OIS and expects interns to draw on and synthesise evidence from a wide range of different sources (e.g. observations of experienced teachers, research in Second Language Acquisition, discussions with teachers and young learners and reflections on their own practice). In preparing interns to teach within the requirements of the National Curriculum the emphasis of the programme is on the development of pupils' communicative competence, with a particular focus on approaches to teaching in each of the four language learning skills. This does, however, lead to some tensions where the realities of day-to-day schooling often lead to a focus on coverage of a scheme of work which does not always allow for the mastery of each of these skills.

The way in which pupils' competence in the foreign language is assessed also gives rise to certain tensions. The GCSE examination (and in particular its 'speaking' component) has, in many ways, militated against spontaneous use of the language, and encouraged instead the memorisation of pre-prepared blocks of text to be produced during an assessment carried out by the teacher, rather than equipping pupils with the linguistic capacity to be able to use the language effectively in an unplanned context. Many MFL teachers rely heavily on published course books, which tend to be heavily 'topic'-oriented and which invariably include end of unit assessment materials, resulting in a tendency to 'teach to the test' in order for pupils to be able to perform adequately in these assessments. Topic language and relevant grammatical structures are developed within each topic area, but once pupils move to a subsequent topic there is often little 'recycling' of previously learned language. This creates tensions for the interns who often find that they are expected to plan for the delivery of prescribed content without a clear sense of the pupils' overall linguistic progression. Whilst the programme encourages them to develop coherent planning over a series of lessons, the content of these lessons is often determined by the relatively prescribed focus of the departmental scheme of work, which is in itself usually based on the structure and content of the textbook. The National Curriculum for languages is promoted within the university taught sessions as a potentially valuable tool to inform lesson planning, but many interns find that it is rarely referred to in school-based discussions around planning because it is assumed that the requirements are adequately covered by the course book and overall scheme of work.

Finally, many interns express the desire when applying to the programme to be able to develop in their pupils a strong sense of the culture of the countries in which the language is spoken; many have studied and/or worked in these countries themselves and are able to draw on personal experience as well as wider cultural knowledge and understanding. They also recognise that this can be motivating for pupils (Williams, Burden & Lanvers, 2002; Dörnyei, 2003), who otherwise express the view that learning a foreign language is difficult and more challenging than many other school subjects. The interns find, however, that the curriculum allows for little other than cursory coverage of cultural aspects of learning a foreign language and that attempts to integrate such aspects into their planning are not fully realised because of the pressures to cover other aspects of the curriculum in the limited amount of time available.

The internship

The 'Joint Week's' structure of the first term, followed by a second term within the same school is intended not only to support the integration of different sources of knowledge but also to enable interns to acquire sufficient necessary knowledge of a specific school context, of its policies and practices, of its pupils and their individual needs. It thus, affords them the opportunity to plan for pupil progression over a significant period of time and to measure the effects of this more sustained teaching on pupil learning outcomes. Working within a context with which they have become familiar also puts the interns in a stronger position to be able to try out new ideas in their teaching and to evaluate the outcomes effectively since they have a detailed knowledge of the learners and of their prior achievements. The second school placement provides them with a context in which they can start to take greater responsibility for their own professional learning, identifying for themselves those aspects of planning, teaching and evaluation on which they particularly wish to focus, through the further elaboration, exploration and testing of new ideas. They are thus, initiated into the processes of ongoing professional learning, which is intended to establish a firm foundation for future learning.

The role of research

Research is central to the OIS. Engagement in research, both into the nature of effective subject pedagogy and also into teacher learning and development has always featured strongly in the academic work of faculty staff at the Department of Education. This, and other research, informs the teacher education programme in a number of different ways. First, interns are introduced to a broad field of educational research (both general and in relation to the teaching of their particular subject) and are asked to draw on this appropriately when making decisions related to their own practice. Second, research into the nature of experienced teachers' knowledge is used to consider how such knowledge may be made more explicit to student teachers. Third, research into student teachers' learning (see for example, Burn, Hagger & Mutton, 2015) has been used to inform the structure and approaches within the teacher education programme. Finally, interns are required, through their assignments, to adopt a research approach to specific issues in their teaching, which necessitates both drawing on existing research and adopting a practitioner enquiry approach, involving the collection and analysis of relevant data leading to explicit conclusions and clear implications for their own developing practice.

Summary

The OIS, as one of the first programmes to offer a radically different approach to teacher education in England has, since its inception, been required to operate within the substantial policy changes that have taken place at the national level in England. Broadly speaking, policy direction in the latter years of the 20th century could be seen as compatible with the underlying philosophy of the programme (for example, recognition of the value of learning that takes place in school settings and of the value of collaborative partnership working), although the 'market-driven' approach inherent in more recent teacher education policy has led to particular challenges for established teacher education providers, including the University of Oxford.

Whilst the most recent government allocation of training places has offered longer-term guarantees to some providers, making it possible for programmes such as the OIS to envisage a degree of stability in the immediate future, there is no evidence, as yet that the recent period of extensive policy turbulence in England has ended. Our expectation is that the programme will be required to respond to further challenges, seeking new ways to accommodate fresh imperatives, insofar as it can without compromising its core principles.

The United States and teacher education at Michigan State University

Michigan State University (MSU) has distinctive teacher education programmes located in a distinctive university context. MSU is a large land-grant research university with large teacher education programmes. The elementary and secondary programmes each usually prepare from 150 to 200 candidates yearly. This is atypical in the United States, where it tends to be the large public teaching universities that have large teacher education programmes, whilst those of research universities are usually much smaller. This unique combination of a large programme within a large research university has allowed the programme to flourish and maintain its reputation as the number one in the nation (recognised as such for the past 22 consecutive years by the U.S. News & World Report[1]). The research approach followed by the programme has supported continuous improvement and diffusion.

Over the last 10 years educational policy in the United States has shifted to follow a market-driven system with increased demands for accountability and regulation, and a 'technical rationalist vision of schooling and of teacher professionalism' tends to dominate (Schön, 1990). Within this context, helping teachers learn to teach represents a careful balance between larger accountability demands, the programme's vision and what future teachers need to be successful.

The technical rationalist notion of the knowledge needed for teaching is at odds with the model that MSU has followed to prepare teachers for many years, which emphasises the central role both of content knowledge and of pedagogical content knowledge and reflection on one's own practice. The teacher education programme at MSU was reformed along those lines in the mid-1990s to offer a teacher education 'model for the 21st century' (Stuart & Tatto, 2000), and to transform the role of the teacher educators within universities through their engagement in research that could be used to inform the programme's curriculum and practices, as well as those of the schools within a partnership model.

The re-definition of Qualified Teacher Status (QTS) as a result of the No Child Left Behind (NCLB) legislation, described in Chapter 3, whilst resisted by many in the educational area, served if anything, to support the approach of the teacher education programme at MSU, which had long focused on the importance of content knowledge on teaching. Because of the United States' decentralised system of governance and the state's role in controlling education, the programme has been relatively immune to the value-added accountability demands that have affected their counterparts in other states. Thus, the NCLB legislation whilst impacting schools all over the country, and encouraging the creation of alternative routes into teaching[2] did not necessarily have a direct negative effect on MSU's teacher education programme.

In contrast with other teacher education programmes in the United States that require only 15 weeks of student teaching or less, the MSU programme is highly unusual in that it requires a lengthy mentored student teaching lasting 30 weeks; an experience which has prompted some school principals to remark that graduates during their first year in post are equivalent to second-year teachers.

Gradual changes and enduring tensions

The programme at one point represented a partnership between the state, the private sector, schools and teacher educators all supporting its transformation from a 4-year to a 5-year route, conceived of in a consecutive configuration to include a 1-year internship in the partner schools (Holmes Group, 1995).

Entry into the newly reformed programme became more rigorous than previously, with prospective student teachers evaluated on academic and personal criteria. Since then a grade point average (GPA) of 2.5 (on a scale that ranges from 0 to 4) has been a requirement to enter the programme. Yet a 2.5 GPA is already comparatively low within the university, where the average high school GPA of the admitted freshmen (first years) is 3.62. The relatively low GPA requirement for entry into MSU's teacher education programme is balanced by the strong focus on content and methods courses. Most students that enter the teacher education programme enrol as undergraduates at MSU and take academic courses similar to those of students who will go on to a variety of career paths or in the recently created option of alternative 'integrated' or 'interdisciplinary' programmes designed for individuals intending to teach particular school subjects.

Unlike tutors within the OIS in England, MSU's programme faculty (also referred to as teacher educators) visit interns in schools for supervision purposes with less frequency than when the programme was reformed and was linked to Professional Development Schools (PDSs). Currently, the role of faculty is clearly distinct from those both of the university supervisors (field instructors) and of the school-based mentor teachers (or mentors). Both of the latter, however, interact frequently around school practice concerns. Yet recently, the role of the field instructor has begun to change. Previously field instructors spent considerable time in the schools in dialogue with intern and mentor, facilitating a more coherent experience for the intern. Now field instructors spend a significant amount of time collecting data (for example, through periodic observation of the intern) needed by the programme to document effectiveness in preparation for accreditation reviews. These important changes in roles meant breaking a key link with the original MSU model, which sought to maintain a high level of coherence between university and school practices.

More significant, however, has been the transformation of the reformed programme's original transversal organisation – designed to cut across subjects and contexts – to a more disciplinary one, and reflecting the organisation of schools in which programmes for pupils of different ages and in different subject areas tend to operate in isolation from each other. Faculty attempts at maintaining coherence at the time of the study included bi-weekly meetings across the subject departments, and a meeting with the field instructors each semester. Programme coordinators meet frequently with school personnel.

The vision of the programme is consistent with a constructivist approach to teaching and learning and provides a coherent view about the goals and purposes of learning to teach across the entire programme. The programme emphasis is on ensuring that trainees have a deep understanding of both subject matter and pedagogical knowledge, and can use their own experiences to inform their practice. The programme envisages a teacher who is prepared to challenge the status quo in schools and to work proactively towards stated societal as well as instructional goals. Terms such as reflection on learning, teaching subject-specific strategies to promote understanding in diverse learners, democracy, community, social justice, equity and inclusion of minorities, has characterised the aims of both the primary and the secondary programmes since it was reformed (Stuart & Tatto, 2000, p. 500).

Maintaining and enacting this vision, however, represents a continuous challenge. Scholars have explained the tension around teacher education in the United States as a struggle between progressive ideas, which have tended to dominate the teacher education curriculum and general ethos, and efficiency concerns, which have tended to dominate school governance including the school curriculum, and the lives of teachers and pupils (Labaree, 2008). Such a situation has created a long-term mismatch between what teachers are expected to do in schools (summarised perhaps in terms of teaching academic subjects according to standards and as preparation for the world of work), and what schools of education are preparing them to do (make use of child-centred pedagogies, intended to teach children how to learn within an inquiry-based approach).

The secondary programme at Michigan State University

The secondary teacher education programme works in partnership primarily with school districts across Michigan and comprises academic and professional programmes and a mentored internship.

The academic programme

Candidates to the secondary programme have to fulfil course requirements as stipulated by the university to be eligible for secondary certification to teach grades 6–12. These include completing a bachelor's degree in integrative or interdepartmental studies in their disciplinary area (arts and humanities, biological and physical sciences or social sciences). For mathematics, whilst the university requires all student teachers to demonstrate proficiency beyond the level of college algebra, there are additional requirements mandated by the college and degree major. In addition, they must demonstrate first-year competency in a foreign language and in the use of educational technology.

Professional education courses

Students take two common foundational courses during their first and second years in university, prior to admission to the teacher preparation programme. After admission, during their third and fourth years they take three courses that introduce candidates to the notion of reflection on practice, issues that are foundational to the teaching of subjects to diverse learners, and the craft of teaching at secondary level.

Preparation in the subject areas[3]

In addition to obtaining a major in their subject area as part of their bachelors' degree, the programme offers four methods courses in the subject areas over 2 years, two in the fourth year, and one in each semester during the internship. These courses help student teachers re-contextualise subject matter knowledge for diverse learners.

Literacy

English, literacy and language arts as a school subject occupies a central place amongst the subjects given emphasis in the United States. As such, the curriculum is constantly under scrutiny and discussion concerning content, design, delivery and assessment. This state of affairs is reflected in the MSU secondary teacher education literacy programme curriculum. The syllabus states that the programme is designed to prepare student teachers to teach 'literacy' rather than 'English', as the faculty sees literacy not as a 'school subject' but rather as foundational to all other school learning. Consequently, in the programme, literacy is conceived as broader than English as a subject, a notion that aligns with the position of the National Council of Teachers of English:

> Literacy has always been a collection of cultural and communicative practices shared among members of particular groups. As society and technology change, so does literacy [...] the 21st century demands that a literate person possess a wide range of abilities and competencies, many literacies. These literacies are multiple, dynamic, and malleable. As in the past, they are inextricably linked with particular histories, life possibilities, and social trajectories of individuals and groups.
>
> (NCTE, 2008/2013)

The literacy programme is based on Schwab's (1976–1977, 1983) and Schwab and Thomas (1986) and engages student teachers in investigations about how pupils: *learn* language, *learn about* language and *learn through* language. These three language components are present in the curriculum, instruction, assessment, within the school and classroom contexts. The literacy programme engages student teachers in reflection and inquiry and encourages them 'to become activists in addressing the needs of marginalised populations, and in the analysis of political oppression'.

The programme vision of English and literacy teaching can be at odds with the schools' visions where the climate of accountability has created tensions for teachers as they attempt to align the standards with the needs of their students, schools and communities. This tension is also reflected in the work with the teacher education programme as teachers, already walking a delicate balance between standards and their pupils' needs have to negotiate the induction of idealist interns in their classroom. These tensions affect student teachers who are already struggling with notions of agency and identity as they take on the role of a teacher and engage in the multiple demands of teaching the school curriculum (writing, reading, comprehension and appreciation of the literature), plus learning to plan instruction, conduct classroom discussions, assess pupils' learning, collect data on their practice and their pupils' learning, and use the analysis of that data to reflect and support their own learning. Thus, whilst the programme urges interns to engage in activism, reflection and inquiry, the school internship requires readiness and action in a fast-paced environment.

Mathematics

Mathematics is one of the subjects that has a privileged place in the school curriculum at the national and local levels, and it is seen along with literacy as key to school success. The teaching and learning of mathematics has focused on critical thinking and reasoning since 1989 when the National Council of Teacher of Mathematics (NCTM) standards were released. These standards were important since they were designed to replace the previous curriculum, which emphasised mathematics as the learning of rules and procedures. The 2009 Common Core Curriculum Standards for mathematics complement the NCTM standards and contain 'content' standards for grades 6–8, and 9–12 for each of the five content strands: Number and Operations; Algebra; Geometry; Measurement; Data Analysis; and Probability. There are also process standards, which regulate the methods by which mathematics knowledge can be acquired and includes problem-solving, reasoning and proof, communication, connections and representation. The new standards occasionally represent a challenge for middle school teachers who unlike high school teachers may have not been prepared as specialists.

The teaching of mathematics has become increasingly regulated by the curriculum standards, by student testing and by school ranking according to student achievement targets, and represents a significant challenge for student teachers who are urged by the programme to use inquiry-based methods, which often conflict with the strategies used by schools and their mentors to help pupils do well in tests.

Student teachers find themselves negotiating the programme message and the school message, and whilst knowledgeable in the subject, find it difficult to shape instruction in ways that balance their own sense of how one learns mathematics, and how mathematics should be taught to comply with programme and school demands and with curriculum mandates. Thus, after years of emphasising constructivism in mathematics teaching and learning, now teachers are given what to them seems a mixed message: 'mathematical understanding and procedural skills are equally important, and both are assessable using mathematical tasks of sufficient richness' (NCTM, 2014).

Science

Science in the United States has been seen, along with mathematics, as essential for creating and sustaining a strong economy. Yet for more than 50 years there have been concerns with the degree to which United States schools can prepare a science competent society (NAEP, 2016). This situation has led to the development of the Next Generation Science Standards (NGSS), which have stated as an explicit goal the creation of curriculum and classroom conditions to enable teachers to help students develop a deeper understanding of science beyond memorising facts, and to experience similar scientific and engineering practices as those used by professionals in the field (NGSS Lead States, 2013). Whilst the development and adoption of these standards received general support, not all states engaged in this reform of the science curriculum. Important challenges have been the development of assessments to measure learning and the preparation of teachers to engage with these standards, which depart in important ways from the way they themselves learned science, as they embody a high level of complexity.

Science represents a complex challenge for teachers and teacher education, especially for middle school teachers, because it requires comprehensive knowledge of science to teach the integrated curriculum. In contrast, in high school, teachers are required to teach in their area of specialisation.

The Secondary Science Teacher Preparation Programme at MSU is distinctive in its curriculum, which has been designed to prepare teacher candidates to teach science using an inquiry approach within a social justice mandate. Thus, the new orientation of the science curriculum as expressed by the NGSS found a welcoming reception amongst science teacher educators in the Secondary Science Teacher Preparation Programme.

Course instructors support student teachers to learn to 'work within a teaching cycle: planning based on standards, learning theories and research on students' ideas; teaching and assessing based on plans and students' interactions with the activities; and reflection on/revision of teaching in which enactment of teaching is analysed and ideas for improvement are considered (Gotwals & Birmingham, 2015). Courses are designed to produce an interactive dynamic between the university classes and classroom practice as many of the assignments are centred in student teachers' classroom placements. In middle schools, science departments have typically developed lesson plans and other resources to help teachers effectively teach the integrated curriculum.

Science educators have identified important tensions between what the programme expects of their student teachers and what the school context requires of them especially as concerns pupil learning. The complex demands of what is considered a high-stakes subject are compounded by student teachers' own ideas as to what counts as knowing and learning science, given emerging standards and how they themselves learned science in school.

Social studies

In the United States, and in contrast with England, history and other such disciplines, are embedded in the 'social studies' curriculum. The National Council for Social Studies (NCSS) issued its first standards in 1994, yet the content of the social studies curriculum is decentralised and highly variable across the different states. The revised standards provide a framework for teaching, learning and assessment in social studies and are wide-ranging, including 10 themes encompassing global, national, institutional and individual dynamics. According to the framework, the aim of social studies is 'the promotion of civic competence – the knowledge, intellectual processes, and democratic dispositions required of students to be active and engaged participants in public life' (NCSS, 2010). Thus, teaching social studies in schools is a complex undertaking. In teaching history, for instance, the framework expects that pupils' understanding of the theme of culture would also require an understanding of aspects of time, continuity and change and of power, authority and governance.

The NCSS standards also make clear that they should not be seen as substitute for the content standards (civics, history, economics, geography and psychology), which 'provide a detailed description of content and methodology considered central to a specific discipline' (NCSS, 2010). Yet the grouping of the disciplines into the 'social studies' umbrella has served to dilute a more discipline-based curriculum and has created a 'generalist' rather than a more specialist approach to preparing future social studies teachers. Whilst student teachers may understand the rationale for this kind of approach, it creates tensions for those from a specific disciplinary background (history, geography, etc.) who find themselves having to teach a broad ranging curriculum. The programme prepares student teachers to deal with this by promoting the interdisciplinary character of 'social studies'. It is guided by five core precepts:

> *One,* the notion that teachers and students co-create the curriculum.
> *Two,* the principle that teachers are expected to value the cultural, social and intellectual funds of knowledge that pupils bring with them to school and the classroom.
> *Three,* that teaching is a learning profession.
> *Four,* that teachers and students are citizens.
> *Five,* that teaching social studies is an interdisciplinary endeavour that connects pupils to the world around them.
>
> (NCSS, 2010)

The social studies university courses and school experiences thus, bring together standards in social studies, language arts, inquiry and health.

For unit planning the social studies secondary programme uses the Understanding By Design format (see Wiggins & McTighe, 2005), regardless of the approach that particular districts and schools may be using, on the assumption that this format will help guide future teachers in their curricular thinking by placing the emphasis on the outcomes they want their pupils to achieve as a result of implementing the unit.

It is difficult to understand how student teachers make sense of all these demands relating to what they are expected to know and do as they enter the school environment. It is possible that the very wide scope of knowledge and functions that are assumed for social studies teachers, whilst providing freedom and flexibility, also allows schools to create different roles for student teachers according to ever-changing day-to-day needs. Whilst in high school, there is a disciplinary focus, in middle school the all-encompassing school curriculum may make it possible for student teachers to spend little time teaching the disciplines, and more time teaching other aspects of the curriculum.

The internship

The internship programme enrols applicants who come from within the university. To be placed in secondary schools, interns must pass the subject tests within the Michigan Test for Teacher Certification[4] in relation to their teaching majors.

The MSU teacher education guide describes the goals of the secondary internship as one of 'collaborative learning among interns, faculty and teachers in schools combining theory and practice, university courses and classroom experience, where content knowledge is re-contextualized to ensure that it fits the notion of inquiry-oriented teaching' (MSU, 2017a).

The 1-year internship includes six professional education courses half of which can be used towards a master's degree. These courses and experiences are designed to help prepare students to be engaged in the work of practising 'like a teacher, putting it all together in actual supervised and mentored practice'. One set of two courses constitutes the practicum and it is implemented in the school, whilst the other two sets of two courses are delivered at the university.

The first course set provides a guided progression towards independent teaching. Its objective is to 'allow students to utilise the tools that they have developed over the course of the teacher education programme and put those educational experiences to work within a classroom setting'.

The second course set is based on educational foundations and guides interns as they examine teachers' professional and ethical responsibilities including classroom management, the development of lesson plans and the use of assessments and other resources to improve practice and support student learning.

The third course set is subject pedagogy-based and immerses interns in the use of qualitative and quantitative research methods on teaching and learning. It helps interns to think about and understand criteria for judging the validity and applicability of research-based knowledge, and to frame educational problems worthy of inquiry. As part of this experience, interns design and assess studies of their own teaching practice.

The internship for secondary teachers includes a period of 'guided practice' during the fall semester, and a period of 'lead teaching' during the spring semester.

The interns' designated mentor is expected to introduce them to the school and the subject department norms and to meet frequently with them, as they get more familiar with the school, the classroom and the work of teaching. Interns have a *focal* class in which they begin to teach as soon as they feel ready. Interns receive monthly visits from the field instructors who typically observe them teach and provide feedback on their teaching. The university faculty teaching the academic or professional courses typically do not go to the schools to work with interns, but the interns attend the university 1-day per week for 7 weeks of each 14-week semester to take courses on educational foundations and subject pedagogy.

With some exceptions, the sporadic involvement of programme faculty with the interns at schools, and with the mentor teachers and field instructors some-times results in lack of coherence (or alignment) of what interns are expected to do in the school and what the university courses intend them to do. Higher levels of alignment come about when programme faculty and field instructors visit schools frequently, and particularly when the mentors are former MSU graduates, or when they have deliberately sought to engage with the pro-gramme's philosophy. Successful mentors seem to be able to provide interns with a framework to think about accountability demands whilst attending to pupil learning, and to help them create a bridge between programme vision/requirements and school demands.

The role of research

As the MSU programme website makes clear, research-based evidence has been fundamental to its design:

> We are guided by research about the critical role of expert subject matter knowledge in quality teaching. The research suggests that possessing general pedagogical skills is not enough. Teachers who know the content well have pupils who learn more. The knowledge such teachers possess, however, is not simply knowledge of the content. It is knowledge of how learners learn the content – what they struggle with, what they are likely to misunderstand, what questions they are likely to have – and knowledge and skills for designing instruction to capitalize on the way learners learn par-ticular content.
>
> (MSU, 2017b)

MSU has long been associated with pioneering, high-quality research on teacher education, not least through its research centres on teacher learning and learn-ing to teach. The MSU's Institute for Research on Teaching initiated a pro-gramme of pioneering work on teachers and pupils thinking, and on the importance of learning to teach school subjects, which ran from the mid-1970s to the early 1990s.[5] Later, with federal support, the college launched a 10-year research programme on teacher education and teacher learning. In the early

2000s, the Teachers for a New Era project positioned MSU as an exemplar amongst teacher education programmes in the nation.[6] In the mid-2000s, the federally funded cross-national study the Teacher Education and Development Study in Mathematics (TEDS-M)[7] (Tatto et al., 2012) created an innovative programme to engage in teacher education research at a global scale for another 10 years.

Thanks to this research agenda, the MSU teacher education programme, remains in a relatively strong position, allowing it to defend the integrity of its programme and to serve as an important exemplar. External demands for accountability, however, which seem to be shaped more by market-based rationales and political ideology than by evidence, make it increasingly difficult to focus sufficient attention on nurturing and growing healthy school partnerships.

Summary

We used the MSU programme as a lens through which to analyse the changes that have occurred in teacher education in the United States over the last 35 years. These changes can be briefly summarised in the following sequence of events. From a more general programme in the 1980s that enrolled a large number of students, to a smaller programme with a distinctive emphasis on teaching and learning as inquiry, connecting research with teaching and practice across academic subjects; to a selective programme initially working formally in partnership with schools under the PDS model and seeking to maintain those partnerships even when the PDS model was abandoned; to a programme more closely aligned with the university disciplines designing a curriculum that involves the whole university in the responsibility of preparing knowledgeable teachers. Over the years, MSU teacher educators have continuously responded to internal and external demands to create and recreate a programme consistently ranked as the national leader.[8]

MSU teacher educators and education scholars were able to use the criticism that emerged in the early 1980s to energise not only the programme but the profession as a whole. They did so by creating an inquiry-based curriculum and using a well-structured research agenda to support it. They argued that teachers are professionals and as such must have a kind of knowledge beyond that gained simply by attending schools (Lortie, 2002) or applying common sense to the deployment of disciplinary knowledge learned elsewhere. They engaged in their own research on teaching, reaffirming previous findings (Good & Brophy, 1978) and learning more about the complex nature of inquiry-based subject matter teaching, and what it takes to learn to teach it well (Clark & Peterson, 1986). The wave of subject-specific pedagogical research, pioneered by MSU (and taken up elsewhere), challenged previous, generic notions of teaching as the ability to manage classrooms.

The programme however, has not been immune to the waves of market-style reforms affecting teacher education, which have according to a number of scholars, weakened schools and schools of education (Darling-Hammond, 2010; Sleeter, 2008; Zeichner, 2010).

There is evidence to support these scholars' claims. At MSU at least, programme faculty are introducing data collection systems, standards and assessments to evaluate programme outcomes. Whilst acknowledged as important and necessary, compliance with these mandates has intensified work demands and has made it necessary for members of the faculty to cut down in some areas (such as intense involvement in schools) to sustain the scholarship that is not only expected by the university but that forms the basis of the teacher education programme.

Challenges for the field, given the MSU experience and that of other schools of education, are the increased development of disciplinary silos as a response to alignment with content standards and the school curriculum more generally, the bifurcation of staffing structures to create a distinction between 'research faculty' and 'teaching faculty' and, possibly, a turn to more school-based training.

Social enterprises: Teach First as a new kind of partnership in teacher education

Criticism of existing forms of teacher education on the basis of pupil outcomes has also given rise, in both the United States and England, to alternative routes into the profession, led not by government but by charitable organisations or social enterprises, backed by corporate sponsors. Indeed, this is a worldwide phenomenon: with Teach for All now representing some 35 teacher education projects around the world. Although the movement has been described as a 'globalising travelling reform', each national programme operates as a separate entity, 'mediated by and grown within local cultures' (Ellis et al., 2016, p. 62).

As with our study of more traditional routes, in examining these new partnerships we have focused on a single, detailed case, setting institutional decision-making and development in the context of wider societal changes and national policy making. Our particular focus is the Teach First partnership as it operated in London, involving *three* partners: the Teach First organisation; the regional university training providers; and the schools in which the participants were employed, initially as unqualified teachers.

Launched with a first cohort of 186 participants that began teaching in London in 2003, the Teach First programme enjoyed consistent government approval and encouragement to expand, so that by 2013–2014 it included more than 1,200 primary and secondary participants across nine regions. Its stated ambition, conceived during an investigation by management consultants McKinsey and Company into how businesses could help improve outcomes for pupils in London, is that no child's socio-economic background should 'limit the opportunities they have in education and in life'.[9] Working on the premise that pupil outcomes are largely determined by their access to excellent teachers, and informed by the example of Teach for America, the investigative team proposed a new programme, targeted at top graduates to bringing additional excellent teachers into challenging schools for 2 years.

With leadership identified as the attribute lacking in schools judged to be failing their pupils (Wigdortz, 2012), the programme's design and much of its appeal to well-qualified graduates, is rooted in an emphasis on participants' leadership potential and development of their leadership skills. Thus, whilst the programme includes the award both of QTS and of a Postgraduate Certificate in Education (PGCE) at the end of the first year (recently upgraded from a postgraduate *certificate* to a postgraduate *diploma*), it is branded as a 'Leadership Development Programme'. Teaching in disadvantaged schools, is thus, essentially presented as a vehicle through which to gain leadership skills and experiences, also valued by employers in other sectors (Parker & Gale, 2016). Whilst many 'ambassadors' remain in teaching for longer,[10] Teach First emphasises that participants are only expected to commit to teaching for those 2 years.[11]

In addition to considerable support from the business community, establishment of the programme also required official government approval and financial backing. The impetus to involve universities in the provision of training essentially came from the Teacher Training Agency, which agreed to provide similar levels of funding as that allocated to more traditional postgraduate programmes. Whilst Teach First accepted the requirement to involve a university training provider, the organisation's founder originally hoped to choose the university concerned and to remain 'in charge of the messaging, recruitment, training and all elements of the programme' (Wigdortz, 2012, p. 176). The organisation was obliged, however, to put the contract out to tender. The fact that only one university bid was actually received for the contract in December 2000 (and judged to be inadequate) is an indication of HEIs' initial reluctance to engage with this alternative route.

The HEI that eventually won the contract the following year, Canterbury Christ Church University College, had originally been established by the Church of England in 1962 to provide teachers for church schools. It was typical of the many teacher training colleges originally established as religious foundations and brought into established universities or given university status as part of the harmonisation of the higher education sector at the end of the 20th century. It was granted full university status in 2005 – as Canterbury Christ Church University (CCCU) – but its core focus remained the education of those entering public service.

It is perhaps unsurprising that only a relatively new university was willing to accept the kind of partnership that Teach First offered. Wigdortz (2012) described the relationship into which they settled as one of 'deep mutual respect, but also constant bickering'. Vigorous disagreements between Teach First and members of CCCU were 'quickly ratchet[ed] up into huffing and puffing and shouting' (Wigdortz, 2012, p. 185). A key point of contention was the balance of the 6 weeks' intensive training provided before participants started work in school: 'I wanted more broad leadership training at the summer institute, while [Sonia Blandford, the Dean of Education] pointed out that our teachers couldn't gain their qualification if they didn't have enough of a background in teaching pedagogy' (p. 186). The eventual agreements reached will be described below, after a brief explanation of how other universities came to be involved, including the scheme's other London partner, the Institute of Education (IOE), a well-established HEI, with a strong research reputation, that had operated since 1909 as a school of the University of London.

Despite the early tensions, the Leadership Development Programme was judged to be very successful. An evaluation commissioned by the Teaching and Development Agency (successor to the Teacher Training Agency) confirmed that it had successfully targeted elite universities, recruiting those who would not otherwise have considered teaching. The majority of its participants (83 per cent in 2003 and 74 per cent in 2004) came from 'Russell Group' universities, with particularly large groups from Oxford and Cambridge (Hutchings, Maylor, Mendick, Menter & Smart, 2006). Further proof of its impact on perceptions of teaching was its entry at Number 62 in the United Kingdom Times Top 100 Graduate Employers. By 2013, it had reached eleventh position.[12]

Whilst acknowledging early difficulties and tensions between Teach First and CCCU, Hutchings et al. (2006) noted many positive outcomes identified by participating schools, including the high-quality lessons delivered by participants, their contribution to extra-curricular activities and the ways in which their presence sometimes served to reinvigorate established staff members. Although a third of schools did not retain any of the original participants beyond the 2-year requirement, another third retained at least half of them. Whilst the immersion into teaching was undoubtedly 'exceptionally challenging', as Ofsted noted in 2008, very few participants withdrew.

The scheme had by then already expanded to Manchester and the Midlands (with new regional HEI partners). In 2010, the coalition government announced a further doubling of its allocated places and continued expansion beyond the shortage subjects that it had originally prioritised. Faced with the uncertainty created by the introduction of the School Direct route, announced in the same government White Paper (DfE, 2010), the IOE now applied to join the scheme.

Although CCCU also successfully applied to continue as a London region partner, the pattern of allocations to different subjects meant that CCCU not only lost its monopoly as the HEI regional provider, but also suffered an overall reduction in numbers. Several 'university-based professional tutors' originally recruited by CCCU directly from schools to work on the Teach First programme found themselves seeking new posts within the same regional programme as IOE employees. Of the five subjects included within our case study, responsibility for English and science was retained by CCCU, whilst maths, modern languages and history were assigned to the IOE. The relatively limited time devoted to subject-specific input meant, however, that fewer new university-based *subject* tutors were recruited into the HEIs. Subject-specific elements were more likely to be provided by established PGCE tutors, working part-time on the Teach First programme.

The secondary programme

Given the imperative for participants to make a significant impact on pupil outcomes within 2 years and the assumption that high-attaining graduates, recruited for their leadership qualities, will quickly learn to become effective teachers, participants on the secondary programme assume sole responsibility for classes from the beginning of September, teaching up to 80 per cent of a full timetable. This means that all essential training has to be accommodated within the 6-week 'summer institute' undertaken in June and July.

During the year that follows, participants are released for just 6 further subject training days within the HEI. In school, they are supported by a subject mentor required to meet with them weekly and by a professional mentor with oversight of all the participants across the school. They also receive fortnightly visits from a university-based tutor, usually the participant's professional tutor. In the early years of the programme, only three of these visits were made by subject tutors, reflecting the emphasis on broader professional studies that had characterised CCCU's traditional PGCE programmes (in contrast to the stronger subject emphasis within the OIS). This pattern was also more cost-effective for a programme that depended so heavily on tutor visits to schools. It was only after Ofsted recommended that the London region should consider how to 'support the more progressive development of participants' understanding and application of subject pedagogy throughout the course' (Ofsted, 2011), that the number of subject tutor visits was officially increased to six.

Alongside their regular teaching commitments and assessment against the QTS standards, participants are expected to complete several written assignments examined by the university, on which the PGCE award also depends. During the subsequent summer break, participants may choose to participate in a short internship offered by the charity's business sponsors. They are also required to return to summer institute for a week to share their experiences with the new cohort and engage in further leadership development.

During the second year, for which participants are paid as newly qualified teachers and assume a 90 per cent timetable, in-school support or coaching is provided entirely by leadership development officers, directly employed by Teach First. Participants are also encouraged to undertake further modules (building on credits achieved through the PGCE) within the IOE's Masters in Leadership.

The academic programme

The structure and content of the summer institute varied considerably between regions and from one year to the next as the programme expanded. In 2013–2014, London region participants spent 4 weeks in London, including 10 days in the university, split between a leadership component (led by Teach First), professional studies and subject pedagogy. The other 10 days were spent in schools: 4 days in individuals' placement schools and 6 days within subject groups, supported by subject teachers and tutors in planning, teaching and evaluating a short sequence of lessons. A further 2 weeks were spent with the national cohort at the University of Warwick, with time again divided between the Teach First leadership component, professional studies and subject pedagogy.

Whilst a further 6 days during the year were devoted to subject pedagogy within the HEI, professional studies input was thereafter, limited to tutors' advice during their fortnightly visits and the reading suggestions and guidance linked to participants' assignments. The fact that these assignments had to satisfy validation panels in different institutions meant that the criteria tended to be quite generic, making only vague reference to 'learning theories' and 'reflective practice'. Whilst different HEIs and different tutors responsible for subject leadership across all the HEIs might promote particular conceptions of learning or subject pedagogy, these could not be explicitly acknowledged in the shared assessment criteria. Thus, for example, whilst all the participants were obliged to complete a reflective journal, there was little agreement amongst the university-based tutors about the particular model of reflective practice that should underpin this practice.

Integration within the teacher education course

The inclusion of 2 school weeks within the summer institute demonstrates the programme's emphasis on classroom experience. After just 3 days in the university, participants were expected to plan, teach and evaluate a short lesson sequence, with the support of subject teachers, working alongside the university tutors. Joint observation of those experienced teachers by both the participants and their tutors also provided them with practical examples and a shared frame of reference to which they could subsequently refer.

Unfortunately, this kind of close school/university collaboration was difficult to achieve in the rest of the programme. Whilst tutors could plan collaboratively with the school departments that hosted the summer institute subject groups, the process of assigning participants to particular schools and recruiting mentors was conducted entirely by Teach First. Subject mentors were invited to attend just one afternoon of subject-specific training that coincided with the programme's launch. Whilst subject tutors expected to meet mentors during their visits to participants, this was rarely guaranteed and often proved impossible. The fact that smaller departments rarely hosted participants in consecutive years, made the development of shared understandings even more difficult. It is unsurprising that the variable quality of school-based mentoring was identified as a concern in the evaluations conducted by Hutchings et al. (2006) and by Ofsted (2008) or that their subsequent inspection (Ofsted, 2011) called for better development of participants' subject pedagogy.

Integration was perhaps easier in relation to the professional studies strand since professional tutors visited each school on a fortnightly basis. Nevertheless, this did not necessarily mean that participants had access in school to the distinctive expertise and research-based knowledge of academic experts. Many professional tutors had been recruited to the programme directly from schools and were employed on teaching-only contracts, giving them little scope to develop a research perspective.

The issue of integration as it related to the leadership programme and participants' development as classroom practitioners also remained problematic. Schools claimed to find the partnership confusing and reported that 'communication between Teach First, CCCU and themselves was not always working well' (Hutchings et al., 2006, p. 66). Despite a widely acknowledged commitment to constant improvement of participants' experiences, new tensions inevitably arose as the partnership expanded, not only between Teach First and its new partners, but also between different universities required to reconcile different accreditation systems and competing priorities.

Preparation in the subject

In total, the subject-specific component of the Teach First programme amounted to 12 university-based days and 6 school-based days during the summer institute along with a further 6 subject days. Participants were also expected to receive six subject tutor visits. Despite the appointment of national subject leads and the use of standard templates for subject handbooks, the challenge of coordinating subject tutors across nine different regions made it very difficult to ensure coherence for all participants. Subject-specific input had increased considerably in the light of Ofsted's (2011) recommendation, but tutors had relatively little opportunity to discuss priorities with mentors or to plan the university-based programme in collaboration with them.

Summary

Teach First has proved highly successful in relation to many important criteria. It has attracted significant numbers of academically successful graduates into teaching and continued to improve its high rating as a graduate employer as it expanded. It secured outstanding Ofsted ratings and, despite early difficulties in attracting even a single academic partner and in building a productive working relationship with them, the scheme had, within a decade, found several enthusiastic HEI collaborators, including the IOE, a world-renowned research institution. Whilst longer-term retention rates amongst Teach First graduates are well below those of more traditional providers, the organisation has never defined success in these terms. Its Leadership Development Programme is marketed as a 2-year commitment, and thus, the proportion of participants continuing beyond their 'training' year to become newly qualified teachers is much higher than amongst graduates of more conventional PGCE programmes.

The only significant weakness identified by Ofsted in 2011 related to the subject-specific dimension. This strand is much weaker than within either the OIS or the MSU teacher education programmes, both of which have invested heavily in the development of interns' pedagogical content knowledge, supported by deeply-rooted research traditions in subject pedagogy and pupil learning. Despite regular visits from university personnel, the scope for Teach First participants to engage with research remains limited by the fact that their professional tutor (whom they see most often) is rarely a research-active member of the university. The extent of the collaboration that has been achieved, not merely between schools, HEIs and Teach First but also between different HEIs, is very impressive within the constraints of a programme that has expanded annually and adapted the structure of its summer institutes almost as frequently. Nonetheless, this constant change has placed enormous strains on effective communication and programme guidelines have tended to prioritise generic pedagogical approaches and shared course procedures rather than focusing on subject-specific pedagogical research and professional knowledge. Professional tutors generally build supportive relationships with individual participants, but participants' learning about teaching their subject depends profoundly on the quality and nature of their school-based mentoring and the scope for regular interaction between subject tutors and mentors is severely limited.

Conclusion

In this chapter, we have described how HEIs in England and the United States have responded to the shifting policy contexts, which were portrayed in Chapter 3. We have done this through the lenses of two particular universities engaged within long-standing initial teacher education partnerships (the University of Oxford and Michigan State University) and by examining the establishment and operation of a new kind of training provider – the charitable organisation Teach First, operating in the context of London with two further HEIs.

We have seen how increasing external intervention into teacher education in both national contexts has created new pressures and challenges for existing HEIs as well as opportunities for new kinds of private/public social enterprises. Whilst all institutions have had to respond in some way, our argument is that from a sociocultural perspective it is important to be sensitive to the particular forms of response made, as these will shape the distinctive learning experiences of the student teachers in the respective sites.

Both HEIs involved in more traditional forms of teacher education can claim a track record of excellence in provision. Their responses to the external challenges are therefore, made from a position of relative strength, which has been developed historically. Developments in England in the 1990s associated with the promotion of 'partnership' generally echoed what had already been happening at Oxford, and may, indeed, have been influenced by it. At MSU, the faculty were already attuned to the challenges associated with subject teaching and could therefore, respond positively when criticisms were made at a national level. Both these programmes are based on a vision of what a teacher is and how such a teacher may develop – elaborated at Oxford, in an explicit list of underlying 'principles', and at MSU as a progressive trajectory. Whilst vision plays a vital role too in the success of the Teach First programme, very different kinds of principle – rooted not in expertise in subject pedagogy but in the qualities and importance of leadership – underpin the Teach First Leadership Development Programme.

The nature of the respective teacher education programmes and their relationship with the wider provision is in each case quite different. The OIS is a discrete 1-year programme, which may be entered by graduates from any university in the country, or indeed beyond. At MSU, teacher education is a 3-year programme of study enmeshed within an overall 5-year undergraduate programme, with the fifth year being the internship. Teach First participants are essentially defined by the nature of their relationship to the charitable foundation that recruits and assigns them to particular schools, although the latter are actually their employers. The participants are supported by different kinds of tutors, who may well even come from two different HEIs.

One important similarity however, that informed, in part, our selection of these particular institutions, is the fact that all three of them can afford to be very selective in their admissions. Good degree classes and high GPAs respectively are required of applicants to these teacher education programmes, although it is necessary to acknowledge that for Teach First participants, the subject of their degree may very well not be the same as that which they are teaching. It is the quality of their degree classification – the capacity to learn and to lead that it represents – and not the participants' subject knowledge per se that is specifically valued.

The content of the respective programmes also differs in that the practicum constitutes a full two-thirds of the Oxford programme, complemented by studies in the pedagogy of the relevant subject and a course of general professional studies. At MSU, there is a much more differentiated programme which includes 2 years of previous study within the initial teacher education programme as the precursor to a year-long internship (which continues to be supported by weekly courses in the university for 7 weeks of each semester). Whilst the first year of the Teach First programme could perhaps be regarded as a 1-year practicum, supported by 6 occasional days back in the university, the only specific preparation that participants receive for it is an intensive 6-week summer training programme that seeks to combine introductions both to professional studies and to subject-specific teaching (of a subject that the participant *may* not have studied as an undergraduate). Whilst university staff regularly visit the Teach First participants in school, the most frequent visitor is the tutor concerned with general rather than subject-specific dimensions of pedagogy. Whilst the visits of the Oxford tutors are much less frequent in total, the key role here is played by the subject tutor. In contrast to both these programmes, MSU faculty members do not go into school to supervise interns. The relationship between the programme and the school is primarily mediated by the field instructors, which makes the nature of the interaction between school and university significantly different again.

Whilst each programme has specific terms used to describe the particular roles of university and school-based staff, the nature and quality of the programmes depends profoundly on effective interaction between the holders of these various roles. The tension between teaching and research for university faculty members is increasingly apparent at MSU. Although this is also a concern at Oxford, it appears to surface less strongly there. The relationship of research activity to the respective programmes is however, an apparently critical factor that is part of what may distinguish both the OIS and the MSU programmes as particularly successful. A commitment to research-informed practice is implicit within HEIs' involvement in the Teach First partnership, but the programme is essentially promoted as one of leadership rather than pedagogical development. Although participants are expected to undertake academic assignments (leading now to a postgraduate diploma) the limited time that they spend in the university and the limited research experience of many of their professional tutors means that their own research engagement is limited. The espoused model of professional learning is one of reflective practice rather than the kind of practical theorising promoted at Oxford, or the inquiry-based approach to social justice promoted at MSU.

In the next chapter, we offer equivalent accounts of how schools that are engaging with teacher education in England and the United States within these different programmes have responded to the shifting policy contexts. Having thus set out the institutional responses and the experiences of both HEIs and schools – the two key social situations of development identified in Chapter 2 – we will then be ready to look at how the student teachers and those who work with them experience the processes of learning to teach.

Notes

1 The U.S. News & World Report (2017a) programme rankings are based on surveys of education deans, external grants, editorships and selectivity of doctoral admissions (www.usnews.com/education).
2 For example, the online, self-paced American Board for Certification of Teacher Excellence, Teacher Certification Programme created as a more affordable and faster way to place a 'highly qualified' teacher in every classroom albeit bypassing the school practicum (e.g. practice teaching and mentoring) which have been considered key experiences in learning to teach (American Board, 2017a, 2017b: www.american-board.org/ and http://abcte.org/).
3 The information on the subject areas in this section comes from programme syllabi analysis.
4 www.mttc.nesinc.com/ (Pearson Education, 2017).
5 http://education.msu.edu/irt/default.asp (MSU, 2017c).
6 https://education.msu.edu/epc/library/papers/Teachers-for-a-New-Era-Project.asp (MSU, 2017d).
7 Funded by the National Science Foundation and sponsored by the International Association for the Study of Educational Achievement (IEA).
8 www.usnews.com/best-graduate-schools/top-education-schools/michigan-state-university-06103 (U.S. News & World Report, 2017b).
9 www.teachfirst.org.uk/why-we-exist (Teach First, 2017a).
10 https://graduates.teachfirst.org.uk/why-teach-first/what-were-doing (Teach First, 2017b).
11 www.teachfirst.org.uk/blog/how-many-our-teachers-stay-classroom (Freedman, 2014).
12 www.teachfirst.org.uk/about/our-history (Teach First, 2017c).

References

American Board. (2017a). *Online, self-paced teacher certification.* Retrieved from www. americanboard.org/.

American Board. (2017b). *Become a teacher.* Retrieved from http://abcte.org/.

Burn, K., Hagger, H. & Mutton, T. (2015). *Beginning teachers' learning: Making experience count.* Northwich: Critical Publishing.

Clark, C. & Peterson, P. (1986). Teachers' thought processes. In M. Wittrock (Ed.), *Handbook of research on teaching* (3rd ed.) (pp. 255–296). New York: Macmillan.

Darling-Hammond, L. (2010). Teacher education and the American future. *Journal of Teacher Education, 61*(1–2), 35–47.

Department for Education (DfE). (1992). *Initial teacher training (secondary phase), Circular 9/92.* (London: DfE).

Department for Education (DfE). (1993). *The initial training of primary school teachers: New criteria for course approval, Circular 14/93.* London: DfE.

Department for Education (DfE). (2010). *The importance of teaching: The Schools White Paper 2010.* London: HMSO.

Department for Education (DfE). (2013). *History programmes of study: Key Stage 3: National curriculum in England.* Retrieved from www.gov.uk/government/uploads/system/uploads/attachment_data/file/239075/SECONDARY_national_curriculum_-_History.pdf.

Dörnyei, Z. (2003). Attitudes, orientations, and motivations in language learning: Advances in theory, research and applications. *Language Learning, 53*(S1), 3–32.

Ellis, V., Maguire, M., Trippestad, T. A., Liu, Y., Yang, X. & Zeichner, K. (2016). Teaching other people's children, elsewhere for a while: The rhetoric of a travelling education reform. *Journal of Education Policy, 31*(1), 60–80.

Freedman, S. (2014). *How many of our teachers stay in the classroom?* Retrieved from www.teachfirst.org.uk/blog/how-many-our-teachers-stay-classroom.

Good, L. T. & Brophy, E. J. (1978). *Looking in classrooms.* New York: Harper Collins.

Gotwals, A. W. & Birmingham, D. (2015). Eliciting, identifying, interpreting, and responding to students' ideas: Teacher candidates' growth in formative assessment practices. *Research in Science Education, 46,* 365–388. doi: 10.1007/s11165-015-9461-2.

Holmes Group. (1995). *Tomorrow's schools of education: A report of the Holmes Group.* East Lansing, MI: Holmes Group. Retrieved from https://eric.ed.gov/?id=ED399220.

Hutchings, M., Maylor, U., Mendick, H., Menter, I. & Smart, S. (2006). *An evaluation of innovative approaches to teacher training on the Teach First programme: Final report to the Training and Development Agency for Schools.* London: London Metropolitan University.

Labaree, D. F. (2008). An uneasy relationship: The history of teacher education in the university. In M. Cochran-Smith, S. Feiman-Nemser & D. J. McIntyre (Eds.), *Handbook of research on teacher education: Enduring issues in changing contexts* (3rd ed.) (pp. 290–306). Washington, DC: Association of Teacher Educators.

Lortie, D. C. (2002). *Schoolteacher.* Chicago: University of Chicago Press.

McIntyre, D. (1997). A research agenda for initial teacher education. In D. McIntyre (Ed.), *Teacher education research in a new context* (pp. 1–15). London: Paul Chapman.

McIntyre, D. (1990). Ideas and principles guiding the internship scheme. In P. Benton (Ed.), *The Oxford Internship Scheme: Integration and partnership in initial teacher education* (pp. 17–33). London: Calouste Gulbenkian.

McIntyre, D. (1993). Theory, theorizing and reflection in teacher education. In J. Calderhead & P. Gates (Eds.), *Conceptualizing reflection in teacher education* (pp. 39–52). Lewes: The Falmer Press.

Michigan State University (MSU). (2017a). *Secondary education internship guide.* Retrieved from http://education.msu.edu/teacher-preparation/secondary/internship/.

Michigan State University (MSU). (2017b). *Teacher Preparation Program: Becoming a secondary education teacher.* Retrieved from http://education.msu.edu/teacher-preparation/secondary/.

Michigan State University (MSU). (2017c). *Research: IRT publications.* Retrieved from http://education.msu.edu/irt/default.asp.

Michigan State University (MSU). (2017d). *Education Policy Center: Teachers for a new era project, 2002–2007.* Retrieved from https://education.msu.edu/epc/library/papers/Teachers-for-a-New-Era-Project.asp.

Miller, R. & Osborne, J. (Eds.) (1998). *Beyond 2000: Science education for the future* The report of a seminar series funded by the Nuffield Foundation. London: King's College London, School of Education. Retrieved from www.nuffieldfoundation.org/sites/default/files/Beyond2000.pdf.

National Assessment of Educational Progress (NAEP). (2016). *The Nation's Report Card: 2015 Science at Grades 4, 8, and 12.* Washington, DC: National Center for Education Statistics (NCES) No. 2016162. Retrieved from www.nationsreportcard.gov/science_2015/files/overview.pdf].

National Council for Social Studies (NCSS). (2010). *National curriculum standards for social studies: A framework for teaching, learning and assessment.* Washington, DC: NCSS. Retrieved from www.socialstudies.org/standards/introduction.

National Council of Teachers of English (NCTE). (2013). *The NCTE definition of 21st century literacies.* (Updated February 2013. Adopted by the NCTE Executive Committee, February 15, 2008). Retrieved from www.ncte.org/positions/statements/21stcentdefinition.

National Council of Teachers of Mathematics (NCTM). (2014). *Principles to actions: Ensuring mathematical success for all.* Reston, VA: NCTM. Retrieved from www.nctm.org/uploadedFiles/Standards_and_Positions/PtAExecutiveSummary.pdf.

NGSS Lead States. (2013). *Next Generation Science Standards: For states, by states.* Washington, DC: The National Academies Press. Next Generation Science Standards. Retrieved from www.nextgenscience.org/.

Office for Standards in Education, Children's Services and Skills (Ofsted). (2008). Rising to the challenge: A review of the Teach First initial teacher training programme. London: HMSO. Retrieved from http://teachfirstnz.org/images/uploads/Documents/tf2008ofsted.pdf.

Office for Standards in Education, Children's Services and Skills (Ofsted). (2011). *Modern languages: Achievement and challenge 2007 to 2010.* London: HMSO. Retrieved from www.gov.uk/government/publications/modern-languages-achievement-and-challenge-2007-to-2010.

Parker, S. & Gale, T. (2016). *Teach First, ask questions later: A summary of research on Teach First's alternative vision of teaching and teachers.* Produced on behalf of the Scottish Teacher Education Committee at the invitation of the General Teaching Council of Scotland and the Scottish Government.

Patton, M. (1990). *Qualitative evaluation and research methods.* Beverly Hills, CA: Sage.

Pearson Education. (2017). *Michigan Test for Teacher Certification.* Retrieved from www.mttc.nesinc.com/.

Riley, M. (2000). Into the key stage 3 history garden: Choosing and planting your enquiry questions. *Teaching History, 99*, 8–13.

Schön, D. A. (1990). *Educating the reflective practitioner.* San Francisco, CA: Jossey-Bass.

Schwab, J. J. (1976–1977). *Transcriptions of seminars taught at the Institute for Research on Teaching at Michigan State University.* Archived at the Museum of Education, University of South Carolina.

Schwab, J. J. (1983). The practical 4: Something for curriculum professors to do. *Curriculum Inquiry, 13*(3), 239–265.

Schwab, J. J. & Thomas, R. (1986). *The practicals 5 and 6: Finding and using commonplaces in literature and psychology.* Archived at the Museum of Education, University of South Carolina.

Shulman, L. S. (1986). Those who understand: Knowledge growth in teaching. *Educational Researcher, 15*(2), 4–14.

Shulman, L. S. (1987). Knowledge and teaching: Foundations of the new reform. *Harvard Educational Review, 57*(1), 1–22.

Sleeter, C. (2008). Equity, democracy, and neoliberal assaults on teacher education. *Teaching and Teacher Education, 24*(8), 1947–1957.

Stuart, J. & Tatto, M. T. (2000). Designs for initial teacher preparation programmes: An international view. *International Journal of Educational Research, 33*, 493–514.

Tatto, M. T., Schwille, J., Senk, S. L., Ingvarson, L., Rowley, G., Peck, R., Bankov, K., Rodriguez, M. & Reckase, M. (2012). *Policy, practice, and readiness to teach primary and secondary mathematics in 17 countries. Findings from the IEA Teacher Education and Development Study in Mathematics (TEDS-M).* Amsterdam: International Association for the Evaluation of Student Achievement (IEA).

Teach First. (2017a). *Why we exist.* Retrieved from www.teachfirst.org.uk/why-we-exist.

Teach First. (2017b). *What we're doing.* Retrieved from https://graduates.teachfirst.org.uk/why-teach-first/what-were-doing.

Teach First. (2017c). *Our history.* Retrieved from www.teachfirst.org.uk/about/our-history.

U.S. News & World Report. (2017a). *Education.* Retrieved from www.usnews.com/education.

U.S. News & World Report. (2017b). *Michigan State University.* Retrieved from www.usnews.com/best-graduate-schools/top-education-schools/michigan-state-university-06103.

Wigdortz, B. (2012). *Success against the odds – five lessons in how to achieve the impossible; the story of Teach First.* London: Short Books Limited.

Wiggins, G. & McTighe, J. (2005). *Understanding by design.* Alexandria, VA: Association for Supervision and Curriculum Development. Retrieved from www.storyboardthat.com/articles/e/what-is-ubd-understanding-by-design.

Williams, M., Burden, R. & Lanvers, U. (2002). French is the language of love and stuff: Student perceptions of issues related to motivation in learning a foreign language. *British Educational Research Journal, 28*(4), 503–528.

Winch, C., Oancea, A. & Orchard, J. (2015). The contribution of educational research to teachers' professional learning: Philosophical understandings. *Oxford Review of Education, 41*(2), 202–216.

Zeichner, K. (2010). Competition, economic rationalization, increased surveillance, and attacks on diversity: Neo-liberalism and the transformation of teacher education in the U.S. *Teaching and Teacher Education, 26*, 1544–1552.

5 Schools as settings for learning to teach

Responses to policy and social pressures in England and the United States

This chapter describes the role that schools play as spaces for educating teachers within the challenging societal and policy environment that affects education in both countries. Increasing critiques of schools and teachers, seen as the key causes of low pupil performance, have given rise to important variation in how schools frame their mission and their policies in relation to teaching and learning. Within this variation, schools are constantly responding to accountability demands primarily characterised by increased testing, and teacher and school evaluations. Within this context of continuous pressure and change and as the movement towards school-based teacher preparation gains more currency, we discuss the way in which schools in both countries are managing to change and adapt to constant societal pressures whilst supporting future teachers as they learn to teach. We look in particular at the schools that are working in partnership with the three programmes examined in Chapter 4. We consider these schools as special cases, acknowledging the key assumption throughout this book that institutions produce different responses to the aforementioned pressures.

School-based teacher education in England

Stability and change

Notwithstanding the different models of partnership in operation (Furlong, Barton, Miles, Whiting & Whitty, 2000), schools in England have – since government Circulars 9/92 and 14/93 (DfE, 1992, 1993) established new requirements for partnership arrangements – become used to playing a significant role in initial teacher education. With over 30,000 teachers in training each year, securing sufficient school engagement is vital, although there is no statutory requirement for schools to participate. Inevitably, levels of engagement vary: whilst some seek more limited involvement, others regard initial teacher education as a central part of the school's overall activity (Mutton & Butcher, 2008). Most schools see the benefits of involvement outweighing the costs (Allen, Belfield, Greaves, Sharp & Walker, 2016), with the potential advantages from their perspective ranging from 'increased continuing professional development opportunities and fresh teaching ideas to the trainee contributing to teaching – or expecting to hire the trainee' (Allen et al., 2016, p. 20). The opportunity that this involvement affords schools to recruit the new entrants is particularly significant, given the well-publicised issues around teacher recruitment and retention in England.

Accountability, teacher education reform and the rise of school-based teacher preparation

The emergence of alternative routes into teaching in England (described in Chapter 3) has led to further significant change in schools' involvement in initial teacher education, particularly following reforms introduced by the coalition government from 2010 onwards. The rationale for reform came from the government's view that 'schools should take greater responsibility in the system' (DfE, 2011), based on the assumption that the current system was not providing an appropriate number of suitably qualified teachers, with the kinds of knowledge and skills that schools required.

The emergence of the School Direct programme enabled those interested in learning to teach to apply directly to a specific lead school, which would design its initial teacher education programme in conjunction with, but not determined by, a university partner. Those training on such courses would continue to pay tuition fees to the university partner with individual agreements reached as to the amount of funding transferred to schools. The School Direct salaried scheme also enabled schools to employ new entrants to the profession as unqualified teachers and to train them 'on the job', again working in conjunction with a university provider. In both schemes, wider accountability rested with the university, which would be subject to the usual regulatory and inspection systems.

This increase in the level of responsibility assumed by schools has also been reflected in the growing number of School-Centred Initial Teacher Training (SCITT) providers. SCITTs are accredited providers in their own right and many work entirely independently of universities, although those that do so are only permitted to award Qualified Teacher Status (QTS) rather than a Postgraduate Certificate in Education (PGCE), which depends on university accreditation. SCITTs that would like to offer PGCE qualifications can only do so in collaboration with a university.

The result of this policy drive at the macro level has been to reshape many practices within the new models of 'school-led' teacher education, operating at the meso level. Recent research (Brown, Rowley & Smith, 2016) has highlighted key areas in which this is happening, in addition to the changing role of the university and the inevitable adjustment to the 'balance of power' within partnership arrangements. The researchers discuss the way in which '[t]he composition of trainee pedagogical experience is being reconfigured' (Brown et al., 2016, p. 23), concluding that this results from differing beliefs about the nature of such a learning experience. They note, furthermore, that '[c]onceptions of substantive subject and pedagogical subject knowledge vary between school and university teacher educators' which may 'affect coherence of provision across different locations' (Brown et al., 2016, p. 24). Finally, they highlight the way in which competing views of the value of particular types of research affect the manner in which 'teacher educator professionalism and agency is understood and enacted' (Brown et al., 2016, p. 25).

It is also important to recognise that many schools are frequently working not within a single model of partnership but within different models, simultaneously negotiated with a range of different providers. These overlapping partnerships may create tensions in terms of achieving overall consistency and coherence within each programme and across programmes within a school.

Change and diversification

The policy changes described above reflect just one aspect of recent education reforms in England. School reform has continued unabated, with each successive government implementing a wide range of changes, including, for example, three iterations of the statutory National Curriculum since 2000, each accompanied by alterations to the assessment frameworks, with the most recent version leaving primary and secondary schools entirely responsible for determining their own framework of assessment for National Curriculum subjects. Furthermore, frequent revisions of the school inspection framework have reflected current government priorities – such as pupil behaviour – and have placed a strong focus on pupil outcomes, as reflected in standardised test results and examination grades. Significant reforms have also been made to the public examinations undertaken at 16+ and 18+, with each change requiring the teaching of new specifications, often at relatively short notice. All of the above have been subject to critical commentary but, most importantly, all have required schools to implement change at a rate that many find extremely demanding and in a way that appears increasingly tightly regulated, at a time when other government education policy reflects a greater sense of de-regulation.

Such de-regulation has been enacted primarily around issues of school governance, particularly during the period of the coalition government from 2010 to 2015 and continued by subsequent Conservative administrations. The 2010 White Paper (DfE, 2010) set out proposals for expanding the 'academies' programme, allowing successful schools to become 'converter' academies, independent of local authority control and receiving funding directly from government. 'Converter' academies could deviate from the requirement to follow the National Curriculum and were also given the freedom to appoint teachers without QTS. The White Paper also heralded the introduction of free schools, which could be set up by groups of parents, teachers, charities or businesses and given the same levels of autonomy as academies. Latest government statistics (DfE, 2017) show that, in January 2016, 69 per cent of all secondary school pupils and 24 per cent of all primary school pupils were being taught in schools with academy status.

It is highly likely, therefore, that student teachers will be working in contexts that have been subject to rapid change over a relatively short period of time. It has also been argued that particular governance models (and related accountability regimes) can create a climate in which 'teacher values are mostly suppressed in the face of the coercive compliance imposed by performative managerialism' (Wilkins, 2015, p. 1156), raising issues of professional identity.

Finally, schools in England, which meet specific criteria (see DfE, 2014) can apply for government designation as Teaching Schools. One criterion for selection is that the school should have '[a] track record of delivering high-quality school-led Initial Teacher Training' and have the support of an accredited initial teacher training provider. Schools with this status work in partnership with other schools as part of a Teaching Schools Alliance and are accountable for the outcomes of their engagement in, amongst other areas, initial teacher training, continuing professional development, school-to-school support, leadership development and research.

Partnership

This increasing focus on accountability follows a trend evident in many countries, but practice in England appears to be amongst the most extreme in terms of its focus on the accountability both of schools (Figlio & Loeb, 2011) and of teachers working within them (Leat, 2014). Whilst universities may conceive of partnership in particular ways, schools may have a different perspective, perhaps placing more emphasis on the need for teachers in training to be 'classroom-ready' at an early stage. The *Carter Review of Initial Teacher Training* (Carter, 2015) used the findings from an annual survey of the National Association of Head Teachers in England to highlight head teachers' concerns about newly qualified teachers' understanding of behaviour management, awareness of assessment practices and capacity to assess effectively. In such a context it is easy to understand, from the school's perspective, the importance of equipping student teachers with the practical skills necessary for them to function effectively in the classroom. Essential as these skills are, an increasing focus on 'school-led' models may result in other important aspects of professional learning being obscured. Brown et al. (2016) in their report on the introduction of the School Direct model, found that 'in contrast to those based in universities, school teachers were positioned as not having the time or the access to research or theoretical models, meaning that they had a less developed understanding of pedagogical concepts specific to their subject' (2016, p. 19).

Thus, policy changes at the macro level, may lead, in turn, to changing expectations – at the meso level – of the way in which student teachers respond to and learn from the practicum experience. It is also not unusual for different approaches to be in operation concurrently within individual schools.

School-based learning in the Oxford Internship Scheme

The Oxford Internship Scheme (OIS) 'partnership agreement' drawn up between the university and partnership schools sets out the roles and responsibilities of all those working within the programme, as well as outlining expectations of the interns and detailing the learning opportunities that should be available to them. It also explains the overall governance and management structures of the programme and funding arrangements within the partnership. Essentially, internship schools agree to provide opportunities that will enable interns to learn how to teach pupils with differing levels of prior attainment, across the full age range, and to provide school-based training related to interns' need to meet the statutory requirements for the award of QTS.

The curriculum strand

Within the programme, school-based subject mentors (or mentors) and university-based subject tutors (or tutors) take joint responsibility for planning and implementing a coherent and integrated curriculum strand and for assessing interns' competence. There is an agreed approach to supporting interns in order to enable them to demonstrate the essential skills, knowledge and understanding required and to analyse and evaluate their own teaching throughout the year. The roles of the mentor and the tutor complement each other, although each has a distinctive contribution to make to the development of the intern in relation to classroom practice.

Mentors, who receive training from the university before taking on this role, are expected to coordinate the interns' school-based experience and to support them as they assume increasing levels of responsibility for planning lessons and teaching a range of pupils. Mentors specifically support interns in developing their subject pedagogy, whilst helping them to understand any specific contextual factors, which they will have to take into account in planning and teaching.

The subject tutors each work with a number of schools, supporting the interns in that subject within the school (usually one or two per subject area). This ensures a breadth of knowledge about local practice. Whilst they are committed, like the mentors, to developing the interns' ability to be effective classroom practitioners, subject tutors are also particularly focused on cultivating interns' critical understanding of the curricular and pedagogical possibilities inherent in various approaches to teaching. In addition to the shared features of the role, the subject tutor will lead university-based sessions, assess the interns' written assignments and, through a minimum of five school visits to each intern, spread across the year, support interns' learning and moderate assessments of their competence on a cross-school basis. Additionally, subject tutors have a responsibility to undertake research that will be of direct benefit to classroom practice.

The professional development strand

The professional development strand of the programme focuses on more general aspects of schools and schooling and is planned and delivered by both tutors at the university and staff in schools. A university-based general tutor (or general tutor) oversees the wider practicum experience of all the interns in any given school, in collaboration with a school-based professional mentor (or professional mentor). Working together these colleagues coordinate the weekly sessions of the school-based professional development strand, to complement those held in the university and enable the interns to be integrated gradually into the ethos and workings of their internship school. The general tutor is expected to develop an understanding of the particular school ethos and ways of working by meeting and building relationships with members of staff, particularly the head teacher and the subject mentors.

The professional mentor (or mentor) has three distinct, but complementary roles: ensuring effective channels of communication within the school, relating to the wider initial teacher education programme; coordinating the work of the subject mentors in relation to appropriate provision for individual interns; and supporting those mentors, by working proactively with them when interns are experiencing particular difficulties. The role of professional mentor is a vital one within the school and the professional mentor bears much of the responsibility for overseeing the way in which the school operates within specific programme or national policy level requirements. Beyond these managerial roles, however, the professional mentor also has a pedagogic role in ensuring that the principles of the internship scheme are reflected in the delivery of the professional development strand. Ideally, the role involves more than the organisation of a series of school-based training sessions and extends to an exploration of why things are done in particular ways, leading to 'questions about alternative practices and their relative merits, and to issues about the criteria being used, the evidence available, and the interests being served' (McIntyre, Hagger & Burn, 1994, p. 49).

The general tutor, based at the university, liaises with the school's professional mentor, serving as a channel of communication between school and university. The general tutor also has responsibility for supervising interns' assignments and other enquiry-based projects linked to the professional development strand.

School settings

The two schools selected for our study within the OIS are both long-standing local partnership schools that were actively involved in setting up the programme. Both schools are academies and both are now designated as Teaching Schools, working together within a wider organisation, the Oxfordshire Teaching Schools Alliance. Within the OIS each school regularly hosts a larger than average number of interns.

Riverside Academy

Riverside Academy is a secondary school of 1,700 pupils aged between 11 and 19. It is located within the city on two sites, a short distance from each other. It became an academy in 2012 and then, in 2013, the lead school within a multi-academy trust, which includes a number of local primary schools, another secondary school, the local SCITT and a new free school, due to open in 2019.

Riverside is a high-performing school, judged 'outstanding' by the Office for Standards in Education, Children's Services and Skills (Ofsted) that consistently performs above the average in league tables of examination results for schools, both locally and nationally. It includes a significant number of pupils from above average socio-economic backgrounds but also a significant number from less advantaged backgrounds. Eligibility for free school meals is in line with the national average. The proportion of pupils from minority ethnic backgrounds is higher than the national average, as is the percentage of pupils with English as an Additional Language (EAL). The proportion of pupils with learning difficulties and/or disabilities is about average, but the percentage of pupils with statements of special educational need is higher than average.

The school has a distinctive character, reflected for example, in the fact that it does not have a school uniform policy (which is highly unusual for secondary schools in England) and in its travel policy: it boasts the highest proportion of pupils in the country travelling to school by bicycle (over 58 per cent) and almost 90 per cent using sustainable means of transport.

As a Teaching School, Riverside Academy extended its involvement in initial teacher education by being designated as a SCITT provider in 2014. Working within the wider Oxfordshire Teaching Schools Alliance, it provides both salaried and fee-paying School Direct programmes for just over 80 trainees at both primary and secondary level (the latter in a range of subjects). Several members of staff (many of whom previously acted as mentors within the OIS) have designated roles within the SCITT. Alongside its work as an accredited teacher training provider, the school also continues to accept interns from the university. The latter are thus, working in a context where national teacher education policy at the macro level is being re-contextualised at the meso level, as the school formulates its own training programme alongside an existing partnership model.

Riverside School has thus, responded enthusiastically to a range of policy reforms first set out in the 2010 government White Paper (DfE, 2010), allowing it greater autonomy and the opportunity to reinterpret national policy at a more local level.

Groveside Academy

Groveside Academy includes more than 1,800 pupils, aged between 11 and 19. Again it is a split-site school, located in a small town approximately 20 miles from the university, with each site accommodating pupils from a specific age range. It became an academy in 2011 and is the lead school in a multi-academy trust, established in 2013, which, at the time of writing, includes five primary school academies and another secondary school academy in the local area. The multi-academy trust's vision statement includes the assertion that 'each academy has its own distinctive nature and ethos [... underpinned by ...] our shared vision for high-quality education for local children'.

Groveside Academy is a high-performing school, judged to be 'outstanding' by Ofsted. It consistently performs above the average (locally and nationally) in league tables of examination results. The school's most recent inspection report noted that relatively few children from minority ethnic backgrounds attend the school and that the proportion of pupils with special educational needs and/or disabilities is also well below average (related mainly to moderate learning, or behavioural, emotional and social difficulties).

The school timetable is unusual in that its 70-minute lessons are longer than in most schools, and a break between each lesson enables teachers to travel between sites. The school also offers some 'elective' classes, essentially extra-curricular, after-school sessions that enable teachers and pupils to undertake some form of enrichment activity.

Groveside Academy was designated as a Teaching School in 2014, working closely within the local SCITT as well as receiving student teachers from other initial teacher education providers, including the University of Oxford. The school has acted as a lead 'School Direct' school, working in collaboration with both Oxford and other university providers, and also hosts salaried School Direct trainees through the local SCITT programme.

The school has, like Riverside Academy, embraced national policy reform and used the resulting freedom to lead developments at school level and within the local area in both initial teacher education and in programmes to support teachers' ongoing continuing professional development.

The Teach First agreement with schools

Since Teach First is an employment-based training programme, the schools are the participants' employers, paying them as unqualified teachers for the first year, to teach up to 80 per cent of a full timetable. Although government funding is allocated to the schools to provide subject and professional mentors, the school also pays a recruitment fee to Teach First, which controls the selection and placement of the participants (in line with the schools' requests for particular subjects). Participants can express a preference for a particular type of school or area of London, but there is no guarantee that this will be taken into account.

During the year, the schools are expected to release participants for 6 days of subject-specific training, and for a week's experience in a second school (often a direct swap with another participant). Whilst the government grant is expected to provide for subject-specific and more generic support, subject mentors and professional mentors can perhaps best be described as providing different kinds of personalised support around the participants rather than each offering a distinct stand of a jointly planned programme. The leadership component, prominent within the summer institutes, is much less emphasised during the first year in school, although it becomes more significant in the second year, when Teach First leadership development officers assume responsibility for coaching the participants.

In the early stages, the schools were invited to send a representative to regular meetings of the Teach First London Advisory Group, which drew up the list of 'Key requirements for school placements'. This list has been successively refined to try to ensure that all staff involved have sufficient knowledge of the scheme to meet the agreed expectations and to eliminate wide disparities between participants' experience in different schools.

The subject strand

As in more traditional initial teacher education programmes, participants are assigned a subject mentor, expected to meet with them weekly, to provide guidance and support. Although regular observation is also expected, this might be relatively infrequent – perhaps only once every 6 weeks. Whilst most of these mentors are subject specialists, the fact that Teach First participants are often recruited to address shortages in particular subjects may mean that, there is no experienced teacher available within their subject to take on the role.

As explained previously, support for the development of subject pedagogy was also provided during the 6 university-based subject days and, from 2011 onwards, through the subject tutor's six visits. But mentors were often unavailable to meet the tutor on these occasions. Although Teach First offered a formal 'mentor recognition scheme' (Ofsted, 2011), this programme ran independently of the subject tutors. The core document that structured the participants' professional learning over the course of the first year was their reflective journal, which supported regular processes of target-setting and review. The subject handbooks, in contrast, which sought to reflect well-articulated, research-based models of subject pedagogy, were intended to coordinate the regional and national elements of the summer institute at the subject level and were not really used by, or with, school-based mentors. With the exception of the subject departments involved in the school-based subject days within the summer institute, subject mentors' collaboration with subject tutors was very limited, as Ofsted had observed, when they called for increased support for 'the more progressive development of participants' understanding and application of subject pedagogy' (Ofsted, 2011, p. 9).

The professional development strand

As noted in Chapter 4, the weighting given to the professional development strand of the Teach First programme was much greater than within many more traditional courses. Alongside the programme of regular training events organised by the professional mentor, the university-based professional tutor visited the participant on 12 occasions.

Both professional mentors and professional tutors observed the participants' teaching and coordinated formal assessment of their progress, bringing evidence from their own observations together with those of the subject mentors and tutors at termly assessment points. The fact that the professional development strand ran exclusively in school (once the summer institute was over) meant that it was most strongly shaped by the specific assumptions and practices of each particular context. Professional tutors might introduce research-informed perspectives, especially when setting up formal assignments, but the scope for participants to consider the implications of those research insights for their own practice always depended heavily on the particular expectations of teachers within their placement school. The high expectations of participants even within their first year meant that they were subject to acute pressures to comply with established norms and to demonstrate that they could operate existing procedures effectively. As noted in Chapter 4, many professional tutors had been recruited directly from roles in school. Whilst they often brought a depth of experience in different contexts to their work, this was not necessarily rooted in familiarity with, or engagement in, research.

School setting: Eastside Academy

Eastside Academy, where we collected our case study data, was, in 2013–2014, a smaller than average, inner London secondary school, with just over 1,000 pupils. It had converted to academy status the year before and had just opened its first sixth form (to accommodate 16- to 19-year-olds). It had recently benefitted from the government-funded 'Building Schools for the Future' scheme, allowing it to invest £17 million in much-needed renovations and reconstruction.

When Eastside Academy first joined the Teach First programme only 34 per cent of pupils achieved the nationally recognised measure of five A*–C grades at General Certificate of Secondary Education (GCSE) (including English and maths). The school had continued to struggle and been placed in 'special measures' by Ofsted, under threat of closure when a new head was appointed in 2006. Thereafter, its results had steadily improved, to such an extent that 80 per cent of pupils achieved the expected standard of five A*–C grades at GCSE and Ofsted rated it as 'outstanding'.

In 2013–2014, a large proportion of pupils (53 per cent) were eligible for free school meals and the school was particularly proud of the fact that these pupils made progress in line with that of other, less disadvantaged young people at the school. The proportion formally identified as having a special educational need or disability was also high, at 14 per cent (compared with a national average of 7 per cent). The school included a very diverse pupil population, including 52 per cent of Bangladeshi heritage, and 10 per cent identified as Black African. Thirty-three languages were spoken in the school and 77 per cent of pupils were identified as learners of EAL. The school population was also highly mobile, with almost 40 per cent of those in the 16+ examination cohort having joined after the first year of secondary school.

The school opted to join the Teach First programme in its second year of operation. The new head was fully persuaded of its potential and went on offering places to four or five participants every year. By the time of our data collection, three members of the senior leadership team had joined the staff through Teach First. This steady influx of new teachers (and the rapid staff turnover which gave rise to it), meant that the teaching body was relatively young, with almost two-thirds of staff under the age of 35.

Whilst we have acknowledged the lack of 'typical' Teach First schools, Eastside Academy clearly represents a 'best-practice' case study in that it met the scheme's original selection criteria and its head teacher continued to endorse it enthusiastically as he presided over a period of transformation in the school's results. Eastside Academy appears to have benefitted from its engagement in the scheme precisely as its founder had intended. The professional mentor, herself a Teach First graduate, had rapidly risen to become an assistant head teacher and was now in charge of professional learning. The head teacher, who was fully convinced of the participants' classroom impact and of their leadership potential, deliberately sought to give those who completed the 2-year programme new roles that quickly broadened their responsibilities 'pushing them hard to expand their experience' (Wigdortz, 2012, p. 197).

The school's enthusiasm for Teach First did not mean however, that it was uninvolved in other forms of initial teacher education. Eastside Academy accepted small numbers of student teachers from other London providers and made a strong commitment to the School Direct salaried route, indicating a clear preference for employment-based training.

Summary

Significant policy changes at the macro level have resulted, in many ways, in the transformation of the school contexts in which beginning teachers are placed for their practicum experience. Whilst the schools, profiled above, may have been at the forefront of engagement with the opportunities and freedoms afforded by new models of school governance, they are by no means atypical. An increased focus on accountability, ongoing curriculum reform, a 'high-stakes' inspection regime, and the constant drive to secure good standards of pupil behaviour, are all potential contributors to the 'performative culture' (Ball, 2003) that permeates many schools in England. This changing context has developed alongside equally significant reforms to teacher education, which have prompted both universities and schools, at the meso level, to re-appraise traditional ways of working; re-conceptualising roles and responsibilities within partnerships and addressing more fundamental philosophical questions around the sort of teachers that we want and how such teachers can be developed.

School-based teacher education in the United States

Stability and change

Teacher education in the United States has been, since its inception, based in higher education institutions (HEIs); this trend continues in spite of the emergence of alternative certification routes. According to the U.S. Department of Education, in the academic year 2011–2012, the most recent period for which data is available, a total of 62,961 candidates enrolled in alternative certification route programmes, compared with 551,166 in traditional routes; thus, traditional certification draws close to 90 per cent of those aspiring to become teachers (USDOE, 2015). This means that in contrast with England, decision-making and management of programmes occurs within colleges and universities where the majority of teachers are prepared. Funding is regulated by the state and via HEIs. Some preparation in school settings real or simulated has, nevertheless, always existed alongside formal teacher preparation although, given the decentralised character of education in the United States, its nature varies widely across the country and even within states. School-based teacher preparation may range from short field experiences to year-long internships depending on the approach to teacher education adopted by the programme and the extent of funding offered to support school mentors or more formal partnerships such as those originated by the Professional Development School movement (Holmes Group, 1990; Holmes Group, 1995). The notion of linking theory with practice as a duality has been a constant concern of teacher educators since teacher education moved to higher education, and an enduring tension that programmes and schools are continually striving to resolve (Grossman, Hammerness & McDonald, 2009).

Accountability, teacher education reform and the rise of school-based teacher preparation

Since the Eisenhower years (1953–1960), tensions had begun to emerge around school accountability, mostly about the learning outcomes of school funding, but it was not until the Carter years (1977–1980) that these concerns began to turn to teachers (New York State Education Department, 2006/2009, p. 41), and soon prompted questions about the effectiveness of teacher education programmes. Beginning in 1980, a fertile political climate, fed by increased calls for accountability, the publication of national tests results, and the publication of *A Nation at Risk* in 1983 (USDOE, 1983), resulted by the early 1990s in the development of school-based routes. School-based routes were seen as alternatives to the traditional teacher education programmes, based on the assumption that effective preparation required more and more authentic school teaching experiences. Subsequent administrations especially that of President George W. Bush, gave added support to alternative route programmes and currently 48 states and the District of Columbia have alternative route programmes to teacher certification where the universal requirement is that candidates possess a bachelor's degree and fully engage in school teaching for a significant amount of time before becoming certified.

Characteristically, alternative certification requirements vary by state[1] with some including some pedagogy training, subject content examinations and school teaching, amongst other requirements (USDOE, 2015, p. 4). In Michigan, there are three main alternative routes to certification. One is a 1-year 'accelerated certification in education', whilst the other two, a 'university pathway', and a 'Troops to Teachers' programme, which recruits and places 'quality retiring active duty and reserve military personnel into classrooms', take about 3 years to complete whilst teaching in a Michigan school district. To date, alternative route programmes are seen as essential to staff schools in inner cities and rural areas and in high-demand subjects such as mathematics, sciences and special education.

Change and diversification

A parallel development to the emergence of school-based teacher preparation has been the steady creation of the so-called charter schools (publicly funded, but privately run). Whilst the majority of schools in the United States are public schools (publicly funded, and run by school districts and the states), the number of charter schools has continued to grow. According to a report from the National Center for Education Statistics called the 'Condition of Education' (Kena et al., 2016), the number of charter schools reached 6,500 at the start of the 2013–2014 school year, yet according to Barshay (2014) writing for the Hechinger Report, 'charters represented only 6 per cent of the United States public school system of 98,454 elementary, middle and high schools' with the largest increases in California, Texas and Florida. Some states have resisted the operation of charter schools including Alabama, Kentucky, Montana, Nebraska, North Dakota, South Dakota, Vermont and West Virginia. The emergence of charter schools represents a challenge for improving the quality education amongst underserved populations as teachers in these schools tend to drop out and report higher levels of dissatisfaction and high turnover rates due in part to the practice of hiring uncertified, non-union teachers (Roch & Sai, 2016).

Whilst the number of charter schools in Michigan has increased sharply, we do not discuss them further in this book because at the time of this study participating teachers within the MSU programme were only undertaking their internship in public schools.

Partnerships

The teacher education programme at MSU was probably one of the first in the country to engage in vigorous reform by creating partnerships with schools as part of the Professional Development Schools movement, as described in Chapter 4 (Holmes Group Report, 1986, 1995) and by creating a year-long internship. Whilst the programme had operated in close partnership with a number of schools for a long time, increased regulations and standards have more recently altered the delicate ecosystem. Some partner schools were forced to close when they were not able to demonstrate 'adequate yearly progress', a measure conceived by the *No Child Left Behind Act of 2001* (NCLB) (U.S. Congress, 2002) to determine how public schools and their districts were performing academically (e.g. pupils' expected annual achievement growth) according to results on standardised tests. Some partner schools opted not to continue collaborating with the programme, whilst others have continued accepting interns.

Nevertheless, school regulations, including the requirement for schools to demonstrate that they are compliant with state education standards, which began evolving in the early 1990s, were not the only sources of stress for the university-school partnership. The demands on traditional teacher education programmes to secure accreditation by proving their effectiveness created additional pressures for programme faculty (teacher educators), and mentor teachers or mentors. Teacher education programmes have had to increase data gathering efforts to satisfy increasing demands for evidence as required by accreditation standards. In addition, continuous changes in state standards forced on teachers and teacher educators have required a constant process of adaptation to new agendas (Anagnostopoulos & Rutledge, 2007; Tatto, 2007/2009; Tatto et al., 2016).

Whilst the MSU programme and its partner schools continue to productively collaborate in the preparation of future teachers, external accountability efforts, as felt differently in schools and universities, often put programmes and schools at odds with one another.

Yet and in spite of these pressures, the vision of the MSU programme partnership reveals a strong commitment to collaboration:

> One of the primary goals of our program is to develop a partnership between practising teachers and teacher educators, working toward making meaningful connections between classroom fieldwork and university coursework. We believe that people do not learn from experience alone, but through experience in combination with careful preparation, good mentoring, discussions with colleagues, and well-designed courses. Therefore, we seek to develop sustained connections among teacher candidates, MSU staff, and practicing teachers.
>
> (Secondary Teacher Preparation Team, 2015, p. 6)

In sum, programmes confront a paradox as teacher educators, their future teachers and their mentors are all focused on survival and, often disparate efforts, not all consistent with the programmes' goals, are needed to achieve it. The survival of partnerships depends on the strong commitment to collaborate in preparing future teachers.

School-based learning in the MSU internship

The MSU teacher preparation programme, in which the final year is dedicated to an internship in a school, emerged as a result of discussions that led to the release of the *Tomorrow's Schools of Education* report (Holmes Group, 1995), which took the position that universities needed to reconnect with schools and classrooms. The internship was described in detail in Chapter 4. Here we focus in detail on particular elements of the school-based experience, including the vision that guides learning to teach in schools, the responsibilities of interns, mentors and field instructors, and the contexts of the particular schools in which our case study interns were located for the full academic year.

Interns

Student teachers become interns when they move into their final year internship. The interns are students who have completed 4 years in university as required for an undergraduate degree – BA or BSc – in their major subject including 2 years of teacher preparation in the university. During their internship, in their 5th year, they gradually engage in teaching for an academic year in a school designated by the programme, working on their teaching practice with a mentor teacher and a field instructor (university supervisor), whilst at the same time are enrolled in graduate courses in the teacher education programme in the university.

Interns are expected to begin co-teaching in a 'focus class', to engage in 'guided lead teaching' during the fall semester, and engage in 'lead teaching' over the course of 10 weeks in the spring semester, when they become responsible for a substantial portion of the mentor teacher's duties.

The beginning of the internship is a highly stressful time, full of uncertainty and high expectations for individuals, not less because the programme encourages interns to fully engage as a teacher in their focal class. At this stage in their programme the mentor teacher and the field instructor play key roles in securing interns' success.

Mentors

According to the programme, 'mentor teachers are experienced teachers who [...] provide guidance, insight and opportunities for supported practice' (Secondary Teacher Preparation Team, 2015, p. 9). They are expected: to support intern learning by co-planning and co-teaching; by facilitating observations and reflection; by allowing interns to learn about assessments (of pupils and of their own practice); and by helping them prepare for their future careers.

Field instructors

The programme sees the field instructors as the bridge between the programme and the schools. Field instructors are in many cases graduate students but also former teachers or principals who are expected to

> make five scheduled visits each semester and hold five conferences with the intern and mentor during the academic year [...] supply information about programme expectations to both interns and mentors in schools, offer an additional perspective on classroom events, and support the interns in meeting the programme standards.
>
> (Secondary Teacher Preparation Team, 2015, p. 10)

In addition, they collect data, including observations, assessments and judgements of the intern's' progress, for accreditation exercises. Importantly, they are expected to facilitate communication between mentors and course instructors in the university.

School settings

This section provides a summary portrayal of the schools where interns that participated in our study were doing their internship. The schools presented here represent the diverse characteristics of Michigan schools where interns learn to teach within the MSU's partner school network. In Michigan, schools are organised within districts and thus, regulated centrally by them. Districts are responsible for reports of accountability to the state and the community. The districts typically have one high school and one middle school, and one or more elementary schools depending on size.

The MSU teacher education programme has long-standing partnerships with a wide range of Michigan schools, some very close to the university and some that are more distant. The interns that agreed to participate in this study were placed in a diversity of schools both close and far away from campus. Most of the schools serve a mixture of rural and urban populations and all had a long history of collaboration with the MSU programme. In this chapter, we describe in detail the schools in two districts where the interns who agreed to participate in this study were learning to teach.[2]

The Michigan Far Fields schools

The Michigan Far Fields School District had recently adopted an inquiry approach to teaching and learning with real-world applications and thus, offered important learning opportunities to interns. Their curriculum framework had an interdisciplinary focus and emphasised 'critical thinking', 'learner-centred instruction', 'communication skills', and the 'development of the whole student'.

In addition, at the time of the study, the schools were following a curriculum aligned with the Michigan Department of Education (MDE) standards and benchmarks. In all areas, including mathematics and science, the departments had sought to align their curriculum and assessments with the Common Core Standards.[3] The school district organised district-wide professional development leaving the school departments the tasks of planning, teaching and assessing students and of communicating with parents.

The middle and high school in the Michigan Far Fields School District are seen as favourable settings for the MSU interns, in part, because of the quality of its teachers (all with BA degrees and with a large proportion holding MA degrees), and in part, because of its strong affiliation with MSU including some who are graduates from the teacher education programme.

Midfield Middle School

Midfield Middle School is the context for the case of the mathematics and the history interns we will examine in later chapters. At the time of the study, the school served close to 700 pupils (51 per cent males), in grades sixth, seventh and eighth in the school district, bringing together students from different elementary schools. The majority of pupils in the school were white (94 per cent), 4 per cent were Hispanic and the rest were other ethnicities. About 62 per cent of the pupils were eligible for free or reduced lunch. As is the situation with a number of public schools in Michigan, Midfield Middle School was under a school improvement plan because it had a large achievement gap in 30 per cent of its student achievement scores.[4] The summary report stated that the school had to close this achievement gap, which was seen as predominant amongst the special education and at-risk students as they typically perform poorly on standardised tests. The school was working with special programmes (such as tutoring) to help address these needs. The school had doubled the time allocated to English classes, and continued to monitor students' reading levels throughout the school year.

In contrast with the school's learner-centred instruction philosophy, the school administration attributed its performance to the special and 'at-risk' populations they served, including the number of pupils whose native language is not English.

Whilst in Midfield Middle School the pedagogical discourse was expected to be mediated by their adoption of an inquiry-based curriculum, in reality the pedagogical discourse in the school was dominated by the language of accountability (standards, assessments, pupils' performance, teacher and school evaluations) as the school was under pressure to comply with the school improvement plan and state standards.

The pedagogical practices in the school originated in the subject departments. For instance, in the case of the mathematics intern, she worked closely with the team of teachers who jointly planned, interpreted the curriculum and decided how to tackle accountability challenges. Thus, whilst the intern relied on her mentor, the whole department served as a resource and as a source of ideas and materials. The pedagogical practice at least in mathematics was organised around curriculum maps and periodic and final assessments, which were seen as high-stakes in the school district. In the classrooms, the principles of inquiry-based learning figured prominently, yet compliance with accountability demands via pupil assessments seemed to dominate. Whilst the intern reported her desire to help pupils figure things out for themselves, an approach valued by the MSU programme, contextual practices overpowered her personal motives (what she said she wanted to do in the lesson) which were somewhat mismatched with external (driven by the school) motives.

This tension between the programme's philosophy, the school expressed ideals, and accountability demands made working in these schools a tall challenge for interns as knowledge had to be re-contextualised to fulfil all aims. Yet in practice, the key priority becomes that of the school: the re-contextualisation of knowledge to ensure that it fits the requirements of the curriculum standards and of the assessments, the results of which will in turn be used to evaluate the school.

Highfield High School

Highfield High School is the context for the case of the science and one of the English interns we will examine in the following chapters. At the time of the study, the school served close to 1,000 pupils in grades 9–12. The great majority of the pupils were white (92 per cent), 4 per cent were Hispanic, and the rest were other races with a larger percentage of males (53 per cent). About half of the student population was considered economically disadvantaged. Highfield High School in contrast with Midfield Middle School was highly ranked amongst schools in the nation. The criteria used for the rankings examined whether the school 'serve their entire students well, using performance on state proficiency tests as the benchmarks; and the degree to which schools prepare students for college level work' with the least advantaged students performing better than average for similar students in the state in mathematics and reading tests.

The school is very large, has many different tracks (or programmes) with one of those the 'traditional college prep programme' and serves a very diverse student population. This high degree of diversity is seen as a plus by the MSU programme as interns get to experience a wide range of learning abilities and styles. Whilst the school was reported as amongst the top in the nation, the statistics in the annual report made clear that much needed to be improved especially in the areas of mathematics and science. The wide range of programmes at Highfield High School represented important demands for the teachers and the interns. For instance, interns were often called to teach outside their specialist area typically in technology application laboratories or other similar.

Highfield High School characterises its pedagogical practices as framed by an inquiry approach to teaching and learning, and for both interns observed, their lessons seemed to be consistent with these principles. For instance, in the case of the science intern, the lesson was a fully applied one (a laboratory) so students and intern moved around the room and everyone seemed fully engaged in the laboratory activities.

As expected by the programme, the mentor teachers were very supportive of the interns. The English and science interns' pedagogical practice (e.g. lesson plan) occurred in close interaction and constant dialogue between mentor and intern. Interns maintained a high academic level throughout the lesson as did the students and managed to create a highly interactive classroom environment. In sum, in the case of the science intern, and also in the case of the English intern, the class seemed to be consistent not only with inquiry principles but also with the MSU inquiry-based approach to learning to teach.

The Michigan Near Fields schools

The Michigan Near Fields School District is located in central Michigan. In contrast with other school districts, the website for the Michigan Near Fields School District did not have a philosophy or a goal statement at the time of the study. Instead, the website included links to the 'District Report Card' and other links to school data and reports. The Annual Education Report highlighted the progress and the goals ahead for the school.

Near Field High School

Near Field High School is the context for the case of one of the English interns we will examine in later chapters. At the time of the study, the school served about 300 pupils in grades 9–12, most of them were white (87 per cent), 5 per cent were Hispanic, 3 per cent were African American and 2 per cent were each American Indian, multiracial and Asian. Fifty-three per cent were female, and about 33 per cent of the pupils were eligible for free or reduced school lunch. During the time of the study, Near Field High School was under a school improvement plan with a large achievement gap in 30 per cent of its student achievement scores. The school report mentioned that Near Field High School was affected by having a 'transient' student population and a significant gap between the high and low achievers. The school curriculum in all subjects were aligned with the latest standards at the grade levels, for instance, mathematics and language arts curriculum was aligned with the Common Core Curriculum Standards, the social studies curriculum was aligned with the content standards at the grade levels, and the science curriculum was aligned with the Next Generation Science Standards. The leadership team at the school held high expectations for the whole student body and was determined to close the achievement gap that affected the school.

As with the other schools, this school has a long history of collaboration with the MSU teacher education programme. Its teachers are highly qualified and often take in MSU interns.

Pedagogical practices at the school are considered as very supportive of MSU interns and the school is recognised as having strong departments including the English department. The process of learning to teach in this school by some teachers however, was seen as apprenticeship firmly based on practice in the school setting.

Summary

Whilst the MSU secondary teacher education programme is seen as one of the best in the nation and has a strong history and the solid support of the university, some of the basic tenets of the programme have been altered in great part because of the strong societal pressures that are affecting other programmes across the nation and also more globally. The need to develop strong indicators of accountability and the need to comply with accreditation pressures consumes a great deal of time and energy from programme coordinators and programme personnel. The need to comply with university level expectations that continue to apply a traditional model to evaluate faculty work, makes it difficult for faculty to even envision getting more involved with the schools unless it is to do research that can be published. Whilst the programme faculty have been able to reframe their work so that it can respond to the university's demands to demonstrate productivity in teaching, research and service, neither the college nor the university evaluation procedures reward productivity in school work (e.g. supervising interns in schools). Thus, the college and the programme will soon need to look into the future and look back to the programme's origins to decide whether to invest in developing a stronger partnership structure in order to benefit the preparation of future teachers, or comply with university and state demands widening once more the gap between universities and schools.

Conclusion

This discussion of the role of schools in our two settings demonstrates a number of common themes that exist in both of these national settings. There are clearly some important differences between the two settings as well as within each national context, including the use of different terminology and the deployment of different programme structures.

However, amongst the similarities, the most obvious are two particular tensions: (1) the tension for schools between responding to the changing policy environment for schooling at the same time as responding to the changing policies on teacher education; (2) the tension between the agendas for schools and universities in initial teacher education and thereby, for the respective staff in each site. These are overarching themes that can be readily detected in both accounts given above and which in this final section of Chapter 5 we wish to explore further in order to prepare for the close analysis of the learning experiences for beginning teachers in these various settings that will follow.

There is no doubt that schools in England and in the United States have experienced increasing pressures over recent years, including major and continuing reforms in curriculum and assessment practices and increasing accountability measures, such as Ofsted inspections and NCLB (now ESSA) respectively. Such initiatives have led to a very strong focus on pupil attainment, which has created anxiety in some school settings about the quality of teaching that pupils experience and has introduced a degree of risk into engaging with inexperienced teachers who are currently undergoing training. Nevertheless, many of the same schools are simultaneously concerned about being able to recruit and retain teachers of high quality and one of the most effective ways of doing this is to engage very directly in initial teacher education. Indeed, we have seen through the introduction of 'alternative routes' and 'school-based' routes how schools in both countries may seek to attract people into their schools even before they are qualified. Such an approach of course does tend to make the learning experience of the trainee teacher highly context-specific; they are effectively being trained to work in that particular school, with its own demographics and practices, rather than being prepared to enter a national (or even state) cadre of teachers.

On the second tension, it may well be widely acknowledged that some of the highest quality teacher education programmes are based on very significant partnerships between schools and universities, but that does not necessarily mean that such partnerships are easily established or maintained. In both settings, we can see for example, how university faculty are under considerable pressure to undertake high-quality research, which may distract them from simultaneous engagement in high-quality teacher education. Or put the other way around, university faculty who are highly committed to working with schools on teacher education, may find themselves ostracised for their reduced or poorer quality research outputs. For school staff wanting to engage in teacher education, the rewards may or may not be very tangible. In some settings, the school receives some financial resource in acknowledgement of their contribution, but this may not benefit the individual teachers who are doing the work. However, it may be that those teachers do recognise the significant opportunities for their own professional development that may result from their engagement in teacher education.

Some other common concerns and issues that arise, especially for the secondary school sector, include the significance of subject departments in the schools. Given that each teacher in training is in the process of becoming a specialist in teaching one or more subjects within the curriculum, to what extent can the schools be confident that the approaches of the teacher education programme incorporate recognition of the particularities of learning and teaching in that subject? On the Teach First programme in England for example, the external subject input offered to participants has recently been significantly reduced. Does this mean that the schools will have to compensate in some way for this by increasing their focus on this element? Most likely not in the way teacher education programmes may approach it and instead participants may be limited to learn solely from curriculum materials.

Common to the challenges that schools face in both settings, we may identify two further themes that emerge strongly from the respective accounts – complexity and communication. Programmes of initial teacher education tend to be inherently complex. As we have established in Chapter 1, there are many aspects of knowledge and skills for the student teacher to acquire and develop. Whatever the balance in the provision of these aspects between the school and the university sites, it is necessary to ensure that the full range of learning experiences required is being made available to them. Effective communication is similarly essential if the student teacher is to have a coherent and positive learning experience. This does not only imply effective communication with the student teacher herself or himself. It also means that within the school there must be clear understandings and channels of communication about the programme the student teacher is undergoing and the roles and responsibilities of those school staff who play a part. But then in the majority of cases (all of those in this study) where universities also have a role, whether it be major or minor, then the communications between the school and the university will be critical for successful provision of the programme of learning. This is the essence of 'partnership', the concept that underlies so much that happens within initial teacher education, but which is often not understood fully or has become increasingly difficult to implement. Indeed, it is only when complexity and communication are taken together that the full significance of partnership is likely to be recognised and a positive relationship achieved.

These then are some of the considerations to be borne in mind as we start to present the lived experiences of a number of teachers in training and the experiences of those working with them in Part II of this book.

Notes

1 www.teaching-certification.com/alternative-teaching-certification.html (Teaching Certification, 2017).
2 The names of the schools have been changed to maintain confidentiality.
3 www.corestandards.org/ (Common Core State Standards Initiative, 2017).
4 The State of Michigan has identified some schools with the status of Reward, Focus or Priority. A Reward school is one that is outperforming other schools in achievement, growth, or is performing better than other schools with a similar pupil population (MDE, 2017a). A Focus school is one that has a large achievement gap in 30 per cent of its student achievement scores (MDE, 2017b). A Priority school is one whose achievement and growth is in the lowest 5 per cent of all schools in the state (MDE, 2017c).

References

Allen, R., Belfield, C., Greaves, E., Sharp, C. & Walker, M. (2016). *The longer-term costs and benefits of different initial teacher training routes*. London: Institute for Fiscal Studies.

Anagnostopoulos, D. & Rutledge, S. A. (2007). Making sense of school sanctioning policies in urban high schools: Charting the depth and drift of school and classroom change. *Teachers College Record, 109*(5), 1261–1302.

Ball, S. J. (2003). The teacher's soul and the terrors of performativity. *Journal of Education Policy, 18*(2), 215–228.

Barshay, J. (2014). *Number of U.S. charter schools up 7 percent, report shows. The Hechinger Report*. Retrieved February 17, 2017 from www.usnews.com/news/articles/2014/11/03/number-of-us-charter-schools-up-7-percent-report-shows.

Brown, T, Rowley, H. & Smith, K. (2016). *The beginnings of school-led teacher training: New challenges for university teacher education*. School Direct Research Project Final Report: Manchester Metropolitan University. Retrieved from www.esri.mmu.ac.uk/resgroups/schooldirect.pdf.

Carter, A. (2015). *Carter review of initial teacher training (ITT)*. London: DfE. Retrieved from: www.gov.uk/government/publications/carter-review-of-initial-teacher-training.

Common Core State Standards Initiative. (2017). *Preparing America's students for success*. Retrieved from www.corestandards.org/.

Department for Education (DfE). (1992). *Initial teacher training (secondary phase), Circular 9/92*. London: DfE.

Department for Education (DfE). (1993). *The initial training of primary school teachers: New criteria for course approval, Circular 14/93*. London: DfE.

Department for Education (DfE). (2010). *The importance of teaching: The Schools White Paper 2010*. London: HMSO.

Department for Education (DfE). (2011). *Training our next generation of outstanding teachers: An improvement strategy for discussion*. London: DfE. Retrieved from www.gov.uk/government/publications/training-our-next-generation-of-outstanding-teachers-an-improvement-strategy-for-discussion.

Department for Education (DfE). (2014). *Teaching schools: A guide for potential applicants*. Retrieved from www.gov.uk/guidance/teaching-schools-a-guide-for-potential-applicants.

Department of Education (DfE). (2017). *Schools, pupils and their characteristics, January 2017*. Retrieved from www.gov.uk/government/statistics/schools-pupils-and-their-characteristics-january-2017.

Figlio, D. & Loeb, S. (2011). School accountability. *Handbook of the Economics of Education, 3*(8), 383–417.

Furlong, J., Barton, L., Miles, S., Whiting, C. & Whitty, G. (2000). *Teacher education in transition: Reforming professionalism*. Buckingham: Open University Press.

Grossman, P., Hammerness, K. & McDonald, M. (2009). Redefining teaching, re-imagining teacher education. *Teachers and Teaching, 15*(2), 273–289.

Holmes Group. (1986). *Tomorrow's teachers: A report of the Holmes Group*. East Lansing, MI: Holmes Group. Retrieved from https://eric.ed.gov/?id=ED270454.

Holmes Group. (1990). *Tomorrow's schools: Principles for the design of Professional Development Schools*. East Lansing, MI: Holmes Group. Retrieved from https://eric.ed.gov/?id=ED328533.

Holmes Group. (1995). *Tomorrow's schools of education: A report of the Holmes Group*. East Lansing, MI: Holmes Group. Retrieved from https://eric.ed.gov/?id=ED399220.

Kena, G., Hussar W., McFarland, J., de Brey, C., Musu-Gillette, L., Wang, X., Zhang, J., Rathbun, A., Wilkinson-Flicker, S., Diliberti M., Barmer, A., Bullock Mann, F. & Dunlop Velez, E. (2016). *The condition of education 2016 (NCES 2016–144)*. Washington, DC: U.S. Department of Education, National Center for Education Statistics. Retrieved February 17, 2017 from http://nces.ed.gov/pubsearch.

Leat, D. (2014). Curriculum regulation in England – giving with one hand and taking away with the other. *European Journal of Curriculum Studies, 1*(1), 69–74.

McIntyre, D., Hagger, H. & Burn, K. (1994). *The management of student teachers' learning: A guide for professional tutors in secondary schools*. London: Kogan Page.

Michigan Department of Education (MDE). (2017a). *Reward schools*. Retrieved from www.michigan.gov/mde/0,4615,7-140-22709_62255---,00.html.

Michigan Department of Education (MDE). (2017b). *Focus schools*. Retrieved from www.michigan.gov/mde/0,4615,7-140-22709_62253---,00.html.

Michigan Department of Education (MDE). (2017c). *Priority schools*. Retrieved from www.michigan.gov/sro/.

Mutton, T. & Butcher, J. (2008). We will take them from anywhere: Schools working within multiple initial teacher training partnerships. *Journal of Education for Teaching, 34*(1), 45–62.

New York State Education Department. (2006/2009). *Federal education policy and the states, 1945–2009: A brief synopsis*. Retrieved from www.archives.nysed.gov/common/archives/files/ed_background_overview_essay.pdf.

Office for Standards in Education, Children's Services and Skills (Ofsted). (2011). *Teach First. Initial teacher training inspection report*. Retrieved from: https://reports.ofsted. gov.uk/inspection-reports/find-inspection-report/provider/ELS/70270.

Roch, C. H. & Sai, N. (2016). Charter school teacher job satisfaction. *Educational Policy*. Retrieve from http://journals.sagepub.com/doi/abs/10.1177/0895904815625281.

Secondary Teacher Preparation Team. (2015). *Internship guide*. East Lansing, MI: College of Education, Michigan State University.

Tatto, M. T. (2009). *Reforming teaching globally*. Charlotte, NC, USA: Information Age Publishers. (Reprinted from *Reforming teaching globally*, M. T. Tatto, 2007, Oxford, UK: Symposium Books).

Tatto, M. T., Savage, C., Liao, W., Marshall, S., Goldblatt, P. & Contreras, M. L. (2016). The emergence of high-stakes accountability policies in teacher preparation: An examination of the U.S. Department of Education's proposed regulations. *Education Policy Analysis Archives, 24*(25). doi: http://dx.doi.org/10.14507/epaa.24.2322.

Teaching Certification. (2017). *Alternative Teaching Certification*. Retrieved from www. teaching-certification.com/alternative-teaching-certification.html.

U.S. Congress. (2002). *No Child Left Behind Act of 2001*. Public Law 107–110. Washington, DC: Government Printing Office.

U.S. Department of Education (USDOE). (1983). *A nation at risk: The imperative for educational reform. A report to the Nation and the Secretary of Education*. Washington, DC: National Commission on Excellence in Education. Retrieved from http://files. eric.ed.gov/fulltext/ED226006.pdf.

U.S. Department of Education (USDOE). (2015). *Highly qualified teachers enrolled in programs providing alternative routes to teacher certification or licensure*. Washington, DC: USDOE, Office of Planning, Evaluation and Policy Development, Policy and Program Studies Service. Retrieved from www2.ed.gov/rschstat/eval/teaching/hqt-teacher-certification/report.pdf.

Wigdortz, B. (2012). *Success against the odds: Five lessons in how to achieve the impossible; the story of Teach First*. London: Short Books Limited.

Wilkins, C. (2015). Education reform in England: Quality and equity in the performative school. *International Journal of Inclusive Education, 19*(11), 1143–1160.

Part II

Case studies of learning to teach in specific contexts

6   Selection of the case studies

In this section of the book, we report in detail on the experience of a number of individuals learning to teach in the context of the different teacher education programmes and specific institutions described in Part I. As explained in Chapter 2, our analyses of their teaching practices combine a sociocultural focus on the complex social situations of development of student teachers with a sociological concern about institutional pedagogic practices and discourse.

Summary of the research design and principles for selection

Whilst significant recent developments in teacher education policy operating at national level (in the societal plane, as described in Chapter 3) exercise a considerable influence on the possible structures, content and assessment criteria of the different routes open to beginning teachers in both England and the United States, each individual's experience is also profoundly affected by the particular policies adopted by the specific institutions within which they have chosen to train. At this meso level, within a partnership programme of any kind, beginning teachers' social situations of development are obviously shaped in part by the assumptions and practices of *both* partners – the school and the higher education institution (HEI) – whilst in the context of the Teach First programme, the charitable organisation itself acts as a third partner and potentially a powerful source of influence. The predominant views and official practices of each of these institutions have been outlined in Chapters 4 and 5, but it is only in the experience of individual beginning teachers that they are actually brought together and mediated by particular teacher educators (faculty members and school-based mentors). As this happens, the guiding principles and habitual ways of thinking within each institution also interact with the final source of influence in shaping each individual's social situation of development: their own personal histories, which underpin their assumptions, both about the processes of learning and teaching a particular subject and about the process of learning to teach. It is therefore, only in the experience of individuals that we can effectively explore the interplay between the micro, the meso and the macro levels, and so come to understand the range of ways in which learning to teach is currently experienced in England and the United States.

Obviously, this acknowledgement of the complex interplay of different factors operating within and between levels means that we cannot claim to offer a definitive account of the nature of all beginning teachers' experiences. As explained in Chapters 4 and 5 we have chosen to focus on just one university in each context, each with a long-standing commitment to initial teacher education and on a small number of their partner schools, some of which have also embraced newly-developed 'school-led' forms of partnership, such as School Direct. Because neither of these universities was involved in any of the most radical employment-based routes into teaching, we also chose to focus on one of the more well-known 'alternative routes' by selecting a school in England that had embraced the Teach First programme in its earliest years and remained fully committed to it.

As we were concerned with initial teacher education at secondary level, we were also alert to the fact that important ideas about the processes of teaching and learning were likely to be shaped by individual and institutional assumptions about the nature of particular subject disciplines and the implications of those views for pupils' learning. To make it possible to compare these assumptions and their implications for the re-contextualisation of subject knowledge and the development of subject-specific pedagogy, we therefore, chose to focus on five different subjects within the secondary curriculum: maths and science, along with English, history (taught within social studies in the United States) and Modern Foreign Languages.

In selecting a sample of beginning teachers that would encompass those five subjects, and allow us examine the complex realities for each individual whilst adequately reflecting the diversity of practice represented by new routes into teaching and new forms of partnership, we therefore, sought to ensure that we included at least four beginning teachers in each subject, with at least four of the total associated with each of the different institutions (schools and universities) involved. This resulted in a total of 26 beginning teachers, 18 of them in England, following three different programmes (a 'traditional' Postgraduate Certificate in Education [PGCE] course, a school-led 'School Direct' route and Teach First), associated with three different universities and undertaking placements in three different schools. The sample from the United States included eight beginning teachers, all completing the final 'internship' year of the Michigan State University (MSU) teacher education programme but undertaking their placement in four different schools. Whilst we were able to ensure that the sample in each country included schools with differing proportions of pupils from economically disadvantaged backgrounds, the range of demands meant that it was impossible to accommodate all the variables of potential importance. The sample within the United States is confined to rural schools although each of the three English schools operated in a different kind of geographical context – inner city, urban and rural.

Selection of cases to represent different categories within the analytical typology

In selecting a number of cases from amongst these 26 to present in sufficient detail to explore the ways in which individuals' social situations of development were shaped by the different practices, assumptions and histories of the school/ HEI partnership in which they were embedded, our choices were determined by the typology that emerged from the process of analysis explained in Chapter 2.

In brief, the first stage of that analysis involved using the full range of data that we had collected for each individual in the context of a particular programme operated by specific partners to construct a detailed table that mapped their social situations of development according to the planes of analysis set out in Table 2.2. This process allowed us first, to map out at the societal and institutional levels, the cultural and historical demands and motives for engagement and as well the pedagogic practices and discourse within which all the individual transitions took place. We then used our lesson observations and all the associated interview and questionnaire data to create a summary account of the ways in which each student teacher, in that specific instance, re-contextualised subject knowledge for their pupils, through the processes of planning, teaching and evaluation and of the ways in which those processes were related to the particular context in which they were placed; to their declared beliefs about teaching and learning and to previous teaching or learning experiences that they cited as influential. By bringing all this data together in a single table we were able to examine the extent of alignment between each of the cells, vertically and horizontally, identifying the possible tensions or contradictions that arose for each individual in light of the assumptions and experiences that they brought with them into the process of learning to teach within a specific and unique, culturally and historically determined, institutional context.

Informed by this focus on the extent of alignment within and between the different planes, our second stage of analysis involved identifying and examining the intensity or availability of particular features within each individual's social situation of development. The first of these were 'opportunities for development (OfD)'; that is the potential for development specifically created by the experience of tension or contradiction – a sense of 'crisis' brought about by a lack of alignment, for example, between the ideas and practices espoused by the school and the HEI for example, or between those espoused by the individual and those endorsed in their internship school. The second were 'opportunities for change (OfC)' – the individual's recognition of the limitations of the situation in which they currently found themselves and their capacity to identify a new way of being a teacher. This capacity depends on the 'tools' that they each perceived as being available to them – either amongst their own resources or from within the institutions that made up the particular partnership.

Reading across and up and down the analytical tables that we had created, we characterised the experience of each individual in relation to five specific features:

1   The extent of the OfD created by a sense of 'crisis'.
2   The extent of the OfC, which depended on the mediational tools to which they had access from their HEI, their school or amongst their own resources.
3   The individual's disposition to recognise and respond to both the OfD and the OfC.
4   The relative prominence of their particular subject discipline within their sense of the OfD or OfC.
5   The extent of the alignment (and thus, of the scope for tensions or contradictions) between the individual, the HEI and the school.

After creating a descriptive table that mapped the extent or intensity of each of these features for each individual participant, a further stage of inductive analysis resulted in the identification of five categories that encapsulated most of the different kinds of experience that we encountered amongst the 26 teachers who took part in the study:

a   Vertical and horizontal alignment with few apparent tensions or contradictions/tensions.
b   Vertical alignment across institutions with a high level of tension or contradiction evident at the individual level that was successfully resolved through effective mentoring.
c   Unacknowledged contradictions between the two institutions (the school and HEI), which resulted in low levels of support for the individual.
d   Vertical alignment between the individual and the school culture and practices, but not with the HEI.
e   Vertical alignment between the individual and the HEI, but not with the school.

Each of these categories is outlined in a little more depth in Chapter 2, and is described fully in the chapters that follow (Chapters 7 to 11) through a detailed case study of one particular student teacher and more limited description of two or three others that fall within the same category. The process of choosing which cases to include in the presentation of our sample was thus, determined by the need to select one student teacher whose experience most clearly typifies this characterisation and a small number of others that would serve to illuminate particular dimensions and to illustrate the variety found within it. It is this process of selection, informed by the final typology constructed through successive stages of analysis that resulted in the final list of research participants whose details are set out in Tables 2.3, 2.4 and 2.5. The final sample of 17 thus, includes at least three teachers of each subject and at least one from each of the six schools involved in the study (three in England and three in the United States). Whilst we are not claiming that theirs are the only patterns of development to be found in the experience of beginning teachers in diverse and rapidly changing partnerships, this typology serves both to represent the range of experiences that we encountered at this particular moment of change and to reveal the sheer complexity of the processes that shape the experiences of diverse individuals learning to teach in specific institutional contexts, each responding in different ways to successive changes in national policy.

Following the five case studies, the final chapter within this section will examine the significance of these different typologies and raise important questions for the future of initial teacher education about the way in which they are distributed across the different routes into teaching and different kinds of institutional partnership in England and the United States.

7 Cases of alignment at the meso level of institutions (schools and HEIs) and at the micro level of the individual

Doug's experience of close alignment and effective mediation

The first typology that we have chosen to present using the nested structure that combines Hedegaard's (2012) sociocultural approach to the social situation of development with a sociological concern to understand institutional practices and the particular forms of pedagogic discourse operating within them (Bernstein, 1990) is that of essential alignment at the macro and meso levels, with few apparent contradictions, either horizontally or vertically. This kind of alignment was relatively rare, although we found examples of it in England and in the United States and on both traditional and alternative routes into teaching. It was most obviously exemplified in the experience of Doug, a beginning teacher of history in England undertaking a Postgraduate Certificate in Education (PGCE) within the Oxford Internship Scheme (OIS), with his main placement at Riverside Academy.

Doug was observed at the end of January teaching an introductory lesson to a Year 10 class (of 14- to 15-year-olds) embarking on a new topic, a depth study of Weimar and Nazi Germany 1919–1945 that would feature as one of the main subjects in the General Certificate of Secondary Education (GCSE) for history that the pupils would take the following year. Doug's practice throughout the lesson was strongly focused on encouraging the pupils to take responsibility for their own learning. Before starting the new topic, pupils were asked to respond in writing to individual feedback on a previous task, each answering a specific question intended to develop and strengthen their initial argument. The next phase of the lesson was focused on eliciting the pupils' prior knowledge of Nazi Germany to engage their interest and guide Doug's subsequent planning, and he harnessed a degree of competition to encourage them to work quickly in pairs on the task. The main activity was built around the use of photographs as visual sources, used both to establish initial hypotheses and provoke new questions. The task involved a carefully modelled sequence of steps from identifying specific features within each image to drawing inferences from them by relating what pupils could see to their existing knowledge.

Whilst the lesson was strongly collaborative, there was relatively little whole class discussion. Most conversation took place in pairs and Doug interacted with all the different pairs at some point as they were working. Whilst he shared some information as he did so, he presented little other information directly to the class as a whole. The lesson thus, reflected strong social-constructivist principles with the emphasis being on pupils' articulation and use of their existing knowledge in relation to new stimulus material that they were encouraged to subject to detailed observation. However, whilst the lesson gave considerable responsibility to the pupils, its main task also closely reflected the format of one particular type of examination question, effectively giving them direct practice of a task that they would be required to carry out in a very similar way (albeit with more knowledge) in their GCSE History.

Opportunities for development (OfD)

There was virtually no sense of 'crisis' – in the Vygotskian sense of contradictions between the individual's own psychological development and the demands of the learning situation – either as Doug taught the lesson or in his subsequent reflections upon it. The lesson essentially proceeded smoothly and effectively and several pupils expressed their appreciation by thanking Doug at the end. In structuring the debriefing afterwards, Doug's school-based subject mentor (or mentor) encouraged him to identify the positive features of the lesson and of pupils' progress within it before moving on to any aspects for development. Whilst Doug expressed some concerns, suggesting that he ought perhaps to have managed the pupils' behaviour more effectively, his mentor consistently refocused his attention on the learning objectives that he had planned, asking him to identify how the strategies that he had employed and the way in which he had responded to pupils had served to support the achievement of those objectives. The main suggestions for further development that the mentor did put forward were essentially about building on strengths of the lesson: a proposal that Doug could afford to devote more time to pupils' reflection on the quality of their work, and that given the aptitude of this particular class for productive discussion, he might have extended those elements further. Thus, whilst there was clear evidence that Doug was learning from his experience and from the supported reflection on it – a lack of crisis here certainly did not reflect either complacency or stagnation – this learning was rooted in careful reflection and refinement of what had essentially proved to be very productive.

Opportunities for change (OfC)

OfC provided by mediational tools from the HEI

At the institutional level, it was clear from the pre- and post-lesson questionnaires and from comparison of Doug's approaches with principles embedded in the history curriculum programme at the university, that the teaching and learning strategies he employed were at least strongly supported, if not directly inspired, by the pedagogic discourse and practices promoted at the university.

Two of his early decisions – to give the pupils a significant period of time in which to respond to the feedback on their previous written work and to elicit their existing knowledge as the starting point for the new topic on which they were embarking – were rooted in a commitment to formative assessment that explicitly underpinned one of the core themes of the history curriculum programme, the evaluation of learning. Both strategies were specifically promoted in set readings, including texts by Black and Wiliam and their colleagues (1998; Black, Harrison, Lee, Marshall & Wiliam, 2003), that were introduced in Week 9 of the history curriculum programme.

More broadly, Doug's commitment in these activities and in the central lesson task to social-constructivist theories of learning – for example, by developing inferences from specific features of the visual sources that would serve as hypotheses to test – was also in line with, even if not explicitly driven by the promotion of such a conception of learning to teach within the professional studies element of the programme delivered in the university. Doug's use of enquiry-based planning, driven in this case by engagement with primary sources, in which pupils were expected to answer a genuine historical question, rather than merely master tightly defined subject content knowledge was also entirely consistent with the endorsement of historical enquiry as the starting point of the history curriculum programme theme 'planning for learning'.

Whilst the nature of the history curriculum had recently provoked intense debate and public controversy at national level – with the draft proposals for a new National Curriculum advanced by the Department of Education opposed by 96 per cent of teachers (Burn & Harris, 2013) – the university-based history tutors had formally rejected the Secretary of State's (Michael Gove's) traditional view of teaching history as 'children sitting in rows, learning the kings and queens of England' (Sylvester & Thomson, 2010). They took the view that learning history involves the development not merely of substantive knowledge but of conceptual understanding (of the second-order concepts that shape the nature of the discipline) and of the processes of enquiry and communication by which such knowledge is generated and shared. In bringing these elements together, the university programme deliberately promoted an enquiry-based approach (Riley, 2000) to planning the structure of schemes of work and individual lessons, in which pupils are seeking to answer a genuine historical question, framed in relation to one or more of the key second-order concepts (such as cause and consequence, continuity and change or similarity and difference) that underpin the discipline.

As noted in Chapter 4, this approach, whilst widely endorsed by teacher educators (Byrom & Riley, 2007; Counsell, 2011; Husbands, Kitson & Steward 2011; Burn, McCrory & Fordham, 2013), and strongly reflected in teachers' published discourse (see, for example, Woodcock, 2005; Foster, 2013), was far from universally accepted. Indeed, the university tutors acknowledged within their subject programme that some schools regarded an enquiry-based approach as unworkable and stressed that the beginning teachers would need to test out and develop their own views of it, in part through the series of school-based tasks planned within the joint curriculum programme. Nonetheless, the curricular resources and set readings that the tutors provided both exemplified and endorsed the approach. Doug had therefore, been equipped by his university-based history education programme with arguments in favour of an enquiry-based approach and had seen sufficient examples of its use (within teachers' own published accounts of individual lesson plans and medium-term schemes of work, issued as core readings) to be able to develop an appropriate activity for the start of this particular enquiry, using a collection of photographs that the head of history and another colleague within the department (a newly qualified teacher) had both recommended to him.

OfC provided by mediational tools within the school

As his reference to these recommendations in the pre-lesson interview suggests, Doug felt very well supported by the history department in his placement school. He was offered direct advice and specific suggestions for practice that reflected the principles that the teachers espoused. The principle of allowing pupils to respond to feedback on marked work was a standard routine (to which the pupils settled very quickly). The plan that he followed for the remainder of the lesson was based around an existing pack of resources that he had been encouraged to adapt as he thought appropriate. Doug also referred specifically to ideas gleaned from an in-service professional development session about formative assessment that he had attended with other staff, which also seemed to have influenced his commitment to determining pupils' prior knowledge; to using questioning to elicit their developing understanding (particularly 'hands-down' questioning, so that all pupils appreciated that they might be expected to contribute); and to making formative use of a previous forms of summative assessment (responding to the pupils' homework exercise with specific questions intended to further develop their arguments or explanations).

As noted above, one of the key suggestions for development made by Doug's mentor was that he should allocate more time to pupils' reflection on the quality of their work, suggesting a strong departmental commitment to the development of metacognitive skills and capacity for self-regulation. This was consistent with the wider school's focus on intervention strategies identified through the Education Endowment Foundation/Sutton Trust toolkit (Higgins et al., 2014) in raising the achievement of more disadvantaged pupils. Whilst Doug tended to describe the class as 'very strong', his mentor advised him on several occasions to think of those who would struggle to understand the next step rather than those who would readily grasp it for themselves.

When Doug raised the question of whether he had managed the pupils' behaviour appropriately, his mentor consistently reframed the discussion of his management strategies and responses to pupils in the context of his objectives for their learning and how this had been structured and supported. Thus, at no point in the debriefing did behaviour management become detached from pedagogical considerations.

OfC provided by the individual's mediational tools

At the level of individual transitions, Doug's orientation towards his own professional learning meant that he was alert to all the opportunities available to him in the different contexts of school and university. Even before starting the course, in completing a summary of his previous experiences that would be used to introduce himself to his mentor in advance of their first meeting, he had claimed that his own experience of learning (at school and university level) had 'revealed to him the importance of understanding the context of what it was he was learning and of being able to make connections between new and existing knowledge'. He had no qualms about seeking advice from different sources and in subjecting his own practice to detailed critique. The fact that he had adapted his central lesson activity from an existing pack of resources, discussed with both the head of department and a newly qualified teacher, and that he was drawing on insights from a recent staff development session as well as echoing the structure and requirements of a common exam-style question, was perhaps only to be expected from a beginning teacher who had declared before starting the course that he was both fully aware of the attention to detail that learning to teach demanded and that he loved the process of learning itself:

> I love learning; more accurately I love the process of learning, of attempting to discover the combination of teaching techniques and environment, which can help pupils achieve to their full potential. This is the enthusiasm, attention to detail and attitude towards my own development, which I would bring to my placement school.

The individual's disposition to recognise the scope for development and change

As this quotation makes clear, the nature of Doug's orientation towards his own professional learning meant that he was alert to all the opportunities available to him in the different contexts of school and university. He paid attention to detail in seeking to understand what was happening in his lessons and what was being proposed by his mentor, and was always ready to ask critical questions about how effective his practice was.

Although Doug did not experience any kind of tension or sense of 'crisis' that motivated his learning, he was alert to ways in which aspects of the lesson were not as productive as he had hoped and raised questions with his mentor about the appropriateness both of his planning and of his interactions with pupils, particularly in restoring a productive working atmosphere. His mentor's insistence that Doug re-focus first on the positive aspects of the lesson, before moving to look at possible refinements, meant that he was then in a secure position to reflect on how the advice and strategies that he was being offered could enable him to achieve his ambitions.

His willingness to learn was evident at all stages of the planning, teaching and evaluation cycle. He recognised the freedoms that he had been given in the design of the lesson, but whilst he took advantage of them to tweak resources in ways that he thought would be effective, he also sought advice in so doing from other teachers. He made sure that the lesson would conclude in a fairly routine manner, with an exam-style question that demonstrated to pupils the direct value of what they had learned in relation to the specific demands of GCSE, but he also sought to ensure that the design of the lesson drew extensively on specific insights from the recent staff development session.

The relative prominence of the subject (or subject pedagogy) in consideration of the need for development or change

Doug had a strong sense of identity as a historian and shared the views of both his university tutors and his school-based mentor that there are important subject-specific dimensions of effective teaching. Although there was a point in the lesson debriefing when he began to focus specifically on the management of pupil behaviour, Doug's mentor refused to allow him to focus on this element in isolation. He directed Doug's reflection back to the question of how well the pupils understood and engaged with the tasks that he had planned for them, and thus, how effectively they had achieved the lesson objectives. The issues that emerged from their further discussion as points for development essentially focused on passing more responsibility to the pupils for the development of their historical thinking and explanation in response to the directed advice and prompts that Doug had given them.

Similarly, although there were certain core principles underpinning Doug's lesson that were being consistently promoted across Riverside Academy (such as the importance of giving pupils time to respond to feedback and eliciting pupils' current knowledge and conceptions of a particular topic before introducing new material), the lesson was essentially driven by a specific focus on the kinds of historical thinking that are required in using sources effectively as evidence – the process of drawing inferences from sources and of interpreting them effectively in the light of wider contextual knowledge. Doug focused the pupils' attention on the distinction between observation of specific features in the photographs and the inferences drawn from them and alerted pupils to the fact that on this particular occasion their contextual knowledge was relatively limited, explaining that they would be acquiring further knowledge over the course of the next few lessons to enrich this process and amend or strengthen the conclusions that they could draw.

The extent of alignment (and thus, of the scope for tensions or contradictions) between the individual, HEI and school

As we have demonstrated in this account of his planning, teaching and lesson evaluation, Doug experienced a high degree of consistency across all elements of the PGCE programme. This was true both in relation to the ideas about effective teaching promoted within the school and the university (social-constructivism, metacognition and formative assessment) and in relation to the way in which his own conceptions of the process of learning to teach and of himself as a learner corresponded with those promoted by the structure of the course: an encouragement for beginning teachers to draw on a wide variety of sources, to embrace the notion of continuous professional learning and to retain strong links with their particular subject community.

The extent of alignment between the individual and the school

Doug's ambitions for his pupils' learning were clearly in line with regular practices promoted in the school and endorsed by his mentor. He followed the standard policy of giving pupils time to respond to feedback on their work before introducing new material. He recognised the value of establishing pupils' existing knowledge rather than simply embarking on the topic and assuming that it was new to them and he made extensive use of paired discussion as a strategy for allowing pupils to articulate and test out their ideas. In drawing on an existing set of resources created within the school, he sought specific advice from the head of department and another teacher who had made use of them, before deciding exactly how he would adapt the activity for his own lesson.

The extent of alignment between the individual and the HEI

Doug's own conception of learning history was entirely consistent with the university tutors' promotion of an enquiry-based structure, in which hypotheses about cause and consequence, change and continuity, similarity and difference, for example, can be consistently developed and refined in the light of further knowledge. He read voraciously and whilst he fully recognised his obligation to prepare pupils effectively for the specific demands of the public examinations that they would sit, he ultimately looked, as his tutors urged him to do, to the works of historians rather than simply to the examination criteria for his models of successful practice.

Moreover, Doug's declared commitment to his own learning – as a historian and as a teacher – closely mirrored the explicit principles of the OIS that pre-service teachers should be encouraged to see themselves as learners (rather than merely demonstrating their competence as classroom practitioners) and that they should expect to learn from a wide variety of sources.

The extent of alignment between the school and the HEI

As Doug's experience has revealed, there was actually a very strong consensus between the university history programme and the principles espoused and promoted within the Riverside Academy history department, which owed a great deal to the longevity of the partnership, sustained at the subject level by regular recruitment into the department of teachers trained within the joint programme. Although Doug's mentor had trained elsewhere, the head of the history department and two other colleagues (at the early stages of their career) were graduates of the partnership programme. Moreover, the head of history had been seconded 1 day a week for the past 2 years to work as an associate tutor within the university. Thus, whilst the partnership programme explicitly stated that consensus was not necessarily to be expected between ideas presented as suggestions for practice by the university (which are inevitably de-contextualised and derived from research-based knowledge) and those proffered by experienced teachers working with specific pupils in particular contexts (McIntyre, 1990), this particularly school-university pairing had actually resulted in a very high level of consistency.

Although the school had in recent years played a leading role in the development of the new School-Centred Initial Teacher Training (SCITT) programme, this had been driven at least initially by a concern to recruit teachers in subjects other than those offered by the OIS. Although the SCITT subsequently started to recruit teachers in all subjects, the history department actually refused to accept School Direct trainees, preferring instead to continue working on the established PGCE programme – a departmental commitment to the partnership that helps to explain why ideas promoted within the university were considered so seriously by the school-based mentor and other colleagues and that ensured that there was always scope for Doug to engage in all the suggested school-based tasks.

Other examples of alignment at the meso and micro levels

Although Doug's case was highly unusual for the closeness of the alignment that he experienced between the school and university partner, particularly in relation to the teaching of history, but also in terms of general pedagogical principles, we found two other examples of such consistency, one within the same programme and another an English intern at Michigan State University (MSU).

Joseph: vertical and horizontal alignment overcoming contextual constraints

Joseph, another student teacher undertaking a PGCE in History within the OIS enjoyed similar levels of consistency between his own conceptions of history teaching and the kinds of pedagogy promoted both by the university and by his mentor. In his case, this consistency played a vital role in overcoming powerful contextual constraints that had given rise to a developmental crisis.

Joseph's Year 8 lesson (for 12- to 13-year-olds) was directed towards pupils reaching their own substantiated judgement in response to the question 'Was Africa *really* a 'dark continent' before the Europeans arrived?'[1] Joseph first invited pupils to articulate their own understanding of the quotation then illustrated the idea of stereotyping to help pupils formulate a vision of what the claim meant, before providing them with information with which to challenge it. The main activity was intended to build from shared reading of an information sheet, through coding and organising relevant material from it, to the process of decision-making and justification of their claims. As in Doug's case, the plan reflected a commitment to establishing pupils' own assumptions as the starting point for engaging with the enquiry and the eventual definition of stereotyping was negotiated and refined in response to pupils' suggestions.

It was clear throughout, however, that Joseph was struggling to achieve the kind of sustained attention and on-task behaviour that he sought. He had revised the seating plan following poor behaviour on previous occasions and faced initial complaints and resistance before establishing compliance. Whilst he could generally secure quiet, he frequently had to pause to issue reminders, formal warnings and sanctions to particular individuals. As a result, the latter stages of the lesson were rushed and Joseph realised that the modelling had been inadequate for some pupils who had struggled to develop a coherent, structured summary on which to base their judgement. More seriously, one or two pupils had been entirely unable to use the ideas generated in their initial discussion of possible meanings of 'dark' to establish clearly what the original claim meant.

In some respects, the lesson reflected real tensions between social-constructivist views that relied on pupils' engaged interaction and the need to constrain pupil interactions to make clear explanation and demonstration possible. But the conflict was not between the perspectives of school and university, which he perceived at the institutional level as presenting similarly challenging models of practice. Whilst each provided important advice and support – mediating tools in response to the crisis – Joseph was in large part sustained by the tools that he brought with him from his previous experiences of teaching.

In school, Joseph was able to draw on advice from his mentor about how to manage the pupils' behaviour. All the strategies he used had been previously recommended to him (and had also been captured in the subject tutor's summary of their most recent three-way review meeting): a revised seating plan; the principle of choices and consequences reinforced through the graded system of warnings/sanctions; and the retention of certain pupils at the end of the lesson. But the mentor's advice had been equally focused on the importance of securing a clear line of development from the lesson's central question and learning objective to the sequence of activities and on ensuring that the conceptual focus at the heart of the lesson – in this case, similarity and difference – drove the enquiry.

These same concerns were reiterated in the interview with the university-based curriculum tutor. Along with their shared commitment to enquiry-based planning and to the inter-relationship between substantive knowledge and second-order concepts, both mentor and tutor also endorsed Joseph's somewhat erratic but increasingly strong commitment to more inclusive questioning as a key feature of formative assessment (again reflecting emphases promoted in the work of Black and Wiliam 1998; Black et al., 2003).

Despite this coherence at the horizontal level (again owed to the fact that the mentor had also trained within the same partnership), Joseph's social situation of development presented him with significant challenges, essentially because the support structures offered by mentor and subject tutor working in partnership could not be sustained across the history department. The existence at Groveside Academy of three entirely separate sites, each at least 10 minutes' drive from the other, meant that all teachers spent much of their 'free' time travelling. There were few opportunities to seek advice or learn from informal conversations and the operation of official school policies, such as break or lunchtime detentions, became impossible for the pre-service teachers to operate. The strategy of detaining pupils for a short time at the end of the day was actually proposed by Joseph's mentor as an alternative to the official policy because he simply could not be available to hold them at the right time on the appropriate site.

Teachers' essential isolation meant that although Joseph received general support and encouragement from other subject teachers, no one other than his mentor had given him specific advice about his teaching of this particular class and she rarely observed him with them. In these circumstances, what seems to have sustained Joseph's persistence in the use of challenging historical questions and interactive strategies was his individual background. In part, his determination to challenge stereotypical assumptions about Africa was strengthened by a 2-year period working in Kenya. His willingness to persist with an enquiry-based approach seems to have been stimulated by previous experience teaching the 'middle years' programme of the International Baccalaureate which prioritises critical thinking and the processes involved in informed decision-making. This is not to claim that such an orientation would have been inevitable. The fact that Joseph's teaching had been carried out at a private school in Kenya, with highly motivated, paying pupils may have led him to conclude that such strategies simply could not work with a less committed, more diverse cohort. But in this instance the alignment of certain aspects of his previous experience with the ambitions of his mentor and subject tutors appeared to sustain his determined persistence.

Jason: effective mediation within close alignment threatened by economic constraints

The experience of Jason, an English intern on the MSU programme, undertaking his internship at Highfield High School, was very similar to that of Joseph both in that there was a strong sense of alignment between his own ambitions for pupils' learning and the approaches endorsed by his school-based mentor and the MSU programme, and in that his learning was threatened in some respects by significant contextual constraints. The challenges were not directly evident in the observed lesson, and only really became apparent in subsequent interviews with Jason and his mentor. It was therefore, not entirely clear how they would play out in the longer-term.

Within the lesson itself, the strong alignment between Jason and his mentor in terms of their assumptions about effective pedagogy for teaching English was evident. Although the lesson was based in a computer room (about which Jason expressed some regret, since he felt that the particular focus on the use of technology would not reveal as clearly as other lessons his commitment to the creation of a social environment for learning), the way in which he worked with the pupils clearly reflected the commitment to dialogic teaching that he had described as being important both to him and his mentor. He appeared confident and relaxed in promoting discussion and managed the dialogue well to draw pupils in and encourage them to explain their thinking as they responded to one another's ideas. The effectiveness of his practice in this respect was particularly evident in the tactful but firm manner in which he dealt with a potentially difficult situation where a white pupil made a controversial statement about a racist fraternity incident.

Whilst there was no sense of 'crisis' stimulating OfD, it was clear that Jason's own orientation towards learning to teach and the encouragement and guidance provided by his mentor meant that he was well-equipped with mediating tools to support his learning. His mentor expressed an explicit commitment to allowing Jason to take risks and experiment in his practice, suggesting that 'mistakes' or difficulties would provide a useful stimulus for reflection and adaptation. Jason's own ambition meant that he appeared very receptive to such opportunities; the school principal described him as 'very intentional ... and reflective'. He was prepared to take the initiative in lesson planning and to use the process to seek out challenges to address his own developmental priorities – most obviously his concern to develop more dialogic teaching, despite the risks that it might (and did) present.

Jason identified strongly with his subject, which he regarded as central to young people's education. Although he had specialised in English literature, he recognised the importance of teaching the 'mechanics and grammar of the English language' and was confident in doing so. His confidence was boosted both by the fact that he felt so strongly supported within the school and by the close alignment between the programme aims advanced within MSU and those endorsed by both his mentor and the school principal. The former had been an MSU student and regarded his own training as excellent preparation for teaching, whilst the latter praised Jason's emphasis both on building relationships and on adopting a 'real-world focus' through project-based learning.

The strength of this partnership was only threatened by growing financial pressures and the specific demands of high-stakes testing on the way in which the partnership could operate. Whilst Jason's mentor was keen to give him opportunities to experiment, economic pressures on the school had led to an increase both in class sizes and in the number of lessons that he was expected to teach. He was concerned that this pressure and a growing sense of obligation meant that he would dedicate any time that he gained as a result of Jason assuming responsibility for particular classes to supporting pupils' SAT preparation. As a result, he would not actually be able to allow Jason to experiment in the way that he wanted since he could not provide the necessary back up and feedback. Thus, whilst the programme appeared to be operating highly effectively at the moment it was observed, the mentor in particular felt that its continued operation was under threat. Whilst Jason's intentional orientation to learning might well have helped to sustain his commitment to experimentation in line with the ideals espoused by MSU and endorsed by his mentor, the scope for such risk-taking and the opportunities to learn effectively from it would be significantly reduced if the mediation provided by his mentor was reduced or withdrawn under the pressures of a more intensive timetable and a narrowing focus on high-stakes testing.

Conclusion

Two important conclusions can be drawn from these examples of strong alignment in both the horizontal and vertical dimensions of our analytical framework. The first is that effective learning does not always have to proceed from a developmental 'crisis' experienced as a profound conflict between competing visions or between one's envisioned practice and the reality of classroom experience. Doug was undoubtedly still striving to bring the processes of teaching and learning within his classroom more closely into line with the ideals that he espoused, but the observed outcomes of his practice served to reassure him that he was making effective progress in realising those objectives. The close alignment between school and HEI in terms of their conceptions of learning history – and the fact that the Riverside Academy history department had developed approaches to enquiry-based teaching that effectively enabled them to address the requirements of particular exam specifications – meant that Doug felt he was responding to a well-defined and consistent agenda that drove him forward.

The second conclusion to be drawn, however, from the range of cases illustrated here, is that even when strong alignment is achieved between the individual student teacher and those working most closely with them as teacher educators (school-based mentors and HEI subject tutors) that coherent, supportive framework is not always easy to maintain, given other kinds of pressures operating at the institutional and societal level. In Joseph's case, the purely practical constraints created by a split-site school structure made focused guidance and support difficult to sustain. Even where the strategies that he had been encouraged to adopt chimed strongly with approaches rooted in his previous teaching in a very different context, Joseph encountered real difficulties that prompted him to question what he was doing. Whilst Jason's observed practice looked much more secure and suggested highly effective and coherent partnership working, external pressures created in part by financial difficulties and partly by the imperative to address the demands of the national testing and accountability regimes were beginning to undermine the kind of sustained focus on the intern's learning and willingness to allow him to experiment (and thus, risk initial difficulties and early failure) that the development of dialogic teaching to which both school department and the HEI-programme aspired.

Note

1 This description of Africa is attributed to the explorer, Henry Morgan Stanley who used it in the title for his 1878 account of his expedition *Through the Dark Continent* (Stanley, 1878). Whilst Doug wanted the students to understand the 19th century European/American assumptions and attitudes that underpinned this description, his main aims were that students would learn about specific features of pre-colonial African life and culture and use that knowledge to challenge and counter the negative and false stereotyping that it presented.

References

Bernstein, B. (1990). *Class, codes and control. Volume IV: The structuring of pedagogic discourse.* London: Routledge.

Black, P., Harrison, C., Lee, C., Marshall, B. & Wiliam, D. (2003). *Assessment for learning: Putting it into practice.* Buckingham: Open University Press.

Black, P. & Wiliam, D. (1998). *Inside the black box: Raising standards through classroom assessment.* London: King's College.

Burn, K. & Harris, R. (2013). *Survey of history in schools in England 2013.* London: Historical Association. Retrieved from www.education.ox.ac.uk/wordpress/wp-content/uploads/2013/12/HA-Survey-of-History-in-Schools-in-England-2013.pdf.

Burn, K., McCrory, C. & Fordham, M. (2013). Planning and teaching linear GCSE: Inspiring interest, maximising memory and practising productively. *Teaching History, 150*, 38–43.

Byrom, J. & Riley, M. (2007). Identity-shakers: Cultural encounters and the development of pupils' multiple identities. *Teaching History, 127*, 22–29.

Counsell, C. (2011). Disciplinary knowledge for all, the secondary history curriculum and history teachers' achievement. *The Curriculum Journal, 22*(2), 201–225.

Foster, R. (2013). The more things change, the more they stay the same: Developing pupils' thinking about change and continuity. *Teaching History, 151*, 8–17.

Hedegaard, M. (2012). The dynamic aspects in children's learning and development. In M. Hedegaard, A. Edwards & M. Fleer (Eds.), *Motives in children's development* (pp. 9–17). New York: Cambridge University Press.

Higgins, S., Katsipataki, M., Kokotsaki, D., Coleman, R., Major, L. E. & Coe, R. (2014). *The Sutton Trust-Education Endowment Foundation teaching and learning toolkit.* London: Education Endowment Foundation.

Husbands, C., Kitson, A. & Steward, S. (2011). *Teaching and learning history, 11–18: Understanding the past.* Maidenhead: Open University Press, McGraw-Hill Education.

McIntyre, D. (1990). Ideas and principles guiding the internship scheme. In P. Benton (Ed.), *The Oxford Internship Scheme: Integration and partnership in initial teacher education* (pp. 17–33). London: Calouste Gulbenkian.

Riley, M. (2000). Into the key stage 3 history garden: Choosing and planting your enquiry questions. *Teaching History, 99*, 8–13.

Stanley, H. M. (1878). *Through the dark continent.* London: Samson Low, Marston and Company, Ltd.

Sylvester, R. & Thomson, A. (2010, March 6). It's not about class, it's about the classroom, says Gove. *The Times,* Retrieved from www.thetimes.co.uk/tto/news/politics/article2463151.ece.

Woodcock, J. (2005). Does the linguistic release the conceptual? Helping Year 10 to improve their causal reasoning. *Teaching History, 119*, 5–14.

Cases of alignment at the meso level of institutions, with a high degree of tension or contradiction at the micro level of the individual

Leslie's experience of 'crisis' in her development as a teacher

Our next case study exemplifies alignment across institutions at the meso level, but with a high level of tension or contradiction at the micro level. This pattern is potentially more common in situations where student teachers are trying to re-contextualise knowledge for their pupils within the specific school context but where the approach they take is strongly influenced by adherence to beliefs about the 'ideal' way in which they think they should be planning and teaching. Such an approach may actually be at odds with the institutional values of, at the meso level, either the school or the teacher education provider, or it may be that an outwardly expressed desire to reflect such values in their own planning and teaching masks strong personal inclinations and preconceptions (which may not have been made explicit) that give rise to potential tensions and contradictions. It was Leslie, a student teacher of modern languages enrolled on the Postgraduate Certificate in Education (PGCE) programme at the University of Oxford who most strongly exemplified this typology. Like Doug, in the previous chapter, she was undertaking her extended first placement at Riverside Academy.

The lesson in which Leslie was observed took place at the end of January, when she had recently taken over the teaching of this Year 8 German class (12- to 13-year-olds). This was essentially a lesson in which Leslie had wanted to give formative feedback to individual pupils on some assessments she had carried out in a previous lesson, which had been focused on the pupils' competence in speaking in the foreign language. During the lesson she also wanted to address, with the whole class, some of the difficulties that they themselves had identified in a self-evaluation, which had followed the assessments; these difficulties focused mainly on producing accurate pronunciation and on the memorisation of key vocabulary, both essential for effective communication in modern languages. In order for this to work at a practical level, all the pupils needed to be occupied for most of the lesson so that she could have time for individual feedback and Leslie had spent a long time looking for appropriate activities to facilitate this. She had identified a range of activities but had essentially adapted them from existing materials, rather than designing the tasks herself, without

perhaps appreciating either the extent of their complex organisational requirements, or the need for each activity to be explained in the context of the pupils'
overall learning. She acknowledged that this had been a lengthy process ('I
searched online for a long time and could find nothing suitable. Eventually I
found a PowerPoint for learning phonics and I adapted it.').

The lesson began with a starter activity, which involved the pupils working
together in pairs in order to practise their pronunciation – they were given a
worksheet for this activity but no specific instructions as to how to carry out the
task. Whilst the pupils were working on this activity, Leslie spent the time
arranging her own resources and checking that the classroom computer was
functioning properly. This was followed by a whole class, teacher-led pronunciation activity but the lack of pace and failure to engage the pupils led, almost
inevitably, to some issues with behaviour and Leslie experienced some difficulties in maintaining effective control, leading to a key incident where the
class teacher intervened and quickly re-established order. Sensing that she
needed to organise and hand out the worksheets for the subsequent activities,
Leslie asked the pupils to revert to the starter activity in order to give herself
time to organise this. She then went on to explain the series of activities that the
pupils were to complete in the remainder of the lesson, some of which required
quite complex organisation. During this time, Leslie displayed an outwardly
positive stance, but it was clear that the complexity of the organisation required
at this stage of the lesson was beyond what she was able to manage given her
limited amount of experience to date. When eventually all the pupils seemed to
have something to do, Leslie started to hand out her written feedback on the
previous speaking assessments and she discussed her comments with individual
pupils.

Whilst this was happening many of the pupils did not appear to be fully
engaged with the tasks they had been asked to complete but Leslie was nevertheless, able to go round and give feedback to most of the pupils. She was
clearly striving to be as effective as possible, but the overall working environment within the classroom seemed to militate against what she was aspiring to
achieve and there were times when she appeared to be out of her depth or even
at a loss as to what to do next. She praised effusively those pupils who responded
to her requests, but overall there was little sense of purpose. There was no
indication on Leslie's lesson plan as to how the lesson would conclude and at
that stage she appeared to be 'thinking on her feet'.

Opportunities for development (OfD)

In contrast to Doug, the lesson that Leslie taught reflected, both in the planning of the tasks, the delivery of the lesson and the subsequent evaluation of
what had taken place, many aspects of the 'crisis' that she was experiencing as a
learner of teaching. Overall, it reflected the way in which Leslie was trying to
get to grips with the complexity of the classroom whilst lacking, at that stage in
her development, some of the technical skills that would be necessary to enable

her to achieve her goals. As a result, the pedagogical aims of the lesson were undermined by the poor behaviour of the pupils whom she had failed to engage. She acknowledged that she generally had more control over behaviour when she limited tasks to written exercises, but at the same time she felt driven by the desire to develop the pupils' communicative competence in the foreign language itself, which required practice in speaking. Providing opportunities for the latter, however, meant that Leslie had to take the risk of having less control over the pupils' behaviour. This alone was, perhaps, challenging enough but Leslie also revealed in her reflections on the lesson, further competing motives, which were underpinned by her strong aspiration to be like the teachers whom she observed around her. Her aim, she explained, was to try to replicate the teaching approaches that she observed others using so that they would become 'automatic to me and I don't need to spend time reflecting on what might work'. Furthermore, she wanted to build up a bank of resources since she believed that this would reduce the amount of time she needed to spend on lesson planning. The issue here appeared to be that Leslie was still primarily focused on her own needs as a teacher and had not yet fully engaged with the importance of addressing the learning needs of the pupils. Her response, at this stage, appeared to focus on limiting the potential complexity of teaching so that she could become more efficient. She was struggling to cope with the multidimensional, spontaneous and unpredictable nature of the classroom (Doyle, 1977) and sought to reduce the amount of time spent on planning and self-evaluation in the hope that she could reproduce for herself the routinised practices that she observed in the experienced teachers in the school's Modern Foreign Languages (MFL) department.

Opportunities for change (OfC)

OfC provided by mediational tools from the HEI

Leslie came to the PGCE programme with excellent subject knowledge and quickly displayed a strong interest in second language acquisition theory which underpinned much of the university-based MFL curriculum sessions, particularly the focus on oral interaction in the classroom and the use of the target language by teachers and pupils (as reflected in the work of both theorists and teacher educators; see Lightbown & Spada, 2013; Macaro, 1997; Macaro 2005; Meiring & Norman, 2002). She engaged fully with the ideas, read widely and contributed well to discussions during the university curriculum sessions. Her thinking in terms of her planning before the observed lesson indicated that she was concerned with developing automaticity in vocabulary recall (Hulstijn, 2001) and was keen to perfect pupil pronunciation. Thus, she was not considering merely the delivery of prescribed lesson content within the school's scheme of work but rather saw the lesson as an opportunity to develop the pupils' communicative competence in German, which she had been encouraged to do through the university sessions.

Furthermore, her clear aim of using formative assessment effectively is another aspect of her pedagogy that would have been supported by the university programme. She was aware of the value of analysing the outcomes of the pupils' attempts at speaking in German, which she had assessed in a recent lesson and it was the results of this analysis that she was sharing with the pupils during the observed lesson in two different ways. First, she provided whole class feedback in relation to common issues with pronunciation and second, she provided written feedback to individual pupils during the lesson and discussed this feedback with them, reflecting key features of the 'assessment for learning' approaches with which she was familiar.

Finally, within the learning model of the programme, Leslie had been encouraged to draw on a range of different perspectives to inform her developing thinking as a student teacher and to formulate her own rationales for the decisions that she took in relation to her practice. She was therefore, keen to draw on different sources in order to inform her own planning and teaching.

OfC provided by mediational tools within the school

As well as embracing the pedagogic discourse of the *university-based* components of the programme Leslie was also keen to engage with the established policies and practices within the *school*, particularly with regard to integrating effective assessment for learning procedures into her day-to-day classroom teaching, something that was a key feature of the school's practice. The ideas of both asking the pupils to carry out some self-evaluation of their speaking competence and of providing individual feedback on their performance in the recent assessment task, came from the class teacher (who was also the school's professional mentor as well as having previously been a subject mentor).

The feedback following the lesson was structured in such a way as to allow Leslie to express her frustrations at what had occurred during the lesson in terms of the pupils' behaviour and their general level of engagement and to consider possible reasons for this. Behaviour management had recently been identified by Leslie and the teachers working with her as a key area for development in her teaching; the feedback here enabled her to understand that this lesson was probably too complex in other respects to enable her to focus effectively on strategies for managing behaviour. The teacher went on to identify some important aspects of classroom dynamics that she might consider which required Leslie to re-appraise her original view of the reasons as to why the lesson had not been successful as it might have been and to discuss teaching strategies that might be more effective in the future. The teacher in question also helped Leslie to understand that there were no 'shortcuts' to achieving what she wanted to achieve – she could not simply replicate what she had observed other teachers doing in the classroom in order to become an effective teacher herself.

OfC provided by the individual's mediational tools

At one level, Leslie had a strong sense of agency, supported by her intellectual capability and her view that if she applied herself fully to the process of learning to teach she would achieve success. In spite of strong theoretical underpinnings, Leslie was, however, to some extent anxious about many of the practical aspects of her teaching including behaviour management, as noted above. She was aware of this, but initially found her lack of competence in being able to fulfil the pedagogical aims she had identified frustrating; furthermore, it compromised her desire to develop the sort of routinised practice that she observed in her more experienced colleagues. In many ways she felt that she was doing the things that she needed to do in order to get the respect of the pupils but seemed frustrated once again that this did not come automatically. Leslie also had the intellectual tools to be able to plan lessons effectively yet, when faced with the day-to-day demands of planning saw the answer as being to cut down on the amount of time it was taking; thus, planning efficiently seemed to take on more importance than the need to plan effectively.

The individual's disposition to recognise the scope for development and change

Leslie's focus on the aim of routinising her teaching as quickly as possible (both in terms of emulating what experienced teachers seemed to have achieved and in terms of reducing the time spent planning) meant that she appeared reluctant to focus on some significant issues in her teaching. Her initial evaluation of the observed lesson highlighted few issues and she concluded:

> I think the session went quite well, as I was expecting it to be more chaotic. I was very organised with my planning and resources and the pupils never lacked things to do – there were no gaps.

In terms of the pedagogy, however, she acknowledged that she had been:

> Less comfortable, because normally the pupils would be doing activities that are less rowdy, more structured and more calming; i.e. a writing or translation exercise.

She appeared to evaluate her teaching at this stage of her development in terms of the behaviour of the pupils and not necessarily in relation to the academic progress they were making. It appeared that she planned tasks with a view to the extent to which they would be 'calming' and in spite of her strong desire to develop the pupils' communicative competence in German she nevertheless, resorted to written exercises or translation work in an attempt to establish a calmer working environment in the classroom.

In addition, Leslie's apparent lack of recognition of the potential for development is further emphasised by what *did* become a key focus for her post-lesson reflections. What exercised her greatly was the effect of the teacher's intervention in order to restore order to the classroom: 'But I wish the pupils had been quiet when I told them to and that Gill had not had to intervene'.

Leslie's preoccupation with this incident was reflected in two ways. First, she felt that this very public demonstration of an experienced teacher's ability to restore order immediately highlighted her own inexperience in this area; and second, she just could not understand why the experienced teacher was so effective in getting the pupils quiet just by asking them to do so. Her preoccupation with this intervention in many ways diverted her from a more analytical evaluation of the outcomes of the lesson, which only became possible when the same class teacher conducted a carefully managed debriefing after the lesson itself.

With this careful mentoring Leslie started to see some of the pedagogical choices that were possible and that there were strategies that she could adopt in order to develop her behaviour management skills (rather than relying on her status as the class teacher or her subject expertise), and so her recognition of the scope for change seemed to have increased significantly by the end of the debriefing session.

The relative prominence of the subject (or subject pedagogy) in consideration of the need for development or change

Although Leslie's focus was on developing a particular pedagogic approach, which would take into account the principles of second language learning with which she had so fully engaged when at the university, this was not the area which led to the significant challenges that she needed to work through in terms of her classroom practice. The 'crisis' that she experienced came rather because the pupils did not respond in the way that would have made it possible to explore these pedagogic approaches more fully, but her initial lack of recognition of this meant that she was not able to see the scope for development that these challenges afforded. She was not yet aware that an adherence to a set of pedagogic principles and a tendency to design tasks that would occupy the pupils rather than educate them were not in themselves sufficient to bring about effective teaching and learning.

The establishment of appropriate classroom conditions was nevertheless, intrinsically linked to the nature of the subject, since effective language learning (that requires the active participation of pupils in a context in which many do not feel competent or confident) has to be enacted in a secure learning environment. Ultimately, Leslie's pupils were not engaged in this lesson because the tasks had not been planned in such a way as to be meaningful or even relevant to the learners, and she was thus, required to address the factors, which would enable change to occur.

The extent of alignment (and thus, of the scope for tensions or contradictions) between the individual, HEI and school

Leslie's case illustrates the way in which points of crisis in the development of student teachers have to be understood and managed effectively if they are to lead to productive learning rather than having a potentially negative effect and leading ultimately to a sense of demoralisation. In many ways she could easily have been an example of, like Doug, somebody representing a high degree of alignment between the meso and micro levels since she so clearly espoused the approaches taken by both the university and the school context in which she was working. What made this less possible was the way in which, for a while, she struggled to understand the reasons for the difficulties she was experiencing and therefore, there appeared to be fewer OfD. What helped her through this period was the intervention of others who supported her in making sense of the crisis and to see a way forward that would ultimately (although not immediately as a 'quick fix' of the sort that she had wanted) lead her to identifying the strategies that she could develop in order to become a successful teacher.

The extent of alignment between the individual and the school

Leslie had no difficulty in aligning herself with the pedagogical practices of her more experienced colleagues, which were generally in tune with her own conception of teaching the subject, as well as with their wider practices in relation to assessment, behaviour management, etc. She enjoyed working in a high-performing school and was keen to contribute to the overall school ethos, particularly as a highly qualified subject specialist. What she was not able to do during the first part of her placement at the school was to emulate the practice of those more experienced teachers in the way that she had initially hoped.

The extent of alignment between the individual and the HEI

Leslie had a good understanding of language acquisition theory and wanted to draw on this knowledge as much as possible in her own teaching since it fitted with her own instinct as to what would lead to good quality learning outcomes. In the observed lesson, her underlying principle (to develop good pronunciation) was one that would have reflected what she had learned at the university and what she had read in the literature. Alongside this subject-specific dimension, she was also attempting to enact sound principles of formative assessment, similarly promoted at the university. In doing so, however, she perhaps gave less emphasis to those aspects of the programme that had emphasised the need for thoughtful planning, including the design of appropriate tasks (Mutton & Woore, 2014), which would allow the defined learning objectives to be met.

The extent of alignment between the school and the HEI

The partnership between the schools and the HEI is exemplified in the strong alignment between the MFL department at Riverside Academy and the university. Many of the teachers in the department trained at the university and have worked closely with it over a number of years, with some also having studied for a professional master's degree, again working with the university tutors. Many of the modern languages teachers (within a large subject department) had previously acted as mentors and so, there is a sufficient level of expertise distributed across the department to enable interns to be supported by a range of colleagues at the school. Furthermore, the university has collaborated with these teachers on a number of different research projects, most recently, for example, one that investigated new approaches to subject-specific assessment in modern languages.

Michael: a further example of 'crisis' shaping development and change

Leslie's experience of crisis was ultimately resolved due to the support she received in helping her see the way through her difficulties. The challenges faced in reconciling the tensions and contradictions she experienced were transformed from being potential barriers to her learning to becoming the catalyst for change. There are few others in our sample who experienced quite the same crisis as Leslie (with the accompanying sense of resolution) but one such teacher is Michael.

Michael was a PGCE Mathematics intern at the University of Oxford and carried out his first extended placement at Groveside Academy. In the observed lesson, Michael's objective was for his pupils to be able to calculate the measures of central tendency (mean, mode, median and range) and he began the lesson with a short discussion of these concepts before introducing the problems he had chosen for the pupils to practise. Whilst not stated in his lesson plan, he also expected the pupils to be able to recall the definitions of these concepts (which he said they had learned previously). Very soon, however, it became apparent that many of the pupils needed further reminders of what had been covered before – some began volunteering definitions, which Michael promptly accepted, even though they were not quite correct or conveyed misconceptions. His lack of anticipation of this in his planning, and his view that the fact that the pupils were making contributions was more important than the accuracy of the responses, caused some conceptual difficulties at the start of this lesson, which could have created or perpetuated serious misconceptions amongst the pupils had not the classroom teacher intervened. Michael's judgement as to what might work at any given moment caused him to deviate from his plans at different stages, resulting, for example, in an unplanned discussion or in extending an activity beyond what was planned as a result of one-to-one interactions with individual pupils. At the end of the lesson, he ran out of time and failed to complete the carefully drafted lesson plan. This reflected general trends in Michael's practice – the need to develop a deeper concern for pupils' learning and the need to anticipate and address unexpected events. In spite of these obvious concerns, Michael's demeanour during the lesson coupled with his response to the feedback he received, did not reveal a strong awareness of these specific issues either during or after the lesson.

More broadly, however, there were clear opportunities for him to benefit from the mediational tools that both the university and the school could provide. Michael was positive about the fact that his teacher education programme was providing him with the opportunity to take time to learn to teach properly and he said that he had received support from the university sessions in terms of ideas for engaging pupils in the discussion of concepts. The carefully developed dynamic PowerPoint he used in the lesson indicated that he was aware of what he needed the pupils to understand and the classroom teacher commented on the careful selection of exercises that Michael had provided as: 'perfectly pitched to pupils' levels' indicating that the programme had prepared him well in these respects. Likewise, it was clear that the classroom teacher also cared deeply about Michael's learning and was mindful of his limitations, pointing out in the detailed feedback those occasions where lack of precision in definitions or terminology might have had a detrimental effect on the pupils' learning. The classroom teacher was also concerned that Michael's spontaneous ideas and unplanned actions were, at times, taking up valuable time, denying pupils the opportunities they needed to re-affirm their knowledge. Whilst the classroom teacher was very conscientious in mentoring Michael and providing detailed feedback, he also seemed frustrated by what seemed to be an established pattern in Michael's otherwise acceptable performance. Michael indicated that whilst he saw himself as a learner, he also considered that he was close to being a competent teacher and therefore, had to be prompted continually to reflect on the implications of his imprecise handling of conceptual language rather than identifying these issues for himself.

Some of the issues in Michael's apparent failure to take on board the feedback from colleagues and thus, become an agent of change for his own professional learning may have been as a result of his reliance on what he perceived to be his own strong subject knowledge and his previous successful teaching experience abroad (albeit in a very different context). Yet his discussion of mathematical concepts with the pupils in the observed lesson revealed problems – for example, when failing to highlight incorrect definitions from the pupils or failing to recognise and address the pupils' misconceptions. The fact the apparent issues in his teaching related to his own subject knowledge, which he saw as his strength – may have gone some way to explaining his inability to recognise the OfD emerging from the lesson.

Michael's own reflection on the lesson (following the teacher's feedback) provided some further insight. His view was that 'the session went OK, the main lesson objectives were achieved – most pupils can calculate the averages from the lesson and many understand and can apply the definitions to solve more complex problems'. He also noted that the pupils were responsive to the material in general and participated as expected. When asked if there was anything he would improve, he referred selectively to the more positive aspects of the teacher's feedback (relating to the pupils' participation in class) and to concerns with class and time management. When prompted further, he did briefly refer to the need to have pupils review what they had learned, only to refer again to issues of classroom management: 'keep pupils engaged and avoid disruptive noise levels, develop an environment for people to feel safe discussing ideas and to encourage investigation'. Whilst the experience of teaching the lesson offered Michael rich OfD, it is difficult to gather from his reflections the degree of commitment to change and how he might have activated the tools at his disposal to achieve such change because at no time did he acknowledge the key issue of addressing the pupil's errors and their misconceptions. His reflections revealed that, like Leslie, he seemed to prefer not to engage with the specific difficulties he was encountering in spite of the evidence of what actually occurred in the classroom, even though the opportunity to consider these issues was provided.

In spite of these tensions, there is evidence of significant alignment between the micro and meso levels. In terms of the latter, the structure and content of Michael's lesson plan seemed to be in strong alignment with the general standards and the culture of the school. The objectives of the lesson and the way in which the classroom was managed with periods of guided and individual practice as well as mini-plenaries and the need for a larger plenary at the end of the lesson were indications of this. Furthermore, there was evidence of alignment with the curriculum goals of the university programme; the opening activity (notwithstanding the issues around the accuracy of the pupils' responses) was one designed to elicit previous knowledge and understanding and his wish for them to engage further in discussion of concepts around complex questions was something that he would have been encouraged to develop, as was the development of collaborative working in the classroom. In commenting on his own pedagogic approach, he said: 'I prefer to give students tasks to solve, where they are required to think mathematically and come up with solutions and methods themselves, rather than just explaining methods and procedures for them to apply', reflecting again a strong sense of alignment.

Overall, Michael said that it was important for him to take time to learn how to teach properly, which reflected in the evidence of alignment with both the school and university elements of the programme. Yet, there were underlying tensions. First, his lack of acknowledgement of the issues around his failure to deal with the pupils' incorrect subject-related concepts and their misconceptions may have been influenced by the implied challenge to what he saw as his strong subject knowledge. Having identified 'in advance many possible misconceptions they might have', he seemed unable to deal with further examples when confronted with them in the classroom – a situation exacerbated perhaps by a desire to establish a good rapport with the pupils, which may have influenced his decisions not to challenge incorrect responses. Second, Michael had a strong view of himself as a competent teacher and resented somewhat his status as student teacher in the school, in spite of his affirmation that he wanted to learn. These somewhat conflicting dispositions were heightened by the comparisons he made between himself and those in the school who were following the School Direct route, whom he believed received greater recognition of their teacher status from the beginning:

> I feel that the school seems to value and respect trainee teachers following the School Direct route more than the PGCE internship route. There seems to be an accepted way to treat PGCE interns as students, as an inconvenience, or not as worthy of social interaction as full teachers.

Conclusion

Classed within the same category, both cases presented here show a number of similarities, as well as obvious differences. Leslie and Michael each came to the programme with previous professional experience and both were well-qualified candidates (with strong first degrees and qualifications at master's level) giving them a clear sense of identity as subject specialists. They valued the university programme and also appreciated the separate school contexts in which they had been placed, including the support of the mentor and other colleagues with whom they were working. Their approaches to the teaching of their respective subjects were clearly influenced by the subject pedagogy to which they had been introduced at both the university and in school (i.e. alignment between the micro and the meso level) and they were keen to fit in with the established norms of the latter and to be respected as colleagues, albeit ones at the start of their career. Both expressed a positive disposition to learning, as much as they could, from the opportunities provided by the teacher education programme.

What was interesting, however, was the response of each of them to having taught what was, in many ways, a problematic lesson, in which there had been a necessity for the usual classroom teacher to intervene in order to avert further issues. In each case, the intervention proved to be a significant moment. For Leslie, the intervention was promoted by behaviour management problems resulting from her inability to engage the pupils sufficiently well; in Michael's case, it was because of the failure to correct errors in pupils' knowledge. In both cases, significant contradictions were being played out at the micro level, which related to a perception of professional status. Leslie and Michael clearly wanted to see themselves as teachers. Leslie was eager to replicate what she saw as the automaticity evident in the practice of her more experienced colleagues, but had failed to understand that at this stage of the programme she lacked the necessary skills and expertise to be able to achieve such automaticity. Although she was spending a long time planning her lessons, she was not doing so efficiently or effectively since she was preoccupied with classroom management issues and was planning tasks to keep the pupils busy, rather than focusing on their learning. In Michael's case, he was eager to be accepted as a teacher by the pupils, and was envious of the status that he felt was accorded to trainees in the school on other training routes; although expressing a desire to learn, he also indicated that he somewhat resented his learner status in the school.

For both Leslie and Michael, the focus on teacher status may have led to their inability (or unwillingness) to face up to the challenges they were experiencing in the classroom and their tendency to ignore the OfD. Whilst there was strong alignment between both of them as individuals and the university and school contexts, neither was initially able to acknowledge the significant points for development needed in order for them to be able to move forward. It was only through careful mentoring and explicit feedback that the issues were highlighted. Whilst Leslie needed to be guided, through careful mentoring, to engage with the potential OfC, the feedback for Michael did not appear to have influenced his subsequent reflections.

Finally, both these student teachers experienced tensions because of the way in which they conceptualised the planning of their respective lessons. Whilst both had spent a long time thinking about the correct sequence of activities and the overall lesson content demonstrating, in doing so, clear alignment with the frameworks in which they were working, they had failed to recognise that 'planning was the anticipation of what *might* happen rather than their determination of what *would* happen' and that they needed to consider 'planning as visualisation, rather than planning as a template' (Mutton, Hagger & Burn, 2011, p. 408).

References

Doyle, W. (1977). Learning the classroom environment: An ecological analysis. *Journal of Teacher Education*, *28*(6): 51–55.

Hulstijn, J. H. (2001). Intentional and incidental second-language vocabulary learning: A reappraisal of elaboration, rehearsal and automaticity. In P. Robinson (Ed.), *Cognition and second language* (pp. 258–286). Cambridge: Cambridge University Press.

Lightbown, P. M. & Spada, N. (2013). *How languages are learned* (4th ed.). Oxford: Oxford University Press.

Macaro, E. (1997). *Target language, collaborative learning and autonomy*, Clevedon: Multilingual Matters.

Macaro, E. (2005). *Teaching and learning a second language: A guide to recent research and its applications*. London: Bloomsbury Publishing.

Meiring, L. & Norman, N. (2002). Back on target: Repositioning the status of target language in MFL teaching and learning. *Language Learning Journal*, *26*(1), 27–35.

Mutton, T., Hagger, H. & Burn, K. (2011). Learning to plan, planning to learn: The developing expertise of beginning teachers. *Teachers and Teaching: Theory and Practice*, *17*(4), 399–416.

Mutton, T. & Woore, R. (2014). Designing tasks to promote learning in the foreign language classroom. In I. Thompson (Ed.), *Designing tasks in secondary education: Enhancing subject understanding and student engagement* (pp. 129–151). Abingdon: Routledge.

9 Cases of unacknowledged contradictions at the meso level of institutions, which result in low levels of support or challenge at the micro level of the individual

Our next series of case studies exemplify unacknowledged contradictions across institutions at the meso level (school and higher education institution [HEI]) leading to low levels of pedagogic support or challenge for the individual as a learner at the micro level. The five cases presented in this section, illustrate a range of possible tensions that may arise from a lack of alignment across institutions. In all of the cases, the school and HEI were nominally aligned and the student teachers were perceived by the schools to be making good or steady progress. In four of the five cases, the student teachers also perceived themselves to be making progress and most of them also felt supported by their mentors and other teachers. However, contradictions and tensions in these individuals' social situations of development which created opportunities for development (OfD) and opportunities for change (OfC) that were apparent to the research team on issues such as pupil learning or subject pedagogy, were neither acknowledged nor addressed by the actors involved. As a result, fewer mediational tools were apparent.

Sophia: a declared commitment to learning not matched by genuine challenge – for intern or pupils

We begin with the case of Sophia, an English intern on the Teacher Education programme at Michigan State University (MSU). She was a Post-Bachelor's Teacher Certificate student who held a BA in English and History. Sophia believed that English was an important subject and that she had good subject knowledge. She was quite critical of her training and of the university in particular for the organisation and structure of the programme. Like most student teachers, she viewed the school as the primary source for her learning. In some respects, she colluded with her mentor who did not see the relevance of the MSU curriculum and felt that it detracted from the central focus of learning to teach in a school setting. Sophia seemed untroubled by her mentor's critical views of the MSU programme and was happy to concentrate on delivering the school curriculum as they both felt that this was more important. Being a team player, who followed school practices and procedures, was deemed sufficient by the mentor. It is worth noting here that, because the MSU programme coordinator discusses the programme with the school when a mentor takes on the role reaching agreement about what is expected, and because the teacher education approach at MSU is so well known across the state, it would be reasonable to assume that mentors support the approach of the programme when they agree to sponsor a student teacher. Whilst the programme acknowledges that there are diverse views about how one learns to teach, a situation such as this, would once known, have been attended to by the programme coordinator, who would have been concerned by the mentor's critical orientation to the MSU programme and how it was affecting the student teacher.

Sophia, however, was not fully enculturated into the school and she was aware of differences between her own teaching style and that of her mentor. Despite the fact that she felt liked and generally supported in the school, she was also critical of a lack of direction in some subject areas of her teaching. Nevertheless, she recognised that she was much further ahead in her development as a result of sessions at MSU than a student teacher in the school from another programme.

Sophia was not uncritical of herself as a student teacher and she recognised that:

> There are certain areas where I know that I have weaknesses, but I feel confident in my ability to seek assistance, guidance and help in those areas. I am confident in my ability to utilise the resources available to me through my school community to become a better teacher. Were I to rate myself on a scale of 1–10 in my comfort in teaching English, I would give myself about an 8. There are areas I am not as comfortable, and areas where I feel I have not yet received adequate guidance from my mentor, but for the most part, I am comfortable teaching in an English classroom.

This sense of critical reflection suggests that Sophia was open to change. A contradiction is revealed here between her stated confidence to actively seek mentoring and what she perceived as inadequate guidance from her mentor. She placed the blame for lack of progress in some areas both on her mentor and the structure of the MSU programme. Sophia believed that her development as a teacher 'really depends on the mentor teacher'. Whilst she felt that all of the interns in her school were valued as individual teachers, 'it varies by mentor teacher whether or not we have support for the MSU side of the internship experience'. There was little sense in the interview of Sophia taking individual responsibility for her learning or her understanding of the dialectic between university and school. She felt that her greatest developmental need was the pacing of lessons so 'that I am not racing through material and stressing myself out by being a slave to my calendar'. She was of the opinion that her mentor teacher tended to pack a lot of different material into her lessons but did not deal with much of this material in any great depth, which she regarded as reflecting a different philosophy from her own and indicated alignment with the views of the university. Further, Sophia also wanted to work on formative assessment, the transitions in lessons and the clarity of her instructions. She talked about developing her use of 'progressive scaffolding where pupils are tangibly building on what they did throughout the year/unit/lesson' an inclination that aligns with the constructivist vision and teachings at the university.

Sophia had taught the class that was observed in April 2015 since September 2014 and had developed a very good rapport with the group. Her lesson was part of a unit on what she described as 'informational reading' that she had designed to reflect recent changes in the SAT national examination. Her focus in the unit was on reading comprehension and understanding authorial purpose and style. In particular, the lessons were designed to highlight the tools writers use to convince their audience. In previous lessons, she had introduced a text evaluation strategy with the acronym SOAPPSTone (Subject, Occasion, Audience, Purpose, Point of view, Speaker, Tone). In this lesson, she reminded the pupils of rhetorical strategies, particularly Aristotelian traits of argument in order to explore authorial intention and style. She also wanted the pupils to use this knowledge of rhetoric in their own writing as well. Sophia was relaxed and humorous throughout the lesson. She was in command of the classroom and established and maintained control with the use of facial gestures and her movement around the room. She had built strong relationships with pupils and she clearly knew them well. Although the pupils were generally receptive to Sophia as a teacher, a minority were disengaged and frequently looked at their phones and tablets.

Sophia claimed to be confident in her ability to teach rhetoric as an English teacher. However, her lesson was very functional in its approach to teaching rhetorical devices and their uses in writing. Much of the opening part of the lesson consisted of 'feature spotting' from a text, which they had read in a previous lesson. There was no attempt to describe the purpose of the lesson. Sophia asked the pupils to find examples of rhetorical devices from a text and to comment on the subject, audience, purpose and tone. This focus on authorial lexical choice was misleading to some pupils who completely misread the tone and purpose of the text. As a result, when some pupils identified examples of what they perceived to be 'ethos' and 'pathos' they were unable to justify these choices effectively. For example, one pupil claimed that 'I found a pathos' rather than 'I found an example of pathos' and then singled out a word devoid of the context of the sentence in which it was used.

Sophia then asked the pupils to read a second text on the effects of Hurricane Katrina on residents of New Orleans. The text was engaging and Sophia led a very strong whole class session where she related her personal experience of children from New Orleans being moved as refugees to her home town. She asked the pupils to use their expressed feelings of empathy for the city and its inhabitants in order to look at the point of view in the text. The pupils appeared to understand the task and they responded well. At times, they built on examples made by other pupils. Sophia was both affirmative and questioning. At times, she skilfully pointed out the ways in which pupils were drawing inferences from the text. The class worked effectively as a group led and conducted by her. However, instead of building on this strong sequence Sophia then repeated the feature spotting task from the opening sequence of the lesson, as pupils were to take notes about 'rhetorical appeal (logos, pathos, ethos)', subject, audience, tone and purpose. This safe choice lacked the challenge of the group task and may have reflected Sophia's stated aim not to rush the lesson. She had explained that she felt that asking the pupils to identify features of rhetoric was an effective way of assessing their understanding.

Sophia had intended to ask the pupils to use their knowledge of rhetoric in their own creative writing. The repetition of the rhetorical feature identification task meant that she ran out of time for this task. In preparation for the next lesson Sophia asked the pupils to indicate whether they were more 'maths- or English-minded'. The class was evenly split. Sophia then commented that: 'If you are more maths oriented you probably enjoy looking at rhetorical devices a little more than creative writing'. This statement revealed Sophia's belief in an essential disconnect between what she saw as the technical side of understanding language features and their use in texts and the affective task of creative writing.

In this lesson, there was much to admire in Sophia's effective classroom presence and rapport with the pupils. However, the lesson neither seemed to challenge nor developed pupils' understandings or use of rhetoric. Sophia was confident after the lesson that the pupils were generally on-task and engaged and she saw the lesson as reinforcement of learning. The English task design (Thompson, 2015) of the curriculum challenge focused on a functional understanding of language use rather than a conceptual one.

At the end of the lesson her mentor congratulated her for work well done.

Opportunities for development (OfD)

Sophia's case is a good example of a missed OfD. Sophia wanted to become an excellent teacher and she was not uncritical of her practice. The lesson observed was not wholly without merit as a form of revision on rhetorical devices. Yet, there was a clear contradiction apparent within it between Sophia's perception of herself as a competent teacher of rhetoric and writing and the reality of the lack of challenging learning for both her pupils and herself. Sophia did not experience this as a crisis because she was unaware that her planning and delivery did not stretch the pupils. If she had been made aware of the contradiction between her lesson task design and the intended learning outcomes, and had acknowledged this contradiction, then Sophia may have been able to move beyond a simple reflective model. However, her resistance to the MSU programme combined with her blaming of her mentor for her own shortcomings, and the mentor's reluctance to intervene in the lesson or give her productive and critical feedback at the end, meant that Sophia's OfD were minimal.

Opportunities for change (OfC)

OfC provided by mediational tools from the HEI

Sophia felt that MSU interns had 'a very awkward schedule that causes a disruption in routine for pupils and sometimes even a disconnect with what is happening in our classroom/school overall'. She described having to return to MSU for Friday sessions as illogical and stressful. Sophia felt that although her mentor teacher really liked her as a teacher and colleague, she was exasperated by the MSU curriculum and questioned both the relevance of the curriculum and the logic for taking the intern out of the classroom by scheduling university sessions on Fridays. Sophia also felt that many of the MSU assignments 'were not pedagogically relevant given what was happening in my school and did not always fit well given our other responsibilities as teachers'. The level of the OfC provided by the HEI was potentially high, but in practice there was little scope for change because of Sophia's predispositions towards the MSU programme.

OfC provided by mediational tools within the school

Sophia's critiques of MSU and indeed of her own mentor stemmed from her perception of the school and the teaching of lessons as the dominant source of learning. She also felt that many of the MSU assignments were not relevant to her teaching and that there was a disconnect between the university programme and the school's demands. This suggests that the demands of the school dominated Sophia's practice. Her object motive was to conform to these demands rather than her own development as a teacher.

As a result, Sophia did not see the relevance of the HEI/school partnership despite the fact that she compared her development favourably to a student teacher in the same school connected to a different HEI. She viewed the central role of both the HEI and the school as providing support rather than challenge:

> I do have to say that I received much more support as a person, teacher, and individual from Nearfield High School than I did from MSU. However, again, I do have to say that that likely varies between schools and definitely varies between mentor teachers.

Her OfC were also low because of the lack of effective mentoring interventions. The school support amounted to ensuring that Sophia aligned her practices with those of the school rather than challenging her to reflect critically on her teaching.

OfC provided by the individual's mediational tools

Sophia relied heavily on her own sense of what she recognised to be important in the practices in the school environment. Her lack of critical reflection on these practices meant that her experience was mediated through her perception of what validated support. As a result, she relied in the lesson observed on a very functional sense of semantic use in the chosen text without considering the possibilities for extending the very good cultural and historical discussion on the effects of Hurricane Katrina.

The individual's disposition to recognise the scope for development and change

Sophia understood the need for development and she was able to list her own targets. She was not uncritical of herself and had some recognition of her strengths and weakness as a student teacher. However, she tended to blame what she perceived as shortcomings in support and this limited her ability to recognise how change and development might happen. The lack of critical discussion of Sophia's pedagogical choices by her mentor also limited this opportunity.

The relative prominence of the subject (or subject pedagogy) in consideration of the need for development or change

Sophia saw English as a very important subject for her pupils. In the observed lesson, Sophia's confidence in her own mastery of subject matter was misplaced. As a result, her pedagogical choices of task failed to challenge many of the pupils. The fact that she did not recognise this meant that her assumptions about the ways that knowledge about language is developed in both reading and writing remained unchallenged. Sophia also felt that it was her subject mentor's role to intervene in areas where her subject knowledge was not secure. There was little sense of the dialectic between developing subject knowledge and subject pedagogy.

The extent of alignment (and thus, of the scope for tensions or contradictions) between the individual, HEI and school

The extent of alignment between the individual and the school

Although Sophia felt strongly aligned with the school, and indeed colluded with the school mentor in critiquing the MSU programme, she was also critical of her school mentor. Although this meant that Sophia was able to partially stand outside the culture of the school department she was at the same time eager to conform to what English teachers in the school saw as important. This contradiction remained unacknowledged.

The extent of alignment between the individual and the HEI

Sophia placed far more importance on alignment with the school practices than with the MSU curriculum. Her critique of the organisation of the programme stemmed from her belief that real learning took place in the school setting. The criticism of the MSU programme by her mentor compounded this misalignment.

The extent of alignment between the school and the HEI

The school mentor's criticism of MSU displayed her misunderstanding of the role of the HEI in setting challenges and criticality when learning to teach. Whilst Sophia did well in the university courses, demonstrated strong knowledge of the subject and attempted to follow MSU teachings, as noted on the Hurricane Katrina part of the lesson, the influence of the school department and of the mentor teacher was dominant. The dismissive attitude towards the MSU curriculum as expressed by her mentor undermined the alignment between the school and the HEI in this case.

Further examples of unacknowledged contradictions

Jacqueline's experience of a lack of challenge

Jacqueline, a second Modern Foreign Languages (MFL) teacher, was placed at Groveside Academy in the Oxford Postgraduate Certificate in Education (PGCE) programme. The lesson was observed at the end of February and was only the third occasion that she had taught this class of Year 7 (11- to 12-year-olds) pupils. The focus of the lesson was on telling the time in French as part of a unit designed to enable the pupils to be able to talk about their 'daily routine'. Jacqueline was a native speaker of French and had previously taught French and English as foreign languages, both in France and in the United Kingdom; she was confident in her subject knowledge and felt that she also had a significant amount of classroom experience on which to draw. She felt particularly strongly that French should be used where possible in the classroom for all regular interaction and instructions, in line with the approach promoted by the university and this policy was in keeping with practice at Groveside Academy. Overall, she recognised the close alignment between the university-based programme and the school-based experience, emphasising that: 'there is not a clear division between theory at the department and practice in school but the two are intertwined', but did feel that some of the requirements of the university in terms of specific school-based tasks had been unrealistic, given the capacity of the school for these tasks to be realised. She cited, for example, the university's expectation that the interns would gain experience, during their time in school, of Content and Language Integrated Learning and explained that this had not been easy to arrange at Groveside Academy, perhaps because of the need to liaise with teachers outside the immediate subject department in order to set up a lesson (or programme of lessons) in this way.

Within the observed lesson, two areas were of particular interest in terms of the alignment of Jacqueline's practice with wider language teaching pedagogy.

The first was the role of the target language, which she used fairly consistently throughout the lesson, indicating close alignment between the two contexts; and the second was her approach to presenting new language, which was perhaps less consistent. She tended to rush through this stage, rather than following a sustained sequence of presentation, repetition, question and answer and consolidation. She acknowledged, when talking about her planning of the lesson, that she would need to spend time drilling and practising the new language (if effective acquisition were to take place) but had not achieved this in practice, leading to subsequent problems with pronunciation and recall. There was an acknowledged tension between her wish to keep the learners engaged (which led her to plan a number of short practice activities) and the need for sufficient pronunciation practice, which in her estimation, could lead to lower levels of engagement. The pace of her teaching meant that she was ultimately able to get through all the activities that she had planned and she therefore, felt that she had accomplished what she had set out to achieve. Moreover, her classroom organisation appeared to be strong, which enabled her to manage transitions smoothly and she clearly adhered to the school's (and MFL department's) accepted practices in terms of established routines for the lessons.

The recognition by the mentor that Jacqueline was a competent and confident teacher, able to act independently and to fit in well with the behavioural norms of her school colleagues (with which her own practice and pedagogic discourse seemed to be closely aligned) belied perhaps the need for more challenging developmental targets for her teaching. Before the lesson in question, she was able to set out her goals in terms of the pupils' achievement, affective state and behaviour and in terms of her relationships with them, revealing a complex interplay between the different goals that is not untypical of student teachers at this stage of their development (Burn, Hagger, Mutton & Everton, 2003). But she appeared to be dealing with this complexity by an over-reliance on shorter, well-paced classroom activities, which undoubtedly engaged the learners, but may not necessarily have secured the progression in pupil learning that she ultimately wanted to achieve. Whereas Leslie, another MFL beginning teacher from the same programme (see Chapter 8) had been challenged to address the complexity of her classroom teaching and work through the issues (as a result of effective mentoring). Jacqueline did not appear to be in need of such support and the relative inexperience of her mentor may have been a contributory factor. Although the *school* had engaged fully with the training of student teachers over a number of years, mentoring expertise in the MFL department was less well distributed than at Riverside Academy: the department tended to replace one mentor with another only when necessary and often only after the original mentor left the school. At Groveside Academy mentoring was therefore, seen to be very much the domain of one designated member of staff who had taken on the role and, whilst there was support for student teachers from other members of the department, this was often at a practical level (support with lesson planning and resources) rather than at the level of pedagogical development. Jacqueline's mentor had been carrying out the role for just over a year and whilst she had held regular weekly mentor meetings with her, Jacqueline's university-based subject tutor had noted that previously agreed targets (agreed at three-way meetings) had often not been followed up and remained as ongoing targets on the occasion of subsequent tutor visits. In general, it appeared that, because there were no serious concerns and Jacqueline could be regarded in many respects as a competent teacher, the mentor's role could therefore, be primarily one of monitoring.

Jacqueline's case thus, demonstrates that outward signs of alignment may, in some cases, mask the need to examine more closely how the student teacher actually conceptualises the process of learning to teach and addresses its inherent complexity. Jacqueline appeared to be a confident and competent student teacher who fitted in well with the pedagogic practices of the school and who successfully integrated selected theoretical aspects of subject pedagogy within her teaching (whilst, perhaps, discounting other aspects for pragmatic reasons) and, as such, seemed to face few challenges in terms of individual transitions. The fact that she was, perhaps, judged by others to be 'good enough' meant that the identification of targets for further development was not perceived as a particular priority.

Aneesha's case: structural barriers to effective challenge

Aneesha was a Teach First English participant at Eastside Academy where she had been teaching 18 hours a week since September (a normal expectation for a Teach First participant). She was observed and interviewed in January 2015. She described this as being hard 'as you don't have time to think how to improve or to serve others'. She wanted to be reflective and to improve her teaching but she also felt that other pressures were taking her time. Aneesha lacked confidence as a teacher despite, or perhaps because of, the responsibility that the course gave her. She had struggled to cope with the demands of teaching so many lessons right from the start of the course. On the other hand, Aneesha was very well supported by teachers in the school and to a lesser extent by Canterbury Christ Church University (the HEI supporting the English participants within the Teach First London programme).

There was a clear contradiction between Aneesha's feelings of inadequacy as a teacher and her need to demonstrate competence as a teacher rather than as a trainee. Aneesha clearly had the potential to be a good teacher and given her critical self-reflection there was potentially an OfC. However, she was overwhelmed by the responsibilities of her role despite the strong support she received. In a telling statement, she added that: 'there may not be the need to support so much if the workload was less'.

The school-based subject mentor, a former Teach First candidate, gave a balanced view of what she saw as the strengths and weaknesses of the programme. She valued the independence and sense of responsibility. However, she was aware that this was dependent on the culture of a school and she felt there was little time to be reflective.

There are pros and cons in Teach First. You are given ownership, thrown in the deep end, learning in classroom. But with only 6 weeks training you do feel inadequate and compensate by overworking. You don't get a chance to go to another school.

The mentor felt that her role was to 'support her in how to teach the subject of English. Planning to teach the skills needed in English'. She worked closely with her university tutors. The mentor's degree was in Law as Teach First only required an Advanced level qualification in the subject for teaching. She did not believe that her lack of a degree held her back, but she had been worried about teaching English as a subject. The mentor explained that she had struggled to develop a strong teaching persona in her own first year but after 3 years in the school she felt herself to be a confident English teacher. The experience of going through the Teach First programme meant that the mentor empathised with the multiple demands on Aneesha who was solely responsible for the progress of her pupils, albeit with support from the school. Although the mentor felt that Aneesha was a calm and reflective learner she explained that:

> She is responsible for the progress of her pupils and has to enter data. Roughly a level of progress a year. She needs to be more efficient with planning and marking. She tries to do too much.

The discourse around English pedagogy in the department in which Aneesha taught reflected the school's successful commitment to achieving strong examination results. Performativity pressures, of course, were not unique to the school, but pupils in the school were expected to make almost a grade level of progress a year (under the assessment levels within the previous National Curriculum), considerably higher than the expected norm. Whilst these high expectations had undoubtedly made a difference in raising overall attainment in the school, the pressures on a Teach First participant to match these expectations whilst learning on the job were intense. The English department was also very aware of the large variation in pupils' proficiency in the English language. Indeed, across the school there was a strong awareness of issues of diversity and individual need concerning English as an Additional Language (EAL) pupils. However, Aneesha's mentor described the EAL issue as a 'language barrier' rather than seeing knowledge of other languages as an opportunity within the English classroom.

From the evidence of Aneesha's lesson, and from the interviews with her and the mentor, it was clear that the department had very well-defined views about the pedagogic choices made in planning. Aneesha explained that generally she would be provided with a scheme of work with aims and shared assessment objectives. The scheme might come with PowerPoint slides but it was up to the teacher to adapt these. This structure is not unusual in English departments in England.

In the observed lesson, Aneesha taught a bottom set Year 7 class (11- to 12-year-olds). The lesson showed evidence of a teacher concerned with the structures of the English language rather than the reasons for language choices. This reflected Aneesha's concern with the language proficiency of the pupils, most of whom were classed as EAL learners. This emphasis on form over content perhaps accounted for the limited learning that went on in the lesson. Aneesha had explained before the lesson that her pupils struggled to explain the effects of writer's language choices. She had chosen a series of verbs taken from extracts from David Almond's teenage novel *Skellig* and she wanted the pupils to comment on the choice of the verb and the effect on the reader. The objective for the lesson was of relatively low demand for the pupils and many of the pedagogic choices in the lesson were very procedural. She did not explain to the pupils why they were doing the tasks and did not refer to the plot or structure of the book in the lesson. Often Aneesha resorted to feature spotting:

> Find what verb the writer uses when he describes Skellig eating. Underline the verbs to do with eating. Give yourself a star and a wish. I want everything neat.

However, Aneesha did at one point use a freeze frame where pupils modelled a representation of the meaning of identified verbs such as 'hissing'. The pupils clearly enjoyed this task.

Aneesha's reflections after the lesson focused initially on the good behaviour of the pupils. Nevertheless, she felt that the lesson did not really meet her learning objective, which was to explain the connotations of word choice in a fluent paragraph. She did not question the validity of her lesson objective. Aneesha's concerns were to do with what she perceived to be a lack of clarity in her instructions and a need to model more. She worried both about teaching the whole class and the need to work individually with pupils.

In a feedback session after the session involving her subject mentor and professional mentor, the former reassured Aneesha that her instructions were clear. The feedback session in general focused on Aneesha's use of assessment for learning and her questioning in the classroom. Both the professional and subject mentors were warm in their support and praised her establishment of a relaxed and focused classroom environment. The mentor questioned some of the procedures of the lesson and agreed with Aneesha that the pupils needed an overall frame for the lesson. She also pointed out the need to explain to pupils why they were doing tasks. However, she did not address the apparent weaknesses in the lesson structure itself. Her focus was heavily on what she perceived to be grammatical mistakes made by the pupils, although her judgements about this reflected her lack of subject specialism. For example, she believed that a pupil who described stillness in his writing as 'feeling quiet' should have written 'being quiet'. It was deemed sufficient that she had involved the pupils rather than thinking about the reasons for setting objectives and learning outcomes. The professional mentor, on the other hand, highlighted the successes in the lesson such as the use of praise and checking understanding whilst pointing out ways that it could become more productive.

Both the professional mentor and the subject mentor felt that Aneesha should spend more time planning and thinking through her lesson plans. Yet Aneesha felt under pressure to deliver the lessons she was already teaching. She wanted to be able to plan together with her mentor and to watch other English teachers but was unable to do so due to time constraints. The support offered by the school was very strong but the structure of the Teach First programme and the performativity demands on the school inevitably affected the quality and type of advice given. These constraints meant that her OfD and OfC were limited.

Nereen: a missed opportunity for development through lack of attention to subject-specific contradictions

Nereen, a beginning history teacher, was also on the Teach First route at Eastside Academy. In Nereen's case, as might be expected of a participant on an employment-based training route, there was a very strong alignment between the strategies that she adopted in planning and teaching her lesson and those espoused by the school-based subject and professional mentors who supported her. As was the case with Aneesha, Nereen's teaching practice and her assumptions about effective teaching were essentially shaped by the standards and culture of her school. These routine expectations were evident in the structure of her lesson with three sections, each concluding with a form of plenary that in theory allowed her to assess what has been achieved. Whilst these practices were only partially aligned with those endorsed by the history programme offered by the university partner in the Teach First programme, Nereen was essentially unaware of the differences. The lack of time for more sustained subject-based input and advice was one of the constraints of the programme that she particularly resented (at least, at the point when the observation and interviews were carried out); but she clearly felt that the structure of the programme also limited her opportunities for *school-based* learning. She lamented the lack of time to observe more experienced colleagues who would be able to demonstrate, for example, precisely how they dealt with persistent low level disruption and lack of student focus.

The observed lesson had been planned in with three distinct sections for exploring a new topic (How people in the Middle Ages saw their world – which would provide the context for subsequent study of the Crusades), with a final reflective task that invited the pupils to sum up what they had learned and their new questions about the medieval period. The first part of the lesson focused on a simple comparison of two images of the same location at different periods in time (contrasting the Middle Ages with the present day); the second was intended to generate more detailed descriptions of the differences between the scenes at particular London landmarks; and the third, using a vivid account of a traveller's entry into medieval London, was to be used as the basis for a series of six illustrations created by each pupil to encapsulate the most vivid scenes, although there was no time to complete this within the lesson.

Nereen had expected the lesson to go well and the fact that it did not do so, provoked an acute sense of 'crisis' for her, which meant that it might *potentially* have served to stimulate new learning. The 'crisis' was perhaps particularly extreme because of her expectations. She had envisioned pupils being excited by the topic – particularly the account that of the sights, sounds and smells of medieval London – and therefore, to be engaged by it. Yet the lesson was constantly threatened by low level disruption and Nereen found herself repeatedly reiterating her basic expectations and seeking to secure quiet in order to proceed. Unfortunately, her sense of frustration was largely channelled into questioning the training route on which she was enrolled, rather than providing a stimulus to take specific action to address the concerns that she had identified.

In addition to the poor behaviour, and lack of interest that this seemed to reflect, Nereen also recognised that the pupils' written responses lacked detail and any awareness of the *continuities* (and not just the changes) between the present and the past. Although these concerns might perhaps have prompted her to reflect on the adequacy – and indeed the compatibility – of her objectives for the lesson, her essential focus on the problem of the pupils' behaviour meant that she effectively closed down the options for her learning. Because the data projector failed, Nereen had to resort to showing the pupils the images that she wanted them to compare on her laptop. The reflection on the screen necessitated turning off the classroom lights, and Nereen argued that student behaviour, which would have been much easier to monitor and address in daylight, deteriorated as a result.

Nereen's frustration was perhaps exacerbated by the fact that the main strategy on which she was relying was essentially guided by her school-based mentor, who kept reiterating her own commitment to arousing pupils' 'passion for history' and yet it had apparently failed. She was unaware of potential flaws within the lesson to which a sharper focus on subject-specific pedagogy might have alerted her: the fact that by exaggerating the shocking and gruesome nature of life in the past she was tending both to reinforce pupils' misconceptions that people in the past were 'stupid' and to obscure the elements of continuity between past and present that she had also been hoping that pupils would be able to identify. Whilst insights from the university-based subject programme might have supported Nereen's learning in school, she made no reference to specific ideas from that source, merely lamenting in general terms her lack of opportunity to learn from more sustained input at a pace that she could handle. The perspectives offered by her tutors were clearly not an obvious resource for her at this point.

Interviews with Nereen and her mentor revealed that she had access to considerable support in school, provided regularly by her subject mentor and the professional mentor and motivated by a strong commitment to Nereen's learning; but the extent to which this support was enabling her to identify ways forward appeared limited. Certainly, her subject mentor's emphasis on inciting passion or curiosity seemed to have failed her. The mentor's own route into teaching had been through the previous employment-based route of the Graduate Teaching Programme and although she referred extensively in interview to a current focus on developing Nereen's 'subject knowledge', she did not provide many specific details about the nature of the development that she thought was needed. It was therefore unclear, for example, whether the development that she envisaged related only to substantive knowledge or to enhancing Nereen's understanding of common misconceptions, for example, or supporting her appreciation of the relationship between substantive and second-order concepts in the development of pupils' historical understanding. One element that the mentor was clearly seeking to address related to enhancing Nereen's capacity to envisage pupils' progress in the medium-term, rather than focusing all her attention on individual lesson objectives. This had the potential to guide her in determining what knowledge and what kinds of conceptual understanding would prove *most* important to secure – but there was no indication that Nereen was actually drawing on this perspective in her analysis of the particular lesson that she had taught.

At the time of the lesson observation, Nereen seemed to bring few resources from her own experience of learning at school or her successful study of history at university to bear on the challenges that she was facing. Whilst she referred to the boost that recruitment to Teach First had given her and the sense of flattery in being recognised as an 'outstanding' graduate, she was by this point finding the programme's expectations of her a burden that she was struggling to bear. Her mentor referred repeatedly to the pressure that Nereen put upon herself (as well as the intense demands of the course) and her tendency to dwell on her failings, which prompted the mentor to keep highlighting the positive features of her practice in order to try to boost her self-esteem.

Nereen's strong feelings of failure may help to explain why the obvious 'crisis' provoked by the lesson was interpreted more as confirmation of her continuing difficulties rather than as a stimulus for new learning. She recognises that she was effectively sinking into a downwards spiral, but the suggestions that she made about what would help her or how she might learn to do things differently all effectively point to the need for a different kind of training programme, with more opportunities to watch experienced teachers and fewer challenges to seek to address at the same time.

Irene: an extreme example of unacknowledged contradictions

The final case presented here of Irene at Midfield Middle School was in many respects an extreme example of unacknowledged contradictions, which was reflected in a very weak lesson delivered by an apparently confident teacher. This misplaced confidence meant that the attempted re-contextualisation of knowledge exemplified in the lesson was insufficient to meet the learning needs of her pupils. In Irene's case, the very fact that she had been asked to teach a technology lesson when her training was in social studies and EAL, reflected a profound lack of alignment between the school's objectives and those of the programme, which formally placed a strong emphasis on subject knowledge (alongside knowledge of pedagogy and of learners). Limited connection between the programme and the intern's experiences in school was also reflected in the lack of feedback on her plan and the fact that the researcher was unable to secure the involvement either of Irene's mentor or the regular class teacher who was absent throughout the lesson. The case exemplifies an instance where the intern was neither supported nor challenged.

Whilst there were a number of profound inconsistencies between her stated objectives and the outcomes of the lesson, Irene appeared entirely unaware of these problems. As far as she was concerned, the lesson had been a successful one. There was thus, no sense of 'crisis' that might provoke new learning. The first of these inconsistencies related to the fact that Irene spent considerable time stating and reiterating quite complex instructions about specific features that she expected pupils to include on their planning sheets (in preparing to create an iMovie) and yet provided no written instructions or visible reminders to the class to support her oral instructions. The second inconsistency derived from the fact that this planning sheet eventually proved to be inaccessible to the pupils online (because the resource collection had not been updated), negating all the effort that she had invested in her explanations and reminders about what should feature in each box. The third inconsistency was the fact that despite the emphasis of the whole lesson on the need to *plan* before embarking on their creative project, one group of pupils reported back to Irene at the end of the lesson that they had entirely ignored this instruction and pressed ahead within the creation of their film. Whilst Irene remained calm and composed in the face of all these difficulties there were no suggestions in her post-lesson interview either that she regarded these elements as problematic or that she had learned from any of them.

In every respect, the scope for Irene's learning to be mediated by tools available to her within the school or derived from her previous experiences was very low. Her presentation of the lesson's central objective – expressed purely in terms of accomplishing activities (correctly filling in the 'think-sheet') – was incompatible with the HEI's conception of learning and even that of the school. The school did not appear to have engaged with Irene in any way to support her planning or evaluation of the lesson, nor did she refer to any other perspectives that might have alerted her to the fundamental problems with the lesson plan and its implementation. Despite her anxiety that the pupils might 'not understand the rubric', she had devised no strategy with which to strengthen their understanding (for example, by providing them with a visual display that would summarise the basic requirements for them, freeing her to focus on their awareness, for example, of the level of detail that might be required for the plan to provide an adequate guide to the creative process). Despite the clear evidence that at least one group had entirely ignored her instructions to begin by completing the planning sheet, Irene confidently declared afterwards that the class now 'understood the importance of planning'.

Irene's disposition to change was therefore, very low. She offered no suggestions at all about how her plan might be developed or refined, not even to liaise with other technology staff to ensure that resources are accessible when they are needed. Indeed, her only regret related not to her planning or teaching, but to our research: the fact that she did not have a lesson that involved more direct instruction for the researcher to observe.

Whilst it is unsurprising that subject did not feature at all within Irene's concerns of as a focus of evaluation, there was no evidence that she even sought to engage with the subject-specific principles that she was encouraging the pupils to apply to the design process: 'Investigate, Plan, Create, Evaluate'. Indeed, she moved pupils straight from their choice of subject matter directly to the planning process and made no effort to help the pupils *themselves* to identify the elements that might go into the planning process; her focus was simply on ensuring that she had told them what elements they needed to include and that they had remembered which ones needed to be listed where.

The fact that Irene was so calm in her conduct of the lesson and did not identify any problems with it, suggests that she felt confident that her teaching was consistent with the standard approaches expected in the school, in spite of the school, at least in writing, advocated an inquiry approach to teaching and learning. Whilst we have assumed that there were extensive contradictions between the university programme and the school, and between Irene's conception of learning and that espoused by the university, she did not acknowledge these in any way. It would appear that her practice was valued by the school, in that they had effectively left her to get on with the lesson, and that this was sufficient endorsement for her.

Conclusion

At first glance, these cases may appear to have relatively little in common. Some of the student teachers appeared calm and confident, both about their own performance and about what the pupils had achieved in the lesson observed; others experienced an acute sense of failure. Most of the student teachers were obviously receiving regular and sometimes very close support; others seemed to have been essentially left to their own devices.

What unites them, however, is that when the cases are considered with reference to the objectives of the teacher education programmes within which they were each located, each of them reveals important tensions or contradictions, which were essentially unidentified. In the extreme case, represented by the example of Irene, the intern herself was entirely unaware of the issues and it seems entirely possible that those responsible for her learning in school may also have regarded her teaching as unproblematic. Whilst Sophia and Jacqueline's mentors were much more engaged in offering support and guidance than Irene's mentor, they too seemed oblivious to particular tensions associated, in each case, with subject-specific features of their interns' teaching that conflicted with the emphases of the subject pedagogy promoted by their university partners (MSU and Oxford, respectively). Aneesha and Nereen both recognised that their practice had fallen far short of their ideals, but whilst their mentors sought to offer further advice and considerable reassurance and encouragement, there was again no indication that they had identified the kinds of concerns with effective learning in their respective subjects that would have formed the basis of the subject-specific component advanced in this case by the different university partners within the Teach First programme.

It is interesting to note the importance of subject knowledge and subject pedagogy in giving rise to most of the contradictions revealed in these cases: Sophia and Aneesha both tended to settle for a highly functional or technical approach to teaching about specific features of English rather than developing pupils' capacity to make informed choices about their own use of language. For both Jacqueline and Nereen, concerns to secure the pupils' interest or to sustain the pace of the lesson tended to obscure fundamental aspects of subject pedagogy: the need for adequate repetition and practice when introducing new language or the risks to pupils' understanding in over-emphasising the strangeness of people in the past. Whilst it is perhaps unsurprising that the most extreme example of unacknowledged contradictions should have occurred in Irene's case, where an intern was teaching entirely outside her own area of subject expertise, it is also perhaps significant that Aneesha's mentor did not have a background in English, whilst Nereen's mentor had followed an employment-based route into teaching with limited subject-specific input.

Whilst their sheer diversity obviously illustrates the extent of variation between individual student teachers' social situations of development, it is also very apparent from this collection of cases that praise, reassurance and extensive emotional support are vital, but not sufficient as mediational tools, and that there is no substitute for systematic analysis of student teachers' practice in relation to a range of diverse criteria, including those valued by the university as well as those most apparent both to the student teacher and to their mentor.

References

Burn, K., Hagger, H., Mutton, T. & Everton T. (2003). The complex development of student teachers' thinking, *Teachers and Teaching: Theory and Practice, 9*(4): 309–331.

Thompson, I. (2015). Communication, culture, and conceptual learning: Task design in the English classroom. In I. Thompson (Ed.), *Designing tasks in secondary education: Enhancing subject understanding and student engagement* (pp. 86–106). London: Routledge.

10 Cases of alignment between the micro level of the individual and the meso level of the school (but not with HEI)

Our next series of case studies exemplify alignment between the individual at the micro level and the school at the meso level, but misalignment, tensions or contradictions at the meso level with the higher education institution (HEI). The cases presented in this section illustrate a range of tensions that may emerge from the individual as a learner when the demands of the school conflict with those of the programme. This pattern is potentially more common in situations where student teachers are trying to align their teaching with the specific school context, taking an approach that is strongly influenced by adherence to school practices as reinforced by their mentors and their school department norms and may depart in significant ways from HEI ideals. In high-stakes situations for pupils and schools such as those introduced by current accountability demands and frequent testing, student teachers' tendencies are to relegate the HEI approach to planning, teaching and assessing for that of the school, although with unacknowledged tension at the level of the individual who often attempt to bring in what they have learned in the HEI, albeit without much success. This situation is more likely to occur when there is some misalignment between the goals of the school and those of the HEI or between mentors' and student teachers' individual motives in spite of what otherwise can be seen as healthy partnerships and often as a response to external pressures. This kind of misalignment was common in England and in the United States and on both traditional and alternative routes into teaching. We begin with Alyson a highly competent mathematics intern who finds herself negotiating school and HEI competing demands.

Alyson's struggle to reconcile competing demands

Alyson was learning to teach on a programme at Michigan State University (MSU) that required a 1-year internship before graduation, and she was placed at Midfield Middle School. She came to the programme with a BA degree from MSU with a major in mathematics. She decided to become a mathematics teacher because she was good at mathematics when she was in school herself and also because she was aware that there was a need for mathematics teachers. She said that she felt 'quite comfortable teaching maths and understanding the subject'.

At the time of the observed lesson, Alyson was in the last month of the programme. She was teaching an algebra lesson to an eighth grade class of fairly successful pupils; she had been with this class since the beginning of her internship, first under her mentor's guide and in the final semester as a lead teacher. In the observed lesson, she was revising work with the pupils in preparation for a test that they would have the following day. In thinking about the lesson in question she wanted to encourage her pupils to engage in discussion with one another, using as a model work developed by Pijls and Dekker (2011) to enable pupils to show, explain, justify and reconstruct their own mathematics work. According to Alyson, her goal was to move away from 'product help' (i.e. which assists the pupils in figuring out what the answer is by offering specific mathematical hints), towards 'process help' (i.e. which aids pupils in working together in order to solve a problem). She stated that she wanted 'to make the transition towards offering more process help so that the pupils are more able [*sic*] to discuss their own mathematics without relying on me for help every step of the way'. In terms of the detail of the lesson, Alyson's intention was to 'guide them during the first activity, by giving them questions and checking their answers, and during the second activity, I will just monitor progress and answer any questions that they may have'. The questions that guided the first activity, to be completed on a whiteboard, were included in a worksheet entitled 'Key Concepts for Quiz: Equivalence, Distributive Property, Factoring, Income, Expense, Profit'. During the second activity, the pupils were to work together (in table groups) in order to match different forms of the same expression to show their understanding of equivalence. She also planned to use the activity to evaluate whether her objectives had been met, to see 'where the pupils are still struggling so that I can know what material to explain further before they actually begin the quiz or carry on in the course'.

In the lesson itself, she began by collecting in homework and then distributing the worksheets, which led straight into the work in table groups. During this activity, she monitored what was happening and offered help to individual pupils who seemed increasingly frustrated at not being able to do the task (most pupils at this stage were working individually rather than as a group). When she judged that some pupils were able to get the correct answers she moved on to the second 'whiteboard' activity (which had originally been planned as the first activity) and this took the remainder of the lesson. Throughout, she reminded the pupils that they would need this knowledge for the assessment (quiz) the next day.

When asked how she thought the lesson went Alyson said, 'I think that the session went fairly well; all the pupils were engaged and that was what I was most concerned about since this was a review for their quiz, the next class period.' She did, however, reveal that she had a preoccupation with behaviour management with this class and that it is not unusual, as in this observed lesson, for some pupils to be off task. She observed that '[a]lthough most of the pupils were engaged and on-task, there were still some that tried to derail the others and I think having a better structure could have helped with that'. In terms of her own pedagogy, she said that she felt comfortable with the approaches she had adopted and that these reflected her regular practice. She appeared to know the class well but acknowledged that 'teaching the class is often a struggle between determining what enough support is for those who don't understand, and not so much [support] that those who do [understand] are completely bored and unchallenged'.

Opportunities for development (OfD)

The lesson created a moderate sense of crisis in that Alyson realised, as she was teaching them, that about half of the pupils still had difficulty with the material she was reviewing with them for an upcoming test. The way in which the lesson was structured, however, and the way in which the need to comply with accountability requirements had influenced teaching more broadly helped to moderate this sense of crisis as the expectation was that some pupils would be more successful than others. Alyson justified the problematic situation by explaining that she had, in effect, been expected to teach two separate groups within the same classroom – the pupils who kept up with her fast-paced lesson and problem-solving routines, and those who seemed lost. Yet, in spite of the number of pupils who were obviously not able to understand the work in the way that she had anticipated, she moved ahead with her lesson plan and did not change the pace or the content of her teaching. The plan had been worked out with the classroom teacher and in accordance with the school's mathematics department and Alyson felt a strong expectation that she should comply with the school's demands. Whilst she said that she had planned the lesson according to mathematics education research directed at encouraging pupils to show, explain, justify and reconstruct their own mathematics work (a goal consistent with her teacher preparation programme) the structure of the lesson, framed by the requirement for the pupils to answer a worksheet, did not allow this. Thus, this inherent contradiction between Alyson's stated goals for pupil learning, the demands entailed in preparing pupils to successfully answer a test, and the inquiry-based model of learning advocated by the programme could be observed throughout the lesson. Yet, her goal seemed to shift from making sure that the pupils understood the work to going through the complete worksheet, which given the number of problems to be solved, moved at a very fast pace and allowed little opportunity for the type of group work and collaborative thinking that she had expected to occur.

Opportunities for change (OfC)

OfC provided by mediational tools from the HEI

Whilst Alyson did not explicitly mention the teacher education programme as a source of ideas for the lesson, the fact that she cited a research article as inspiration for what she would have liked to have happened in the lesson indicated the influence of the programme in her planning and in her reflections, though not yet in her practice. The lack of alignment between the educators who taught the classes and those who observed them (the field instructors) led to an important gap, which significantly reduced the mediating tools, provided by the programme, which could help interns better re-contextualise programme norms with school norms, and which might result in conducive OfC. In spite of a weekly class at the university, in which interns were expected to reflect on their school-based experiences and to discuss challenges and successes, it is not clear how Alyson might conciliate a rationale for 'teaching to the test' within a programme that strongly instructs future teachers to teach following an inquiry approach, and to attend to issues of access to knowledge as a matter of social justice.

Whilst it is not possible to fully appreciate the extent to which Alyson is able to pursue an inquiry-oriented approach to teaching mathematics in a class that was designed to help pupils prepare for a test, the fact that about half of the pupils had trouble engaging with the material was very noticeable, yet went unsolved throughout the class. The absence of the mentor teacher in the classroom made it impossible for Alyson to seek advice or gain insights during or after the lesson.

This situation caused a sense of crisis, which Alyson endeavoured to brush aside in order to go through with the lesson plan. This situation which would be seen by the MSU programme as problematic especially from the point of view of social justice, signals an unresolved opportunity to learn for Alyson.

OfC provided by mediational tools within the school

The school was seen as a very supportive environment for learning to teach and Alyson seemed to have a very strong relationship with her mentor. The lesson she taught was designed by and with teachers in her department, and Alyson was committed to implementing it faithfully. The fact that the mentor teacher was not, however, in the classroom observing Alyson effectively, reduced Alyson's opportunities to change or adjust the lesson to the learning pace of her pupils, as the mediating role of the school mentor was absent and she was not able to intervene during the lesson in question. Further, the structure and objective of the lesson plan de facto reduced the opportunity to learn for several of Alyson's pupils. Since the mentor teacher did not observe this, Alyson found herself with no clear way of knowing how to change, and whether the school would support her in changing the lesson, with the inherent risks this would bring. The school's message was clear: the worksheet needed to be completed as this was necessary in order to ensure that the pupils were ready to take the upcoming test. Alyson did what she had been expected to do, in spite of her attempts at reaching all the pupils and her desire to engage them critically in learning the subject. As she mentioned in the debriefing interview, pupils' overall grades are based on 90 per cent assessment and 10 per cent assignment work and so her main concern had been to get through the lesson and for the pupils to pass the test. At the end of the period, the mentor teacher came into the classroom and asked Alyson how the lesson went. Alyson said that it had gone fairly well, and that all the pupils were engaged (which later she said had been her main concern), so the potential role of the mentor in mediating change had been lost because the underlying tensions that she had experienced were not observed by the mentor or articulated by Alyson.

OfC provided by the individual's mediational tools

Alyson organised the pupils as work groups and provided tools (hand-held 'whiteboards' so that individual pupils would write the answers to the problems and show them to her for quick feedback) to change the dynamic of the lesson from a simple review that would entail filling out worksheets. Her hope was that, whilst the activity required the pupils to answer many problems in a short period of time, by organising the pupils in this manner they together would work out the solution to the problems in the worksheet. As she indicated when talking about her plans for the lesson, the idea was to help the pupils to move from 'product help' (where the goal is to get the correct answer) to 'process help' (where the goal is to encourage pupils to show, explain, justify and reconstruct their own mathematics work). Whilst this did not work for about half of the pupils, it did for some, and to a certain extent Alyson did change the way in which pupils were traditionally prepared for tests.

The individual's disposition to recognise the scope for development and change

Whilst it was evident that Alyson had put thought into planning a different kind of review lesson, her reflections after the class did not indicate that she recognised an opportunity for development. Reflecting on her teaching she said that: 'I ask the pupils several times how they got the answer or why the answer is what it is; however, that still tended to focus on the computational aspect rather than the conceptual'. Thus, she failed to recognise areas where she might improve her planning and her practice and rather placed the burden of learning on the pupils.

In her reflection on the class, she said that she was able to review the material in an engaging way for pupils (rather than just having them do a practice quiz and go over the answers for that). She also intimated that she deviated from her original goals by providing more support for the more challenging questions, yet this revealed that if pupils did not know the basic concept related to the question it would be quite difficult for them to answer the many problems provided on that topic. She said that she had also deviated from her original plan by selecting the questions where she thought the pupils needed to spend more time reviewing. Yet, these reflections did not result in her recognising areas for growth, rather her reflections again seemed to place the difficulties encountered in the lesson on the knowledge level of the pupils.

The relative prominence of the subject (or subject pedagogy) in consideration of the need for development or change

It is obvious that Alyson had very good knowledge of the mathematics she was teaching. She herself said that she had strong subject knowledge and that her choice to become a teacher was based on her facility with the subject. In the observed lesson, the goal had been to help pupils become fluent with the concepts they were learning. 'Fluency' in mathematics is one of the goals stated in the United States' 'Common Core Standards' and assessments have been designed to measure this skill in the pupils. There is no question that Alyson was fluid in this area, yet this fluidity might have had detracted from the pedagogical goals that she wanted to achieve. The fast pace of the lesson and a very high number of problems to solve, might, it is true, have indicated fluidity and given the lesson a good sense of momentum, but the cost of this appears to have been a lack of opportunity for the pupils to acquire deeper understandings of the key concepts. Given her own comfort with her subject knowledge, Alyson did not see OfD in this area; it was, however, obvious that she needed more support in learning what is understood as the *pedagogy* of the subject (referred to as pedagogical content knowledge in Chapter 1).

Alyson was aware of her limitations in being able to find multiple ways to convey concepts and in being receptive to her pupils' feedback and said that her 'most pressing learning needs is to be able to create several different ways of explaining the concept and also developing methods of switching between those different explanations to make student understanding smoother', yet she did not elaborate on how she would do this. Because she attributed the difficulties in the lesson to the pupils (in that her reflection was that some understand and some do not), and because of her own security in her mathematics subject knowledge, it was unclear how she might try to change or where would she go for help. Returning to the professional knowledge needed for teaching, she did seem to think that she needed to make connections across the different curriculum topics she was teaching, and needed to explain things in different ways, but did not seem to be concerned with learning more about how to help pupils who lacked understanding of the subject, or how to teach the subject to those pupils beyond that. She saw her role 'as more of a facilitator, where I presented the questions and then leading them to the answers where needed' – a notion that seemed to conflict with her aim of 'process help' and one, which might be unhelpful for her and her pupils in the long run.

The extent of alignment (and thus, of the scope for tensions or contradictions) between the individual, HEI and school

Alyson's case provides us with an understanding of the way in which beginning teachers struggle to realise their own pedagogical goals when they have neither the sophisticated pedagogical knowledge that they require nor the experience on which they need to draw in order to reflect effectively on the outcomes of their teaching. Whilst her goals at this stage of the programme seemed to reflect an approach that would be consistent with that offered by the university programme and whilst she was keen to realise these goals in her practice, the situated demands of the school required her to align that practice to the established norms, which in this case meant preparing pupils sufficiently well for their upcoming assessment. In trying to attempt something different during the lesson before the assessment, it is not surprising that she failed – she was not experienced enough herself to be able to address issues around the pupils' conceptual development in this way; she did not have the support of her mentor in helping her navigate this difficult territory; and, crucially, the pupils themselves were not familiar with what she was trying to achieve so ended up feeling frustrated and confused in some cases. Faced with such difficulties it is understandable why beginning teachers might go for the easier option of following the 'tried and tested' practices of others with whom they are working, in line with accepted institutional norms.

The extent of alignment between the individual and the school

Alyson was in a programme that required a 1-year internship before graduation. Because of the high-stakes placed on the school internship and on the mentor's assessment of interns' performance for graduation, alignment with school and standards/assessments tended to be very high, and this was the case for Alyson. In addition, over the last 10 years, mathematics performance in schools in the United States has received much attention. During the time of the study, schools across the country were struggling to implement the Common Core Standards (as was evident both in this school and in Alyson's teaching). As Alyson herself explained, a pupil's grade is determined 90 per cent from assessment and 10 per cent from assignments. Thus, Alyson's lesson plans and practice were strongly shaped by the culture of the school and all the pressures coming from curriculum alignment and demands for accountability. There was therefore, strong alignment with the school department and with the teachers.

The extent of alignment between the individual and the HEI

Within the increased frequency of testing and accountability the teacher education programme would have approved of Alyson's attempt at both changing a review for a test to make it a more dynamic and meaningful review of mathematical concepts, and at forming a learning community in her classroom. The programme would also have approved of Alyson's stated goals and of her use of research as a reference to increase pupils' constructive engagement with challenging mathematics topics. Yet, Alyson ran into difficulty when she tried to put her plans into practice. The theory to practice connection (also mentioned in Chapter 1) may help to explain some of Alyson's difficulties; her key problem, however, was in the lack of alignment between the goals of the school and those of the programme. For instance, dedicating a full lesson for a drill before the test goes against the constructivist approach of the programme. Accepting the premise that some pupils understand and some do not also goes against the programme's commitment to prepare teachers to educate all learners, to embrace diversity and to teach for understanding. Finally, the programme would expect Alyson to be able to integrate theory with practice and teaching experience with reflection on that experience. Unfortunately, the distance between the programme goals and the school goals left Alyson in a difficult position. The supervision of the internship by the programme does, however, rely on field instructors to be the key providers of feedback, which can occur five times per semester and requires programme professors contact with the interns for 3 hours per week, so it could be argued that the influence of the programme once interns are deeply immersed in teaching is less than it would be ideally.

The extent of alignment between the school and the HEI

Alyson's goal, at least in this lesson, was to help pupils engage in discussions with the notion that they would help one another learn, yet this dynamic did not seem to be happening, in part because the curriculum standards explicitly ask for 'fluency', which by definition does not allow much time for thoughtful discussion. Her idea of the teacher as a 'facilitator' appeared to be preventing her from intervening when pupils needed clear explanations and guidance. Instead, a number of pupils seemed to be very confused and frustrated and as a consequence, were falling behind. Can the idea of being a teacher of fluency combine well with the idea of the teacher as facilitator? The analogy of learning a new language is illustrative of how difficult it might be to understand what is going on if one lacks an understanding of the basic structures and of the vocabulary. Whilst arguably she was preparing her pupils for a quiz, the glimpses of the previous class, a day earlier, showed the pace and the basic structure to be the same. In the quiz preparation worksheet, even the problems with the most text (profit equations) lacked sensible context. She herself admitted that she needed more knowledge to be able to see the connections across concepts and themes. Can there be a way to begin working from the 'inside' and from that starting point to develop a pedagogy that will help underserved pupils to become more knowledgeable, compassionate and successful? Whilst Alyson had internal drive (based on what she said that she wanted to achieve in the lesson) there was clearly a mismatch with external drives coming from the institution, the school and the subject department.

Further examples of alignment between the individual and school culture and practices (but not with HEI)

Alyson's case is one of several that reflected alignment between the beginning teacher and the culture and practices of the internship (or placement) school, but with less strong alignment with the university. The three cases below offer further examples. Interestingly, the first two cases both deal with beginning teachers in England recruited to the School Direct programme, delivered in collaboration with the university. In this model, aspiring trainee teachers apply to the designated lead school, not the university, for a place on the programme and this school has a key role to play in both the selection of candidates and in the planning and delivery of the teacher education programme. A School Direct lead school must also offer the expectation of employment at the school (or in a partner school) at the end of the training period, although there is no legal requirement to provide such employment. Within this context, as in Alyson's case, it is perhaps to be expected that there will be strong alignment between the beginning teacher and the school, but it is not the case that this should imply any necessary reduction in the alignment with the university, although this appears to be what occurs in the two cases that focus on School Direct student teachers, as well as in the third case presented here.

Megan: a shared concern with managing behaviour that restricted the focus on subject pedagogy

Megan was an English intern at the University of Oxford who had been recruited by Riverside Academy under the School Direct programme (in association with the university). She was highly qualified (with a first class degree in English and Modern Languages and a doctorate in Applied Linguistics) and with a specialist research interest in pupils who have English as an Additional Language (EAL). The observed lesson took place in January, in the third week of her full-time placement in her internship school where she had been placed since September during the 'Joint Weeks' part of the programme (2 or 3 days each week in school and 2 or 3 days at the university) and was part of a sequence of lessons focusing on the children's author Michael Morpurgo's (2003) novel *Private Peaceful*, set in World War I (WWI). In planning the lesson, Megan appeared to be conscious of development targets for her teaching that had been set previously, following a joint discussion between Megan, her mentor and her subject tutor shortly before Christmas. Briefly, these were the need to consider providing opportunities for learners to evaluate and improve their performance; making accurate and productive use of assessment and feedback; being more aware of low level poor behaviour/disengagement and using appropriate behaviour management strategies to address this. The latter is unsurprising since much of the ongoing discussion between the mentor and Megan focused on questions of behaviour management, perhaps reflecting the mentor's own priorities as a pastoral leader in the school. For the mentor, the key point of development for Megan was better management of the classroom rather than considerations of learning or assessment.

The lesson planning focused on features of informal letter writing and in Megan's words 'paves the way for the pupils' formative and summative assignments'. The lesson plan itself indicated that the lesson would begin with a period of silent reading (which was the policy of the English department at Riverside Academy), with the main body of the lesson following a 'four part'[1] lesson structure (starter, introduction, development, plenary). Megan's planning highlighted both the pedagogic and curriculum demands that she faced in planning a lesson as well as the school's cultural expectations in relation to pupil participation. She told us that:

> This lesson will introduce two main ideas: one, the fact that letters from WWI are artefacts, which can tell us about this period in history from the individual, personal perspective of soldiers who fought in the war; and two, the idea that informal letters share a number of common features.

There was an attempt here to link the pupils' developing understanding of and empathy for soldiers' lives during the war with a genre-based classification of textual features. However, Megan's lesson objective: 'To understand how we gain insight into what WWI was like for real soldiers', sounded more like a history lesson than an English one and suggested a tension between her pedagogic aims and the message that she shared with the pupils. Megan also mentioned that she was 'currently working on classroom manners with this class (i.e. ensuring that pupils don't speak over me/over their peers; ensuring that pupils put up their hands before speaking, etc.).'

The lesson itself appeared to focus a lot on control: both of the atmosphere of the classroom (particularly pupil behaviour), and learning. Almost half of the 50-minute lesson was given over to silent reading and procedural tasks, with no particular focus on developing the pupils' learning in relation to the lesson objectives. When the main task was introduced there was very little time for pupil discussion and the lesson appeared to be very much teacher directed. Megan's reflections after the lesson revealed that she did not explore in any great detail why she thought the lesson objectives were not met and, furthermore, her comments suggested unease with mixed-ability teaching because she seemed to equate lower attaining pupils with disruptive behaviour:

> There are a few quite immature pupils in this class who can be disruptive. This is a mixed-ability classroom, with the full range of abilities. We have five pupils on the SEND register, three EAL pupils and two pupils who receive the Pupil Premium.[2]

The possibility for OfD were clearly there, given the potential tensions evident in both the planning and delivery of the lesson, but they remained hidden for Megan because of strong alignment with the values of the school and the particular areas of emphasis on which her mentor chose to focus. Despite Megan expressing that she did not achieve her lesson objectives, there was no real reflection on her part on the extent of pupil learning within the lesson. Her reaction that the pupils were at least well behaved was mediated by the concerns of her mentor (who was also primarily concerned with behaviour management issues) and hence, most of Megan's references to pedagogical decision-making were related to the implications in terms of pupil behaviour:

> However, I felt a bit more comfortable. I often include activities, which allow pupils to do more group work. I love doing group work but it can get rowdy!

The school context was only partially able to afford Megan the OfC because the dominant relationship was that with the mentor who focused on social issues and behaviour management rather than pedagogy. Whilst Megan reported feeling appropriately challenged by her subject tutor (who encouraged her to develop a sense of criticality) her own sense of agency in determining how she would move forward appeared to be low in the face of the nature of support from her mentor. Although well-meaning, this tended to be over-protective and meant that Megan was not challenged on the effectiveness of her task design or delivery.

Overall, her strong alignment with the school's expectation of the way she should do things (including specific policies and practices, as well as the strong mediation from her mentor) and a desire to conform, meant that Megan was not able to recognise the potential OfD. It was not, however, that she was inherently averse to change since her decision to move from an academic career to a professional one showed a willingness and commitment to change, but in the context in which she was now working she saw little incentive to do so. Her apparent acceptance of a lack of challenge and criticality in the process of her own development was also reflected in her approach to the teaching of the subject itself. The lesson indicated that the primary concern was the management of student behaviour rather than the development of their understanding of the subject, and the task she had planned (to consider the common feature of informal letters) was one that she later acknowledged had been 'low access' and not sufficiently challenging for some of the pupils. The OfC resulting from this evaluation were, however, low because one of the key issues – Megan's weak understanding of genre theory – had not been identified by her mentor nor subsequently addressed.

Megan's strong alignment with both the policies and practices of her internship school (including the emphasis given to the need to prepare pupils adequately for both formative and summative assessments) and her mentor's priorities contrasted with the low level of alignment with the university programme. Although there was apparent consensus between the latter and the principles espoused and promoted within the Riverside Academy English department, this was not borne out in the relationship between Megan and her mentor who focused predominantly on issues around behaviour rather than subject pedagogy.

Sandrine: a deep sense of coherence as she was socialised into school practices

Sandrine was a well-qualified French native speaker who had worked previously as a Foreign Languages Assistant at Riverside Academy, which then recruited her to the School Direct programme where she was a Modern Foreign Languages (MFL) intern. The observed lesson, which took place in late January, was slightly unusual in that she was preparing a small group of Year 10 pupils (14- to 15-year-olds) for an imminent 'controlled assessment' writing task, the results of which would count towards each individual pupil's final French General Certificate of Secondary Education (GCSE) score. The planning included opportunities to explain the controlled assessment procedures to the class, some further coverage of the language content (focusing on talking about 'my town') and some opportunities for the pupils to think about what a good piece of writing at this level might look like, with opportunities for them to evaluate some examples themselves. She said she wanted to 'give them the tools to prepare their writing independently'. She was keen that the pupils should feel reassured about the impending assessment. In terms of the ideas for the lesson, she drew mainly on her own previous experience with the class, the MFL department's scheme of work and her knowledge of the GCSE examination requirements. The usual class teacher helped by making suggestions for activities for the lesson, but Sandrine planned the actual lesson itself independently. The structure of the lesson followed the lesson planning format recommended by her subject tutors, and she anticipated some of the things that might happen to upset her plans (such as the overhead projector not working, as had been the case in the previous lesson); she had prepared printed resources just in case.

During the lesson itself, Sandrine worked through most of the activities she had planned and she demonstrated that she was confident in her own subject knowledge, both in terms of the language itself (as a native speaker of French) but also in her knowledge of the examination syllabus, including the specific nature of the 'controlled assessment' and what pupils needed to have done in preparation for them. The class appeared to trust her and recognised that the guidance she was giving was relevant and appropriate. She herself was 'really happy with the way the lesson went' and she demonstrated many of the behaviours of a competent teacher (for example, there was a good rapport with the pupils; she knew exactly what they needed at this stage of their learning as far as examination preparation was concerned; there was a lesson starter that revised previous work; she got the pupils to apply assessment criteria to a sample of work themselves; and she managed behaviour effectively). Sandrine nevertheless, missed various opportunities for the pupils to develop their knowledge and understanding (for example, in providing developmental feedback to the pupils following completion of the content-focused tasks, or structuring the tasks themselves so that there was progression and increasing levels of challenge). Her own evaluation of the lesson indicated that there were not significant development areas for her to consider:

> I do not feel that I need to improve anything with that particular class. I am really conscious of each of the pupils' level, I know the curriculum for KS4 [Key Stage 4] perfectly (because I have been working in the school with

exam classes for 2 years before my training) and I am really confident with my subject knowledge (which is also my mother tongue).

Overall, there was no sense of 'crisis' in Sandrine's experience of learning to teach because she was confident in her subject knowledge, was able to integrate the policies and practices of the school effectively into her teaching and was able to replicate the practice of her colleagues successfully. Sandrine's socialisation into the MFL department of the school had taken place before her initial teacher education programme began and she was already familiar with the ways of working of her colleagues and of the school in general. There were few tensions in her pedagogic practices and her general pedagogic discourse, and Sandrine's own approaches to teaching resonated with the established practices of those around her. Although the HEI programme had explicitly encouraged her to think critically about what she was learning from a range of different sources, her decision-making was influenced primarily by her desire to fit in with the established practices of the school. There were few internal tensions between what she was trying to achieve and what actually happened in the classroom and, because she was a competent teacher, there appeared to be less need for a mentoring approach that highlighted and addressed any such potential tensions and challenges – the approach taken appeared to be one that affirmed her practice rather than one that set new challenges for her. This, coupled with her own disposition to be satisfied that she had achieved enough, did not lead her to consider alternative approaches nor to reflect on potential learning opportunities for the pupils that might have been missed – she saw no need to change an approach that she believed to be working sufficiently well.

Given the nature of the programme (with its strong emphasis on language acquisition) and Sandrine's own identity as a native speaker of French, and given that Sandrine had few issues with behaviour management, which might have otherwise been the focus of her classroom practice, there were certainly OfD in relation to her own subject pedagogy. Again, however, the sense that she was doing enough to plan and deliver successful lessons in more generic terms may have masked any awareness of the potential for further development in her subject pedagogy.

There was clearly strong alignment with the standards and practices of the school in which Sandrine was training. As a School Direct trainee she hoped to be employed by the school at the end of the training year (which did, in fact, happen) she appeared to take on the policies and practices of both the MFL department and the school in an uncritical way. Furthermore, she was at ease with her colleagues and keen to be seen as a reliable member of a team. This strong predisposition to fit in meant that there was less alignment with the underlying principles of the Initial Teacher Education programme as a whole and it appeared to have little impact on her overall development. She saw herself as coming to the programme with good subject knowledge, experience of teaching in the school in question, good knowledge of curriculum and examination frameworks and some previous theoretical knowledge of language acquisition, and now, perhaps, only requiring the opportunity to demonstrate her competence in order to gain Qualified Teacher Status. There were no outward tensions in relation to this strong alignment to the school and a less strong alignment to the HEI because Sandrine did what she felt was required of her, aligned herself effectively with the policies and practices of the school and was confident in her planning and teaching, and in the relationships that she established with the pupils.

Jane: anxious to conform to school expectations but aware of subject knowledge deficiencies (that the school did not expect to – and the university had not managed to – address)

Jane was a PGCE Science intern at the University of Oxford who came to the programme with a BSc in Biochemistry and who offered chemistry as her subject specialism; she was placed at Groveside Academy and the lesson which was observed took place towards the end of February after several weeks in the placement school on a full-time basis (having been placed in the school on a part-time basis during the 'Joint Weeks' of the programme before Christmas). The lesson was a physics lesson taught to a class of Year 7 pupils (11- to 12-year-olds) in which there was to be revision of previous content (electricity and magnetism) in preparation for a forthcoming assessment. The actual lesson plan indicated that the pupils would be asked to complete a 'carousel' of seven different activities during the lesson, each lasting just over 5 minutes, with some questioning and further information following the completion of the activities by all the pupils. The lesson was planned independently but was supported by the class teacher in this process; the activities selected were all taken from either the textbook or from a website of published resources for teachers. Jane indicated that the content might 'be difficult for dyslexic pupils and slow readers and writers due to the activities involving reading and writing', but appeared not to have made any adjustments either to the plan or the materials to take account of this factor. She also anticipated that some activities might be completed more quickly than others and might require some extension work, but had not prepared for such a contingency.

The lesson did not proceed totally in the way that Jane had intended and there were issues around time management. First, some of the activities required different amounts of time for completion, so some activities were completed well within the time allowed and others required longer; second, there was not time to complete all the work that she had planned for the lesson. For Jane, the situation of crisis in this lesson was having to teach physics when her specialty was biochemistry. She understood that in order to be a science teacher in England she had to be able to teach all three science subjects, which meant that she had to develop her subject knowledge in physics rapidly, as well as learn to teach the subject itself. In the observed lesson, there was less challenge in terms of her subject knowledge because it was a revision lesson and carried a lower level of difficulty (the assumption being that the pupils, and Jane, had already learned the material) but nevertheless, Jane was still clearly uncomfortable. She had been asked to plan the lesson herself (with some support from the classroom teacher), and in addition to her limited knowledge of the subject she also seemed to experience problems with classroom management and time management.

Jane had not been left alone to develop her subject knowledge in physics and the PGCE programme provided strong support at the university to science interns as they responded to the challenges of teaching out of their immediate subject specialism. Mentors were also encouraged to support the interns in developing their subject knowledge where necessary and the question of how to do this had been addressed regularly at regular meetings of the science mentors with the subject tutors. Yet, in spite of this, Jane did not mention the programme as a source of support or ideas in her struggle to prepare and teach this lesson.

The feedback from the mentor immediately after the lesson was direct: Jane needed to plan for differentiation; needed to manage her time better (as she had run out of time); and needed to learn to think on her feet. Jane also received feedback from the classroom teacher who advised that Jane needed to improve her presence 'as a teacher' in the classroom, to focus on classroom management issues, and to anticipate the different learning needs of individual pupils. For the mentor, whilst knowledge of the subject is important, it is 'not what would make or break a novice teacher'. In fact, her view was that not knowing the subject well as a subject specialist meant that Jane had to approach her teaching as a learner herself and would therefore, be better able to anticipate the needs of her pupils. Therefore, whilst Jane had strong school support and was receiving feedback related to specific aspects of classroom practice, in the specific area where she believed she needed more guidance (i.e. teaching outside her subject specialism) support from the school was lacking.

Jane therefore, had to rely on her own initiative to address her lack of subject knowledge in physics, and the way that she appeared to do this in this particular lesson was to rely on published resources and activities and then to structure the lesson around these activities in a fairly prescriptive way, relying on the response from the pupils to generate any further discussion of the topic as necessary. Nevertheless, she was supported in the planning itself by the class teacher. She was very receptive to feedback and was aware of the areas that had been identified by her mentors as needing further development. Furthermore, Jane was aware of her limitations in terms of her subject knowledge in physics, but she was not able to identify how the school or the programme could help her develop the knowledge and skills that she needed and seemed to be unwilling to accept that this had had an obvious negative effect on the lesson observed.

At one level, Jane was working very hard to meet the school expectations of her, as communicated by her mentor and classroom teacher. Her lesson plan followed the structure that was used in the school and at the end of the lesson the feedback provided by the classroom teacher and the mentor was in terms of her compliance with the structure (for example, the lack of a plenary activity meant that she was not able to make a summative evaluation of the level of learning that had taken place and this was seen as a deficiency by both her mentor and the classroom teacher). Whilst the school assumed that Jane would naturally be able to work out how to teach in general (and more specifically in relation to teaching outside her subject specialism) she may, however, have needed stronger direction.

Furthermore, Jane felt pulled by the programme's expectations concerning the development of deep subject-specific understanding, and its strong emphasis on knowing the subject well. Where this became evident as an opportunity for development was in the tensions that arose between the pragmatic approaches that Jane took (which resulted in her trying to teach in a way that followed certain effective procedures promoted by the school) and the need to develop the pupils' conceptual awareness within the subject. By teaching in a procedural way – and receiving feedback and development targets that were likewise related to procedural issues, such as suggestions as to how to manage group work more effectively – she was not challenged to address the question of her lack of sufficient knowledge to be able to develop the pupils' appropriate concepts in the subject (evidenced, for example, in the limited surface reasoning when she attempted to respond to the pupils' questions or deal with their claims that they had not fully understood the content).

Overall, it was clear that Jane was trying both to teach in a way that would gain the approval of the school colleagues with whom she was working and to address the subject issues in pragmatic ways that she had developed for herself. These approaches, however, were masking the underlying issues in her subject teaching, which she herself was not able to recognise. Her sense that the observed lesson 'ran smoothly' concealed the key question as to whether or not the pupils were now able to master the complex subject material on which the lesson had been focused.

Conclusion

The cases presented here within the same overall category, reflect a number of tensions, particularly in the way in which the student teachers in question were trying to develop their own professional practice whilst at the same time being conscious of the need to fit in with the expected behaviours and practices of the school in which they were placed. The strong alignment with the school context and the relatively low level of alignment with the university programme, in each case, resulted in the identification of fewer OfD than might have otherwise been the case, and fewer resultant OfC.

As has been seen elsewhere amongst other cases, some of the lessons described here were problematic in that they appeared to fail to present the pupils with an appropriate degree of conceptual challenge, yet in the student teachers' own evaluations of these lessons they chose not to focus on this as an issue and in several cases were satisfied with the outcomes (Jane's assertion, for example, that the lesson 'ran smoothly' and Sandrine's view that she did not need to improve any aspect of her teaching with that particular class). The lessons appeared to be evaluated in terms of the extent to which the student teachers had achieved what had been expected of them. Even Alyson, whose aspirations were to move towards a 'process help' approach, ended up having to resort to the 'product help' that she hoped to avoid, mainly because of her lack of experience in planning and delivering the sort of lesson that ideally she would have liked to have taught. Faced with a lack of sufficient experience themselves, the student teachers represented in the four case studies in this chapter tend to deal with this challenge by adhering closely to the practices of their more experienced colleagues in order to demonstrate their competence – what Edwards and Protheroe (2004) have referred to as 'teaching by proxy' (p. 183). One way in which this emerges in these cases is the way in which the student teachers in question are expected to adopt (often uncritically) the tools, which have been judged to be appropriate by the school for these specific purposes. So, for example, Megan began her lesson with a period of silent reading as this was the policy of the English department at her school; Alyson was required to use a specific worksheet; and Jane was required to use the school's own lesson-planning format. Whilst all of these policies and practices may have intrinsic value, what is noticeable is that the student teachers do not have the opportunity to form their own judgements about such value through exploring and evaluating possible alternatives.

The particular contexts in which this occurs throughout these cases also reveal other common features. In all four cases, the emphasis is on preparing the pupils for an impending assessment of one sort or another. In three of the cases (Alyson, Sandrine and Jane), the purpose of the lesson was to revise specific content ahead of a school test or, in the case of Sandrine, a controlled assessment that formed part of the GCSE examination. The accepted school practices for such preparation were adopted by the student teachers and the lessons were to a great extent 'scripted' within such requirements, thus, limiting the scope for more creative planning, yet the need to prepare pupils adequately for regular assessments is a feature of both the United States and English school contexts so ultimately has to be part of the repertoire of these student teachers. What singles out what happened in each of these cases, however, is not the adherence to a pre-determined approach, but rather the lack of responsiveness to the opportunities that arose in each of the lessons when the pupils' learning might have been developed more fully.

Another feature of these cases appears to be the tendency of the student teachers to categorise their pupils in particular ways, often reflecting the discourse prevalent in many schools. So Megan talks about the 'range of abilities' of pupils in her class and those who may have specific barriers to learning or those from particular types of background; Alyson talks about 'those who don't understand' and 'those who do' and the level of support required for each of these groups; and Jane discusses how the content she had prepared might not be appropriate 'for dyslexic pupils and slow readers and writers'. Such a way of seeing pupils may reflect the pedagogic practice of many schools, based on notions of fixed ability and where 'differentiation' is the tool by which the learning needs of a range of different pupils might be addressed. Even though these student teachers may have aspirations to provide challenging learning opportunities for all their pupils, they often lack the experience needed to enable a more expansive view of learning to be enacted in the classroom, and so it is perhaps unsurprising that they resort to an approach that leads them to categorise pupils in such a way that they can then demonstrate that they have taken sufficient steps in their planning to address these diverse needs.

Pupil behaviour (and the related issue of pupil engagement) is another common area of focus for all of these student teachers. Alyson acknowledges her preoccupation with behaviour management and for Megan it is one of the key aspects of her teaching, supported by her mentor's own views as to what lies at the heart of effective teaching and learning. Jane is advised that she needs to develop a stronger classroom presence in order to keep the pupils more engaged and for Sandrine it is the fact that she has no behaviour problems at all that enables her to deliver what she considers to be a successful lesson, but nevertheless, one in which there is perhaps insufficient challenge for many of the pupils. For these student teachers, managing pupil behaviour effectively represents perhaps one of the key measures by which experienced teachers are recognised and it is therefore, unsurprising that this issue dominates much of their thinking, given that they demonstrate alignment between themselves as individuals and the culture and practices of the school in which they are working.

Finally, these cases reflect the way in which these student teachers focus on what might be considered the more generic skills of teaching at the expense of the development of subject-specific pedagogy. Alyson does start off trying to develop a 'process help' approach that will develop the pupils' conceptual understanding, but eventually fails to put this into practice since she has to cope with the many other demands of the classroom. For Megan, Sandrine and Jane the subject itself seems to be a secondary consideration. Megan ends up planning what resembles a history lesson rather than an English lesson because she fails to address the key English concepts that might be developed within the study of the WWI texts; Sandrine focuses primarily on coverage of the language the pupils will need in order to cope with the forthcoming controlled assessment, but in doing so presents only formulaic language and misses the opportunity to develop the pupils' wider communicative competence; and Jane is concerned with providing enough activities to keep the pupils occupied, but pays little attention to the level of conceptual difficulty of each of these activities.

Whilst there are clearly differences between the four cases presented in this chapter, it is clear that the policies and practices of the school have exerted a large influence on the way in which these student teachers develop. The OfD that are identified relate predominantly to the acquisition of behaviours and skills, which are necessary for what is judged to be effective teaching in each of these contexts and the OfC are therefore, mediated by the teachers with whom they are working most closely, using the cultural tools particular to those contexts. Whilst the criteria for success are clearly identified and performance is measured against these criteria, there is perhaps the danger, from the evidence here, that what may be neglected is the opportunity to develop the student teachers' subject-specific pedagogy through innovation in their own teaching.

Notes

1 This suggested lesson structure was adopted by the majority of secondary schools in England following the implementation of the National Literacy Strategy (later becoming part of the wider National Strategy) by the Labour government from 1998 onwards (DfE 2011). The 'National Strategy' was discarded by the new coalition government in 2010 but many schools continue to use this, or a similar planning structure.
2 Pupils with a learning difficulty or disability which calls for special education provision to be made for them are identified on the special educational needs and disability (SEND) register. Approximately, 20 per cent of pupils in schools in England appear on the SEND register. EAL pupils are those who have a language other than English as their first language. In primary schools, EAL pupils currently make up just over 20 per cent of the school population; in secondary schools it is 16 per cent. The Pupil Premium Grant was introduced by the coalition government in 2011 and comprises additional payments made to schools for each child who is, or has been eligible for free school meals at any point in the last 6 years; for each child from a family in the armed services; and for children in local authority care or adopted from care.

References

Department for Education (DfE). (2011). *The national strategies: English*. Richmond, UK: The National Archives. Retrieved from http://webarchive.nationalarchives.gov.uk/20110113104120/http://nationalstrategies.standards.dcsf.gov.uk/secondary/english.

Edwards, A. & Protheroe, L. (2004). Teaching by proxy: Understanding how mentors are positioned in partnerships, *Oxford Review of Education, 30*(2), 183–197.

Morpurgo, M. (2003). *Private peaceful*. London: Harper Collins Publishers.

Pijls, M. & Dekker, R. (2011). Pupils discussing their mathematical ideas: The role of the teacher. *Mathematics Education Research Journal, 23*, 379–396.

11 Cases of alignment between the micro level of the individual and the meso level of the HEI (but not with the school)

The two case studies in this chapter are examples of vertical alignment between the individual student teacher and the higher education institution (HEI), and some degree of misalignment with the school. In these cases, the dominance of the programme's aims and conceptions of the subject, the subject pedagogy and of pupils' learning as understood and held by the individual, clashed with those of the school. This meant that there were important opportunities for development OfD and opportunities for change OfC tensions/contradictions apparent to the individual and the mentor teacher often emerging from planning and enacting practices that conflicted with established practice in the classroom, or with a highly structured curriculum. Whilst these tensions and contradictions were often present and provided a fertile ground for development, the potential for change represented an individual struggle between 'fitting-in' or 'challenging the status quo', and meant that student teachers found themselves struggling to figure out whether and how programme ideals may have a place in the overly regulated (testing/standards) school climate, in what is for them a high-stakes situation.

William's struggle to convey science content using an inquiry-based approach

William was learning to teach on the secondary programme at Michigan State University (MSU) that required a 1-year internship before graduation. He was placed at Highfield High School for his internship. He came to the programme with a interdepartmental major in biological sciences from MSU. He was a highly energetic individual who was enthusiastic about science and cared about encouraging pupils to take an active interest in science; he did so by adopting an inquiry approach to teaching science as advocated by the initial teacher education programme. He had actively trained himself to use learning technologies in the classroom and was not afraid of implementing his newly learned skills to engage pupils in interacting with him as he taught. At the time of the observation William had been teaching this class since the beginning of the academic year and he was about a month away from obtaining teaching certification.

In the particular lesson observed, William was teaching an 'Egg Osmosis Lab' to a high school biology class in grade 9. This lesson was part of a unit on cell membrane and the complexities of molecule transport. In explaining the plans for the lab, he said:

> We will be talking about osmosis and all different kinds of membrane diffusion. We will also be recording data from our egg osmosis lab that we began on the day prior. I will be explaining how to conduct good lab etiquette as well as guiding discussion about the cell membrane. Students will be recording data as well as working in groups to complete lab and worksheet tasks.

William thought that this lesson would contribute to pupils learning because they would 'get a hands on view of a scientific process and be able to work hands on with biology. Students will have to conceptualise concepts that were discussed and make valid predictions based on their logical connections'. All these ideas demonstrate a high level of alignment with the teachings in the university.

In explaining his approach to teaching, William said that he liked to relate the content to something that is popular in the students' culture:

> A big example during this lesson, 'Clash of Clans' is a popular game that I can make references to, the cell membrane is comparable to the city base walls. Only certain things can get through to the town centre and, similar to the cell membrane, if the object entering is dangerous it can change the city for better or worse.

During the lesson part of the lab, pupils did attend to William's explanations and followed 'lab etiquette'. When the pupils had completed the experiment, however, they did not seem to have a clear idea what to do with their eggs, even though instructions that were given before the experiment were that they should leave their eggs where they found them, but William failed to enforce these instructions or to monitor that in fact all pupils had done so before moving on to the next demonstration. Instead, William moved on to begin a demonstration of how cell membranes work, which required a teabag in a teapot with boiling water. The fact that only some pupils duly deposited their eggs as instructed and others decided to keep it, resulted in a student having an 'accident' with his egg, which broke on his lap and stained his pants much to the concern of the mentor teacher who had to take the student to get cleaned up, and resulted in the class getting distracted as well. Whilst William tried to establish control by moving on to the teabags in the boiling water to illustrate dispersion and their porosity as an example of a membrane, a number of pupils were still laughing and commenting on the broken egg.

Throughout the lesson, William maintained a high level of science language as did the students. To evaluate learning, William introduced the use of the

'Plickers software' (a way to create questions that pupils can see in their iPads and interact with during class). The introduction of this software was one of William's contribution to innovating his teaching and fitted William's vision of the teaching and learning dynamic that he wanted to see in his classroom. The 'Plickers software' is described online as a 'problem posing – solving tool that gives students thinking time to problem-solve' (Plickers, 2017). When explaining his pedagogy William said:

> For today, I wanted students to stay engaged throughout the entire lesson. Using technology through Plickers questions was a great way to bring students back home to reflect on what they learned. Giving them enough time to do their work in the beginning of class gives them well-deserved freedom and trust, but I wanted to also have them start to develop a sense of responsibility for their work.

William's approach to teaching science was consistent not only with the school's philosophy, but also with the MSU inquiry-based approach to learning to teach science. He explained:

> This was Day 2 of the lab, so students are beginning to form observations. I didn't want students to have a full grasp of what is going on next, but I want them to have a decent guess at what their eggs will look like the next day. For example, some of them placed their egg in corn syrup, causing their egg to shrink. After seeing the water at the top of their beaker, I would hope they would hypothesise that water will rush back into the cell if placed in water for another day.

When asked what he did to prepare for the lesson, William said: 'A simple lesson plan, lab write-up, and purchase of materials; making sure I have enough eggs and vinegar'. Whilst he said that, his ideas were drawn from the mentor teacher and peers who suggested the lab, he seemed to have done the planning by himself, likely missing the opportunity to anticipate with his mentor teacher how the lesson may develop.

In reflecting on how the class went, William said: 'it had an "organised chaos" feel which is a great mix for my classroom'. Indeed, that feeling of organised chaos put him at odds with his mentor teacher, who whilst agreeing that William was comfortable with the subject, worried that William had not yet developed habits that might help him to be more successful in the classroom. For instance, his mentor confessed that whilst he gave him a great deal of feedback (often meeting every day of the week) he wondered if 'he is actually listening'. The mentor considered this intern's major weaknesses to be self-reflection and classroom management. The mentor went on to say that the intern needed to understand that 'there are things he must do to be a successful teacher that he may not agree with. Right now I don't think he understands his professional responsibilities outside of actually teaching the students'. The mentors' main strategy was one of 'sometimes allowing the intern to fail when I know it is going to happen and then discussing it with him being the one doing most of the talking and reflecting'.

The mentor was supportive of the intern's use of technology and the intern's level of science knowledge. The mentor emphasised classroom management, and time management in delivering lessons as areas for change. The tension in the relationship between the intern and the mentor was, as the mentor remarked, the very different teaching style by the intern.

William had the idea that a good science teacher is someone who gives pupils the freedom to act and experiment, and felt that the rigid nature of schools made engagement with science difficult. It is possible to say that he saw himself as an advocate of pupils' science learning in spite of schools' procedures and regulations. For him, it was also important to be liked by his pupils and thought that this would happen by trying to become their friend or by being more lenient. Upon reflection and almost at the end of his lead teaching, he thought that this way of acting did not help his students. When asked to consider what he needed to learn to support the science learning of his students, he said:

> My students need to improve on the quality of their work; a big mistake I made in the beginning of the year was being too lenient with student work. Now they feel comfortable to give sub-par answers and presume full credit. My students also need to work on making connections throughout numerous lessons over many days. Science is about making connections and then relating them to material that was discussed in the recent past.

In his own words:

> I think I need to be more stern [*sic*] with the expectations of my students. I know they think they can get away with whatever they want. Perhaps I can start creating rubrics for labs such as these, so I can grade according to a guide more strictly. Many students are simply okay with failing a class, which I have a hard time diagnosing not only why but how to reverse this thought [*sic*] as well.

Opportunities for development (OfD)

William's sense of crisis emerged from the realisation that he lost control of the class in spite of his best efforts to teach a thoughtful and dynamic lesson that should have engaged his pupils, and also from the recognition that he needed to find a better way to manage his class, a notion that his mentor teacher would have favoured and that he seemed to see as of low priority. This particular lesson brought together many of the key elements of inquiry-based science teaching that would meet the standards not only of William's programme but also of the school. In addition, William introduced the use of technology to create a more interactive and participatory environment in class. Whilst there were important

OfD evident in this particular lesson, however, William may not have been fully aware of them. The lesson observed had a high level of difficulty and, as it is often the case when teaching young people, things did not go as expected. William realised that he easily lost control of the class and at least in his lesson plan he took care to structure the lesson carefully. Yet when asked what he did to prepare for the lesson, William seemed to have done the planning by himself.

Whilst much of what happened during the lesson including the 'egg incident' could have been prevented, had William given careful instructions to pupils (not only verbal but written) from the beginning to the end of the experiment (as stated in his lesson plan), this did not quite happen. Failing to follow through and getting distracted by the flow of the class and his enthusiasm for the subject, he forgot to make sure every student took back the egg to the assigned place. One of the eggs breaking half way through the lesson created a great deal of tension between William and the classroom teacher and distracted the class from the next demonstration. Whilst William reflected upon this, he deflected responsibility to the pupils. In a more general way, he noted a pattern of poor class management and a lack of understanding on how to engage the pupils without being too friendly or too lax, and wondered whether at the end this decision had affected pupils' learning. In discussing this, he did not mention how he planned to address this perceived weakness.

Opportunities for change (OfC)

OfC provided by mediational tools from the HEI

William's programme provides a year-long internship designed to support interns learning to teach in schools with strong support from a mentor teacher. The year-long internship includes a 'teaching cycle of planning, teaching, assessing, and reflecting' guided primarily by the programme course faculty, to be followed by support from mentors, and periodically by field instructors. These mediating tools are designed to create opportunities for 'guided' change. Whilst the programme subject faculty is strongly discipline oriented and highly involved in the planning, assessing and reflecting of interns as they implement their lessons, they are less concerned with classroom management and somewhat removed from classroom teaching, which is more the domain of the mentor teachers and of the programme field instructors. It is possible that the lack of subject faculty involvement in the schools creates a disconnect thus, making it difficult for student teachers like William to negotiate the programme's message on the primacy of teaching subject matter under an inquiry approach, which for him also means freedom to experiment and the need to learn how to manage the class, which to him translates into control and possibly decreased likability from the part of his students.

William was well regarded in the programme and had shown significant progress throughout. He fully embraced the programme's vision concerning a strong emphasis in subject matter and access to knowledge as a matter of social justice. Whilst these aspects could have been more fully integrated into the pedagogy of science teaching, for William the programme message materialised more as explicit resistance to controlling pupils' classroom behaviour.

OfC provided by mediational tools within the school

This school and in particular William's mentor and classroom teacher, were highly supportive of him. The mentor, a highly experienced science teacher and a graduate of the programme reported dedicating a great deal of time mentoring William, meeting with him three times a week or more often. Whilst somewhat frustrated, he had been William's mentor and classroom teacher for the year-long internship. In spite of his continuous work with William, however, he still saw much to improve and a lack of willingness or capacity to understand from William's side what was required in taking on the role of a teacher (Buchmann, 1986). Whilst William's level of science knowledge, his teaching approach and use of technology were consistent with the programme and with the school's philosophy, the mentor's criticism of William's classroom management, and time management in delivering lessons seemed to widen the gap between William and his mentor teacher's notions of what is entailed in good science teaching. The tension in the relationship between the intern and the mentor could have been perhaps addressed more effectively had the mentor more deliberately engaged in addressing the pedagogy of teaching science (Gotwals & Birmingham, 2015), and had the HEI field instructors identified it as an issue in their visits. Instead the mentor attributed the problem to the very different teaching style by the intern. Failing to address the interns' notion of how to best teach science for social justice at the school level negated important OfC for William.

OfC provided by the individual's mediational tools

William was a highly motivated individual and took the initiative in learning new technology to bring to his classes, as well as in designing and delivering his lessons. He was also passionate and competent in his subject. This degree of agency, however, often put him at odds with the classroom teacher. As his mentor pointed out: 'The major concern is with classroom management and the intern's understanding of his professional responsibilities'. Whilst William did recognise OfD and he was able to articulate them, he seemed to lack the tools to address these particular weaknesses specially because his main concern was with conveying the subject to pupils with passion and conviction.

The individual's disposition to recognise the scope for development and change

William seemed to be able to recognise OfD, but only to a limited extent, and because of this, it proved difficult to develop a disposition to change. For

William, the most important part of learning to teach science was communicating his enthusiasm for the subject to his pupils and figuring out how to best teach the material. Teaching science within an inquiry approach, as espoused by the programme, and getting along with his pupils were seen by William as the most significant aspects of teaching above and beyond other aspects that were in turn seen as highly significant by the school/mentor. Paradoxically, attention to his mentor's concerns could help William address a classroom that seemed to be frequented by continuous crises, and could create a classroom climate that would be more conducive to learning. For instance, his mentor confessed that whilst he gave him a great deal of feedback (often meeting every day of the week) he wondered if 'he is actually listening'. The mentor considered this intern's major weaknesses to be self-reflection and classroom management, ironically, aspects that were considered very important by the programme as well. The mentor went on to say that, the intern needed to understand that 'there are things he must do to be a successful teacher that he may not agree with; right now I don't think he understands his professional responsibilities outside of actually teaching the students'. But the mentor's separation of the content from the teaching, likely in an attempt to emphasise for William what he saw as the problematic part of his teaching, contributed to a failure in communication.

William's likely misconception of what it meant to develop an interest and actively engage in teaching and learning science within an inquiry approach, seemed to stand in the way of him creating a workable structure with which to manage his classroom and to self-regulate his teaching, and by implication help his pupils to do the same. In spite of the strong support provided by his mentor, William made only small improvements in learning how to regulate himself and others, and to enact the professional requirements of being a teacher.

The relative prominence of the subject (or subject pedagogy) in consideration of the need for development or change

William considered himself to be a scientist, and had a major in interdepartmental biological sciences. Because of his enthusiasm for science, he cared deeply about helping develop the same interest in science on students, and encouraged them to engage through inquiry with the material. To him, discipline was not necessary as long as he was successful in fully and deeply engaging the pupils with the material. He was not afraid of trying new things, such as technology to engage pupils and to introduce elements of surprise in his teaching. Whilst he himself was comfortable with the subject, and his mentor agreed, he had not yet developed habits that might help him to be more successful in the classroom. William seemed to adopt the position that one can be a good teacher if one has a strong knowledge of the subject and can help pupils learn it through inquiry approaches.

William's level of comfort with, and enthusiasm for his subject, may have stood in the way of his development as an effective science teacher. Deeper understandings of how to teach science (or of science pedagogical knowledge) within an ordered environment was something that William still needed to master.

The extent of alignment (and thus, of the scope for tensions or contradictions) between the individual, HEI and school

The extent of alignment between the individual and the school

Whilst William's teaching was highly consistent with the goals of the programme and with the school's philosophy and curriculum, the classroom teacher (and William himself) pointed to inconsistencies in terms of management and professional behaviour.

The extent of alignment between the individual and the HEI

The programme emphasised strong science content knowledge and strategies for teaching science at secondary level. The programme also supported future teachers to learn 'standards-based practices in science planning, teaching and working with students and assessment'. The science programme's curriculum focused on 'inquiry and application-based practices', and engaged interns in a 'teaching cycle of planning, teaching, assessing and reflecting'. The programme had as one of its goals preparing candidates to 'become a successful and functioning member of the teaching profession'. Thus, William's lesson and report from his mentor teacher provided evidence of strong alignment with the programme goals, and some misalignment with school practices.

The extent of alignment between the school and the HEI

This case illustrates the dilemma that William confronted when creating an active and participatory science class allowing his pupils more freedom and responsibility to discover and explore, and still managing to make the experiences instructive rather than just a string of fun activities. In William's case, and at least in this lesson, his objective of involving pupils in collecting data from a science experiment was achieved, but it is difficult to ascertain whether or not pupils learned what was intended. The follow-up activity with the teabags, designed to firm-up the lesson derived from the egg experiment was in part disrupted by changing the dynamic of the class. Upon reflection, William stated that achieving the lesson outcomes: 'boils down to my ability to explain what they are to do beforehand, my ability to instruct pupils prior to their engagement in the lab will decide whether or not they succeed'. Whilst he understood the scientific challenge of the lesson, the need for precise measurement of a very delicate egg membrane and the potential for disruption if the egg membrane were to break, his persistence in believing that learning science requires freedom and room for wondering, created for him a dichotomy between freedom and control, and between giving pupils 'comfort to roam' or providing structure to the class. This way of thinking, made it very difficult for him to acquire the needed skills to create a productive class environment. His lack of follow-up on the mentor's teacher feedback jeopardised his OfD and growth.

Naomi's struggle to teach mathematics using a problem-solving approach

Naomi was learning to teach in the Teach First programme in London. The Teach First contract in London was jointly awarded to the Institute of Education and Canterbury Christ Church University, thus, the programme represented the joint effort of universities and the Teach First organisation to provide a general Professional Development Programme.

Naomi's first placement was at the Eastside Academy, which was judged by the Office for Standards in Education, Children's Services and Skills (Ofsted) in 2012 to be an 'outstanding' school and three members of the leadership team, entered the profession through the Teach First route, which made it a school committed to the Teach First programme and translated into important support for student teachers.

Naomi came to Teach First as a music and mathematics graduate. As such, Naomi reported feeling comfortable with the mathematics she was teaching and said in our interview that she felt very competent on the subject. She had quite a struggle to get there however. After trying a Postgraduate Certificate in Education (PGCE) programme and dropping out, she ended up working as a teaching assistant (not in Eastside Academy) and finally enrolled with Teach First. Although she came close to dropping out within this programme too, Teach First has been able to accommodate her. She complained about too much pressure and heavy emotional costs, but she was starting to feel successful. The support provided through the Eastside Academy via the subject mentor and professional mentor had been key in her decision to stay.

The lesson observed was an 'Introduction to solving equations' and included as learning outcomes for all pupils (ranging from National Curriculum levels 5 to 7) 'to be able to construct an equation with an unknown on one side' (complying with the 'create' curriculum standard), 'to notice that operations must be applied to both sides of an equation in order for it to remain valid', and 'to notice that to get back to an original value inverse operations must be applied in turn (both complying with the "analyse" curriculum standard)', 'to be able to solve an equation with an unknown on one side', and 'to be able to solve more complicated equations with an unknown on one side (complying with the 'apply' curriculum standard)'. The lesson was carefully planned by Naomi according to the Teach First model, and the lesson's learning outcomes were aligned with the Teach First aims and as a consequence with the school's expectations.

Naomi's plans for her class were thoughtful and she enacted them accordingly. The starter activity introduced pupils to thinking about solving an equation and even this starter task had gradations of difficulty. Whilst she asked them to 'guess' in an easy informal tone, the number she used in the 'x' place had a low level of difficulty ($x+3/2=2$), but she provided an 'extra-hard level of difficulty' for the more ambitious students. This 'guessing' activity flowed into the main activity of the lesson, which consisted of a spider diagram with two progressions and multiple levels of difficulty and possibilities for imagining equations from easy to increasingly difficult equations, which pupils endeavoured to do by providing larger and larger numbers. Naomi encouraged them and had no problem modelling how to solve the progressively involved equations. There were, however, groups of pupils who did not seem to be keeping up with the more challenging problems and were happy to 'hide' behind the pupils who enthusiastically continued to volunteer numbers. After modelling the activity and providing an example of guided practice, Naomi asked pupils to work independently in (equal ability pairs), whilst she (and her mentor) walked around evaluating how well pupils seemed to be responding to the task and grasping the intended concepts. As this occurred, Naomi noticed misunderstandings of the task or limitations in what the pupils were doing and repeatedly reconvened the class to explain concepts and procedures using examples from pupils' work.

Naomi seemed very comfortable with the level of mathematics required of her, to support and engage pupils in thinking mathematically in increasingly ambitious steps. She asked questions, asked for answers, and in general encouraged pupils to think of more and more difficult problems (but this occurred by pupils thinking of larger numbers instead of moving deeply along a particular strand of the spiderweb as her mentor later pointed out). At the end of the class session and when discussing the class with her mentor, Naomi shared concerns about pupils at the lower ability levels that may have not advanced as much as she had expected. She was very critical of herself and worried about whether she had helped pupils learn the concepts and whether she had given all pupils equal opportunities to participate in 'co-constructing' the spiderweb.

When asked about how the lesson went, Naomi said that she thought that the lesson had gone well in that the pupils got excited and interested; however, she did not get through as much as she had wanted since the pace was too slow. She would have liked to be clearer with instructions; she had never taught the lesson before, and thought that she talked too much. She would like to teach this lesson in more than in one session. She could have given them more time, she said:

> Some of the brighter ones got a lot whilst others would have benefitted from more time on it, because this is an activity that could be extended, the brighter ones could continue to work ... some were off task and there was silliness ... I was not as stern as I should have been.

She thought that the open nature of the task made it difficult for the pupils to behave. When asked about the pedagogy of the subject, she said she had read the Boaler text about 'the two schools Amber Hill and Phoenix Park School one is unproductive but they [the pupils] are just as good at problem-solving using this pedagogy – which has an effect – even if you do not see it right away'. She thought that 'the quicker the students do the task, the more they get out of it. The trick is to balance fun, learning and quickness'. Then, upon reflection, she said that her pupils needed practice in what they were learning; but since they had exams:

> We cannot do open lessons all the time, the younger they are it is good to do problem-solving and help them be more independent and creative, to get it in when you can, [for instance] some students came up with the rules and conclusions and I did not have to indoctrinate them … I do not think they found it a boring lesson.

She said she was happy to convey her own strategies to students, to help them do mental maths. She tried to give pupils little tricks because 'numeracy is not really reinforced [in the curriculum] but it is really a big problem with say column addition, and subtraction they need reinforcement all the way through'.

Thus, whilst her lesson plan was aligned with Teach First and with the school's expectations, her teaching, her actions in the classroom, and her discourse (which switched from citing the Teach First discourse to reflecting on the fact that there was not enough time to teach, and that the pupils did not seem to be learning mathematics as they should, and that the system was set in a way that disadvantaged the less well-off students) revealed a basic misalignment with the principles of Teach First and therefore, with the school and with the education system more generally. She quoted as her frame of reference a reading that had been recommended, in all likelihood, by a university tutor, written by Jo Boaler a scholar who has successfully promoted mathematics learning as problem-solving, and how this kind of pedagogy can make a difference in both well-served and underserved schools (see Boaler, 2002).

Naomi's practice was attentive to each student and frequently provided feedback to the class as a whole and to pupils individually. As with William, this was in fact a teacher who at the micro level was rejecting the way she was expected to teach in the school in favour of the way she believed was necessary for the pupils to learn the concepts in more depth.

Naomi's sense of crisis came from the realisation that in spite of her efforts, her pupils might not be learning key mathematics concepts and might not be enjoying learning. She expressed a strong sense of frustration associated with the time allocated for learning and the time used to prepare pupils for exams. She expressed the need to try to learn better how to reach the pupils and how to learn how to teach important concepts effectively. Whilst this pressure was experienced as part of working in a school that had successfully transformed itself from failing to outstanding, she saw the problem as systemic and her reaction was on the one hand to recognise her own limits, and on the other hand to escape! She confessed that becoming a teacher had involved heavy emotional and physical costs. She was however, in a school that offered her rich opportunities to learn and she had a mentor, and a professional mentor who were helping her as much as they could.

Whilst this school prepares their teachers through a collaboration of Teach First with a university, in Naomi's case, however, she drew a great deal from the preparation she received whilst at a PGCE programme in a different university, which whilst she did not finish, seemed to be both a source of support, and inspiration and to provide a glimpse of what was possible vis-à-vis Teach First. It was also a source of frustration as she realised that neither the school nor the curriculum or for that matter the system supported thoughtful deeper mathematics learning.

Typical of Teach First, after a short summer course, Naomi received very strong support from the school. Not only had the school managed to offer her more flexible assignments to allow her to learn time management skills and to adapt to the fast-paced teaching and learning required by the curriculum, but her mentor as well was knowledgeable and supportive. Her mentor was a graduate from Teach First, and had been working as a teacher and mentor in the school. The mentor was in the classroom during the lesson and met immediately with Naomi after the lesson to provide feedback, thus, indicating the high priority given to supporting beginning teachers in the school. However, the kind of feedback provided had to do more with classroom and time management than with the content of the lesson taught, as the mentor called for attention to pace and engagement and emphasis on the keywords (to make sure pupils understood what they meant). This was in contrast with the need for development and the search for change expressed by Naomi, which called for more substantive feedback on mathematics pedagogy and in understanding how to adjust school expectations with pupils' learning needs.

As a music and mathematics graduate, Naomi reported feeling very comfortable with the mathematics she was teaching and very competent in the subject. Because she was herself a learner, she had a way of recognising when pupils were not getting the concepts and she quickly stopped the flow of the lesson to attend to her pupils' learning needs. Her insights as a mathematics learner herself both supported and frustrated her as a teacher and gave her the tools to challenge an assessment-driven curriculum as much as is possible within a Teach First framework.

In addition, Naomi had a strong disposition to recognise OfD in the subject she was teaching, in managing time for planning and in limiting her ambitions (and frustration) for the amount of content and the kind of approach (investigations) that she felt she needed to teach. Her need for development was more in the direction of mathematics pedagogy, which was not something she was likely to get at the school.

Further to her ambitions about learning to teach the subject appropriately, she listed a number of things she needed to do, which showed a strong individual disposition to change, amongst which were her need to find time to think about how to teach the concepts, to figure out how to teach them to students and to plan. At the personal level, one of her big concerns was with managing her own time as she admitted that she needed to do one thing at a time, and that she could not tackle everything.

Concerning Naomi's own OfD as a mathematics teacher, her most salient concern was with pupils' learning, and she wondered whether 'the trick' was to balance fun, learning and quickness. Specifically, concerning the subject she said that she needed to learn more about how to teach statistics because it was different from teaching algebra. It was evident that Naomi's main concern had to do with a real commitment to pupils learning mathematics, and she was frustrated with the delicate balance of learning (as fun), and assessments. She recognised that whilst her pupils needed a lot of practice and time for exploration, she also acknowledged the need to prepare them for exams, perhaps the primary concerns of the school and all of the schools in the country. She expressed her frustration at not being able to do 'open' lessons as frequently as she would have liked. Her challenge was to teach pupils at a younger age to 'do problem-solving and help them be more independent and creative, to get it in when you can' within a curriculum that seemed to be designed to frustrate such attempts.

Naomi was critical of the outside forces that led to an apparent reduction in time for deeper mathematics learning. She saw herself as an active agent in challenging these ongoing pressures and as a resource to her pupils to help them become comfortable and knowledgeable with mathematics. This was evident in how she saw her role as conveying her own strategies to students to 'help them do mental maths, to give pupils those little tricks ... because numeracy is not really reinforced [in the curriculum] but it is really a big problem with say column addition, and subtraction they need reinforcement all the way through'.

Whilst alignment with the school culture was very high, since basically teacher training occurred in the school, Naomi found ways of subverting what she saw as restricting opportunities to learn for her students. Naomi's lesson plan, for instance, followed the format of all lesson plans at Eastside Academy, which had three sections that were to be followed when planning a lesson. The first section of the heading showed levels of learning outcomes (derived from Bloom's taxonomy of educational objectives). The second section contained a list of eight lesson features (including arrival activity on board; learning outcomes shared with students; learning outcomes throughout the lesson; work modelled showing students the expectations for the lesson; keywords used in the lesson; student and teacher talks; mini-plenaries throughout the lesson; and learning competencies and humanities skills); and the third section, which referred to assessment opportunities throughout the lesson ending up with a plenary. This highly scripted lesson was a source of stress for Naomi who would rather have spent more time to make sure that all pupils were understanding concepts; yet spending more time with some pupils meant sacrificing the plenary at the end. Nevertheless, she did 'deviate' within the script.

In fact, whilst Naomi was learning to teach as part of the Teach First initiative, she had previously been enrolled in a PGCE programme and compared both experiences frequently. She drew from the research readings (e.g. Boaler, 2002) to which she was exposed when she thought about mathematics pedagogy and the importance of focusing on pupils thinking and doing investigations rather than 'indoctrination'. She dropped out of the PGCE programme, however, which she thought too demanding and not flexible enough. Whilst Teach First works with a university, her main learning context was in the school and with her mentor who worked continually with her and met with Naomi for significant periods of time every week.

In spite of Naomi's resistance and her genuine concern with the level at which pupils were grasping the concepts and their ability to keep the same pace, she was also concerned with their success, so a great deal of the lesson was directed at helping pupils engage successfully in solving equations. Whilst her lesson was creative and dynamic and deviated from the script, it was also procedural and, whilst she mentioned Boaler (2002) and understood the notion of deeper mathematics learning, time limitations and the culture of the school, resulted in more of an emphasis on numeracy fluency than on conceptual understandings. This ongoing tension represented a big source of frustration for Naomi. Thus, she felt caught between helping her pupils learn mathematics conceptually and moderating the pressures that came from complying with standards and assessments.

At the end, and in spite of the strong support she had received from her school, she said that her strongest feeling was to:

> Have freedom from the education system itself, I think because we are stuck inside a grid that students must be able to do this in this time and you cannot make those forays into areas that are really interesting like students' investigations when you see that they can really benefit from more time on something and you cannot do it ... there are too many assessments, too much time pressure.

Her teaching philosophy, was therefore, more aligned with the thinking in the university than with that of the school.

Conclusion

Whilst Naomi's situation was frustrating for her and caused her great personal anxiety she was aware that her teaching did not resemble the principles that characterised Jo Boaler's approach (Boaler, 2002). Yet she found support of some kind, as she overtly expressed concerns to her mentor and her mentor accepted, understood and guided her using her own knowledge as a previous Teach First graduate.

In the case of William, it took a different angle; whilst he was strongly supported by his mentor (who was himself a graduate of the MSU programme), his situation was more openly combative as William seemed to challenge what he perceived to be unreasonable school procedures to exert control over students, and to follow the plans he had developed with the support of the university, feeling empowered to apply it in many cases disregarding the teacher's concerns/guidance as to how to create a conducive classroom environment.

References

Boaler, J. (2002). *Experiencing school mathematics: Traditional and reform approaches to teaching and their impact on student learning.* London: Routledge.

Buchmann, M. (1986). Role over person: Morality and authenticity in teaching. *Teachers College Record, 87*(4), 527–543.

Gotwals, A. W. & Birmingham, D. (2015). Eliciting, identifying, interpreting, and responding to students' ideas: Teacher candidates' growth in formative assessment practices. *Research in Science Education.* doi: 10.1007/s11165-015-9461-2.

Plickers. (2017). *FAQ.* Retrieved from www.plickers.com/faq.

12 The significance of alignments in initial teacher education

Introduction

In drawing up a sociocultural framework for the analysis of student teachers' experiences as they begin to negotiate their initial introduction to teaching, we have endeavoured to create a tool to help us understand better what is occurring in these highly complex and dynamic sites of learning (Doyle, 1977). By drawing on the work of Bernstein (1990) and Hedegaard (2012) (see Chapter 2), we have sought to uncover some of the range of relationships and contradictions that exist in and around the learning that occurs through student teachers' experience of the school placement, mediated by school-based mentors, university-based tutors and personal experience. We have described the contradictions and tensions that emerge from enacting practice as 'opportunities for development' (OfD), and 'opportunities for change' (OfC).

An OfD is characterised by a sense of 'crisis' or critical period caused by a lack of alignment between the views and practices of an individual and one or more of the institutions from which they are learning, or from contradictions between the object motives and practices of the institutions themselves. These critical periods may also be caused by tensions or contradictions that originate from within the learner as they respond to a particularly complex social situation of development. An OfC may be evident in response to a critical period or sense of crisis, but does not necessarily depend on evident contradictions, but rather on individuals' recognition of their own limitations or the limitations of the situation they are in and on their abilities to imagine and enact a different role for themselves as teachers. These abilities rely in turn on the mediational tools made available to them by the higher education institution (HEI) partner or by the school or brought into the situation by the student teacher as a result of their previous experiences and prior learning.

Our interest in the learning of future teachers preparing to work at the secondary level has also prompted us to focus on the relative prominence of different subject disciplines in each individual's developing thinking as a teacher and on the relationship of their own conceptions of teaching and learning to those of the teacher educators in both school and university. All of these elements define the extent of the alignment between learners and institutions, the nature of the stimulus for learning within each social situation of development and the types of support available, and so help us to distinguish between more or less successful experiences. In this chapter, we consider in more detail the importance of alignment in initial teacher education.

The coding system that we developed helped us identify a number of distinctive elements, as described in detail in Chapters 2 and 6. This coding system is not a categorisation tool used to create a model into which the experiences of all student teachers will fit, but rather an attempt to capture some of the complexity in learning to teach across different settings. There is scope for variation across all cases in relation to all four elements of the framework (OfD, OfC, individual dispositions, and the prominence of the subject or of subject pedagogy) that represent specific aspects or dimensions that we have sought to identify or code. We have identified five particular patterns and used them to guide our selection of cases; we could have picked a number of different individuals whose experiences would have represented *different* kinds of combinations. Whilst we have mainly focused in our depiction of these cases on the micro level of analysis, our understanding and depiction of them is richly informed by our exploration of the macro and meso contexts, set out in the earlier chapters (see Chapters 3, 4 and 5). As Vygotsky (1987) argued, 'the unit is a vital and irreducible part of the whole' (1987, p. 46) and the individual cases of learning described in this book are both situated and subject to the dominant pedagogical discourse (Bernstein, 1990).

In relation to Hedegaard's (2012) planes, each of these patterns of alignment demonstrates a particular pattern of tension and/or contradiction between planes, where the object motives of the respective participants may – or may not – be congruent, or, to use the term we have adopted here, in alignment. However, it is important to note that the four elements within our coding system might each appear in different combinations for other cases not represented here.

Our understanding and categorisation of these different elements emerged out of our close analysis of the data derived from video/observation of lessons enacted by our 17 cases of student teachers, together with a range of interviews with them and those close to them, as well as scrutiny of programme and school documentation. We used Bernstein's notions of pedagogic discourse, including his differentiation between vertical and horizontal forms of communication, as well as Hedegaard's concept of planes of analysis (Bernstein, 1990; Hedegaard, 2012). This has enabled us to develop what we believe is an original analytical tool that highlights and is sensitive to the sociocultural nature of the learning that prevails in these situations and is informed by the institutional and societal (meso and macro) contexts in which the learning is taking place.

In presenting the particular cases, our accounts start from what might be seen as a phenomenological approach to the particular situation through endeavouring to find types of a class of phenomena within two strong and well-established initial teacher education programmes. However, through the analysis of the wider contexts undertaken (notably in Chapters 3, 4 and 5) the intention was to ensure that we could make sense of critical points or crises in development (in the Vygotskian sense) that the student teachers might be experiencing and of the contradictions and tensions apparent in that situation in terms that went beyond the immediate existential phenomena that were observed.

Our approach also built upon the work done by Tatto (1996, 1998, 2007/2009) on the influence of coherent teacher education programmes on the opportunities to learn provided to future teachers. Further work examined the macro level of policy, the meso level of institutions and the micro level of acquired teacher knowledge as a result of programmes' opportunities to learn (Tatto et al., 2012). Our approach in the present study also acknowledges the kind of insights about the different 'dimensions' of learning from experience that were identified through the earlier work of the Developing Expertise of Beginning Teachers project (e.g. Burn, Hagger & Mutton, 2015). Those categories related very much to the orientations and understandings of the learner teachers themselves and provided a valuable tool for school or university staff to work with the learner in a more informed way. The wider sociocultural approach presented in this study thus, builds upon this earlier work to illuminate the whole framework for learning that is being created for the student teacher, with light also being shone on the staff involved and on their institutions. It thus, may be seen to draw greater attention to the mediational tools that are available (whether they are used effectively or not) to support the learning of the student teacher.

The use of this framework may also be seen to reduce the direct 'gaze' on the student teacher, which is so often experienced in initial teacher education (Pillen, Beijaard & Den Brock, 2013; Beijaard, Meijer & Verloop, 2004) thereby, reducing the sense of individual responsibility or even culpability – not least when 'things go wrong' – that may sometimes be so damaging, emotionally and professionally, for those who are directly involved, not least the student teachers. This sociocultural framework allows us to concentrate on both the 'volitional, goal directed, tool-mediated action' (Smagorinsky, 2010, p. 26) of the individual within the specific contexts of school departments, and on the interactions between the various agents involved in initial teacher education. At the core of our framework is the notion that learning to teach is a community endeavour, not the lonely task of an inexperienced (and often young) individual.

The five patterns of alignment represented in the case studies

What can we learn from reflecting on this typology? We have identified five particular patterns of alignment in the preceding chapters. It would be facile to suggest that 'good' alignment is simply the desirable situation for all cases. In a sense, that may be what is to be aimed for in all cases, because it suggests that understandings of teaching and learning to teach are agreed upon between the individual learner, the school and the university. However, this may also be the situation where the least 'new' learning is taking place. It may, in other words, be necessary for there to be some contradiction, some tension, some non-alignment in the situation for new learning to occur, for the learner herself or himself to be able to experience significant OfC or OfD. In England, all initial teacher education programmes, including the Postgraduate Certificate in Education (PGCE) and Teach First, require that student teachers switch to a different school, usually in the middle of their main placement experience, precisely to make 'the familiar strange' again. This has the potential to create new situations of crisis or tension, expected to contribute to further development and change in individuals.

Furthermore, it is appropriate to ask if the application of the analytical tools (of OfD, OfC, individual disposition, and the prominence of subject or subject pedagogy), creates the possibility of arriving both at a more sophisticated 'diagnosis' of what is occurring in a particular setting, and a sense of how that diagnosis may then be acted upon – and by whom – in order to improve the conditions for learning and development of the student teacher? If the learning at this micro level is indeed significantly structured by the meso and macro level contexts, then to what extent is any action or intervention at the micro level likely to be effective? In other words, how constrained is the situation of development for any individual student teacher? To what extent can the agency of that person or indeed the agency of individual members of school or university staff bring about change in the conditions of learning in that specific situation? We have seen a positive answer to this question in some of the cases presented, but a less positive answer in others.

The central focus of each case that has been portrayed is a single lesson undertaken by the student teacher. The purpose of our analysis and of the tool in this study was certainly not to 'assess' the performance of the student teacher (as is often the purpose of observations carried out by university or school staff), but rather to gain a deeper understanding of the learning processes going on in that situation, and to develop a tool to help us determine more precisely the OfD and the OfC that exist within that context.

We turn now to offer a brief reflection on each of the main cases and on some of the subsidiary ones.

Doug, Joseph and Jason

The case of Doug represents an example of strong alignment between school and the HEI. Since he was in a situation where the values, understandings and intentions held by university staff, school staff and himself were all congruent, his experience points to the need to consider how such effective alignments come about, and what were the conditions that created such alignment? The tensions and contradictions for Doug arose largely from his ambition to push himself further in his development. He was both supported and challenged in this by his school mentor and subject tutor, but the important point was that Doug recognised the social situation of development and actively sought to change it. Doug's agentic approach, as much as the strong alignment with university and school staff, created these strong developmental situations.

For Joseph, there was also strong alignment between the school and the HEI, both of which supported him in addressing the challenges he faced in the specific context in which he was working, although in school it was only his mentor (rather than other colleagues) who was able to provide the sort of support needed in order to mediate the necessary OfC.

Conversely, for Jason, notwithstanding the strong alignment between the school and the HEI, it was workload issues resulting from other significant areas of responsibility within the school that threatened to take the mentor away from being in a position to support him effectively, and thus, to restrict his opportunities to learn to take the necessary risks in his teaching from which he might continue to develop.

Leslie and Michael

When we move on to consider Leslie, and indeed Michael, in Chapter 8, we can see an example of how an approach taken by the mentor can significantly reduce non-productive misalignments. In other words, we can identify how the agency of the school member of staff has responded to the OfD in the situation for the student teacher, thereby increasing the opportunities to learn and thus, helping to create more positive learning conditions for them, in both cases.

Sophia and others

In Chapter 9 however, we can see that in the case of Sophia the elements of misalignment do not appear to have been identified by any of the participants in the situation. Sophia herself was unaware of the weaknesses in her approach and there were opportunities for her to learn that seem to have been missed. This application of our analytical framework demonstrates the need for some kind of intervention and/or guidance in order to improve the conditions for Sophia's learning. Its application in other cases, such as that of Nereen, also shows that it is possible to provide support that will not actually improve the conditions for learning. Whilst Nereen was getting a great deal of emotional support from those around her, it did not appear to be creating OfD and OfC. It is not simply the provision of support that matters; the nature and the receptivity of that support are critical.

The great lack of self-awareness in a student teacher, the requirement to teach in an area outside of her expertise and the invisibility of this situation to both the school and the university, as in the somewhat extreme case of Irene, presents a very challenging situation calling for significant input. However, devising appropriate strategies and approaches may be far from straightforward in a situation such as this.

We suggest that all of the cases here demonstrate the importance of effective communication between the university and the schools concerned. Misalignments such as these, reflecting contradictions, which are unacknowledged by the school or the university, are far less likely to occur where the relationships are strong and based on professional dialogue. As we suggested in Chapter 9, there appears to be a tendency for school staff to focus on the more generic aspects of pedagogy with less attention to specific issues within the subject, by comparison with the focus taken by university staff. However, if the partnership is a deep and effective one, then such misalignment is less likely to occur.

Alyson and Sandrine

These cases, in Chapter 10, where there was apparently good alignment between the student teacher and the school but not with the HEI, offer some other interesting insights. Alyson's case shows that subject knowledge is not enough. Here was someone with very strong knowledge of her subject but who, in spite of her intentions and her knowledge about how, in theory, to empower pupils to be self-regulated learners, was able to communicate that knowledge to only half of the class, and unable to effectively reach the less advanced pupils within a fast-paced classroom context. The practical theorising approach of the programme did not seem to be fully functional in this case. Whilst Alyson was successful in covering all the material as expected by the school department, she realised that she fell short when considering the programme's norms and her own sense of how to teach mathematics. The absence of her mentor teacher from the classroom however, allowed important OfD and OfC to go unaddressed.

For Sandrine, the problem seemed to derive, in part at least, from the fact that having worked in the school previously (as an assistant) she was relying extensively on her prior experience and her existing 'acculturation' into that context. There were few opportunities for *change* because there was little identification of anything problematic in her teaching; and few opportunities for *development* because her acculturation did not lead her to question her situation as an opportunity for professional learning. Rather her teaching practice was an opportunity to demonstrate technical competence, which she was able to do effectively. She was not achieving change or development to an extent that might be hoped for because the opportunities for this had not been created. There was not enough awareness of the possible alternatives.

William and Naomi

In the final cases that are presented in Chapter 11, William was clearly someone with many positive qualities, but who was somewhat resistant to listening to his mentor teacher in the school and to attend fully to school norms and so was apparently not really learning as much as he could from his experience there. Whilst his own views were well aligned with those advanced by the university and he cared deeply about his pupils' learning, he was not using the experience in the school as a positive learning opportunity. Although he saw OfD and engaged in some active change, such as improving his own knowledge of technology and creating engaging experiments/activities to convey the material to his pupils, he did so without creating a conducive classroom environment that would in turn allow them to engage in more productive learning. His failure to understand the classroom as a system and his reluctance to attend to his mentor's advice underlining the holistic nature of teaching creates an ongoing tension for all involved. Whilst the university programme views and practices would align with those of the mentor teacher, this did not seem so obvious to William who saw the school environment as restrictive to pupils' science learning and thus, resisted becoming a source for control himself. This case, like those in Chapter 10, demonstrates the importance of the HEI-school relationship and communication.

In contrast, Naomi might be expected, given her position as a participant in Teach First, to be aligned with the school. But whilst she was willing to meet the school's expectations and had strong support from them, her previous participation and learning in a PGCE programme made it very difficult for her to achieve full alignment. Her resistance, however, took a different form from that of William. Whilst she understood the classroom as a system and was working hard to learn from and align with the practices of the school, her knowledge of an alternative way of teaching mathematics to diverse pupils challenged the school curriculum at every turn and created much anxiety for her. Even so, she found in her mentor, a supportive listener who allowed her some scope for innovation. Thus, as was evident more in her practice than on paper (i.e. her lesson plans which must align with the Teach First model), she endeavoured, with the help of her mentor, to help pupils make sense of mathematics and to realise that they are capable of developing mathematical ideas, and to create multiple representations. She was frustrated in this attempt, by the lack of time that would allow pupils to develop conceptual ideas and allow her to model and demonstrate how to solve mathematical problems. This tension between what the Teach First framework required and her intent to approach mathematics teaching using an inquiry-based approach resulted in misalignment with the school. This tension, as she declared, was likely to remain unresolved given its systemic nature, yet her intention was to continue to attempt to fit an inquiry-based approach to teaching mathematics within a model that by its very design seemed to undercut such attempt.

Summary

Whilst the analysis of these cases demonstrates differing alignment relationships, the underlying theme that emerges is the importance of the deliberate creation of opportunities to learn, created by university-school partnerships. This implies the investment of significant resources in the creation of shared norms and understandings, and of development of ways of thinking that provide a framework for shaping practice, such as conceptions of teaching for social justice and the value in emphasising the nature of the pedagogy of the content (a value that all the three programmes examined share), and of the learner as a sense-making individual (a value that distinguishes the MSU and the Oxford programmes).

This also includes significant skill in understanding the challenges that young individuals encounter as they begin to take on the role of a teacher, when they stand on the threshold that demarcates the knowledgeable person from the knowledgeable teacher (Buchmann, 1986). The development of these frameworks and ways of thinking come into play as inevitably unproductive misalignment will occur in learning to teach situations. But when one of these institutions does not align with the shared vision, if one exists, it is often the student teacher who would need to decide how to bridge these divergent visions, or to formulate a new vision on their own – a vision likely to be informed by their apprenticeship of observation, other experiences and possibly by peers. In some cases, the alignment would be with the school, if the programme fails in providing a coherent vision; in others the alignment would be with the HEI, if the school fails to sustain the vision. In some cases, and provided that student teachers have internalised a vision of good teaching, this sense of misalignment, whilst creating crises, may result in significant growth for the student teachers as they figure out how to create situations where, for instance, notions of social justice and sense-making can be enacted in their teaching. As we have seen, and provided that both the programme and the schools constitute a mutually reinforcing partnership, the extent to which the student teacher can benefit from the experience will also depend crucially on their own dispositions, knowledge and prior experience. Programmes such as Teach First bring a third partner into play as co-provider, as well as the school and a HEI, and, as a provider, they are directly responsible for selecting candidates to join the programme. This adds further complexity in the relationship between the school, the HEI and the individual as neither institution has any direct prior knowledge of the individual student teacher.

The framework we developed and have used as a research tool in this study, appears to offer insights into the teaching and learning of student teachers that go beneath the surface of what is immediately apparent to the professional observer. The tool is however, very resource intensive in the way that it has been adopted in this study, with much time being devoted to recording, transcription and interviewing and to the analysis of documents (at the meso and micro levels) as well as to the careful analysis of the wider policy context in which the learning processes are taking place. It is therefore, not a tool that could realistically be adopted for supporting the routine practice of school-based or university-based staff engaged in initial teacher education. It is possible however, that the tool could be used as a powerful aid to professional learning and development for such staff. In contexts where university staff are being inducted into their role as teacher educators (Murray, 2008) or indeed where school staff are being prepared as school-based teacher educators (whether as subject mentors or as professional mentors or as field instructors), the explication of this approach may provide some very rich opportunities. Furthermore, it might well be that some kind of introduction for student teachers to this way of thinking about experiential learning and the schema that has emerged from it, could be used in helping the student teachers themselves to prepare for their school experience.

The analysis concerning the prominence of the subject or of subject pedagogy in our framework, may provide a particular opportunity for professional learning, not only for student teachers themselves but for developing shared understandings between subject departments in schools and university-based subject tutors/instructors. We have seen how some of the cases depicted in this section have raised particular questions about subject-specific aspects of practice. At the heart of Nereen's difficulties, for example (in Chapter 9), was a contradiction inherent in her conception of history and how it could be made both accessible and meaningful to young people. Alyson's case (in Chapter 10), illustrated the importance of the difference between learning skills and concepts in mathematics, whilst in Leslie's case (Chapter 8), the significance of knowing how to manage a classroom interacted with the ability to teach pronunciation in Modern Foreign Languages. The value of knowing how to teach for understanding can supersede a limited school curriculum to support pupils' learning (Chapter 11) was illustrated by the cases of both Naomi and William.

These are but small examples demonstrating how issues of particular significance within a subject may be identified and then deliberated upon through adopting this approach. It is in discussions such as these that Bernstein's distinctions between vertical and horizontal discourses may be helpful (Bernstein, 1990). Clearly, both aspects are important and if one is prevailing over the other it is likely that the learning of the student teacher is either superficial on the one hand (where the horizontal dominates) or abstract (or even abstruse) on the other hand (where the vertical excludes or diminishes the horizontal).

Conclusion

We would reiterate and emphasise the point made earlier about the nature of partnership in initial teacher education. The analysis offered through this study has clearly demonstrated how important the relationships are between the respective participants in the processes of teacher education. Much has been written in many places over many years about the importance of partnership in teacher education (Furlong, Barton, Miles, Whiting & Whitty, 2000; Mutton, 2015). It also continues to be a major theme in teacher education research. What this study has revealed, however, is some of the reasons why partnerships are so challenging and at the same time so critical in creating the conditions for the effective learning of student teachers. Partnership is not only a matter of procedural and logistical arrangements, important though these are. What emerges from our review of these cases is a deep sense of the significance of pedagogical partnership. Partnership will be most effective in creating optimal conditions for student teachers learning when it is an active, dynamic and continuing process of dialogue, debate, discussion and interaction. At the heart of these interactions will be matters of pedagogical significance concerning both pupil and student teacher learning, the nature of the respective curricula for these learners and the appropriate pedagogy and assessment procedures in relation to the subject being taught.

Although the field placement or practicum has been the main focus of the cases presented here, it is clear from them that this element in a programme of teacher education cannot and certainly should not be seen in isolation, as it perhaps was in many settings during the 20th century. It is crucial that teacher education programmes are constructed in an integrated way. Certainly, as we have suggested repeatedly in this book, there are two physical situations of development for the student teachers, at least in the great majority of programmes. In some cases, these situations are closely aligned, but in others there may be misalignment between the HEI and school agenda or between the object motives for the actors involved. In some cases, a high degree of alignment may present the best OfD and OfC, facilitating high-quality professional learning for the student teacher, as well as for the other participants in the process. However, this is only so where both the HEI and the school recognise the need to challenge and sometimes disrupt the learning of even the best student teachers. Doug, for example, was continually challenged by his mentor, his subject tutor and by himself. In other cases, what we call productive misalignment led to social situations of development that produced OfD or OfC when the student teachers confronted the situation and changed it. For Naomi, for instance, her experience of misalignment and all the challenges she faced as a result of 'not fitting-in' allowed her to learn how to work with her school, and specially her mentor, to go beyond the limiting curriculum imposed by Teach First towards a richer teaching dynamic. In the case of William, his misalignment with the school was not as productive as that of Naomi and resulted in some missed OfC. Yet William's alignment with the programme's philosophy and his challenge to the school curriculum/constraints, allowed him some OfD and OfC in a way that increased his sense of agency.

Whilst the focus in this section of the book has been very much on experience within classrooms in schools, it is important to remember that we set these experiences very carefully in the wider context of the particular institutions and in the context of the wider state and national settings in which they were taking place. If the pedagogic discussions around learning to teach that occur between the various participants in a particular setting can be constructed in the manner which this study has suggested is important, it is likely that this will lead to an enhancement of the professional knowledge base for staff and student teachers in both school and in university settings. They may in other words become more agentic in their work and develop a stronger professional identity.

In the third and final section of the book, we step back from the detail of the study to reflect on what we have learned from this multi-level and sociocultural analysis of teacher education in England and the United States. We first seek, in Chapter 13, to assess the extent to which the insights gained may be seen as indicating that the processes of professional learning in teacher education may be taken to have universal elements or whether, in fact, they show that the particularities of wider contexts significantly shape the learning experiences, and the situations of development for student teachers. In part, of course, this is to return to the questions of comparative analysis, which we outlined in Chapter 1. In Chapter 14, the final chapter, we venture into a prospective discussion on the future of partnerships in teacher education in both countries as shaped by their distinctive macro contexts, and use the insights gained in this study to set out elements of an agenda for future teacher education research.

References

Beijaard, D., Meijer, P. C. & Verloop, N. (2004). Reconsidering research on teachers' professional identity. *Teaching and Teacher Education, 20*(2), 107–128.

Bernstein, B. (1990). *Class, codes and control. Volume IV: The structuring of pedagogic discourse.* London: Routledge.

Buchmann, M. (1986). Role over person: Morality and authenticity in teaching. *Teachers College Record, 87*(4), 527–543.

Burn, K., Hagger, H. & Mutton, T. (2015). *Beginning teachers' learning: Making experience count.* Northwich: Critical Publishing.

Doyle, W. (1977). Learning the classroom environment: An ecological analysis. *Journal of Teacher Education, 28*(6), 51–55.

Furlong, J., Barton, L., Miles, S., Whiting, C. & Whitty, G. (2000). *Teacher education in transition.* Buckingham: Open University.

Hedegaard, M. (2012). The dynamic aspects in children's learning and development. In M. Hedegaard, A. Edwards & M. Fleer (Eds.), *Motives in children's development* (pp. 9–17). New York: Cambridge University Press.

Murray, J. (2008). Teacher educators' induction into higher education: Work-based learning in the micro communities of teacher education. *European Journal of Teacher Education, 31*(2), 117–133.

Mutton, T. (2015). Partnership in teacher education. In Teacher Education Group (Eds.), *Teacher education in times of change* (pp. 201–216). Bristol: Policy Press.

Pillen, M., Beijaard, D. & Den Brok, P. (2013). Tensions in beginning teachers' professional identity development, accompanying feelings and coping strategies. *European Journal of Teacher Education, 36*(3), 240–260.

Smagorinsky, P. (2010). A Vygotskian analysis of the construction of setting in learning to teach. In V. Ellis, A. Edwards & P. Smagorinsky (Eds.), *Cultural-historical perspectives on teacher education and development: Learning teaching* (pp. 13–29). London and New York: Routledge Taylor and Francis Group.

Tatto, M. T. (1996). Examining values and beliefs about teaching diverse students: Understanding the challenges for teacher education. *Educational Evaluation and Policy Analysis, 18*(2) 155–180.

Tatto, M. T. (1998). The influence of teacher education on teachers' beliefs about purposes of education, roles and practice. *Journal of Teacher Education, 49*(1), 66–77.

Tatto, M. T. (Ed.). (2009). *Reforming teaching globally.* Charlotte, NC, USA: Information Age Publishers. (Reprinted from *Reforming teaching globally,* M. T. Tatto, 2007, Oxford, UK: Symposium Books.)

Tatto, M. T., Schwille, J., Senk, S. L., Ingvarson, L., Rowley, G., Peck, R., Bankov, K., Rodriguez, M. & Reckase, M. (2012). *Policy, practice, and readiness to teach primary and secondary mathematics in 17 countries. Findings from the IEA Teacher and Development Study in Mathematics (TEDS-M).* Amsterdam: International Association for the Evaluation of Educational Achievement (IEA).

Vygotsky, L. S. (1987). Thinking and speech. In L. S. Vygotsky (Ed.), *Collected works: Volume 1.* New York: Plenum Press.

Part III

Comparing trends, contradictions and future trajectories

13 Policy and practice in England and the United States

Comparing trends and contradictions in teacher education

Introduction

In this chapter, we use a comparative framework to examine experiences in the two countries in relation to trends in the policy and provision of teacher preparation with special attention to the responses to pressures brought about by developments in educational policy. We use the conceptual framework introduced in Chapter 2, to compare across the two country contexts: the sociocultural influences on teacher education policy; the institutions where learning occurs; and the individual transitions as observed amongst the study participants.

Sociocultural influences on the reform and practice of teacher education

In England, the reform agenda has been characterised by a move towards what the government has called 'school-led' teacher education in response to a particular policy stance that regards what is taught in university programmes as being largely irrelevant in contrast to practical school-based experience, which alone is able to provide the necessary conditions for effective professional preparation to take place. The changes that have occurred as a result of the policy reforms introduced by the coalition government from 2010 onwards should, however, be seen in the context of the ongoing concern with teacher education as a 'policy problem' (Cochran-Smith, 2005) and the intervention of successive governments for more than a quarter of a century, resulting in increased levels of regulation, a focus on performativity and regular compliance monitoring (McNamara, 2010). Alongside this increased regulation has been de-regulation, in terms of the multiplicity of routes into teaching now available. The effect of the above reforms has been to emphasise the pre-eminence of school-based practice within any initial teacher education programme, consistent with the broader notion of the 'practicum turn' (Mattson, Eilertson & Rorrison, 2011), which has been in evidence internationally. In England, however, this has not been merely an acknowledgement of the importance of school-based experience, but rather a policy view that such experience is not just necessary but also sufficient in itself as a model for 'training' teachers.

In the United States, the reform agenda has been dominated in the last 15 years by increased federal mandates for regulation of schools, teachers and teacher education programmes. The push for regulation came in the form of the introduction of common curriculum standards across the majority of states in the country, and frequent local and national assessments at all levels of K-12 schooling. Several states adopted value-added models to assess schools' performance, including the introduction of teacher evaluations, which have indirectly affected teacher education.

Central to policy reform in both the United States and in England has been the drive to secure an adequate supply of high-quality teachers, able to deliver high-quality outcomes for all pupils. In England, however, this has not extended to the requirement for teacher education providers to collect pupil performance data as a measure of programme effectiveness, as has happened in some states in the United States, although the Office for Standards in Education, Children's Services and Skills (Ofsted) inspection framework (Ofsted, 2014) does indicate both that trainees will be observed during the inspection process in order to 'evaluate the quality of teaching and training, and [the trainees'] contribution to the learning of children/pupils/learners' (p. 15) and that evidence will be collected that includes 'information about children's/pupils'/learners' progress' (p. 16). In the United States, this model of teacher programme evaluation has been rescinded after 3-years of consultation across all education sectors under validity and cost concerns.

The use of the word 'training' and the term 'initial teacher training' reflect the terminology used deliberately by the government in England to provide a contrast with the established notion of initial teacher education. Student teachers – or those following programmes, which are delivered by non-university providers (such as School-Centred Initial Teacher Training schemes) – are consistently referred to as 'trainees', thus, emphasising the focus on 'a technical rationalist approach to professional knowledge' (Furlong, 2008, p. 735). The emphasis on the value of school-led teacher education in England has created cultural changes in the way in which schools engage with teacher education programmes. Whilst many schools still continue to work within traditional, well-established partnership models, others have become more entrepreneurial and have developed their own programmes, often motivated by the need to secure the employment of teachers in subjects where recruitment has become a problem. The idea of schools preparing their own 'home-grown' teachers who are 'classroom-ready' at the earliest opportunity has begun to influence the way in which teachers and teacher educators within these schools view initial teacher education. Furthermore, it is not unusual for such a conceptualisation to inform the approaches also taken with student teachers within a traditional university-school partnership, when they are placed at the school in question.

The policy tensions in England are evident in the findings of the *Carter Review of Initial Teacher Education* (Carter, 2015) and, following its recommendations, the subsequent setting up of 'expert groups' to examine the content of teacher education programmes in England, as discussed earlier in

Chapter 3. The review itself advocates 'careful consideration of the processes of beginning teachers' learning, which calls for a focus on effective pedagogy and curriculum design' (Mutton, Burn & Menter, 2017), but its recommendations ultimately reflect the view that initial teacher education programmes should deliver prescribed content and that evidence to support teachers' decision-making should be drawn from a 'central portal of synthesised executive summaries, providing practical advice on research findings about effective teaching in different subjects and phases' (Carter, 2015, p. 70). Although the status of the recommendations of the expert group that reported on core content are non-statutory, thus, leaving providers to decide to what extent this prescribed content might be incorporated into individual programmes, the expectation that they will do so is implicit in the likelihood that this will be an element of all future Ofsted inspections of teacher education programmes.

In the United States, the discourse around teacher education, now extended to teacher preparation to include alternative routes, has been dominated by the concern that new teachers feel unprepared for 'classroom realities'. The argument is that: too many teacher preparation programmes are weak and do not provide teachers with a rigorous clinical experience (e.g. failing to recruit, select and prepare teachers with the skills and knowledge they need to help their pupils learn); that the teacher workforce does not reflect the diversity of the nation's pupils; and that there is a lack of accountability for teacher preparation programmes' performance (USDOE, 2011).

This discourse was followed by calls to enhance the preparation of prospective teachers and the professional development of current teachers to increase student achievement. The Obama administration strongly advocated the creation of partnerships to improve teacher quality. The U.S. Department of Education created a grant programme (US$5.1 million) known as the 'Teacher Quality Partnership Program', an initiative directed at stimulating the development of model teacher preparation programmes at the undergraduate or fifth year licensing level, or the creation of new teaching residency programmes for individuals with strong academic or professional qualifications but without teaching experience.[1] Between 2009 and 2016, the programme awarded 68 grants to partnership proposals, giving a strong push to the existing teaching residency programmes, which had been running since 2004 in Boston, Chicago and Denver to meet the hiring needs of urban districts. According to the National Center for Teacher Residencies (2017):

> Like doctors training in hospitals, residents spend a full year learning how to be an effective teacher, working alongside an accomplished mentor teacher. With ongoing support, residents train in the district where he/she will launch their teaching career. Successful candidates complete the residency with state certification and a Master's degree.

Other residency programmes have been developed in partnership with institutions of higher education with long histories of preparing future teachers under traditional models, and others with government agencies or even with museums.

Other models such as Teach for America and the New Teacher Project Teaching Fellows[2] (featuring training in core skills in the summer, and intensive classroom practice, expert coaching and personalised training) have been offering alternative routes into teaching with mixed results (Auletto, 2017).

But whilst policy has opened spaces for these and other alternative routes into teaching, the large majority of future teachers are still prepared in pre-service programmes in higher education institutions (HEIs) with a variety of school-based practice modalities lasting from 6 months to a year (87 per cent as of 2015 are prepared to become teachers in traditional programmes). It must be mentioned here, that the decentralised United States system allows states not only to resist alternative approaches into teaching, but also to mediate how policy affects the local education system, including the preparation of teachers. Thus, the emerging modalities are by no means existent across the nation.

In addition to introducing important reforms on the provision of teacher education, the most important federal attempt at regulating teacher preparation programmes was the initiative to implement a value-added system of teacher preparation evaluation under the requirements for Title II data reporting by programmes and states, as required by the Higher Education Act (USDOE, 2016). The federal teacher preparation programme regulations were rescinded in March 2017 after 6 years of development and sustained discussion amongst members of the profession (for more detail see Tatto et al., 2016). Whilst the requirement for accountability data reporting remains, there is not a unified federal mandate on how to proceed. Yet, due to the push to regulate, progress has been made concerning definitions of teaching quality, the role of teacher education institutions and of standards and assessments as discussed in earlier chapters. A significant group of several national organisations and foundations called the Coalition for Teaching (2014) has put forward a telling definition of a 'profession-ready educator':

> Profession-ready teachers have completed a robust preparation process and are fully licensed by the state in which they teach. Profession-ready teachers possess the content knowledge of the subject they will teach and the pedagogical skills and capabilities to translate that knowledge into effective instruction that meets the needs of all students in the classroom. Profession-ready teachers are comfortable leading a classroom because they have had extensive practice through clinical experiences and a teaching residency. By passing a performance assessment prior to becoming a teacher of record, profession-ready teachers have demonstrated that they are capable of leading a classroom. All of these components combined ensure that prospective and early career teachers are on the pathway to accomplished practice and that all students will have access to excellent teachers.
>
> (Coalition for Teaching, 2014, p. 1)

The coalition that produced this document includes: the American Association of Colleges for Teacher Education; the American Federation of Teachers; the Council for the Accreditation of Educator Preparation; the Council of Chief State School Officers; the National Board for Professional Teaching Standards (National Board); the National Association of Elementary School Principals; the National Association of Secondary School Principals; and the National Education Association.

In sum, important changes have been introduced in the last 15 years in the teacher preparation landscape including strong support for school-based partnerships and a regulatory system scheme. The partnership model under the teacher residency programmes route seems to be successful as far as recruitment and retention is concerned; more research, however, is needed to document effectiveness. Whilst there was rejection of the federal regulations early this year, regulation and control of teacher education is still very much on the agenda, albeit at the level of the states.

The institutional activity settings of higher education and schools in the United States and England

The models of partnership that we see in operation in both countries are not, at face value, that dissimilar. Whilst the programmes at Michigan State University (MSU), the University of Oxford and the Teach First model reflect particular approaches, all operate within recognisable paradigms and have at their heart the notion of partnership between the institutions charged with delivering teacher education programmes and the schools, which provide the practicum experience. It is recognised that neither, on their own, would be able to provide sufficient opportunities for those learning to teach to acquire the complex knowledge and skills teachers need, yet university-school partnerships in both countries face significant levels of challenge.

First and foremost, individual schools and universities act primarily as separate activity systems, each with its own history, culture and practices and only come together for the purposes of preparing prospective entrants to the profession. In these traditional models, both universities and schools have much wider goals than the preparation of new teachers. For the university, undergraduate education and research are seen as at least as important as professional education, and for schools, the teaching and learning of the school pupils are undoubtedly to be the most important focus. Indeed, in the school setting, where initial teacher preparation may be seen as a secondary level of activity, initial teacher education may easily become marginalised if the structures do not exist to enable the student teacher to be fully supported in the practicum setting.

Additionally, each institution has its own view as to how student teachers best acquire the complex range of knowledge and skills that they require. This may be reflected in some cases, as we have seen, in tensions between the two institutional activity settings where differing values may determine different approaches. These tensions are evident both in the United States and in

England and emerge from some of the cases highlighted in Part II, reflecting differences in perception as to what it is that student teachers should know and be able to do and the most effective means of acquiring such expertise.

Thus, much depends on the nature of the initial teacher education partnership and the extent to which it is underpinned by commonly agreed approaches and shared pedagogical concerns. In England, the nature of working within partnership has changed significantly as a result of the 'school-led' reform of teacher education (begun under the coalition government) with the clear policy directive to give schools a stronger voice as to the way in which teachers are trained. Questions still remain however, as to whether the rhetoric around 'school-led' provision actually leads to more effective partnerships. In both the United States and in England, the question has to be to what extent initial teacher education has, at its heart, genuinely collaborative partnerships (Furlong, Barton, Miles, Whiting & Whitty, 2000) or those in which separate, but complementary responsibilities are devolved to each of the partners. When looking at what occurs at the meso level, it would seem reasonable to argue that there is likely to be greater alignment between university and school provision where there is a higher degree of integration and programme coherence across both institutions. In the United States, the emergence of teacher residency programmes has the potential to alter the way in which traditional teacher education works with schools to prepare teachers.

Whilst there is, certainly in England, a strong rhetoric around partnership and the nature of working in partnership, we still have to heed Alexander's (1984) warning, made over 30 years ago, that: '*the comfortable language of partnership*', which policy makers and others adopt with ease, will conceal '*more intractable issues*' (1984, p. 142). Some of these intractable issues emerge, to a greater or lesser extent, in both the United States and England through the respective policy backgrounds and individual programme descriptions, which reflect tensions at both the macro and meso level. These tensions are also reflected within the case studies at the micro level and clearly have an impact on the professional learning of some student teachers.

In both countries, political reform has been driven by market forces and has resulted in an emphasis on accountability and regulation, which has to be carefully balanced with concerns at the programme level as to the most effective way of educating teachers as professionals. In England and the United States, the debate has centred around the type of teachers that we might want to produce, with the prevailing policy emphasis in England having been on the 'craft' aspects of teaching, or on conceptualising the effective teacher as a 'technician' (who is expected to be able to follow standard procedures or draw on synthesised evidence of what works, regardless of any specific context). In the United States, the discourse is around the teacher as one who is very knowledgeable in their discipline whilst the craft aspect has tended to remain in the background. Within these contexts, programmes such as the Oxford Internship Scheme (OIS) have instead promoted the need for student teachers to learn from a diverse range of appropriate sources to inform their professional learning and, within a model of research-informed clinical practice (Burn & Mutton, 2013), to engage in 'practical theorising' (McIntyre, 1995). The latter is intended to enable them to 'exercise their own judgement in the classroom and make decisions as to whether and how research-based considerations are relevant to how and what they teach' (Winch, Oancea & Orchard, 2013, p. 6), but is not typical of programmes in England overall. In the United States, context again, it is only some individual programmes, such as the one at MSU, that have attempted to resist the emerging notions leading to 'fast-tracking' teachers into schools, and have instead continued to emphasise the need to have demonstrable knowledge of the subject, to develop the subject pedagogy, the general pedagogy and clinical capacities within a 'learner-centred or active, inquiry-based' model, conceived to be essential amongst effective teachers (Stuart & Tatto, 2000). This has only been possible by creating collaborative partnerships, which embody the programme's underpinning principles. Thus, both programmes, whilst in different contexts, use research to inform their programme design and help student teachers use research to inform and regulate their practice.

Programmes in both countries are subject to a number of binary positions, creating further tensions that potentially militate against alignment at all levels. We have seen how in the United States, for example, there has been an ongoing struggle between 'progressive ideas' on the one hand (which are seen to characterise the university perspective) and demands for efficiency, standardisation and accountability on the other (which tend to characterise the policy discourse) (Labaree, 2008). This results in differing views as to the sort of teacher that we might wish to produce and thus, disagreement as to the nature and purpose of teacher education programmes. In England, the debate around such binaries has often perpetuated the view that universities provide what is regarded as irrelevant 'theory' whilst schools provide the opportunity for relevant 'practice' (Murray & Mutton, 2015). It is against this background that the pedagogic practice of individual programmes is being enacted and where the above tensions are seen to play out, often reflecting the 'disconnect between the campus and school-based components of programs' (Zeichner, 2010, p. 89).

One of the key issues, in both the United States and England, is the extent to which there is coherence in the initial teacher education programme across the partner institutions. In England, the subject mentor is given significant responsibility for the effective delivery of the school-based elements of the programme, but there is evidence that, whether within an employment-based model or a more traditional model, the mentor is more likely:

> To focus primarily on the repertoire of teacher behaviour prescribed by 'the standards' as well as their school's goals, perhaps at the expense of other equally important aspects of professional training and development, such as making sense of wider educational issues.
>
> (Jones & Straker, 2006, pp. 181–182)

The case studies in Part II reveal not only the key role that effective mentoring can play in helping student teachers to recognise the opportunities for change (OfC) and in providing the necessary tools for development to occur, but also the way in which mentoring can restrict such opportunities when the focus is too heavily prescribed by the policies and practices of the specific school context in question.

A question raised by the MSU programme is the extent to which university faculty in general need to be directly involved in the practicum experience of the student teacher. Whilst the OIS scheme, as well as the Teach First programme, is dependent on faculty staff visiting student teachers/participants in school on a fairly regular basis in order to observe them teaching and give feedback, as well as discussing overall progress with the subject mentor, the MSU programme relies on graduate students (or sometimes those who have previously worked in senior positions in schools) to carry out visits to schools. This raises the question as to whether programme coherence is more dependent on the overall architecture of partnership (and the practices within such architecture) or whether it requires university staff to have a significant role in working directly with the student teachers and their mentors both at the university and in school during the practicum experience.

The cases in Part II illustrate the way in which knowledge is re-contextualised within specific institutional contexts. In the university settings in both countries, subject-specific pedagogical approaches, informed by research-informed understandings of learning and teaching, are promoted and student teachers are expected to draw on these approaches in their classroom practice. In order to make sense of their own teaching they are required to evaluate the effectiveness of particular approaches and pedagogic strategies and, in doing so, draw on a range of possible criteria. These criteria may be informed by a range of factors, including: theoretical perspectives underpinning any subject-specific pedagogy; the policies and practices of the school in question; the requirements of the curriculum; national standards; previous experiences of teaching; and the response of the pupils and their learning outcomes. These criteria will not, however, be applied equally to all experiences of teaching and it is not unusual in some contexts for particular criteria to be privileged over others. The way in which this happens depends on what is valued in different contexts and, in the case of approaches to individual subjects, differences across subjects within the same school. As a consequence, student teachers may be supported in different ways and the use of mediating tools may differ significantly from subject to subject (even from student teacher to student teacher) depending on what is being valued in terms of the knowledge, skills and understanding that they are perceived to need.

Individual transitions as they occur in England and the United States

The framework discussed extensively in Chapter 6 provides a useful lens with which to look at the individual student teachers' opportunities for development

(OfD) and their OfC. What is striking is that from the limited snapshots of teaching that were observed and recorded, each offers a rich source of data in relation to OfD and OfC. Each lesson highlighted particular OfDs although not always in the same way. For some student teachers, it was the 'crisis' provoked by the teaching experience, which highlighted the possibilities for further learning, whereas for others, there was less a sense of strong challenge and more a sense of being able to identify aspects of the lesson that might have been approached differently, or capitalised upon more effectively. The way in which the student teachers engage with the OfD also reveals a variety of different responses. Whilst some show positive dispositions to learning from their individual experiences and to confronting specific challenges, others choose to ignore the very issues that are causing problems in their classroom practice, and in doing so, risk closing off the potential of OfDs.

Similarly, the cases show that OfCs may depend on a number of factors. In some cases, the student teacher may be well disposed towards learning and respond to the OfC in a way that enables them to address the issues in their teaching, draw on support where necessary and move forward. In other cases, the student teacher will only be able to progress as a result of the mediating tools provided within the programme by the school or the university. Finally, some student teachers may struggle to engage with the OfC because of their own view as to what needs to occur in order for their teaching to improve. In these cases, student teachers may often see little opportunity for growth as they attribute the issues related to their teaching to contextual factors. Some appear to blame the pupils and their inappropriate responses, poor levels of motivation or poor behaviour amongst other causes; others focus on specific constraints of the school context or what they regard as the unrealistic expectations of the programme.

Subject differences do not appear to be a determining factor in relation to the degree to which student teachers are able to identify and respond to OfD. Yet, whilst all the student teachers were knowledgeable within their subject, subject pedagogy issues were almost uniformly present in the cases observed. In many instances, this was manifest in the cases of individuals who appeared to have a strong identity as a subject 'expert', which potentially militated against them being able to see that the way in which they were presenting subject-specific content or responding to the pupils was perhaps at least partially, or too heavily, influenced by their own preconceptions. The cases illustrate a range of assumptions as to what pupils should know or be able to do at any given stage, and sometimes profoundly unhelpful notions of how a lesson should proceed, or of what might constitute effective ways of evaluating what pupils have learned from it.

The varying degrees of alignment reflected in the case studies indicate a range of factors at work in relation to the social situation of development of individual student teachers. The complex interplay between individuals (at the micro level) with particular sets of beliefs, preconceptions and personal histories and the contexts (both at the macro and meso level) in which they are learning to teach, has to be recognised and addressed if those individuals are to learn effectively. It may be that there is rarely full alignment between these planes (although there are examples within our study of individuals, which come close to such alignment, as in Doug's case), and there may, inevitably, be tensions between institutional practices at the meso level within any university-school partnership, but it is only by recognising these tensions as part of the complex picture of a student teacher's development that we can effectively understand each individual situation of development and the factors that might facilitate or constrain professional learning within it. In terms of the latter, our study suggests that it is the student teacher who is experiencing a sense of crisis at the individual micro level and who is unable to recognise or address the OfD who will struggle the most. Whilst strong alignment at the meso level in relation to the institutional values, practices, pedagogical beliefs and structures for support of either the HEI or the school can mediate these problems, without such alignment the OfCs are unlikely to be realised.

There are important differences in the way that individuals re-contextualise and reproduce knowledge. All student teachers come as graduates of the subjects that they are intending to teach and all see themselves as subject specialists, but the way in which they develop their own subject pedagogy is subject to different influences. For many, this development is tied to the strong message and instruction conveyed by the programme, although in some cases the student teacher is unable to manage the complex transition into teaching, or, once placed in the school, question the validity of the programme message. For others, this development is strongly related to the policies and practices of the placement school, although there are a few examples of those who reject these influences. What is particularly striking is the way in which those who were recruited as School Direct student teachers in England appeared to want, above all, to adhere to the commonly agreed practices of their placement schools (to which they had originally applied – rather than to the university – for a place on the teacher education programme) and seem less inclined to problematise their teaching or to consider alternatives to what they judged to be working effectively. For those student teachers enrolled within the traditional teacher education programme, who may initially find themselves reproducing rather than re-contextualising knowledge following the tacit mandate of their school departments, an understanding of the need to engage in inquiry-driven teaching may persist once the pressures to fit in schools is lessened by the passage of time and the acquisition of experience.

Conclusion

Future teachers are engaged in multi-layered social situations of development within the specific social and cultural contexts of both their placement schools and their university environment. Although these situations can provide fruitful OfC and OfD, problems of misalignment between school and university programmes or a lack of a critical stance on the part of the student teacher or school representatives can limit these possibilities. Edwards (2010) argues that social situations for development for initial teacher education may include learning about relatively stable practices such as a school curriculum. However, student teachers are also engaged in situations where practices are less well defined, such as understanding the learning of children living in poverty, issues of language or the particular special needs of a child. The latter situations might involve a more critical or questioning stance that require the student teacher to adjust their pedagogy. The argument advanced in brief here, is that these less well-defined practices can produce useful social situations of development for student teachers as they negotiate both the national contexts of teacher training and the particular experiences of their school and university contexts. From a sociocultural perspective, the findings reported here, suggest that if teacher educators are to engage meaningfully with the processes of development and change that those teachers undergo, then more attention needs to be paid within initial teacher education programmes to the potentially conflicting object motives of professional subject mentors and student teachers and to the mediating role of individual, social and institutional histories and experiences. Indeed, the foundations of university-school partnerships in initial teacher education were built on distributed and situated expertise in schools and universities. In the strongest cases, these initial teacher programmes are open to scrutiny, critique and re-contextualisation, both by the partnership and by the student teachers engaged in them. This clinical practice approach stresses both the dialectical interplay between theories of education and teaching practice as well as the developmental importance of disrupting and questioning previous assumptions about pedagogy and the ways particular people learn in particular social circumstances.

The research reported here thus, reaffirms the importance of designing initial teacher education programmes on the basis of genuine school-university partnerships that take account of the different object motives that student teachers encounter as they learn to teach. The mediating tools offered by schools, HEIs and individuals may be influenced by a range of different factors, including not only the cultures of the institutions involved but also external pressures. In Bernstein's (1990) terms, the pedagogic re-contextualisation and reproduction of knowledge in schools and by teachers may be subject to external (and often dominant) pressures such as accountability demands, efficiency concerns and often strong criticism of schools and teachers. Discourse of this nature, means that student teachers need both to be aware of such discourse and to be placed in social situations of development where it is possible for it to be interrogated critically.

In this way, future teachers can become more agentic in recognising, interpreting and changing their social situation of development. Such an approach, however, also requires exposure to as wide a range of sources of learning and that programmes acknowledge and encourage the creation of challenges within the social situation of development in question. In short, the research reported here appears to provide strong support for the careful development of research-informed higher education school partnerships, and for research-informed clinical practice in initial teacher education.

Notes

1 https://ed.gov/programs/tqpartnership/index.html (USDOE, 2017).
2 http://tntpteachingfellows.org/ (TNTP Research Fellows, 2017).

References

Alexander, R. (1984). Innovation and continuity in the initial teacher education curriculum. In R. Alexander, M. Craft & J. Lynch (Eds.), *Change in teacher education. Context and provision since Robbins* (pp. 103–160). London: Holt, Rinehart and Winston.

Auletto, A. (2017). *Are teacher residency programs an effective approach to improving the teaching workforce?* Retrieved from http://edwp.educ.msu.edu/green-and-write/2017/are-teacher-residency-programs-an-effective-approach-to-improving-the-teaching-workforce/#sthash.BuXMb9iO.dpuf.

Bernstein, B. (1990). *Class, codes and control. Volume IV: The structuring of pedagogic discourse.* London: Routledge.

Burn, K. & Mutton, T. (2013). *Review of 'research-informed clinical practice' in initial teacher education.* Research and teacher education: The BERA-RSA Inquiry. London: BERA. Retrieved from www.bera.ac.uk/wp-content/uploads/2014/02/BERA-Paper-4-Research-informed-clinical-practice.pdf.

Carter, A. (2015). *Carter review of initial teacher training (ITT).* London: DfE. Retrieved from www.gov.uk/government/publications/carter-review-of-initial-teacher-training.

Coalition for Teaching. (2014). *Profession-ready teachers and principals: For each and every child.* Coalition for Teaching Quality. Retrieved from: http://coalitionforteaching quality.org/images/upload/Profession_Doc.pdf.

Cochran-Smith, M. (2005). The new teacher education: for better or for worse? *Educational Researcher, 34*(3), 3–17.

Edwards, A. (2010). How can Vygotsky and his legacy help us to understand and develop teacher education? In V. Ellis, A. Edwards & P. Smagorinsky (Eds.), *Cultural-historical perspectives on teacher education and teacher development* (pp. 63–77). London: Routledge.

Furlong, J. (2008). Making teaching a 21st century profession: Tony Blair's big prize. *Oxford Review of Education, 34*(6), 727–739.

Furlong, J., Barton, L., Miles, S., Whiting, C. & Whitty, G. (2000). *Teacher education in transition: Reforming professionalism.* Buckingham: Open University Press.

Jones, M. & Straker, K. (2006). What informs mentors' practice when working with trainees and newly qualified teachers? An investigation into mentors' professional knowledge base. *Journal of Education for Teaching: International Research and Pedagogy, 32*(2), 165–184.

Labaree, D. F. (2008). An uneasy relationship: The history of teacher education in the university. In M. Cochran-Smith, S. Feiman-Nemser & D. J. McIntyre (Eds.), *Handbook of research on teacher education: Enduring issues in changing contexts*, (3rd ed.), (pp. 290–306). Washington, DC: Association of Teacher Educators.

Mattsson, M., Eilertson, T. & Rorrison, D. (Eds.). (2011). *A Practicum turn in teacher education.* Rotterdam: Sense.

McIntyre, D. (1995). Initial teacher education as practical theorising: A response to Paul Hirst. *British Journal of Educational Studies, 43*(4), 365–383.

McNamara, O. (2010). Une approche technique et rationaliste: La formation des enseignants en Angleterre. *Revue Internationale D'Education, 55,* 49–60.

Murray, J. & Mutton, T. (2015). Teacher education in England: Change in abundance, continuities in question. In Teacher Education Group (Eds.), *Teacher education in times of change* (pp. 57–74). Bristol: Policy Press.

Mutton, T., Burn, K. & Menter, I. (2017). Deconstructing the Carter Review: Competing conceptions of quality in England's 'school-led' system of initial teacher education. *Journal of Education Policy, 32*(1), 14–33.

National Center for Teacher Residencies. (2017). *Become a teacher: Learn to teach.* Retrieved from https://nctresidencies.org/become-a-teacher.

Office for Standards in Education Children's Services and Skills. (Ofsted). (2014). *Initial teacher education inspection handbook from September 2015.* Number 150033. Manchester: Ofsted. Retrieved from www.gov.uk/government/publications/initial-teacher-education-inspection-handbook.

Stuart, J. & Tatto, M. T. (2000). Designs for initial teacher preparation programs: An international view. *International Journal of Educational Research, 33,* 493–514.

Tatto, M. T., Savage, C., Liao, W., Marshall, S., Goldblatt, P. & Contreras, M. L. (2016). The emergence of high-stakes accountability policies in teacher preparation: An examination of the U.S. Department of Education's proposed regulations. *Education Policy Analysis Archives, 24*(25). doi: http://dx.doi.org/10.14507/epaa.24.2322.

TNTP Research Fellows. (2017). *Homepage.* Retrieved from http://tntpteachingfellows.org/.

U.S. Department of Education (USDOE). (2011). *Our future, our teachers: The Obama Administration's plan for teacher education reform and improvement.* Washington, DC: USDOE. Retrieved from www.ed.gov/teaching/our-future-our-teachers.

U.S. Department of Education (USDOE). (2016). *Preparing and credentialing the nation's teachers: The secretary's 10th report on teacher quality.* Washington, DC: Office of Postsecondary Education, USDOE. Retrieved from www2.ed.gov/about/reports/annual/teachprep/index.html.

U.S. Department of Education (USDOE). (2017). *Programs: Teacher Quality Partnership Grant Program.* Retrieved from https://ed.gov/programs/tqpartnership/index.html.

Winch, C., Oancea, A. & Orchard, J. (2013). *The contribution of educational research to teachers' professional learning: Philosophical understandings.* Research and teacher education: The BERA-RSA Inquiry. London: BERA. Retrieved from www.bera.ac.uk/wp-content/uploads/2014/02/BERA-Paper-3-Philosophical-reflections.pdf.

Zeichner, K. (2010). Rethinking the connections between campus courses and field experiences in college-and university-based teacher education. *Journal of Teacher Education, 61*(1–2), 89–99.

14 The future of teacher education in England and the United States

Introduction

This last chapter is prospective in that it discusses the future of teacher education in both countries, using as a basis what we have learned through our research. The chapter examines the paradoxes of the current policy trends and how these are expected to play out in the future. In both countries, the political situation has changed in dramatic ways: in England with the impending split from the European Union; and in the United States with a new administration that is bent on rejecting past trends and on enforcing exclusionary policies. Teacher education continues to be contested terrain and may become more so given the strong hold that neoliberal policies have on education.

Throughout this chapter, our focus is on the macro level scenarios that are developing, but we hope that the reader will appreciate how significant these scenarios may be at the meso and micro levels, having seen, in earlier parts of this book, how these levels are influenced by wider, political and societal changes. We also remind the reader that we are not seeking to make simple distinctions between the two national contexts; we are not assuming that we are comparing 'like-with-like', except at a very general level of concern with teacher education.

The chapter concludes by reflecting on the research reported in this book and the effectiveness of the methodology adopted. Some suggestions are made about future directions for teacher education research.

Teacher education policy in England and the United States

Given the global context and the drive for all countries to focus on the quality of teachers – who represent the key factor in raising the academic performance of pupils, upon which the prosperity of the nation is deemed to depend (as discussed in Part I) – then governments and policy makers will be more, rather than less, likely to continue to intervene in teacher education in both countries.

In England, direct influence on policy is perhaps easier to achieve because of the centrally regulated system, but national and state level intervention is presumably also highly likely to occur in the United States. In the United States, however, as a result of a new regime that began in January 2017, the educational landscape may change in dramatic ways. As the new administration finds its feet, the new secretary of education may attempt to introduce changes that affect not only the main system of public education, but also the provision of teacher preparation. Even the very existence of the Department of Education may be a matter for change. So far (at the time of writing), there has been strong resistance from Congress to the new administration's policy proposals.

In both jurisdictions, teaching standards are deployed and will continue to be the main instrument by which new entrants to the profession are assessed and judged. There is likely to be a tightening of the way in which the *Teachers' Standards* in England are applied (DfE, 2011), especially in the wake of very recent government pronouncements about 'strengthening Qualified Teacher Status (QTS)'.[1]

In the United States, and under a new administration with tendencies towards more business-oriented approaches and less federal intervention, it is possible that the different states will take more control of education, albeit with considerable variation; yet standards are likely to stay. These may continue to emerge from professional organisations and from the programmes themselves, in collaboration with state level educators, rather than from federal departments. In contrast with England, where a central authority monitors the quality of the programmes, those in the United States are monitored by an accreditation process coordinated after consolidation by a single agency that requires programmes to document effectiveness and evidence of compliance with accreditation standards. Teacher education accreditation requirements, which now run on a 7-year cycle, and the reporting mandates stipulated in Title II of the Higher Education Act (USDOE, 2016), will continue to demand evidence of performance against agreed standards, and other measures of effectiveness.

Interestingly, there has been no equivalent call in England for the re-accreditation of initial teacher education providers, although this is the process that is currently taking place in Wales following the Furlong Review (Furlong, 2015). All providers in Wales have had to submit new bids for accreditation in line with a completely new set of criteria for initial teacher education provision. Although this seems to be a very centrally regulated measure, it does appear to be designed to make providers sign up to much more integrated programmes/ models of research-informed clinical practice, which have, up until now, been lacking in Wales, where there is also no effective teacher education research base.

In England, the quality of provision will continue to be monitored through the Office for Standards in Education, Children's Services and Skills (Ofsted) inspection regime, which will ensure that policy directives that affect both school and teacher education are being implemented.

The unpredictability (and even precariousness for some providers) of the recent allocations system appears to be coming to an end, with the initial granting of guaranteed 3-year allocations to some providers and unofficial policy indications that this will continue and will include a greater proportion of providers as time goes on. The Secretary of State for Education (again in her speech to the Association of School and College Leaders) has encouraged providers to submit bids for innovative programmes to the Department for Education, which if successful, would carry with them the guarantee of 3-year allocations in order to allow for stability of planning and development.

In the United States, the state level budget allocation to universities is highly variable, yet current trends signal greater reductions to occur in the more conservative states including Michigan. Whilst privatisation and school-based routes into teaching are on the rise, the main providers will continue to be those programmes placed in higher education institutions (HEIs).

Yet, the school practice elements in the provision of teacher education may be altered as the definition of teachers' qualified status has been challenged by a powerful coalition of organisations and foundations, so that it is now a requirement that not only makes subject knowledge essential, but that also emphasises extensive periods of clinical experience and the expectation that programmes support the preparation of profession-ready teachers as demonstrated by assessments of competence. Thus, it is not unlikely that at the moment of graduation all future teachers will need to undergo a rigorous examination that is most likely to be developed and administered at the local level. A residency element may be added to the regular 4.5- to 5-year programmes for full certification.

In summary, what we are seeing in both jurisdictions is further evidence of the twin elements of contemporary social policy in this era of neoliberalism. We see the combination of the tightening grip, for example, on standards and on the curriculum, with the parallel emphasis on free market approaches, through diversification of entry routes and inherent competition between providers (see Childs & Menter, 2013, for a fuller examination of these matters in England).

The future of university-based teacher education

Having reached 'almost the edge of the precipice' in terms of the inexorable advance of school-led provision in England, the change of Secretary of State in summer 2016 has led to a change of policy perspective. Universities are now no longer seen in the way that they were seen by the two previous Secretaries of State and Justine Greening has indicated that she wants to see universities fully involved in initial teacher education alongside other providers such as the School-Centred Initial Teacher Training (SCITT) schemes. The possibility of making 3-year allocations represents a step in this direction.

John Furlong has noted the apparent precariousness of universities' involvement in English teacher education. But he urges that this involvement is absolutely essential:

> Being exposed to the best that is known about teaching and learning how to assess evidence and address the values implicit in different courses of action, learning how to utilise such knowledge to inform practical judgements, fostering the abilities and dispositions needed to develop morally

justifiable practical wisdom in one's own work, all of these, then, are critical to effective professional education in a modern world.

(Furlong, 2013, p. 185)

It is in the university that these resources and experiences are most readily available.

In the United States, teacher education provision seems to be relatively safely housed in universities for the near future, with more than 80 per cent of teachers prepared in these programmes. The commitment to prepare 'profession-ready teachers' as described in Chapter 13, seems to reinforce the need for university-based teacher preparation programmes. Given the anti-immigrant and anti-diversity rhetoric of the new administration, it is likely that teacher education programmes will strengthen their dual mission to prepare teachers to teach the curriculum and their historic commitment to prepare teachers to address the learning needs of marginalised populations.

Business-like models in teacher education, if adopted, may affect smaller institutions, a situation that can be made worse if enrolments continue the downward trend observed in the past few years. Individuals are already showing a lack of interest in teaching as a career. Further privatisation of K-12 education, if pursued, may have as a consequence an increase in the number of charter schools, which have typically provided fewer benefits and protections for teachers, and may result in even less interest in teaching as a profession. A real danger, however, would be the proliferation of shorter and less expensive routes into teaching in a highly de-regulated environment. We have seen the effects of these policies across the United States as individuals create profit-making programmes of little market value for individuals after graduation. In other contexts, such as Chile and Pakistan, dynamics like these have had devastating consequences for teacher education programmes.

The future of teaching schools

In the United States, at present and in contrast with England, very few schools or school districts operate teacher education or certification programmes independently of universities. This is a change that has occurred in the last 10 years, which also includes not-for-profit organisations. This however, has not reached the dimensions it has in England. Teacher education programmes depend for their success on the development and maintenance of committed partnerships with schools. Over the years these partnerships have taken many forms and there are likely to be important innovations if the Coalition for Teaching plans (referred to in Chapter 13) come to fruition. Yet at this point, we cannot ignore the many voices within the United States that have spoken for the need to consider a more prominent role for the schools in the preparation of future teachers.

In England, the School Direct model is no longer being promoted as heavily as it was until very recently. Ultimately, many of the smaller School Direct lead schools that only offer a minimal number of training places are likely to with-draw from the scene and be replaced by traditional school-university partner-ships or SCITT provision. The government has indicated that it is not looking to accredit an increasing number of SCITTs but rather to increase the capacity of those already in existence.

Teaching Schools are still being promoted in England as the vehicle for school-to-school and sector-wide improvement. The requirement to engage in initial teacher education, at least as a lead School Direct school, continues to be a requirement of any Teaching Schools bid to the government, although this may change in light of any possible (though as yet not certain) downgrading of the School Direct programme. It is likely that Teaching Schools will neverthe-less have to demonstrate a strong commitment to initial teacher education as an integral part of their work.

In both countries, a key driver for government education policy (and by inference teacher education policy) is to 'close the gap' in terms of the out-comes for pupils from disadvantaged backgrounds. Whilst in the United States, the discourse is often shaped by the country's place in international studies league tables, in England, the government is most concerned about the diffi-culty to reach schools in the 'cold spots', or 'opportunity areas' as they are now called. Many of these are in the deprived coastal towns, and of these, few are close to or involved in partnership working with established initial teacher education providers. In the United States, the imperative has been to reach schools in the inner cities, and to support the learning of all students.

The future of partnerships

In contrast with the United States, where teacher education programmes are autonomous to develop a model that will eventually produce qualified teachers, and satisfy state requirements, in England the structure and modus operandi of programmes is the subject of policy mandates. In England, partnership working remains at the heart of government initial teacher education policy and the reforms of the past 6 years have been focused on drawing schools into more col-laborative working with universities. Whatever we may feel about these reforms and the way in which they have de-stabilised the initial teacher education land-scape, it is nevertheless, the case that universities have had to engage more with schools and include them more fully in the planning and delivery of initial teacher education programmes. Some HEIs have misunderstood (or perhaps over-interpreted) the school-led agenda and hived off most of their provision to schools, resulting in often very generic core content and a lack of subject-specific pedagogy within secondary programmes.

The Carter Review (Carter, 2015) was premised almost wholly on what schools want of teacher education programmes. Written by a head teacher who also heads up a SCITT and drawing on the apparent dissatisfaction expressed by other head teachers, the report concluded that what was required was a common core content so that all 'trainees' receive the same basic provision. It was not prescriptive, however, in terms of models of partnership, but did helpfully flag up the benefits of integrated programmes within genuinely collaborative partnerships.

In the United States, in contrast with England, there is not an official mandate for universities and schools to work in partnerships, yet these typically collaborate in the preparation of future teachers and documentation of successful clinical experiences play an important role in accreditation reviews. Much of the collaboration in the past few years has been around standards and curriculum and how these apply to schools and schools of education as states came together to develop a core curriculum. In the United States, the curriculum had operated in a decentralised fashion, yet under the last democratic administration the need for a common core curriculum was gradually accepted and implemented across most states, albeit not without controversy and some sources of resistance. The introduction of the core curriculum standards brought about important changes including the acquisition of new textbooks, the development of new assessments and professional development for teachers. For teacher education, a common core curriculum meant a more standard content to learn to teach and hopes for the recognition of teachers' credentials across states, this however, has proven to be an elusive goal to this day.

As with any curricular change, the implementation of the common core curriculum meant close collaboration between educators in universities and in the schools. Although the common core encountered resistance in schools, this was not the case amongst university educators, in part, because the development of this new curriculum used the guidelines developed by professional subject organisations, which typically bring together teachers and teacher educators (i.e. in mathematics the National Council of Teachers of Mathematics, and the Association of Mathematics Teacher Educators).

In sum, the rhetoric of partnership is not always reflected in the practice or the pedagogy of teacher education (Mutton, 2016). Both in the United States and in England, individual programmes have adopted innovative approaches to partnership work in an attempt to bring about programme integration and coherence with curriculum and standards work often serving as catalysts.

The role of evidence-based policy and practice in teacher education

Whilst there is a policy rhetoric that talks about evidence-based practice, there is no consensus as to what this means and how it works. At one level in England, this is represented by the notion of a 'central portal of synthesised executive summaries, providing practical advice on research findings about effective teaching in different subjects and phases' recommended by Carter (Carter, 2015, p. 70). But the BERA-RSA Inquiry report (BERA-RSA, 2014) called for a different conceptualisation of the role of research in teacher education and the aspiration for 'research literate' teachers.

Some scholars of teacher education in the United States, would argue that the field has made significant progress since the creation of the American Educational

Research Association's (AERA) Division K, which focuses on teacher education; others would argue that there are still so many disparate views as to what constitutes quality teaching and quality teacher education that it is impossible to argue that there is a defined field for the profession. International studies of teacher education programmes have revealed that indeed there is much variability across and within countries on these issues (Tatto et al., 2012). A recent analysis of the syllabi of secondary teacher education programmes in Germany, Poland, Singapore and the United States reveals that even in the field of mathematics, teacher education, which could be conceivably considered as having a strong grammar (Bernstein, 1990), there is much variability within and across countries (with the exception of Singapore): on the depth of mathematics knowledge that is considered important for teachers to have; on the opportunities to learn mathematics pedagogy; on the general pedagogy provided to future teachers; as well as on the range of clinical experiences they should gain (Tatto & Hordern, 2017). Colleagues across countries, including the United States and England, are investigating these questions as part of a long-term research agenda and are reaching similar conclusions (Tatto & Menter, forthcoming).

The current and future implications of QTS vis-à-vis the knowledge base for teaching

The knowledge base for teaching remains potentially the most contested area. In England, with the government having established a policy landscape in which the rhetoric has, in recent years, been around the value of an apprenticeship model of professional learning in which teaching is conceived of as a craft, it remains to be seen to what extent the need to prepare teachers with adaptive expertise can be brought to the fore. Regaining the ground that has been lost will be difficult and it may be necessary to find new models and approaches in order to do so.

By contrast in the United States, the knowledge base for teaching is widely recognised as that originally proposed by Shulman (1987) with few modifications.[2] The key challenge here, is whether and how different approaches to becoming a teacher are able to result in such a complex amalgam of knowledge, skills and dispositions. Thus, programmes' form, content, methods and evaluation of outcomes have and will continue to occupy teacher educators and policy makers.

The current policy discourse in England is around the 'strengthening of QTS' although it is not actually clear what this means. In essence, it is not necessarily about strengthening the requirements, but rather about when new teachers can be deemed to be fully qualified. The argument is that the end of the training period is too early to confer QTS and that there should be a period of employment before this happens. It seems likely that there will be an initial indication of post-qualification competence followed by the award of full QTS after some time spent working in a school. Original plans for the final decision on the award of QTS to rest entirely with the head teacher in the school, in which the new teacher is employed, appear to have been amended and there is some indication that HEIs will have a role to play in this process (which will not, according to current plans, be implemented until 2019). The analogy that is being made is with accountancy – where final professional qualification would not be gained until after a period of practice.

In the United States, after the re-definition of QTS under the No Child Left Behind legislation in the 2000s (U.S. Congress, 2002), which main requirement was a university degree on a subject, the commitment expressed by the Coalition for Teaching in 2014 (see Chapter 3), the 2015 Every Student Succeeds Act, which represents a big change from the NCLB legislation and the emergence of the teacher residency programmes has brought back the notion that teachers, just like doctors, need a significant period of learning needed knowledge and skills, and monitored in-school practice, although this idea is not currently dominant in the policy discourse.

Teacher education as contested terrain

In both countries, what appears to be most contested is the issue of whether teachers only need a period of practical experience before being sufficiently competent to take on the responsibilities of their role fully, or whether both teaching and learning to teach are both recognised as highly complex activities that require time, appropriate practical and intellectual support, and exposure to an extensive knowledge base, both in terms of the foundation disciplines, generic aspects of teaching and subject-specific pedagogy.

The case studies in our research seem to indicate that if the emphasis is on teachers who merely need to be 'classroom-ready' for one particular school context (as in the School Direct model) then they are likely to be poorly equipped to deal with any contextual change or to recognise opportunities for development (OfD) and opportunities for change (OfC) as they arise in their day-to-day classroom practice. Teachers, who are prepared, however, to adapt their practice in light of unpredictable or changing circumstances, may be better able to cope with the professional demands that they will inevitably encounter.

In summary then, teacher education is a contested domain both in England and the United States. The debates are perhaps more visible and strident in England, not least because of the centrality of the government department con-cerned, compared with the more dispersed, multi-layered system of federal and state governance in the United States. In both settings, however, on the basis of our research, it seems clear that if we are hoping to produce teachers for the future who can demonstrate a high degree of adaptive expertise, equipping them to be flexible and suited to the demands of teaching in the ever more demanding contexts of 21st century life, then careful attention must be paid to the ways in which teacher education programmes are designed and provided in collaborative partnerships that involve schools as well as universities and, where appropriate, other agencies. If these institutions are each to play a part, then those working in them – teachers, faculty members and other professionals working in associated agencies – must all be recognised as having an important contribution to make. But also, when programmes are under way, there needs to be space for the student teacher herself or himself to play a part in shaping their experience so that its learning potential can be fully realised.

Reflections on this study

Our aim in this study has been to bring a rigorous sociocultural approach to bear on the processes of teacher education in two national contexts, through focusing on particular programmes. Central to this approach have been:

1   A commitment to considering different levels of social activity, which we have identified as the macro, the meso and the micro.
2   Deploying Hedegaard's (2004, 2012) planes of analysis to ensure that we are considering the full range of activities that are likely to shape the learning of those involved in these processes.
3   Deploying Bernstein's (1990) theories of pedagogic discourse in acknowledgement of the complexity of the ways in which knowledge is shaped and reshaped during processes of teaching and learning.

Through adopting a comparative approach, involving experiences in two different national settings, we have sought to identify opportunities for considering the extent to which some of the processes involved in initial teacher education may be recognised in apparently very different settings. In terms of the features that have emerged from our study, we do find that there are indeed some very important elements that appear equally pertinent in both settings, though we are careful not to assume convergence.

In particular, through the methodology that we adopted, we have suggested that in the initial education of teachers preparing to work in the secondary school sector, we can identify four features that may significantly affect the learning of beginning teachers. We identified these as:

1   OfD.
2   OfC.
3   The individual's disposition to recognise the scope for development and change.
4   The relative prominence of the subject (or subject pedagogy) in consideration of the need for development or change.

Through closely examining teaching episodes enacted by 17 beginning teachers, we found that the matter of 'alignment' of aims, values, dispositions and understandings, sometimes referred to generically as object motives, between the parties involved in the teacher education processes, are critical to the learning experiences that occur within particular settings. The notion of alignment emerged as crucial as we noted tensions and contradictions within some of the settings that led to critical moments or crises in learning, drawing on Vygotskian thinking about learning (Edwards, 2010).

The central implication arising from this research is that there is a great need for all partners in the processes of teacher education to be very closely engaged with each other in developing shared approaches. In essence, what has emerged is a new perspective on the deep significance of the pedagogical aspects of partnership in teacher education, of partnership as a pedagogical concept. This is not to deny or downplay the significance of institutional or societal factors at work. Indeed, it is to suggest that one part of the engagement between parties in these matters must be to define and make explicit the extent to which factors at these levels are influencing practices within the learning settings – the social situations of development for the student teachers.

Directions for future teacher education research

The study reported in this book, has been relatively small scale, focused on the experience of 17 student teachers of the 26 that we examined in total. Nevertheless, it has been ambitious in its scope and its methodological aims. Its intention was to gain new insights into the processes of learning that are experienced in the activity of initial teacher education, which necessarily demanded a small scale study, using an innovative methodology that would offer much greater depth than that offered by larger scale quantitative methodologies.

Although the collection of empirical data has been small scale, through our commitment to setting our analysis of these data against the wider institutional and social contexts, we have effectively been able to offer an account that has much wider purchase than isolated case studies could offer. It would obviously be valuable to seek to apply the methods over a longer time period with greater numbers of cases in more different contexts on different teacher education programmes. The fact that we have begun to apply the approach in different settings and with a range of different teacher education programmes does, however, give us confidence that the framework that has emerged and the key findings of the study are of wide significance.

The approach we have taken has been avowedly qualitative, but has been strongly informed by educational theory and our previous research. It was also developed in a rigorous, iterative manner. The core research team, of one American and four English scholars, has met and discussed the project very regularly over a period of some 3 years. Indeed, the very drafting of this book has been a key aspect in refining and defining the approach taken.

Finally, we have two main hopes for the future of this work. The first is that teacher education practitioners, whether in schools, HEIs or elsewhere, who read and consider what we have written, will find the insights yielded by this research design of value to them in the development of their practice. The second is that others will pursue similar research in the future, building on and testing its claims, as well as further refining its methodology – just as we ourselves also hope to do.

Notes

1 See Justine Greening, Secretary of State's, speech to the Association of School and College Leaders in March 2017 (Greening, 2017).
2 See Ball and Phelps, (n.d.).

References

Ball, D. L., Thames, M. H. & Phelps, G. (n.d.). https://pdfs.semanticscholar.org/2daa/67d3bbde0d751eab7302c6704f41f9f31f97.pdf.

British Education Research Association/Royal Society for the Arts (BERA-RSA). (2014). *Research and the teaching profession: Building the capacity for a self-improving education system*. London: BERA/RSA. Retrieved from: www.bera.ac.uk/project/research-and-teacher-education.

Bernstein, B. (1990). *Class, codes and control. Volume IV: The structuring of pedagogic discourse*. London: Routledge.

Carter, A. (2015). *Carter review of initial teacher training (ITT)*. London: DfE. Retrieved from www.gov.uk/government/publications/carter-review-of-initial-teacher-training.

Childs, A. & Menter, I. (2013). Teacher education in the 21st Century in England: A case study in neo-liberal policy. *Revista Espanola de Educacion Comparada (Spanish Journal of Comparative Education)*, 22, 93–116.

Department for Education (DfE). (2011). *Teachers' Standards*. London: HMSO.

Edwards, A. (2010). How can Vygotsky and his legacy help us to understand and develop teacher education? In V. Ellis, A. Edwards & P. Smagorinsky (Eds.), *Cultural-historical perspectives on teacher education and teacher development*. London: Routledge, pp. 63–77.

Furlong, J. (2013). *Education: An anatomy of the discipline*. London: Routledge.

Furlong, J. (2015). *Teaching tomorrow's teachers: Options for the future of initial teacher education in Wales*. A report to Huw Lewis, AM, Minister for Education and Skills. Oxford: University of Oxford. Retrieved from http://gov.wales/docs/dcells/publications/150309-teaching-tomorrows-teachers-final.pdf.

Greening, J. (2017). *Justine Greening: Teacher development key to school improvement* (Speech). Retrieved from www.gov.uk/government/speeches/justine-greening-teacher-development-key-to-school-improvement.

Hedegaard, M. (2004). A cultural-historical approach to learning in classrooms. *Outlines: Critical Practice Studies*, 6(1), 21–34.

Hedegaard, M. (2012). The dynamic aspects in children's learning and development. In M. Hedegaard, A. Edwards, A. & M. Fleer (Eds.), *Motives in children's development* (pp. 9–17). New York: Cambridge University Press.

Mutton, T. (2016). Partnership in teacher education. In Teacher Education Group (Eds.), *Teacher education in times of change* (pp. 201–216). Bristol: Policy Press.

Shulman, L. S. (1987). Knowledge and teaching: Foundations of the new reform. *Harvard Educational Review*, 57(1), 1–22.

Tatto, M. T. & Hordern, J. (2017). The configuration of teacher education as a professional field of practice: A comparative study. In J. Furlong & G. Whitty (Eds.), *The study of education around the world*. Oxford, UK: Oxford Comparative Education Series, Symposium Books.

Tatto, M. T. & Menter, I. (Eds.) (forthcoming). *Knowledge, policy and practice in learning to teach: A cross-national study*. London: Bloomsbury Academic.

Tatto, M. T., Schwille, J., Senk, S. L., Ingvarson, L., Rowley, G., Peck, R., Bankov, K., Rodriguez, M. & Reckase, M. (2012). *Policy, practice, and readiness to teach primary and secondary mathematics in 17 countries. Findings from the IEA Teacher Education and Development Study in Mathematics (TEDS-M).* Amsterdam: International Association for the Evaluation of Student Achievement (IEA).

U.S. Congress. (2002). *No Child Left Behind Act of 2001.* Public Law 107–110. Washington, DC: Government Printing Office.

U.S. Department of Education (USDOE). (2016). *Preparing and credentialing the nation's teachers: The secretary's 10th report on teacher quality.* Washington, DC: Office of Postsecondary Education, USDOE. Retrieved from www2.ed.gov/about/reports/annual/teachprep/index.html.

Index

Page numbers in *italics* denote tables.